IN THE SHADOW OF THE BOMB
Physics and Arms Control

Masters of Modern Physics

Advisory Board

Series Editor

Published Volumes

The Road from Los Alamos by Hans A. Bethe
The Charm of Physics by Sheldon L. Glashow
Citizen Scientist by Frank von Hippel
Visit to a Small Universe by Virginia Trimble
Nuclear Reactions: Science and Trans-Science
    by Alvin M. Weinberg
In the Shadow of the Bomb: Physics and Arms Control
    by Sidney D. Drell

IN THE SHADOW OF THE BOMB
Physics and Arms Control

SIDNEY D. DRELL

The American Institute of Physics

Copyright and permissions notices for use of previously published material are
provided in the References section in the front of this volume.

American Institute of Physics
335 East 45th Street
New York, NY 10017-3483

Library of Congress Cataloging-in-Publication Data

Drell, Sidney D. (Sidney David)
    In the shadow of the bomb: Physics and arms control/Sidney D. Drell
      p. cm.
    Includes bibliographical references and index.
    ISBN 1-56396-058-3
    1. Atomic bomb—United States—History. 2. Nuclear arms control.
3. National security—United States. 4. United States—Military policy. I. Title
  QC773.3.U5D74 1993
   327.1'74—dc20

                                                  92-46573
                                                    CIP

This book is volume six of the Masters of Modern Physics series.

Contents

SAKHAROV

COLD WAR YEARS

DETERRENCE AND ARMS CONTROL

STAR WARS AND SCIENTISTS

PROGRESS

Preface

As a physicist, I have tried to understand nature's mysteries. As a citizen, I have worked to decrease the dangers posed by the nuclear weapons of mass destruction that are one of the consequences of scientific progress. Since 1960, my life has been divided between pursuing the dream of discovery and working to avoid the nightmare of a nuclear holocaust. The essays, speeches, and Congressional testimony in this collection touch on both endeavors.

A phone call one evening in 1960 started me on the dual path of scientist and participant in national security policy issues. I was busy minding my own business—probably trying to understand a dispersion relation—when Charles Townes, then the executive vice president of the Institute for Defense Analyses, called to invite me to Washington to attend a briefing for a group of "bright, young physicists." As I remember, Charlie said this was an organizational meeting to bring fresh, new talent together to work on problems of national importance for our security in the still very young age of nuclear weapons, space, and intercontinental missiles. It was the genesis of JASON.

Unquestionably, I was flattered, but I was also very dubious. I had no time to spare. Doing my job as a physics professor, enjoying a family with two small children, and trying like hell to keep up with the exciting new data was already requiring more than 24 hours a day. But the very fact of the phone call from the very distinguished Vice President Townes, plus his cogent arguments, caused me to pause and think. So I talked with my colleague and close friend Wolfgang K.H. ("Pief") Panofsky, whose great personal commitment and enormously valuable contributions to U.S. national security and sound policy I admired very much; and I thought about the value, and even the need, for a new and younger group to add their talents to those of the veterans of Los Alamos, the Manhattan Project, and the MIT Radiation Laboratory, who had already contributed so much. No one, after all, was growing younger.

Encouraged and inspired by Pief, I went to the first JASON briefing that winter. I found the problems interesting— at least some of them. I also found the arguments for involvement compelling and the conditions of broad access to information (without industrial priority restraints and with very strong staff support) very attractive. So I agreed to taste the experience of being a JASON, and I spent several months that summer working in one of the temporary buildings on the hill at the Berkeley Rad Lab (now known as the Lawrence Berkeley Laboratory).

As luck would have it, my colleague Mal Ruderman and I collaborated there on a most interesting problem of calculating what happens in the upper atmosphere following a high-altitude nuclear explosion. We wanted to determine how much nitric oxide was formed by the various collisions and reactions that occur in a layer of hot air, because nitric oxide, a nonhomopolar molecule with a dipole moment, radiates in the infrared region. That radiation was what we wanted to calculate. This problem was of interest then as a possible countermeasure to infrared early-warning satellites—it is of no less interest now as we grapple with some of the technical realities of antiballistic missiles, specifically target discrimination and x-ray propagation.

The problem of infrared radiation from hot air caused by a high-altitude nuclear explosion was fun physics—really fun—but, more than that, this work introduced me to a number of technical issues and practical problems that, today, are still central to thinking about nuclear weapons, arms control, and improved national security. That first summer of work, and what I learned in the first few years thereafter, opened my eyes to a number of issues that now seem more or less obvious, but were then quite new—at least to me.

First, there is the importance of implementing President Eisenhower's goal of "open skies" with effective, reliable, and mutually acceptable and nonprovocative means. The better our early warning, the less trigger-happy or nervous we will be about sudden attacks, especially in times of crisis. The better our reconnaissance and surveillance, the more accurately we can gauge the threat posed by our opponents— particularly then the Soviet Union—and therefore the more rationally and responsibly we can do our national-defense planning; and, most importantly, the more possibilities we can consider for verifiable arms limitations. Remember that, back around 1960, we were still overflying with U-2s, and the era of space-based sensors was just in its infancy. In the 1950s, we had spent hugh sums on a very large, cumbersome, and unnecessary air defense against a presumably enormous, but in reality nonexistent, Soviet bomber threat; and a fictitious missile gap played center stage in the Presidential election of 1960. So much for the virtues or bliss of ignorance. Open skies were—and remain—crucial! The strategic-arms negotiations of the 1970s and 1980s were made possible by the development, during the 1960s, of the national technical means of surveillance that gave us open skies. Happily an open skies treaty was signed in 1992 by member states of NATO and the former Warsaw Pact. In 1993 it is widely recognized that openness is an important asset in world wide efforts to control the spread of weapons of mass destruction.

Secondly, the more I understood the policy implications of new technologies, the more I appreciated the need for making the best technical support available in the government, and especially in the White House. Presidential decisions are fundamentally and more importantly political ones, but, in the area of national security and military planning, they do have crucial technical ingredients that define what can and cannot be done and what should and should not be done, both for weapons systems and for policy, including arms control; and the information available to the president on these technical ingredients should be informed, accurate, and unbiased. Moreover, there is also need for the best projections about what new technologies to bet on with priority support, because of their future potential, and about which ones to deemphasize or terminate, because their promise is poor.

It is no insult to, nor is it a lack of respect for, defense scientists with operational responsibilities in the government labs and executive departments and agencies to emphasize the importance of advice from independent scientific staff to the leaders who must make the decisions, including decisions at the highest levels. When anyone has direct operational responsibilities and is very close to one part of a problem, it is very difficult to step back and see all aspects dispassionately.

Another outgrowth of that first summer of JASON work was my expanding involvement with government committees and agencies applying science and technology to problems of national importance. This included working panels of the president's science advisor, membership on the President's Science Advisory Committee, and advising (among others) the Arms Control and Disarmament Agency and the National Security Council. In one form or another, I have been engaged in "the process" since 1960, sometimes with the executive branch, sometimes with the Congress, sometimes in public in support of, or in opposition to, administration positions. It is, in my judgment, essential that advisors to government retain their freedom to speak out on basic policy issues so long as they protect secrets important to the national security and privileged information gained from access to the political process. It is a strength of the American system that, by and large, this is recognized, although at times and on some issues the bonds between administrations and such critics have been severely tested.

The bonds between JASON members and the academic communities that were our home base were also severely tested during the Vietnam War years. On many campuses, working for a Defense Department that was "doing all those awful things" in Southeast Asia was de facto evidence of evil deeds. With varying intensity, some were personally attacked—I was confronted on several occasions, and once thrown out of a classroom in Europe—for "supping with the devil."

Many defense consultants, including JASONs, felt the strain of having to keep part of our lives secret and off limits to discussions and questions, while working with our students and colleagues in the very open scientific world in which we enjoy the full and open exchange of ideas and the public scrutiny that is traditional and cherished in our purely scientific activities. This contradiction in our lives doesn't cause much of a strain, and it is not really an issue during peaceful times, or in times of national consensus—but, when that consensus breaks down, it can be a very heavy burden.

During those days of confrontation and challenge, it was ever more clear to me how unhealthy it is for a society when its intellectuals and its leaders are split into two warring camps: the intellectual-scientist-academic critics on the outside, and the governmental decision-makers on the inside. Since 1960, I have tried to walk a straight path with one foot in each camp. This collection gives a representative sampling of the public side of that effort.

The three articles in Part 1, " Physics," illustrate the advances in the concepts of elementary particle physics over the past three decades, starting with probing the proton and neutron for their quark constituents ("Partons"). My Richtmyer Memorial Lecture ("When Is a Particle?") describes, in general terms, our understanding of quarks and the unification of forces as of 1978. The Congressional testimony prepared jointly with T.D. Lee ("The Superconducting Supercollider") identifies the major challenges in particle physics as of 1990 and summarizes the physics arguments for constructing the "SSC."

Through the years, my activities in the world of science have brought me in contact with an extraordinary community of creative individuals who have done excellent science and who have also contributed greatly to society as responsible citizens. I have had opportunities on a number of occasions to comment on the achievements of some of my good friends and to describe my admiration for their work. Testimonials for five special colleagues constitute Part 2, "Physicists."

Part 3, "Sakharov," is devoted to that giant of science, who was also a courageous world leader in the campaign for human rights, intellectual freedom, and peaceful coexistence. I cherish the privilege of having known him as a close friend. The three articles in this part of the collection are my greeting to Sakharov at the National Academy of Sciences on his first visit to the United States; a memorial prepared jointly with Lev Okun, which reviews Sakharov's many important contributions to science, human rights, and the arms-control debate; and my talk on his work on disarmament, presented at a memorial symposium in Moscow marking the seventieth anniversary of his birth. This was an extraordinary and moving occasion attended by Mikhail Gorbachev, Boris Yeltsin, and many other notables, including some of Russia's greatest musicians—Richter, Rostropovich, Spivakov—who came to show their respect and admiration for Sakharov with a beautiful musical tribute.

In the next five parts, I chronicle the developing themes in the arms-control and national-security debate. The four articles in Part IV ("Cold War Years") address concerns at the beginning of the decade of the 1980s as the U.S.–Soviet confrontation and continuing arms build-ups followed the ratification in 1972 of the ABM Treaty limiting the development and deployment of antiballistic missile defenses and the signing of an interim agreement limiting strategic offensive arms (SALT I). Although prospects seemed very dim for reversing the arms race, new possibilities were being explored. One such was the proposal to negotiate qualitative restraints as an alternative to numerical limits (prepared in collaboration with Theodore J. Ralston). The civil-defense debates of the 1960s and 1970s were renewed with vigor. Concerns about the environmental effects of nuclear war gained new focus.

During the darkest days of the Cold War, the policy of deterrence between the United States and the Soviet Union, based on the condition of Mutual Assured Destruction (MAD), was challenged by political leaders and threatened by growing arsenals of nuclear weapons.

The next three articles of Part V ("Deterrence and Arms Control") discuss the important rule of a public constituency in the continuing debate about nuclear deterrence as well as the paradoxes and moral issues raised by the condition of MAD.

President Reagan challenged the entire concept of MAD in his 1983 "Star Wars" speech. The three articles (one prepared in collaboration with Wolfgang K.H. Panofsky) in Part VI ("Star Wars and Scientists") are technical and strategic critiques of the Strategic Defense Initiative of President Reagan. The last of these articles, which is an abridged version of my 1986 address on the occasion of my retirement from the Presidency of the American Physical Society, also explores the responsibility of the scientific community in addressing questions of national security. The arrival of Mikhail Gorbachev on the scene in Moscow at this time and the release of Andrei Sakharov and Elena Bonner from confinement in Gorky introduces a new note of optimism.

With the first appearance of "the rose-tipped fingers of dawn" (to quote from Robert Fitzgerald's translation of Homer's Odyssey) following the dark gloom of the Cold War, we saw, in 1986–1988, genuine progress on the political and arms-control fronts. The next two articles (which constitute Part VII, "Progress") analyze the important progress achieved by the Intermediate Nuclear Forces (INF) Treaty and present general guiding principles for managing strategic weapons in the future. (The latter of these was written in collaboration with the late Thomas H. Johnson, a brilliant soldier and physicist as well as a poet of distinction and a patriot of honor.)

The final four articles (Part VIII, "Prospects") are devoted to the bold new accomplishments and the exciting new prospects for further progress fueled by the end of the Cold War, as the United States and the republics of the former Soviet Union work together to reduce their bloated nuclear arsenals and collaborate politically toward building a safer twenty-first century. Prospects for removing all nuclear weapons by the end of the twentieth century are debated (with Theodore B. Taylor). Important verification provisions of the Strategic Arms Reduction Treaty (START), signed in 1991, are described. The third essay considers what science can contribute to national security in the post–Cold War world, and it proposes removing all strategic ballistic missiles—or "fast-fliers"—as first suggested by President Reagan at the Reykjavik summit in 1986. Finally technical arguments for continued underground nuclear tests to improve safety of the remaining arsenal are analyzed and weighed against the political power of a comprehensive test ban.

Although some of the issues in these essays, starting more than a decade ago, are now muted as a result of recent progress, it is of interest to recall how the major issues arose and recurred and how the debates developed. In order to develop the important themes that dominated the debates over nuclear weapons policies, I have included in this volume several essays already contained in *Sidney Drell on Arms Control* (edited by Kenneth W. Thompson; University Press of America, 1988) and short excerpts from *Facing the Threat of Nuclear Weapons* (my Danz Lectures of 1983; updated and reissued 1989 by the University of Washington Press). The individual essays have been edited and abridged for clarity as well as to remove unnecessary repetitions.

References

The articles in this volume first appeared or were presented as listed below.

PHYSICS

"Partons–Elementary Constituents of the Proton?" Physical Reality and Mathematical Description (Ed. by Charles P. Enz and Jagdish Mehra), D. Reidel Pub. Co., Dordrecht, Holland and Boston, U.S.A., p. 111–23 (1974). See p. 3, "Partons-Elementary Constituents of the Proton?"

"When Is a Particle?" (Response of the Richtmyer Memorial Lecturer to the American Association of Physics Teachers, San Francisco, California, Jan. 24, 1978), Am. J. Phys. 46 (6), June 1978; Physics Today, (June 1978). See p. 15, "When is a Particle?"

"The Superconducting Supercollider (SSC)" presented as testimony before the Subcommittee on Energy and Water Development of the House Appropriations committee with T.D. Lee, March 22, 1990 and before the Subcommittee on Energy Research and Development of the Senate Committee on Energy and Natural Resources, April 24, 1990. See p. 41, "The Superconducting Supercollider."

PHYSICISTS

From a talk "Pief," presented at a celebration marking the retirement of W.K.H. Panofsky as Director of the Stanford Linear Accelerator Center, published in Proceedings of the Twelfth SLAC Summer Institute on Particle Physics, The Sixth Quark, PIEF-FEST, SLAC Report No. 281, July 1984, (p. 653–658). See p. 51, "Wolfgang K. H. Panofsky."

Excerpted from "The Many Dimensions of T.D. Lee," presented at the Symposium Commemorating the Thirtieth Anniversary of Parity Nonconservation and Celebrating the Sixtieth Birthday of T.D. Lee, published in Thirty Years Since Parity Nonconservation: A Symposium For T.D. Lee, edited by Robert Novick (Birkhauser, Boston, 1988) p. 85–94. See p. 61, "T. D. Lee."

Adapted from "Viki: Scientist, Humanist, Accompanist, and Friend" presented at a colloquium at CERN, September 19, 1988 honoring V. F. Weisskopf on his 80th birthday. See p. 67, "Victor F. Weiskopf."

Adapted from a talk at a symposium honoring Murray Gell-Mann on his 60th birthday at CalTech, January 1989. See p. 79, "Murray Gell-Mann."

Adapted from "The Voice of the Scientist in the Affairs of Government" presented at a memorial symposium at the Weizmann Institute of Science, November 1989 marking the 20th anniversary of Amos de Shalit's death; published in Rehovot, the Institute magazine, Vol. 11, No. 1, 1991. See p. 87, "Amos de-Shalit."

SAKHAROV

Address greeting Andrei Sakharov at the National Academy of Sciences, November 13, 1988 on the occasion of his first visit to the United States (reprinted in "Sakharov Remembered: A Tribute by Friends and Colleagues," edited in collaboration with S. P. Kapitsa; published by the American Institute of Physics, 1991). See p. 99, "Tribute to Andrei Sakharov."

"Andrei Dmitrievich Sakharov" (with Lev Okun), Physics Today, Vol. 43, No. 8, Part 1, August 1990 (p. 26–36). Reprinted in Sakharov Remembered, op.cit. See p. 105, "Andrei Dmitrievich Sakharov."

Adapted from a talk at a memorial symposium held in Moscow on May 21, 1991 marking the 70th anniversary of Sakharov's birth. See p. 125, "Sakharov and Disarmament."

COLD WAR YEARS

Adapted from "Arms Control: Is There Still Hope?", a talk delivered at the Faculty Convocation in Honor of Jerome B. Wiesner on his Retirement as President of MIT-May 21, 1980. Published in Daedalus Fall 1980: U.S. Defense Policy in the 1980's. Issued as Vol. 109, No. 4 of the Proceedings of the American Academy of Arts and Sciences. Also published in World Politics 81/82, Annual Editions, Dushkin Publ. Group, Inc., Guilford, Connecticut, and in Sidney Drell on

Arms Control, ed. by Kenneth W. Thompson, University Press of America, 1988. See p. 131, "Arms Control: Is There Still Hope?"

Published as a chapter entitled "Restrictions on Weapon Tests as Confidence-Building Measures" (with Theodore J. Ralston), published in Preventing Nuclear War: A Realistic Approach, edited by Barry M. Blechman, Indiana University Press, Spring 1985. See p. 147, "Restrictions on Weapons Tests."

Adapted from "Testimony on the Effectiveness of Civil Defense and Its Role in the U.S.-Soviet Strategic Balance" before the Senate Committee on Banking, Housing, and Urban Affairs, Jan. 8, 1979. See p. 161, "Civil Defense and the U.S.-Soviet Strategic Balance."

Adapted from testimony "Opening Statement to Hearings on the Consequences of Nuclear War on the Global Environment" before the Subcommittee on Investigations and Oversight of the House Committee on Science and Technology, Sept. 15, 1982 (published in Sidney Drell on Arms Control op.cit.) See p. 179, "The Global Effects of a Nuclear War."

DETERRENCE AND ARMS CONTROL

"The Importance of a Public Constituency", adapted from Facing The Threat of Nuclear Weapons, the 1983 Danz lectures, USP University of Washington Press 1983; revised and republished 1989). See p. 191, "The Impact of a Public Constituency."

"The Moral Issue and Deterrence," adapted from Facing The Threat of Nuclear Weapons. See p. 197, "The Moral Issue and Deterrence."

"Newspeak and Nukespeak" published in On Nineteen Eighty-Four (edited by Peter Stansky) Stanford Univ. (Fall 1983 op. cit.). See p. 203, "Newspeak and Nukespeak."

STAR WARS and SCIENTISTS

Adapted from a talk to the annual national meeting of the American Association for the Advancement of Science in Los Angeles, California, May 30, 1985 (Published in Sidney Drell on Arms Control op.cit.). See p. 215, "Star Wars and Arms Control."

Adapted from "The Case Against Strategic Defense: Technical and Strategic Realities" (with Wolfgang K.H. Panofsky), Issues In Science and Technology (National Academy Press), Vol. 1, p. 45–65 (Fall 1984). See p. 231, "The Case Against Strategic Defense."

Excerpted from "Thoughts of a Retiring APS President," Physics Today Vol. 40 (Part 1) August 1987. See p. 257, "Thoughts of a Retiring APS President."

PROGRESS

"Testimony on the INF Treaty" before the Senate Committee on Foreign Relations, February 18, 1988. See p. 273, "The INF Treaty."

"Managing Strategic Weapons" (with Thomas H. Johnson), Foreign Affairs, Vol. 66, No. 5, (published by the Council on Foreign Relations) Summer 1988. See p. 289, "Managing Strategic Weapons."

PROSPECTS AFTER THE COLD WAR

Adapted from a debate at the annual national meeting of Physicians for Social Responsibility in Palo Alto, California, March 11, 1989, "Why not now? Debating a nuclear-free millennium" (with Theodore B. Taylor), Bulletin of the Atomic Scientists, Vol. 45, July-August 1989, (p. 25–31). See p. 307, "Why Not Now?"

"Verification Triumphs," The Bulletin of the Atomic Scientists, November 1991 (p. 28–29). See p. 321, "Verification Triumphs."

Concluding address to the Sixth Annual AAAS Colloqium on Science and Security, Washington, D.C., November 22, 1991. See p. 325, "Science and National Security."

"Testimony on Nuclear Weapons Testing before the Defense Nuclear Facilities Panel of The House Armed Services Committee," March 31, 1992 exerpted from testimony. The Addendum is exerpted from the report to the House Armed Services Committee on "Nuclear Weapons Safety." See p. 335, "Testing of Nuclear Warhead Safety."

PHYSICS

Partons—Elementary Constituents of the Proton?

What are we made of? Throughout recorded history, this has been one of the most important and disturbing questions to challenge our imagination.

Poets through the ages have sung of heaven and Earth and the elements of which all are created. Recall the elegance with which Tennyson phrased his thoughts in "Flower in the Crannied Wall":

> Flower in the crannied wall,
> I pluck you out of the crannies,
> I hold you here, root and all, in my hand,
> Little flower—but *if* I could understand
> What you are, root and all, and all in all,
> I should know what God and man is.

Six hundred years before the birth of Christ, the early Greek philosophers, speaking with more logic and less romance, gave birth to early science in their quest for the fundamental substance of nature. Thales wrote that everything was made of water; Anaximenes suggested air as the primordial substance, and Heraclitus suggested fire. Empedocles proposed that all was made of combinations of the four fundamental substances: air, water, fire, and Earth.

As their ideas and reasoning became more advanced, the early Greek philosophers went beyond appearances and created an invisible world of atoms—that is, of indivisible constituents, or basic building blocks, out of which all is constructed. According to Democritus, who

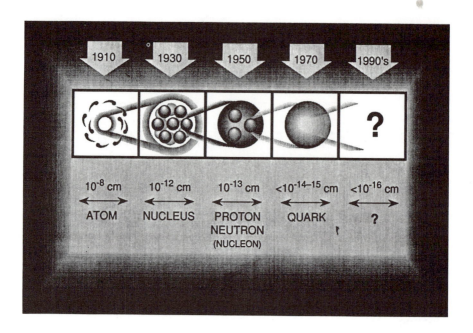

FIGURE 1.

was the most important founder of the atomic theory, the atoms were simpler than all the rich, varied phenomena we see around us, but by their motion and behavior they, though not directly observable, control all we do see. In fact Democritus wrote that, aside from atoms and empty space, the only thing in the world was opinions!

This quest for what the Greeks called the atom—and we now call "elementary particles"—continues, spurred by the increase in the resolving power of the experimental explorations made possible by the giant accelerators. We now know, of course, that there are atoms and nuclei, and we are searching enthusiastically for fundamental building blocks within the proton or neutron on a scale of distances more than a million times smaller than the atomic scale. In little more than 60 years, we have compressed the scale at this new frontier of elementary particle physics by six orders of magnitude, as illustrated in Figure 1. We now have some exciting new clues of possible structure at this new frontier.

These clues, and the experiments performed at the Stanford Linear Accelerator Center (SLAC) that provided them, are fundamentally the same as those that led Rutherford in 1911 to a picture of an atom we are so familiar with today: built of a small, compact nucleus around which electrons circulate in orbits. Recall that this picture of a nuclear atom was derived by scattering alpha particles from matter and observing they were being scattered at large angles and even into the backward hemisphere far more often than one would have predicted on the basis of the then-current ideas of atomic structure. Prior to Rutherford's work, the electric charge in atoms was believed to be diffusely distributed and hence should not have exhibited the concentrated electric fields needed to produce such large deflections of the electrically charged alpha particles. The pattern of scattering told him the original picture of an atom as a homogeneous body—or plum pudding, as described by J. J. Thomson, who discovered the electron—was wrong. In contrast, the atom was found to have a nucleus that was very small and hard, containing all the mass, about which the electrons carrying electricity circulated like planets around the Sun. Figure 2 illustrates the difference between scattering patterns from a nuclear atom and a distributed charge.

On the next scale of probing within the atomic nucleus, structure was once again found. The nucleus itself was revealed to be neither homogeneous nor elementary, but built of individual protons and neutrons that are bound to one another by a still imperfectly understood strong nuclear force. This discovery was made originally by study of the debris emerging from a nucleus when it is given a hard smash by a projectile, such as an alpha particle emitted by a naturally radioactive source.

At the frontier of exploration in the 1930s, on a scale of distances measured in units of 10^{-13} centimeters, or ten-millionths of an angstrom, the world view was simple. This view was that all matter, living and dead, was built of combinations of three fundamental constituents—electrons, protons, and neutrons.

Although appealing in its simplicity, this was indeed a short-lived view that was soon buried in its own debris. We have known now for more than 25 years that, when target protons are hit very hard—as was done in collisions of particle beams incident on hydrogen targets at the large high-energy accelerators—many fragments are produced from them in inelastic collisions; that is, a lot of debris emerges when a target proton is smashed by a high-energy incident beam. That the proton and neutron are not the indivisible objects or basic building blocks of matter sought by the ancient Greeks quickly became apparent when physicists probed with higher energies on a scale of length

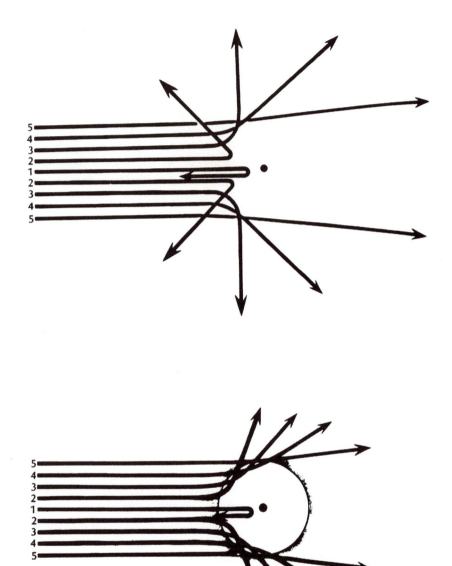

FIGURE 2.

reduced to fractions of 10^{-13} centimeters, or fractions of a Fermi. Typically, the proton changes its internal state of motion when hit by a high-energy projectile, such as another proton. But these internal excitations are very short-lived, and the proton returns to its normal state in less than 10^{-22} seconds with the balance of energy carried off by mesons, or other short-lived, unstable particles of intermediate mass (between that of an electron and a proton). Indeed, some of the fragments emerging from the proton have greater masses than even the proton itself, since the more energy, the greater the mass that can be created, according to the famous Einstein relation $E=mc^2$.

To find new evidence that the proton is composite and has structure is not surprising to anyone at the present time. The great excitement generated by the recent [1968] inelastic electron scattering experiments at SLAC is that they reveal, for the first time, a scattering pattern indicating the presence of strong, concentrated electromagnetic fields within a proton.

This scattering pattern is the same as it would be if the proton itself contained pointlike, electrically charged constituents. More suggestively, the proton seems to have "seeds" and is, thus, more like raspberry jam than jelly or Thomson's atomic "plum pudding."

What, then, is inside the proton? What are those seeds in the raspberry jam? Feynman has called them, with characteristic directness, the "partons," or the parts of the proton. Do they really exist, and are they the unknown elementary particles? Why have they not been already seen in the debris of high-energy proton scattering?

At this time [1970], we do not know what is going on inside the proton. Part of the problem of identifying these elementary constituents—or partons—in the proton is tied up in the question of what holds them together. What are the forces in nature that glue together the elementary parts of the proton? We know only that these forces are very strong—literally hundreds of millions of times stronger than the electrical forces that bind the electrons in their orbits about the nucleus, and at least hundreds of times greater than the nuclear energies binding the protons and neutrons into a nucleus.

This very strong nature of the forces creates the following problem, as illustrated in Figure 3. When we look into an atom, we "see" the individual electrons because they are almost free. The fact they are joined together in a community—the atom—has very little effect on their individual character or appearance. The electrons and the nucleus of the atom are quite clearly identified as such when we ionize, or break apart, an atom. In a system such as an atom, with weak forces—

Atom: $\dfrac{\text{Binding}}{m_e\,C^2} \sim 10^{-5}$

"See" electron

Nucleus: $\dfrac{\text{Binding}}{M_P\,C^2} \sim 10^{-2}$

$\approx$ "See" nucleon, but
environment has
effect on lifetime,
magnetic moment

Proton: $\dfrac{\text{Binding}}{M\,C^2} \gtrsim 1$

Probe of constituents
and debris search may
be very different

FIGURE 3.

such that the binding energies are typically less than ten parts per million of the electron rest energy—we can identify the constituent electrons and nuclei either by a study of the debris or by a study of the inelastic scattering patterns.

Even though the nuclear binding forces are very much stronger than the electrical ones in an atom, this same identification remains clear. Although the constituent nucleons in a nucleus are bound very strongly, their binding energies (typically 10 MeV) are no more than 1 percent of the nucleons' rest energies. Protons and neutrons inside a nucleus are still qualitatively, if not quantitatively, much the same as they would be if they were free and separated from one another—that is, they are similar as nuclear constituents or nuclear debris. However, a difference between the debris and the constituents is already beginning to become apparent.

For an example of the effect of strong forces, consider the nucleus of a deuterium atom, which is composed of a proton and a neutron. Deuterium is a stable substance in nature—that is, if undisturbed by outside forces, it lives forever. If we were to take an instantaneous snapshot of whatever it is that is whirling around inside of the deuterium nucleus, we would see two stable constituents—one proton and one neutron. However, if we separate the neutron from the proton, we would soon learn that, isolated from the nuclear force, a neutron beta-decays in roughly 15 minutes. This example serves to show how strong nuclear forces completely change the character of a neutron. It is stable inside the nucleus of a deuterium atom with a packing fraction of 0.1 percent, whereas it dies off when it is freed and emerges as debris.

When we move up several more orders of magnitude in strength of the binding energy to the study of the structure of the proton itself, this problem is very much more difficult. Now we are faced with a circumstance in which the binding energy of whatever has been observed to emerge in the debris of the proton exceeds its rest energy. The relation between this debris and the fundamental constituents that may reveal themselves to the instantaneous snapshots of very inelastic electron scattering is one of particle physics' greatest mysteries and most profound challenges. We have here a problem—very strong binding—that confronted neither Rutherford nor the nuclear physicists.

Several times now I have alluded to the notion of taking snapshots by studying the very inelastic collisions of high-energy electrons. Electrons have very important and special value as projectiles, or cue balls, for studying the structure of the proton. We have learned from independent experiments done in the past few years at many places that electrons have no detailed structure. Electrons and positrons clashing into one another in colliding rings have been very important in these studies. We know now that electrons are simple and well-understood particles. The existing theory of electrons and electromagnetism successfully meets all experimental challenges extending over the entire range of 24 orders of magnitude in distance from many Earth radii, and our understanding of the Earth's magnetic field, down to the smallest distances of 10^{-14} centimeters, which are probed by the very precise measurements of the electron's gyromagnetic ratio, the Lamb Shift contributions to the hydrogen atom's fine structure, and the hyperfine structure of the hydrogen atom. Indeed, we think of the electron as one of the probable elementary particles, in fact. Therefore, if we scatter electrons from protons, whatever complexities are observed can be blamed on the structure of the proton. This picture is more complicated if, say, two protons collide, because we understand neither the projectile nor the target, to start with, and so we generally have a lot more trouble deciphering the results. A second charm of electrons is that a proton is diffuse, but the electron probes an individual point and so gives a picture of what is happening at one point. In this sense, electrons and protons are complementary probes—electrons for taking

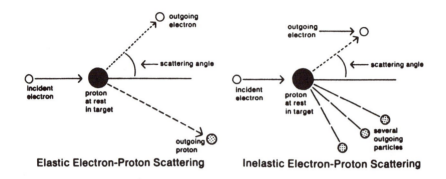

Elastic Electron-Proton Scattering   Inelastic Electron-Proton Scattering

FIGURE 4.

structure pictures with a known electromagnetic interaction, and protons for probing the nucleon forces and producing much debris.

The reason for emphasizing the very inelastic scattering of the electrons is the following: As illustrated in Figure 4, elastic electron scattering refers to an event in which the target particle does not change its internal state but recoils as if it were a rigid billiard ball. Such a scattering measures only the average charge distribution of the target, and this average will be smooth whether the proton does or does not have pointlike constituents. In order to determine the details, we need to take an instantaneous snapshot, and by the uncertainty principle, $\Delta E \Delta t \sim h$, this in turn means a large energy transfer ΔE to the target— that is, a very inelastic collision, if the duration of the interaction, Δt, is to be short. In this case, the target is excited to more energetic states or simply disintegrates, as illustrated, as a result of the energy transferred to it.

The clue that these are pointlike constituents or partons within the proton is shown in Figures 5 and 6 and lies in the appearance of a large continuum tail for very inelastic scattering.

In the case of scattering of electrons from a nucleus, this continuum arises from the electrons bouncing off of the individual protons. Each of the protons scatters as if it were a hard billiard ball, and each scatters independently when the nucleus is given a hard kick with a large transfer of momentum. The total area under the curve tells us that there are Z such protons, and the location of the peak occurs where we expect it to on simple kinematical grounds for elastic scattering from one of the protons inside the nucleus. The disappearing

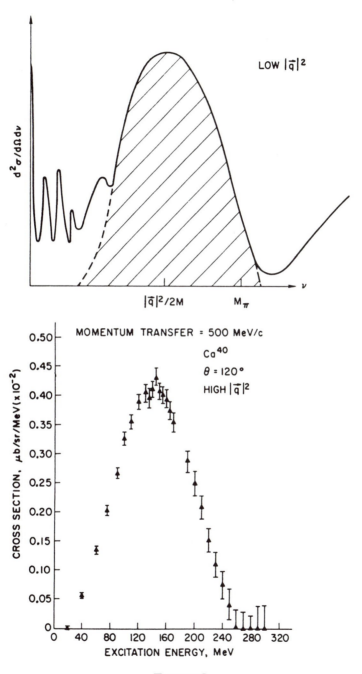

FIGURE 5.

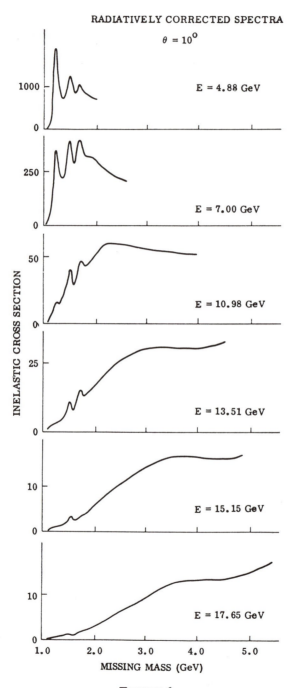

FIGURE 6.

structure in Figure 5, as we go from weak to hard kicks, or from small to large momentum transfers to the nucleus, indicates that the nucleus is unlikely to remain bound together, either in its normal ground state or in one of its many known excited nuclear states, after it receives a hard blow. However, the persistence of the continuum tail is evidence of Coulomb scattering from the individual, rock-hard, pointlike protons within the nucleus. The scattering is inelastic because there is a transfer of energy breaking apart the nucleus; this is very much like a break shot in pocket billiards. The cue ball bounces elastically from the first ball it encounters, but the latter in turn recoils into its neighbors, and several of them fly off in various directions.

When we increase the electron energy by several orders of magnitude to the 20 GeV available at SLAC and scatter from a proton target, we again see the large continuum, as shown in Figure 6. In such hard interactions, the proton is no longer indivisible. It too can be rent asunder. Once again we find that the scattering pattern for disintegrating the proton depends on the scattering angle of the electron and on the energy transferred from the electron in just precisely the way we would predict if the electron were being elastically scattered from hard billiard-ball-like chunks or partons inside the proton. This is the very same pattern that led Rutherford to the nuclear atom.

We have yet to see the tail of the continuum come back down again and, therefore, cannot say how many of these objects there are. We cannot identify their mass since there is no sharp peak. And what is more, as I have already noted, we have no clues about the proton's elementary constituents from searching the debris because of the very strong binding forces. Perhaps there really are elementary constituents—or Feynman's partons—within the proton. We are not yet sure.

Physicists have been searching for some years now for the so-called "quarks," a family of three "things" that are mathematically attractive candidates for the basic building blocks or fundamental constituents of nature. But so far the quarks have avoided detection. They are supposed to have fractional electric charges—either one-third or two-thirds as large as the electron's charge. Do the quarks exist? Are they the same as the partons from which the electrons at SLAC seem to be bouncing? One important new result of the past year has been the discovery that the proton and the neutron have different inelastic scattering patterns. They both scatter as if composed of elementary partons, but their distributions of partons differ. This new clue reminds us of the familiar result that there are also different scattering patterns from atoms with different configurations of valence electrons. More complete and more detailed studies of the differences between the neutron and proton patterns will be valuable additions to this new parton spectroscopy for solving the mysteries of the proton's structure and for establishing the properties of its constituent parts. This is analogous to the earlier atomic and nuclear spectroscopies that provided the basic information on which were built our present understandings of atomic and nuclear structure.

So that is where we are now on the new frontier. Our quest has advanced the frontier to a scale six orders of magnitude smaller than atomic dimensions over the past six decades; by its nature, it is a never-ending quest, for today's candidates for elementary particles may become tomorrow's composite structures. But remember how far we have yet to go—we don't yet know the nuclear forces. I hope that a decade hence we shall have pushed ahead yet another decade on the frontier of elementary particle physics with the aid of the great new accelerators and clashing rings now operating (400 Gev at NAL, ISR at CERN, and SPEAR at SLAC), under study, and being designed. We may then gain understanding of the very strong nuclear forces and, through them, of the cataclysmic origin of our universe.

When Is a Particle?

Our effort to understand what we and our world are made of is one of the greatest adventure stories of the human race. It dates from the beginning of recorded history. Science first flourished 2500 years ago with the quest of the early Greek philosophers for an underlying unity to the rich diversity observed in the world around them. They realized that the search for an understanding of nature at a fundamental level, in terms of basic processes and constituents, necessarily carried them beyond the sensory world of appearance.

In his essay on Lucretius, George Santayana described the emergence of the idea that "all we observe about us, and ourselves also, may be but passing forms of a permanent substance" as one of mankind's greatest thoughts. We now recognize it as the original search, in its most primitive form, for nature's conservation laws and elementary particles. However, the early Greek "metaphysicists" predated by two millenia the modern scientific method, with its insistence on experimental observation. In their inquiry, they relied purely on rational analysis, free from the discipline of direct observational content. Not surprisingly, therefore, they went off in widely differing directions: Leucippus and Democritus to the concept of indivisible atoms; Anaxagoras to the original bootstrap model of infinitely divisible seeds within seeds, each as complex as the whole; and Anaximander, Pythagoras, and Plato to more abstract mathematical concepts of numbers and symmetries.

On occasion since then, scientists have arrogantly alleged that the end of this search for nature's basic building blocks is in sight. However, such delusions have been short lived, especially in modern times, crumbling amidst the debris that emerges from increasingly powerful

FIGURE 1. *The detector, Mark I, with which the "ψ" particle was discovered in 1974 at the Stanford Linear Accelerator Center. The particle was discovered simultaneously at Brookhaven, where it was dubbed "J." The long lifetime and great mass of J/ψ surprised the physics community. The particle's existence decisively supports the concept of charmed quarks.*

atom smashers. We have come to appreciate how much richer nature's imagination is than our own vision of what lies beyond the next frontier, as we explore with ever more powerful and sensitive instruments on ever-shrinking scales of time and space. This is particularly true now, after three explosive years of remarkable discoveries of new particles, starting with J/ψ in November 1974 (see Figure 1). In the wake of these momentous discoveries, it is timely to explore what has happened in recent years to our concept of the elementary constituents—

TABLE 1. Quarks and their quantum numbers in $SU(3)$

Quark flavor	Q	I_3	S
u (up)	2/3	1/2	0
d (down)	$-1/3$	$-1/2$	0
s (strange)	$-1/3$	0	-1

the building blocks—of nature.

Quarks—Fit for the Social Register?

During the past two decades, we have come to the point of accepting into the exclusive family of elementary particles a guest who would not have made the Social Register of an earlier generation. I am, of course, referring to the *quark*, which was introduced in 1964 independently by Murray Gell-Mann and George Zweig[1] in their efforts to summarize and systematize the proliferation of nuclear particles being produced by accelerators on the high-energy frontiers of the 1950s. Regularities had been perceived in the masses of these particles as well as in the characteristics of their creation, their interactions, and their decays. Gell-Mann and Zweig showed that these regularities, as well as new ones found later, could be accounted for in terms of the simple motions and interactions of just three different kinds of fractionally charged spin-1/2 quarks (quarks with one-half unit of spin angular momentum). The quantum numbers of these quarks are shown in Table 1. In this scheme, known as $SU(3)$, several hundred hadronic resonances are successfully interpreted as excited states of just two simple quark configurations: (1) three quarks—qqq—form a baryon and (2) a quark-antiquark pair—$q\bar{q}$—forms a meson. Table 1 lists the quantum numbers and "flavor" labels—up, down, and strange—of the three original quarks. Q is their electric charge in units of the proton charge, I_3 is the third component of their isotopic spin, and S is their strangeness number.

Because the quark hypothesis made correct predictions, provided a systematic organization of a large mass of data, and brought simplicity along with a unifying harmony to our view of nature, it was a crucial step forward, similar in many ways to the discovery of the nuclear atom by Ernest Rutherford in 1911. The role of quarks in subnuclear spectra is similar to that of electrons in atomic spectra, and that of neutrons and protons in nuclear spectra. What is new, however, is that, in contrast in both our atomic and nuclear experience, we do not "see" the individual quarks isolated from one another. When we break apart—ionize—an atom, its electrons and its nucleus are clearly evident and are detected in the debris. The same is true when we identify individual protons and neutrons in the debris stripped away in nuclear collisions. How then do we account for our failure to see quarks in the debris of a shattered proton or of any other subnuclear particle? What does this unprecedented experimental situation do to our concept of an elementary particle?

Indeed, when we now ask what we mean by an elementary particle, we can feel a certain kinship with the modern poet who asks, "When is a poem?" Modern poetry clearly no longer lives by rigid rules of meter and rhyme, and many times even—or should I say especially—the meaning is obscure. As Archibald MacLeish wrote (in his poem "Ars Poetica"). "A poem should not mean / But be." How do we scientists now respond to the question, "When is a particle?"

A Tale of Two Particles

To appreciate how far we have moved in our modern conception of elementary particles, we need look back only to 1930 and the birth of the neutrino. On the historical time scale, this is less than 2 percent of the way back to the earliest Greek metaphysicists of 2500 years ago, but our conception of "When is a particle?" has evolved considerably during this relatively brief period. Before the neutrino could fully establish its credentials as a socially respectable elementary particle in the 1930s and 1940s, many physicists insisted on seeing it carry away both energy and momentum in proper proportion during beta decay; more conservatively, some insisted on being able to observe its arrival. In today's world of quarks, we have apparently discarded such requirements as a standard against which to test the concept of particle. Indeed, according to current dogma, we never can test that concept, nor shall we observe isolated quarks or record the emission and absorption of individual quarks. How and why have we come to such a revolutionary new perception of elementary particles? By way of contrast, let us first recall the story of the neutrino.

The neutrino idea was born in 1930, following the accumulation of experimental data[1] from the microcalorimetric measurements of the average energy of beta particles from radium E [now known to be ^{210}Bi]. This evidence showed that the average energy of disintegration in the decay equaled the mean energy of the continuous beta spectrum, rather than its upper limit, and that furthermore there was no appreciable accompanying gamma radiation.

Wolfgang Pauli was convinced that these results were very significant. In an open letter to Hans Geiger and Lise Meitner, who were attending a meeting at Tübingen in December 1930, Pauli pointed out that, in beta decay, not only the energy but also the spin and the statistics were apparently not conserved. A half integer of angular momentum is missing in beta decay if the beta particle is the only particle emitted.

Incidentally, at this same time, an understanding of the spins and statistics of nuclei based on the fledgling quantum theory provided a strong argument against the hypothesis then current that the fundamental constituents of nuclei were protons and electrons. For example, in those days, prior to the discovery of the neutron, how could one explain Bose statistics for the ^{14}N nucleus if its basic building blocks were in fact 14 protons and 7 electrons!

Emphasizing the importance of spin and statistics, Pauli went on to propose the outlandish idea of introducing a new, very penetrating neutral particle of vanishingly small mass in beta decay to save the situation. However, as Chien-Shiung Wu[2] relates in the fascinating account she prepared as a memorial tribute to Pauli, ". . . he was most modest and conciliatory in his pleading for a hearing." Admitting that his remedy might appear an unlikely one, Pauli commented in his letter:

> Nothing venture, nothing win. And the gravity of the situation with regard to the continuous beta spectrum is illuminated by a pronouncement of my respected predecessor in office, Herr [Peter] Debye, who recently said to me in Brussels, "Oh, it is best not to think about it at all . . . like the new taxes." One ought therefore to discuss seriously every avenue of rescue. So, dear radioactive folks, put it to the test and judge.

Pauli made public his proposal of this strange new particle at the American Physical Society meeting in Pasadena in June 1931. He insisted that the sum of the energies of the beta particle and of the very penetrating neutral particle (or particles) emitted by the nucleus in one process should equal the energy that corresponds to the upper limit of the beta spectrum. In addition to energy, Pauli assumed that linear momentum, angular momentum, and statistics are conserved in all elementary processes.

In his reverence for conservation laws, Pauli adopted an approach very different from that of Niels Bohr, who had suggested some years earlier that energy and momentum may be conserved only statistically and not in individual nuclear processes. Let me quote here from Bohr's 1930 Faraday Lecture[3]:

> At the present stage of atomic theory . . . we have no argument, either empirical or theoretical, for upholding the energy principle in the case of beta-ray disintegrations, and are even led to complications and difficulties in trying to do so.

After conceding some difficulties in so radical a departure from the principle of energy conservation, particularly with regard to time reversal, Bohr remarked:

> Just as the account of those aspects of atomic constitution essential for the explanation of the ordinary physical and chemical properties of matter implies a renunciation of the classical ideal of causality, the features of atomic stability, still deeper-lying, responsible for the existence and the properties of atomic nuclei, may force us to renounce the very idea of energy balance.

Pauli's "Radical" Conservatism

Pauli's hypothesis of a new unobserved particle met with skepticism, as it was too radical for most physicists to accept easily. From our present perspective, the "radical" Pauli, with his insistence on maintaining conservation laws—even at the expense of introducing a new and invisible particle—was really the conservative in his approach. Indeed, Pauli was so conservative that he did not publish his proposal. Only after James Chadwick's discovery[4] of neutrons in 1932 and the consequent collapse of the proton–electron picture of nuclei did Pauli put aside the reservations he had about his neutrino hypothesis.

At the Solvay Congress in 1933, Pauli (correctly) conjectured the neutrino to be a massless spin-1/2 fermion with a penetrating power far greater than that of photons of the same energy. He did this because of conservation laws and in spite of the fact that, as he noted, "experiments do not provide us with any direct proof of this hypothesis"; furthermore, "we don't know anything about the interaction of neutrinos with other material particles and with photons." Pauli argued forcefully against Bohr:

> The interpretation supported by Bohr admits that the laws of conservation of energy and momentum do not hold when one deals with a nuclear process where light particles play an essential part. This hypothesis does not seem to me either satisfying or even plausible. In the first place the electric charge is conserved in the process, and I don't see why conservation of charge would be more fundamental than conservation of energy and momentum.

Pauli also emphasized the crucial importance of investigating the relation between the energy and momentum carried away by the neutrino by means of sensitive measurements of the amount of nuclear recoil.

Shortly after the close of the discussions at the Solvay Congress, Enrico Fermi[5] gave a quantitative formulation of the neutrino hypothesis, and from 1934 on this hypothesis gained enormous strength from its successful predictions of the energy spectrum and of the angular momentum selection rules in beta processes. However, the evidence for the neutrino was still indirect and would remain so for more than 20 years until it was directly observed as a particle. Until the advent of the nuclear reactor, there were no intense neutrino sources. As a result, even though all observations and predictions were as if the neutrino were emitted in beta decay, one could still adopt the agnostic stance of weak faith and worry that nature was simply fooling us. We could invent the neutrino, but did we actually *need* it? Could we do without it?

I remember how real such questions appeared when I entered graduate school at the University of Illinois in Urbana. There I was witness to the first of the series of delicate and ingenious measurements of the nuclear recoils[6] in beta decay that Chalmers Sherwin initiated in 1947. Pauli had judged these measurements to be insurmountably difficult at the Solvay Congress in 1933, but Sherwin accomplished them using a thin-film source of radioactive ^{32}P and time-of-flight techniques with then-fast electronics. He clearly demonstrated that the ratio of the missing energy to momentum was given approximately by the velocity of light. Hence, within the errors of his measurements, the neutrino was, if it indeed existed at all, behaving kinematically as a massless particle.

By then there was, in fact, little if any doubt about the neutrino, and skepticism on this score was hardly stylish. But I remember vividly a physics-colloquium debate in 1948 between Maurice Goldhaber and Sid Dancoff on whether the neutrino really existed. With a conservative logic that, in these days of confined quarks, seems downright reactionary, Goldhaber advised caution, even in the light of Sherwin's results, and emphasized the importance of looking for evidence of neutrino absorption. After all, we may see it disappear, but, before all doubts can be removed, he advised that we should see the neutrino arrive and hit us over the head—the ultimate litmus test for the full respectability of an elementary particle. To which Dancoff replied, in the spirit of the logical positivist, that we had a respectable wave function, a dignified Dirac wave equation, and the unambiguous principles of quantum theory for describing, predicting, and analyzing neutrinos in beta processes. What more did we need? The neutrino was in fact no less respectable than, say, the proton!

No skeptics whatsoever remained eight years later, in 1956, when Clyde Cowan and Frederick Reines[7] used a powerful nuclear reactor as an intense neutrino source and observed its effects. The importance attached by some to being able to detect the arrival as well as the departure of neutrinos is reflected in the 1963 edition of the *Encyclopedia Britannica*:

> Were it not for the quite convincing experimental evidence
> of their existence ... one might regard neutrinos as the
> necessary but undetectable scapegoats whose subtle function
> was to permit the application of conservation of energy and
> momentum to atomic reactions.

I have sketched this history of the neutrino and its development from a radical idea to a respectable particle in order to contrast and compare it with the current quark theory and dogma. Where do we stand now with the quarks? On one hand, we still lack conclusive evidence of ever having "seen" isolated quarks in the laboratory, in spite of many efforts to find them.[8] On the other hand, should we not insist on seeing them if they are indeed the building blocks of the proton? Is such observation not required in the spirit of the modern scientific method, with its primary aim and its central goal, as Herrman von Helmholtz[9] characterized it in paying tribute to Faraday and his work, "to purify science from the last remnants of metaphysics"?

Early in this century, the remarkable art of experimentation developed to the extent that it was possible to study the properties of individual atoms. As a result of this fantastic sensitivity of measurement, our entire conception of "seeing" underwent revolutionary changes. On the atomic frontier, the most profound and radical change was the realization that it is necessary to take into account the effect of the observation itself on the physical system being observed. This fundamental limitation of the measurement process led to a major revolution in our concept of the elementary particle, driving us beyond classical ideas alone to a quantum description. But there is no uncertainty in what we mean when we say that we *observe* an electron as an elementary particle.

Now that we have come upon the quarks, the situation is very different. Are they objects whose existence can be inferred *only* from the properties of larger, complex structures, such as a proton, in which they are the constituents confined to one another by unbreakable bonds? If quarks are indeed not observed singly or in isolation and if they never get beyond being the "undetectable scapegoats" of the *Encyclopedia Britannica* phrase, will we still attach so central and fundamental an importance to them, or even to the elementary-particle concept itself?

Quarks: The Evidence

For the quarks to survive as fundamental, there are two possibilities:

- They will be discovered—that is, observed singly. In this case, they will constitute the atoms of yet another layer of matter, presumably with an internal structure of their own to be studied by another generation to come.
- They will not be discovered, in the same sense as the neutrino was, but they will persist in fulfilling the goal that motivated their being introduced in the first place, of providing a simple basis for the explanation of the observed multiplet structure and properties of subnuclear particles.

We know that there exist simple general laws that explain the rich diversity of nature; this is our fundamental faith as scientists. If the quarks are indeed not observed directly, their survival as vital ingredients in the structure of matter will depend on how successful the quark idea is in unifying, simplifying, and correctly predicting diverse observations, and thereby leading us to such general laws. At least from today's perspective, the quarks seem to have done enough for particle physics that there is little danger of their fading away with the ether. In brief, what is the evidence most strongly supporting quarks?

The original quark idea was put forward to explain why baryons occur with the observed multiplet structure of an octet of spin 1/2 and a decuplet of spin 3/2 and why mesons form nonets of spin zero or one. General features of the hadronic mass spectra, their transition matrix elements, and such static properties as baryon magnetic moments could be understood in terms of their quark content, three quarks for baryons and a quark–antiquark pair for mesons. What emerged was an intuitively simple picture of relatively light pointlike quark constituents moving approximately as independent particles within a hadron.

We had to pay a price for these successes. At the very outset, it was realized that a successful classification scheme for the three-quark baryonic spectra required that the quarks be assigned to *symmetric* configurations. This was in apparent violation of the heretofore sacred relation between spin and statistics that requires half-integral spin particles such as quarks to be in *antisymmetric* configurations. The way out of this dilemma was to assign to the quarks a new quantum number, dubbed color,[10] which could take any one of three values, and to require the baryon wave functions to be antisymmetric in color. This effectively triples the number of quarks, and is therefore reminiscent of Pauli's original proposal for the neutrino. He also introduced a new particle, in part to satisfy the requirements of statistics in beta decay. The added quantum number of color introduces the possibility of many additional but unobserved states, corresponding to hadrons of different colors.

To remove this difficulty, we must insist that the three quarks forming a baryon are in an antisymmetric color-singlet state. Similarly, the quark-antiquark pair composing a meson must form an anticolor pair, with each color occurring in equal parts. All hadronic states that fail to hide their color are ruled out. An explanation of why nature is colorblind is fundamental to a complete theory of quarks. Although a theoretical derivation of colorblindness still remains to be given, we can correctly and simply describe the observed spectra with no unwanted states by insisting that color remain nature's secret.

The existence of pointlike constituents within the hadron also provided a basis for understanding the observed character of hard, very inelastic, high-energy collisions between two hadrons or between the hadron and an electron, a neutrino, or a muon. The nature of the observed scattering patterns between an electron and a proton, for example, required the existence of strong local electromagnetic charges and currents due to pointlike constituents within the proton, which were presumably the quarks.[11] (They play the same role as the nucleus in Rutherford scattering.) Specifically, the constituents of the proton scatter the incoming high-energy electrons in high-momentum-transfer collisions as if they themselves had no inner structure and as if they were relatively light and essentially unbound.

The high-energy inelastic scattering measurements further emphasize the enigma of unobserved quarks. We resort to quark constituents for the most direct and simple interpretation of the observed scattering pattern. However, the proton or neutron, smashed hard and shattered into bits and pieces in the collision, does not spill out quarks in its debris—just other normal hadronic states of mesons and baryons.

The Charm of J/ψ

Unquestionably the most important recent evidence that decisively supports the quark picture was provided by the new discoveries of charmed matter, beginning with the J/ψ in 1974.[12] It sent an explosive shock through the scientific community because, on the subnuclear scale of times, it was an almost stable, very narrow resonance that could not be accommodated in the existing quark scheme. These properties differentiated it from the hundreds of other hadronic resonances with typical decay widths of 10–100 MeV, unless they are suppressed by selection rules. The J/ψ, however, was found to have a total decay width of only 70 keV and a mass of 3095 MeV.

Evidently, there was a selection rule operating to account for the narrowness of this state. Because the new particle is heavy—weighing more than three times as much as the proton—there is no inhibition in its decay due to threshold effects or lack of phase space. Hence the suppression of its decay cannot be explained on kinematic grounds alone. Moreover, the measured quantum numbers of the J/ψ are quite conventional: zero charge, one unit of angular momentum, and zero strangeness—just like the photon, which is the source of the J/ψ in electron–positron annihilation. Furthermore, its decay products are familiar particles—predominantly electrons, muons, and pions. The narrowness of the J/ψ, therefore, cannot be explained in terms of a selection rule corresponding to the conservation of known quantum numbers.

What then was holding it together for such a long time—about 1000–10 000 times longer than expected? A new quantum number was required above and beyond what could be accommodated in the three-quark scheme, which was now found to be too restrictive. This new

TABLE 2. Four-quark scheme, SU(4)

Quark flavor	Q	I_3	S	C
u	$\frac{2}{3}$	$\frac{1}{2}$	0	0
d	$-\frac{1}{3}$	$-\frac{1}{2}$	0	0
s	$-\frac{1}{3}$	0	-1	0
c (charm)	$\frac{2}{3}$	0	0	1

quantum number already had been dubbed "charm" by James Bjorken and Sheldon Glashow. Indeed, the existence of a fourth quark with charm had been anticipated by Glashow and his colleagues[12] several years before, as a simple and natural way of theoretically suppressing unobserved weak decays that lead to a change of strangeness but not of electrical charge between the interacting particles. The easiest way to account for the J/ψ and its long lifetime was to assume it to be a meson made up of a new, massive charmed quark bound to its anti-particle; this is illustrated in Table 2.

The value and beauty of such a simple model lies in its predictive power. The successes for this model have been extensive—and although the new discoveries were a shocking surprise, they are now recognized as contributing importantly to the impressive successes of the quark hypothesis. In the decade preceding these new discoveries, it was established that every known hadron could be explained as a combination of a quark and an antiquark for the mesons and of three quarks for the baryons. Moreover, all possible combinations of the three "ordinary" quarks correspond to a known hadron, without fail. With the discovery of the J/ψ and its interpretation in terms of the theoretically anticipated fourth (charmed) quark, a whole new set of spectroscopic levels had to be hunted for and interpreted.

In particular, we should observe a complete spectrum of charmonium,[13] the bound states of a charmed quark–antiquark pair. This is analogous to positronium, with its spectrum of excited states. In fact, Figure 2 shows how far we have advanced already with charmonium spectroscopy. By way of comparison, Figure 3 shows the fine-structure splitting of the first excited levels of positronium with principal quantum number $n=2$. The $n=1$ level is much lower in energy, separated by an interval of the order of the rydberg relative to the fine-structure splitting, which is smaller by two powers of the fine-structure constant, $\alpha^2 = (1/137)^2$. The energy spacings and branching ratios in charmo-

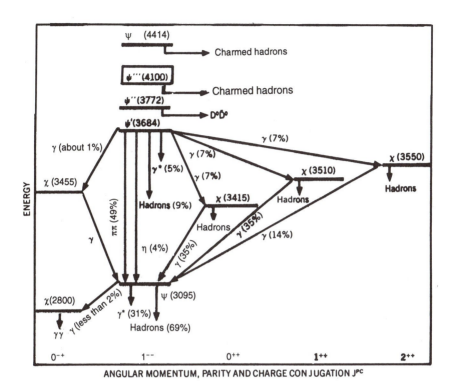

FIGURE 2. *The spectrum of charmonium, the bound states of a charmed quark–antiquark pair, showing decay processes of charmonium levels. Particle masses are given in GeV.*

nium can be understood qualitatively in terms of the binding of a heavy quark–antiquark pair. Detailed analyses of the fine structure reveal information of the shape of their interaction potential.

Furthermore, new mesonic states will be formed when a charmed quark binds with an ordinary uncharmed antiquark, as shown in Figure 4. These, the D mesons, have also been observed and fit into the four-quark classification, $SU(4)$. Already, there are starts toward the spectroscopy of a charmed quark bound to a strange antiquark, the so-called "F meson," and toward the spectroscopy of charmed baryons.

Natural Flavors

A very important parameter for the quark hypothesis is the ratio, R, of the cross section for an electron–positron pair to annihilate to all

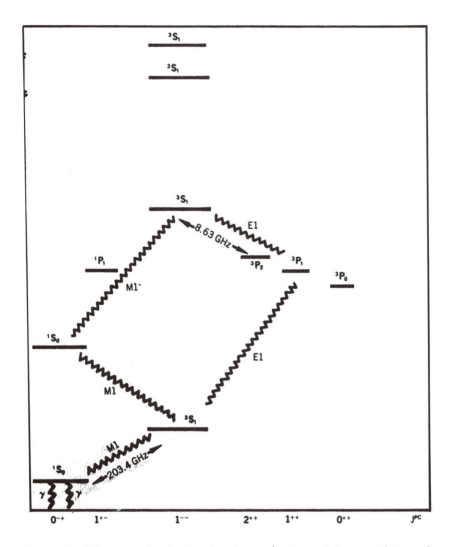

FIGURE 3. *The energy levels of positronium, e^+e^-, provide an analogy to the charmonium spectrum of Figure 2. The first excited levels with $n=2$ show fine-structure splitting.*

possible configurations of hadrons to the cross section to annihilate to a pair of muons, illustrated by Figure 5. Muons, like electrons, are pointlike members of that other family of particles known as leptons—particles that do not experience the strong nuclear forces at all. The muons are charged and, of course, interact through the well-tested

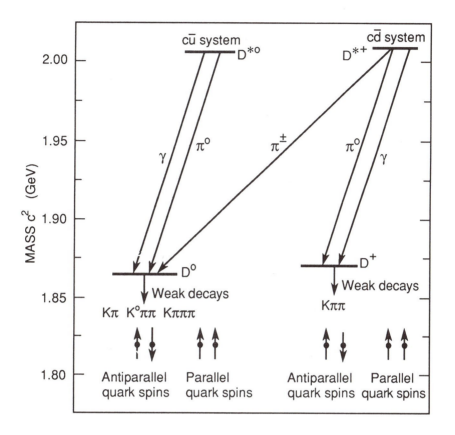

FIGURE 4. *New mesonic states, the D's and D*'s, are formed when a charmed quark binds with an ordinary uncharmed antiquark. The diagram shows the spectroscopy of the four particles.*

electromagnetic forces. In this context, the weak forces are negligible. We believe that, when an electron and a positron annihilate to form hadrons at high energy, a single quark–antiquark pair is the intermediary, even though the quarks themselves do not appear in the final states. If the quarks are pointlike, their contribution should exhibit the same energy dependence as that found in the production of pairs of pointlike muons. The ratio of cross sections therefore should measure the sum of the squares of the quark charges and should be approximately energy-independent.

Figure 6, which shows[12] the measured ratio, adds considerable support to the quark picture by showing two regions of approximately

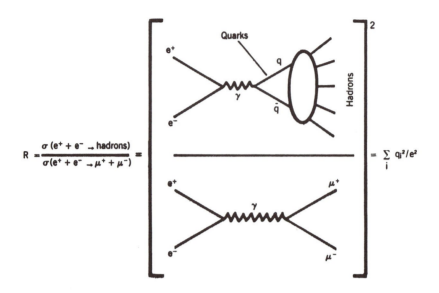

$$R = \frac{\sigma (e^+ + e^- \rightarrow \text{hadrons})}{\sigma(e^+ + e^- \rightarrow \mu^+ + \mu^-)} = \qquad \qquad = \sum_i q_i^2/e^2$$

FIGURE 5. *A schematic picture showing that the ratio R of the cross section for annihilation to hadrons of an electron–positron pair to the cross section for their annihilation to a muon pair is given by the sums of the squares of the quark charges.*

constant R. In the lower-energy region, 1.5–3.1 GeV, which is above the individual resonances but below the onset of the new physics, R has a plateau at about $2\frac{1}{2}$. Above the charmonium region, 5–8 GeV, the plateau rises to about 5. The 4–5 GeV region is very rich in new physics associated with the creation of charmed particles, as well as with the creation of pairs of a very likely new heavy lepton, the tau, of mass 1.8 GeV. These values of R provide clues of the greatest importance about the nature and properties of the quarks. As illustrated, they are close to what one predicts for three varieties—called "flavors"—of quarks below the region in which charm is excited, as well as for the four flavors (including the charmed quarks) in the higher-energy region, provided each flavor occurs in three colors. Otherwise—without color—there would be a sharp discrepancy of a factor of three.

These results thus represent a triumph for the hypothesis of color

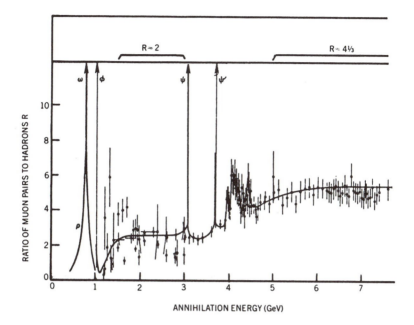

FIGURE 6. *The experimental data for the ratio R of Figure 5 show two plateaus consistent with the calculation indicated there. One of them is near $R \approx 3[(\frac{2}{3})^2 + 2(\frac{1}{3})^2] = 2$, and the other ratio is near $R \approx 2 + 3(\frac{2}{3})^2 + 1 = 4\frac{1}{3}$. The lower-energy region has three flavors and the higher-energy region, where charm is excited, has four flavors plus the heavy tau lepton.*

triplets of quarks. On a descriptive level, the quark hypothesis evidently accounts very well for a broad set of observations. Furthermore, does anyone seriously doubt that R will increase onto a higher plateau when the total energy of the colliding electrons and positrons exceeds 9.4 GeV, the threshold for producing the upsilon meson recently discovered at Fermilab? The upsilon is believed to be a bound quark-antiquark pair like charmonium, but built of yet another new flavor of quark pairs.

By now we have had such a proliferation of quark degrees of freedom—presumably at least fifteen, five flavors times three colors—that it can hardly be said they are entering a very exclusive Social Register.

If we look back once more to the 1930s, we recall that the neutrino became a strong, and to most a persuasive, candidate for the Social

Register of elementary particles long before it was seen, when Fermi provided it with effective and indisputable theoretical credentials. There is optimism, at least among many theorists, that quarks have also been gaining the dignity of a pedigree during the past few years. The reason for this optimism is recent theoretical progress that has identified important features of successful quark dynamics in a well defined class of quantum field theories known as nonabelian gauge theories.[14] These are generalizations, pioneered in 1954 by Chen Ning Yang and Robert Mills, of the precisely tested and unfailingly successful theory of quantum electrodynamics (QED). The photons, which are the vector quanta of QED, are themselves electrically neutral; this is characteristic of an abelian gauge theory. In nonabelian gauge theory, the vector quanta, dubbed "gluons," are themselves also charged. The gluons can exchange this charge between sources or between one another. In the theory of quarks and gluons known as "quantum chromodynamics" (QCD), the color quantum number plays the same role as the electric charge in QED. In QCD, an octet family of colored gluons replaces the single photon of QED as the messenger of the color electric and magnetic fields.

The case for QCD, pioneered in 1973 by H. David Politzer, and by David Gross and Frank Wilczek, is based on the crucial observation that such theories can lead to forces between the quarks, mediated by gluons, that grow weaker at short distances. This behavior is known as "asymptotic freedom." As illustrated in Figure 7, it contrasts with the familiar forces of electromagnetism, which grow even stronger than the $1/r^2$ of the Coulomb law at short distances when quantum effects—in particular vacuum polarization—are included. Asymptotically free forces between quarks provide a basis for explaining the observed behavior of the hard collisions, such as Bjorken scaling, which look like scattering from almost free, pointlike light quarks within the hadrons. These forces must remain in effect for large separations, however, so that the quarks that behave as almost free at short distances on the scale of hadronic sizes will be confined and cannot be pulled apart. Further, the theory must allow only the formation of color-singlet states, to account for the observed spectra and quark structure of hadrons. In QCD, the simplest quark configurations that can form color-singlet states are just the observed ones with three quarks or a quark–antiquark pair.

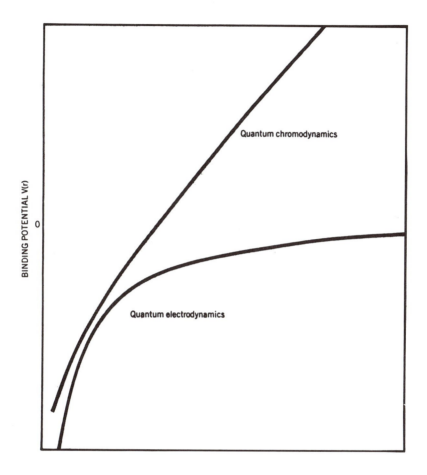

FIGURE 7. *The binding potential in quantum chromodynamics, mediated by gluons, exhibits asymptotic freedom and confinement, in contrast to the electromagnetic potential.*

Color Confinement

In the framework of quantum chromodynamics, quark confinement becomes synonymous with color confinement. This is the other basic ingredient, in addition to asymptotic freedom, that we want to find in QCD if it is to form the basis of a fundamental dynamical theory of hadrons in terms of gluons and of quark constituents. The theoretical challenge to prove whether or not QCD actually confines is formidable because of the difficulty in solving—or even attempting to solve—

quantum field theory when the forces are strong and we cannot resort to weak-coupling perturbative treatments.

With an appropriate dash of the theorists' optimism, let us suppose for a moment that these technical challenges will be surmounted and a convincing case made for color confinement in QCD. We may even further imagine that approximately correct mass spectra will be calculated for the hadrons; this includes understanding why the pion is much lighter than all other hadrons. How compelling will this make the case for quarks as elementary fundamental constituents of the hadron?

The case for quarks might appear more compelling than that of the neutrino back in 1934, because we now see all the elements of a grand synthesis in place. The quantum chromodynamics to which we have turned for a theory of hadrons is a nonabelian local gauge theory of the same formal structure as the one introduced in unifying the weak and electromagnetic interactions. Steven Weinberg discussed this in his article in the April 1977 issue of *Physics Today*. The strong, the electromagnetic, and the weak interactions have very different characteristics, such as their ranges and strengths, as studied at present laboratory energies. It has been conjectured,[15] starting with the pioneering work in 1967 of Weinberg and Abdus Salam, that the difference between the weak and electromagnetic interactions is a consequence of a partially broken symmetry for the weak processes. The intermediate vector mesons of the weak interactions acquire large masses due to the symmetry breaking; only at truly high energies exceeding these masses—thought to be in the range of 70 GeV or higher—will the common characteristics of the weak and electromagnetic interactions be apparent. Some predictions of this approach to a unified theory of weak and electromagnetic processes have already been verified—in particular, neutral-current effects in neutrino scattering.

A further extension of the symmetry considerations underlying the gauge theories to the strong interactions puts the quarks on the same basis as the leptons. The difference between these derives from the fact that quarks carry the color quantum number—the charge of the strong interactions—whereas leptons do not and are immune to the strong forces. Hence leptons, in contrast to quarks, are not confined by the requirement that color remain nature's secret. Such a picture is very attractive. It provides a giant step toward one of the principal goals of modern physics: a unified understanding of all the basic interactions in nature.

Were we to achieve such a theoretical synthesis, the case for admitting quarks to the Social Register as the hadron's basic constituents would clearly be very strong. However, recalling our earlier discussion of the neutrino, do we no longer care that we are now identifying as fundamental constituents of hadronic matter things that, in contrast to all our prior experience, cannot even in principle be isolated and observed? When *is* a particle? Are we now willing to say, as a variation on MacLeish's lines, that, in contrast to a poem, a particle need not be but should mean?

The burden of proof for quarks is very different from the original argument for the neutrino. Whereas the neutrino was postulated to protect energy, momentum, and spin conservation laws, which are based on observable space–time properties, no conservation laws *require* quarks. However, the quarks do present the very strong operational credentials I have described—both experimental and theoretical.

What troubles me most about accepting quarks as the fundamental hadronic constituents is quite simple and has nothing to do with their confinement and Helmholtz's dictum "to purify physics from the last remnants of metaphysics." It is that we already have so many quark degrees of freedom—at least five flavors in each of three colors. The Social Register of particles surely must be more exclusive than that if it is to be valued and honored as it was in those good old days!

Break a Meson, Make Two Quarks

Having said this, I have a sneaking suspicion that quarks may turn out to be somewhat like magnetic poles and nothing more.[16] When broken in two, a bar magnet becomes not isolated north and south poles separated from one another but two magnets, each with its own north and south poles. As many have noted, this is very similar to what happens when a meson made of a quark and an anti–quark is smashed apart, as shown in Figure 8. The debris of the shattered meson consists not of isolated quarks but of more mesons, each with its own quark and antiquark. This is not a literal analogy, of course, because the nonabelian color gauge theory also allows baryons made of three quarks to be formed in color-singlet states. Nevertheless, it is sufficiently close and accurate to be a useful guide.

Our curiosity and present plight with quarks may not be very different from that of an inquisitive mariner at sea some ten centuries or so ago. In a moment of calm on a passage, he might have viewed a compass needle—a spare one, I hope!—with idle bafflement or scientific curiosity, and tried to break it apart to separate the two ends with

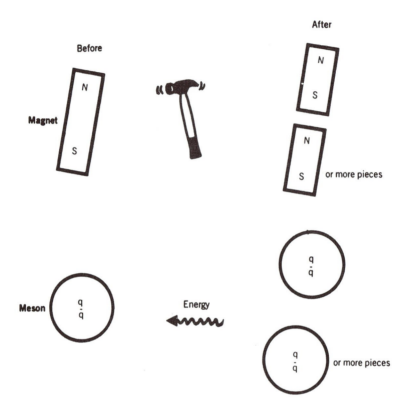

FIGURE 8. *The way quarks break is analogous to the way a bar magnet breaks. Just as the magnet does not break into isolated poles, the meson does not break into isolated quarks.*

opposite properties—that is, the north pole from the south pole. But to no avail, for, with each breaking of the compass needle, he ended up with an additional one having both a north and a south pole. The understanding of this impossibility to isolate single magnetic poles came only when, in 1820, André Ampere explained magnetism in terms of electric currents. In fact, a fundamental theory of magnetism at the atomic level, in terms of the currents of circulating and spinning electrons, was achieved only in this century on the basis of modern quantum theory.

Perhaps the quarks are not the fundamental particles of hadron dynamics, just as magnetic poles are but phenomenological manifestations of amperian currents. Presumably they will remain no less important for the description and understanding of subnuclear processes than bar magnets are for understanding a lot of the physics of magnetism. The quarks have done too much already to be forgotten and discarded. If, however, there are underlying dynamics, the whole question of the meaning of confined constituents as elementary particles will disappear. Whether or not the analogy with magnetism has any merit, the notion of a new "elementary structure" underlying the quarks destroys the very attractive idea of a quark–lepton parallel unless we similarly modify and elaborate our picture of leptons. This hardly appears to be an attractive prospect now, particularly because no one has either seen or theorized creatively as to what these new "elementary structures" might be. On the other hand, the lepton degrees of freedom, along with those of the quark, have also begun to proliferate.

Some physicists were discouraged already 30 years ago with the discovery of the muon, about which I. I. Rabi is quoted as remarking, "Who ordered that?" More recently, we have apparently encountered a new, third strain of leptons[17] in the tau, which is also thought to be accompanied by its own neutrino, as are the electron and muon. As we continue to raise our energy frontier, are we fated to meet proliferating families of leptons as well as quarks? Facing this dilemma, Werner Heisenberg proposed a different viewpoint in a lecture on the nature of elementary particles, which he delivered in 1975, shortly before his death.[18] He raised the possibility that we are asking the wrong question in particle physics when we ask what a proton "consists of":

> I will now discuss that development of theoretical particle physics that, I believe, begins with the wrong questions. First of all there is the thesis that the observed particles such as the proton . . . consist of smaller particles: quarks . . . or whatever else, none of which have been observed. Apparently here the question was asked: What does a proton consist of? But the questioners appear to have forgotten that the phrase "consist of" has a tolerably clear meaning only if the particle can be divided into pieces with a small amount of energy, much smaller than the rest mass of the particle itself.

Heisenberg is referring here to the fact that, in the realm of quarks, in contrast to atomic or even nuclear physics, we are no longer dealing with energies that are but small fractions of the rest masses of the particles themselves. The strong subnuclear forces confining the three valence quarks in the baryon also create many virtual quark pairs and gluons. Retardation effects, as well as the energy–momentum content of the gluon fields that bind the quarks together, will be important. All of these effects and virtual particles—the gluons as well as the fluctuating numbers of quark pairs—must be included in a dynamical description of "life" within the hadrons. When we apply quantum mechanics to a relativistic strong-interaction problem, our basic elements are no longer simply a fixed small number of particles, but field amplitudes that create eigenstates of definite quantum numbers. In view of this, Heisenberg suggested that our quest for simplicity and an underlying level of unification should be formulated in terms of the fundamental currents or symmetries of the theory.

Heisenberg's emphasis on symmetries is reminiscent of the idea of Pythagoras and Plato. Pythagoras first explicitly emphasized the importance of symmetry 25 centuries ago and insisted that, ultimately, all order is capable of being understood and expressed in terms of number. Plato provided a specific form for this idea by identifying the fundamental symmetries as the basic atoms in his scheme. Dressing his idea in modern garb, we should not so much focus on the problem of the many quark degrees of freedom as seek simplicity in the underlying group structure of the fundamental equations. Perhaps in our quest for simplicity we should follow the lead of Albert Einstein by incorporating the sources and forces of a unified field theory in the physical geometry of space–time.

The Hidden One

The fate of the idea of hidden building blocks can be settled only by experiments, including the very fundamental and difficult quark searches already in progress. Whatever their future fate, the concept of confined quarks already has a distinguished history, which dates back to the classical Greek and Roman times and includes the writings of Leucippus, Democritus, Epicurus, and Lucretius. Modern historians of science still debate intensely whether the atoms of Democritus and Leucippus are physically indivisible (because they are solid and impenetrable) or whether they are logically and mathematically indivisible (because they have no parts). Some suggest that both kinds of atoms are to be found in their writings. Apparently, a full development of the idea of indivisible elementary atoms consisting of minimal parts that are permanently confined and can not be pulled apart dates to Epicurus, around 300 B.C. In a charming article,[19] Julia and Thomas Gaisser refer to the elaboration of this idea by Lucretius, who refers to the *minimae partes* of the indivisible atoms in his great poem *De Rerum Natura*. Clearly these were the early versions of quarks—or partons, as we sometimes call the minimal parts of the hadrons.

I was so intrigued by these references to confined quarks, or *minimae partes*, in classical philosophy that I found myself also wondering whether Greek mythology could not provide some roots—perhaps even a name—for these hidden basic things. What I came up with after anything but a scholarly, thorough search[20] was the nymph goddess Calypso, referred to as the hidden one, who kept Odysseus confined to her island of Ogygia for seven years after his shipwreck en route home from the Trojan wars. Calypso offered Odysseus immortality if he would share eternal, blissful confinement with her. However, when the gods called on Odysseus to resume his human destiny and his hazardous journey home, he rejected her offer.

Whether quarks will remain mysterious as hidden elementary "calypsons," be understood as phenomenological manifestations of an underlying dynamics, or reveal themselves directly to experiment remains for the future. So does the fate of those theorists among us who concern ourselves with quantum chromodynamics, asymptotic freedom, and quark confinement. Those theorists who have said that it is impossible to liberate quarks should perhaps look again to Epicurus, the metaphysical father of confined quarks, for a second message that is frequently—and erroneously—attributed to him: Eat, drink, and be merry, for tomorrow an isolated quark may actually be found.

References

[1] M. Gell-Mann, Phys. Lett **8**, 214 (1964); G. Zweig, CERN Preprints TH401, 412 (1964).

[2] C. S. Wu, in *Theoretical Physics in the Twentieth Century, A Memorial Volume to Wolfgang Pauli*, edited by M. Fierz, V. F. Weisskopf (Interscience, New York, 1960), p. 249.

[3] N. Bohr, J. Chem. Soc., **349** (1932).

[4] J. Chadwick, Proc. Roy. Soc. A **136**, 692 (1932).

[5] E. Fermi, Z. Phys. **88**, 161 (1934); Ric. Sci. **2**, Part 12 (1933).

[6] C. W. Sherwin, Phys. Rev. **73**, 1219 (1948); **75**, 1799 (1948); **82**, 52 (1951).

[7] C. L. Cowan, F. Reines, F. B. Harrison, H. W. Kruse, A. D. McGuire, Science **124**, 103 (1956).

[8] L. W. Jones, Rev. Mod. Phys. **49**, 717 (1977).

[9] Reference 3, p. 384.

[10] R. L. Jaffe, Nature **268**, 201 (1977).

[11] J. I. Friedman, H. Kendall, Ann. Rev. Nucl. Sci. **22**, 203 (1972).

[12]F. Schwitters, Scientific American, April 1977, p. 56; W. K. H. Panofsky, talk presented at the Centennial Meeting of the Mathematical and Physical Societies of Japan (Tokyo, 10 October 1977), SLAC-PUB-2025, Stanford, CA.

[13]S. L. Glashow, Scientific American, April 1975, p. 38.

[14]Y. Nambu, Scientific American, May 1976, p. 48.

[15]S. Weinberg, Scientific American, January 1974, p. 50; E. Leader, P. G. Williams, Nature **257**, 93 (1975).

[16]S. D. Drell, Daedalus, March 1977, p. 15.

[17]For an updated discussion and reference see Frank Close: "The Cosmic Onion" (American Institute of Physics, 1983).

[18]W. Heisenberg, Physics Today, March 1976, p. 39.

[19]J. H. Gaisser, T. K. Gaisser, Am. J. Phys. **45**, 439 (1977).

[20]Homer, *The Odyssey*, book 5.

The Superconducting Supercollider

WITH T.D. LEE

The quest to find out what we and our physical world are made of is a mark of civilization dating back to its very beginning. But it wasn't until approximately 500 years ago—about the time of the discovery of North America—that modern science was born. This came about through the realization that theories must be tested by experiment and that certain crucial and precise observations can, in turn, lead to new ideas. Through this strong coupling of experiment and theory, we are able to reduce the great diversity of natural phenomena to a single set of fundamental physical laws. Therefore, any progress that can be made on the fundamental laws will have its effect everywhere and in everything.

The important observations on electricity by Benjamin Franklin in the eighteenth century and the crucial experiments on the electric and magnetic forces by Michael Faraday in the nineteenth led to the unification of these two forces by James Clark Maxwell later in that century. This, in turn, made it possible for us to understand the fundamental nature of light and its identity as a pure electromagnetic phenomenon. From this breakthrough came the development of generators, electric motors, telegraph, television, radar, and, indeed, all modern communications.

At the turn of our century, two crucial, though seemingly esoteric, discoveries were made. One was the result of an experiment by Albert

A. Michelson and Edward W. Morley in 1887 in this country; the other was the black-body radiation formula announced by Max Planck in 1900. The former was the basis for Einstein's theory of relativity and the latter laid the foundation for the construction of quantum mechanics. In this century, all the modern scientific and technological developments—nuclear energy, atomic physics, molecular beams, lasers, x-ray technology, semiconductors, superconductors, supercomputers—exist only because of an understanding of relativity and quantum mechanics. To humanity and to our understanding of nature, these are all encompassing.

Now, near the end of the twentieth century, we must ask what will be the legacy we give to the next generation in the next century. At the end of the 1890s, physicists had a glimpse of a new vista, the existence of exciting and unexplored fundamental areas. Today we also know of the existence of an entirely new class of fundamental forces: the class of those forces responsible for symmetry breaking. We know only of the existence of this new class and very little else. The new superconducting supercollider (SSC) is the key we will use to unlock the door and to take the next big step. As was the case when other great advances were achieved in understanding nature, present progress on the basic physical laws will have a similar long-range and vast impact on the technology of the future.

Since the SSC project is of such a large magnitude and entails so great an expense, it naturally invites a number of serious questions: (1) How important is the SSC in terms of the new knowledge it will provide? (2) Are there alternative possibilities, perhaps more modest in size and cost, for advancing the frontiers of our knowledge? (3) How important is it to the United States to invest in science, and in high-energy physics in particular? What practical benefits to society can be expected to result from the SSC?

How Important Is the SSC in Terms of the New Knowledge It Will Provide?

The very spirit of physics is to explore the unknown. While this makes it difficult for us to predict precisely what we will discover in the future, we *are* in a position to forecast the minimum payoff. Based on our present knowledge, we are confident that the SSC will explore a specific region in which major new discoveries will be made. The SSC specifications were established with this goal in mind, and experience gained since 1983 has strengthened our conviction of the importance of constructing a proton–proton collider with the beam energy of 20 TeV and luminosity* of 10^{33} cm^{-2} sec^{-1}, as originally proposed.

As a result of truly remarkable progress during the past 20 years, we do have one clear benchmark that is crucial as a guide in setting the energy of SSC at 20 TeV. This benchmark comes from our success in unifying the electromagnetic forces with the weak forces of radioactive decay into a single entity, the electroweak interaction (commonly referred to as the standard model). It is an achievement reminiscent of the unification of electricity and magnetism by Maxwell.

Based on our new theoretical structure for unifying weak and electromagnetic forces, the existence and masses of new particles, the W and Z intermediate bosons, were predicted and confirmed experimentally at the European Organization for Nuclear Research (CERN) in 1983. From the predictions of this theory, we are certain that exciting new phenomena *must* appear at the SSC design energy.

At present, we know that there exist three classes of forces—the strong force that binds the nucleus together, the electroweak force, and gravity. We know that all these forces are based on symmetry principles, yet practically all these symmetries are broken. The symmetry breaking lies outside the present scope of our understanding. A major task of the SSC is to understand this new class of symmetry-breaking forces. Our present electroweak theory makes it possible for us to say with confidence that 20 TeV is about the minimum energy needed to see the new phenomena in whatever form they may take.

The masses of all known particles break these symmetries. Consequently, an understanding of the symmetry-breaking forces will lead to a comprehension of the origin of the masses of all known particles. One of the promising manifestations of symmetry breaking may be the existence of particles of a new type, the Higgs mesons. If so, then we would also discover such new particles as well as advancing our understanding of symmetry breaking. In order to make sure that we can unravel the nature of the symmetry-breaking force in the electroweak interaction, we must measure the scattering between the W and Z bosons, and that, we are confident, can be done at the 20 TeV design energy of the SSC.

The recent major advances in particle physics and astrophysics have given us the very first experimentally based glimpse of the history of the evolution of the universe following the Big Bang some 15 billion

---

*Luminosity is the quantity that, when multiplied by the interaction cross section, gives the number of events per second.

years ago. The very high collision energy of the SSC will recreate the physical state that existed in our universe about 1 femtosecond (10^{-15} second) after the Big Bang. Future history books will tell that ours was a time when mankind was able to begin recreating the evolution of the universe following that Big Bang based on solid experimental data, not just on theoretical concepts. The SSC, together with our scientifically productive deep space probes, will enable us to write further chapters in that history.

The search for the smallest building blocks from which everything is made drives us to explore physical phenomena within smaller and smaller distances; that necessitates energies higher and higher in inverse proportion to the distance in question. The SSC energy will enable us to examine the physical space within an attocentimeter (that is, 10^{-18} centimeter, a distance hundreds of thousands times smaller than the size of a nucleus). Since there is no comparable facility being planned anywhere else in the world, the very uniqueness of the SSC insures that we will be exploring an entirely uncharted region. Of course, we cannot definitely predict what kind of new basic particles the SSC will produce. It is precisely this major step into the unknown that poses the challenge, captures our imaginations, and promises the greatest intellectual rewards. This is why the SSC will attract the best creative young minds in the world. It will also restore our cutting edge in both basic science and high technology.

Physics is monolithic. There exists only one universe—our universe. The multitude of forms of all matter obeys only one set of fundamental laws, and we are at the threshold of comprehending that set of fundamental laws. To nature, the same set of laws governs the motion of all particles in every aspect of their manifestations—gas, liquid, solid, living beings, planets, stars, galaxies, from the beginning of the universe to the present. In physics, there is no distinction between the different disciplines of our profession. Our aim is to understand the set of laws that governs everything. The SSC provides a direct route toward achieving this understanding. It will be our contribution to the civilization of the next century.

Are There Alternative Possibilities, Perhaps More Modest in Size and Cost, for Advancing the Frontiers of Our Knowledge?

This question has been addressed by the community of high-energy physicists—the machine builders, the experimentalists, and the theorists—since 1982 in a number of workshops and in collaboration with the Department of Energy through the mechanism of its High Energy Physics Advisory Panel (HEPAP). Encouraged by the dramatic discoveries at the CERN proton–antiproton collider and by the successful operation of the Fermilab Tevatron—the first superconducting synchrotron—the 1983 HEPAP Subpanel on Future Facilities recommended "the immediate initiation of a multi-TeV, high-luminosity proton–proton collider project with the goal of physics at the earliest possible date." That recommendation may be taken as the beginning of the SSC project.

In March 1986, the SSC Central Design Group, composed of physicists and engineers drawn from universities and national laboratories around the world, produced a site-independent conceptual design for a proton–proton collider with 20 TeV per beam and peak luminosity of 10^{33} cm^{-2} sec^{-1}. The two most important ingredients of that recommendation were the following. One, the scientific community was convinced that the technology existed to build a reliable and versatile SSC project designed to those specifications. Two, our scientific understanding provided confidence that the SSC would provide the data necessary for the beginning of an exploration of how symmetries are broken in the basic forces of nature, leading to an understanding of the origin of the masses of all particles.

The SSC Laboratory (SSCL) management has now developed a detailed design, specific to the site selected in Ellis County, Texas, by the DOE. This has led to an increase in the estimated total project cost from the 1986 proposal. The cost increase arises primarily from two types of changes. The first type involves recalculation of labor and materials costs and requirements for magnet research and development and for overall instrumentation to assure reliable accelerator performance. The second type involves technical changes (higher injection energy and a larger magnet aperture).

The main reason for the technical change is that large-scale accelerators using superconducting magnets have only been in operation since 1986, after the original conceptual design of the SSC was made. Over the last two years, beam measurements at the Tevatron at Fermilab and magnetic measurements at the German Electron Synchrotron Laboratory (DESY) have shown the existence of persistent eddy currents that require correction. Based on this experience, the injection energy and the magnetic aperture were increased in order to ensure a reliable machine. New massive numerical simulations using supercomputers now provide us with detailed knowledge of stability under realistic operating conditions. The scientific leadership of the SSCL judges these technical changes to be required for reliable operation and efficient commissioning of the new accelerator.

As a result of these changes, and, in particular, the increased cost, the DOE constituted a HEPAP Subpanel on SSC Physics "to provide advice on the range of useful machine parameters in order to complete the design phase of the facility." It was the unanimous recommendation of this panel and of HEPAP, itself, in accepting and transmitting it to DOE, that implementing these design changes "will ensure confidence in reliable and timely operation of the SSC." The subpanel found that the only cuts that would allow substantial cost savings would seriously reduce the capabilities, as well as the scientific potential of the SSC. It recommended unanimously against redesigning the machine with a reduced circumference, and a proportionally reduced energy. The scientific basis for this recommendation was summarized succinctly in the transmittal letter of HEPAP Chairman Professor Francis Low to Dr. James Decker, Acting Director of the Office of Energy Research:

> The Subpanel has concluded on physics research grounds that any substantial reduction in the energy of the SSC would compromise our ability to elucidate the nature of electroweak symmetry, a truly fundamental problem at the core of the Standard Model. This is because, with 20 TeV beams, there is a confidence that these phenomena can be studied in whichever form they take, whereas, this confidence is quickly lost at lower energies. In addition, no substantial increase of luminosity can make up for a reduction in energy because no multipurpose detector is capable of operating well above 10^{33} cm^{-2} sec^{-1}, the design luminosity of the SSC. Only limited purpose, specially designed detectors can operate at higher luminosities, and these are not capable of thorough exploration of the phenomena in question.

In essence, the scientific judgment is that such a reduction would unacceptably increase the risk of missing important new physics, which is the very goal of building SSC.

Finally, we comment that SSC will be a unique facility well into the next century. It will represent a great step by a factor of ten or more beyond any other accelerator now operating or under construction. The scientific leadership at CERN in Geneva is seriously considering constructing a proton–proton collider in the existing 17-mile-circumference tunnel for its currently operating Large Electron–Positron (LEP) accelerator. However, the SSC, with its 54-mile tunnel and 20 TeV beam energy, will have a major advantage relative to the 8 TeV maximum of the CERN design concept. The SSC will have a unique potential to explore a wide range of physics in the energy range we believe crucial for our discovering the exciting new phenomena for understanding symmetry breaking and particle masses that are the primary goal of SSC physics.

How Important Is It for the United States to Invest in Science, and in High-Energy Physics in Particular? What Practical Benefits to Society Can Be Expected to Result From the SSC?

When construction of the SSC was recommended by President Reagan in 1988, and when it was reaffirmed by President Bush in 1989, it was identified as a national goal. At the same time, a commitment was made to maintain support for a strong and broad-based national program. This is an important commitment, because high-quality scientists and engineers are an important national resource. This technical community is a critical ingredient in our national effort to remain a world leader in technical innovation, to maintain a strong economy and a high standard of living, to flourish in competitive high-tech industries, and to meet our goals in national security.

The SSC will be an important component in training and in maintaining a technological edge for the United States. For many decades into the next century, it will be a unique tool for ensuring U.S. leadership and for helping to train outstanding young American scientists and engineers, and students from more than 100 American universities, in the most sophisticated and demanding new technologies.

More than 50 years ago, Ernest Lawrence at Berkeley and Merle Tuve at the Carnegie Institution in Washington, D.C. built the first large accelerators in the United States in order to study the structure of subnuclear matter. From that day to the present, the excitement and the romance of probing nature's secrets with the most fundamental of all questions—"What are we made of?"—has attracted the best scientific talent of this country.

The SSC will assure continued U.S. leadership in this field, which has been a source of great pride, as well as a stimulus to important technical innovations in superconducting technologies and computer control of complicated systems. It will also be a boon and an important challenge to the leadership of American industries in the highest tech fields, whose experience and expertise will be relied on in building the 54-mile-long system of superconducting magnets and to construct the sophisticated detectors that must be designed to select those few events of crucial importance out of a background of hundreds of millions of interactions occurring each second.

Conclusion

To summarize, the physics community—of the United States and of the world—is excited by the prospect that the SSC will begin to provide data by the end of this decade. Through research, training, and industrial manufacturing, the SSC project will contribute to American technological strength. It will also be a magnet for scientific cooperation worldwide. It will advance our understanding of the universe, and it will help define the quality of our culture. It will, indeed, be an important legacy for us to give to the next generation of scientists of the twenty-first century.

PHYSICISTS

Wolfgang K.H. Panofsky

Beyond any of my words this morning, the presence here today of all you colleagues of Pief's, from places distant as well as close, and from associations long lasting out of the distant past, as well as from very recent times—your presence is the strongest evidence of the respect, the affection, the admiration we all feel for Pief. This admiration has also been warmly expressed in an array of wires and letters from all over the world sent by friends unable to be here today—to their great regret.

Pief's achievements and leadership are so important, so extensive and diverse that there is an almost endless list of reasons for us to welcome this opportunity to be here today to honor him. But, perhaps, no reason is more compelling than the warmth of our affection for this friend we all cherish.

I first met Pief—known more formally as Wolfgang K.H. Panofsky—in 1951. I had just come to Stanford as a physics instructor, and that was the year he decided to move to Stanford from Berkeley, which was then in the painful throes of a crisis over a faculty loyalty oath that poisoned its academic climate and diminished its luster for years to come. Stanford was the winner and, happily for all, Berkeley has since successfully buried that regrettable episode deep into its past. As I look back to that first meeting with Pief in 1951 (33 years ago)— and to my subsequent close association with him since my own return to Stanford in 1956 (28 years ago)—I am amazed at the invariance principles that characterize all of Pief's actions and interactions. His optimism, his warmth, his patience, his integrity, his kindness, his courage, and his persistence—like the gravitational constant or the fine-structure constant—haven't wavered or altered one bit during all these years. Neither has his dress habits or his geometry.

He first arrived at Stanford in an ancient Cadillac—and his current Mercedes is of comparable maturity—probably older and, indicating a slight change of taste, perhaps evidence of weak symmetry breaking. Furthermore, whether dealing with students in elementary physics classes or with presidents, the anonymous or the mighty, theorists or practical scientists, the obtuse or the acute, there is a universality in Pief's interactions. He always shows the same patience. I have heard a liberal defined as one who believes in the improvability of the human being. By that definition, Pief saturates the unitary bound of liberalism—and also of integrity, for I've never heard him hesitate to acknowledge his ignorance when he doesn't know something, as rare as such occasions are.

Pief has contributed extensively and profoundly to high energy physics—in particular, through his beautiful, textbook experiments analyzing the gamma-ray absorption in hydrogen and deuterium, which determined the parity of the pi mesons, showed that neutral pi's were lighter than charged pi's, and determined accurate pion masses. This beautiful work, done in collaboration with Lee Aamodt and Jim Hadley, introduced the term "Panofsky ratio" into the literature. He also collaborated with Jack Steinberger, and their experiments directly identified the neutral pi's produced in the electron synchrotron by observing the two decay gamma rays in coincidence. In addition, after arriving at Stanford, he initiated the study of meson production by electrons, leading to the first information on the electromagnetic structure of the unstable excited states of the nucleon. He has also pioneered the building of beautiful machines and created a great laboratory— immodestly, perhaps, considered here [at Stanford] the greatest high-energy lab. He has been an inspired and inspiring teacher. Throughout his career he has devoted himself unselfishly to effective, wise, and innumerable contributions to science policy and budgetary considerations in Washington, and to improved international collaboration in science and the free flow of scientists and science across national and ideological boundaries.

Pief has also made profound contributions as a government adviser to official deliberations, as well as to the public debate, on vital issues of arms control and international security. Unfortunately for us all, Pief's views have not always been accepted, not because they lacked vision or wisdom or a compelling logic, but because of the shortcomings of those in responsible positions in government to act with a comparable courage and wisdom.

But there is something about the life of the good Dr. Panofsky about which few are aware. I've known Pief for one-third of a century and have been very close to him for many, many years. But I had forgotten this fact, and it took research in the preparation for this tribute for me to be reminded that our one and only Pief was the subject of an article in *Playboy* magazine seven years ago. As the famous saying of Ring Lardner goes, "you could look it up"—June, 1977. No, there was no centerfold picture of him. To quote from *Playboy* magazine: "Dr. Wolfgang Hermann Panofsky was from Berlin and was naturalized in 1942." I will omit the next sentence in order not to embarrass Pief— were I to repeat it, it would say: "Dr. Panofsky may be the brightest man in the world." But, in passing over that, we come to "the beef":

> He is 5' 2" tall, weighs 150 pounds, neither smokes nor drinks and is manifestly, painfully indifferent to clothes. Not that he's a nudist; just that his mind is on higher things.

That clearly is a collection of characteristics that makes it somewhat difficult for *Playboy* to continue on into revealing depths—although the source of Pief's charms that qualified him for *Playboy* was identi- fied by the editors as follows: First he built a straight 10,000-foot "long vacuum pipe that is housed in a heavy concrete casing sunk 25 feet underground that has no practical use whatsoever," and, second, "he is a key figure in the Strangelove business. . . . ; he is smarter than the rest"—among whom *Playboy* included Edward Teller, Herman Kahn, and Eugene Wigner, to mention a random three—and "therefore has helped them avoid potentially embarrassing crushing boo-boos." And I can attest that is indeed true. He *is* smarter, and many a gaffe has been avoided when he has been heard and obeyed. Incidentally, I can think of only one other physicist to make *Playboy*: William Shockley— and he had to found a rather unusual kind of bank down in Southern California to be so recognized.

Another published biography of Pief says that he is 5' 2" and has eyes of blue, which to many automatically suggests one of the famous song lines of the flapper era: "Five foot two, eyes of blue/Oh what those five feet can do. . . ." And now I ask what other physicist you know has been immortalized in song—I have to admit, however, that that verse dates back to Pief's early childhood, so there is hardly a causal connection.

Pief's achievements have, of course, been recognized by his being awarded almost every conceivable honor that exists, and the citations that accompany these awards themselves tell much about the breadth of his accomplishments and the deep respect he has earned from so broad a community. For example, when he received the Enrico Fermi Award in 1979, the citation read:

> For his many important contributions to elementary particle physics; for his leading role in advancing accelerator technology evidenced in the success of the SLAC 20 BeV, SPEAR and PEP machines; for his positive influence on and inspiration of younger scientists; and for the depth and thoughtfulness of advice he has so generously given the United States Government. . . .

Similar words of praise can be found in the citations for the National Medal of Science; the Franklin Medal from the Franklin Institute, "particularly for accelerator design, construction, and successful exploitation"; the Ernest O. Lawrence Medal for his fundamental contributions to meson physics; the Leo Szilard Award for his contributions to society through his arms-control work; the Richtmeyer Lecture by the American Association of Physics Teachers; and the list goes on.

Every facet of Pief's activities has been honored because, in typical Panofsky fashion, he set and achieved the highest standards in each of his many undertakings. In his days as a teaching professor, he was exceedingly popular and beloved by the students from freshman courses on up because of the clarity and excitement of his lectures, the warmth of his personality, and his accessibility. It is characteristic of Panofsky that that's precisely the way he has been running the Stanford Linear Accelerator Center (SLAC) for more than 25 years. His office door is always open; everyone at the Lab has access to him; more than once, running around in shirt sleeves at odd hours, he has been taken for a janitor—and has acted out the role. His patience and energy never seem exhausted; he has led with candor, with an innate ability to resolve conflicts constructively and by being creatively involved in every aspect of the Lab's activities—a fact for which *I* am particularly grateful: it made me a credible Deputy Director. He has created an organization whose spirit and lively intellectual atmosphere have nurtured individual creativity. Indeed, the style and spirit of SLAC are truly a reflection of his own personality.

The world would be a better place if one could point to achievements in the arena of arms control and international security that bear the Pief trademark as clearly and as heavily imprinted as does SLAC, but, as many of us have learned to our great frustration, in the political realm a scientist often encounters insurmountable difficulties of a type not found in our scientific laboratories. In the lab, we are dealing with constant and rational laws of nature; we can do repeatable experiments on well-defined systems; we recognize—and have a well-justified faith—that simplicity and beauty are the marks of understanding and truth. In the world of politics, the situation is anything but that orderly and rational. The ratio of one's accomplishments to one's effort seems so discouragingly small—but there is no doubt that the countless hours and days and weeks and months, the almost countless trips that Pief has devoted to government advising, have indeed left their mark and had an important impact. Pief's involvement dates all the way back to World War II, and he has served since the late 1950s as a trusted adviser at the highest level to presidents from Eisenhower to Carter. President Eisenhower's science advisers, James Killian and George Kistiakowsky, in their individual memoirs as Special Assistants to the President, write of numerous meetings and occasions in which they turned to Pief for his technical advice.

And the reason is clear. Linus Pauling put his finger on it once in a public debate when he described Pief as a man whose vision was free of parallax. That objectivity, and his willingness to roll up his sleeves, to work and master the nitty-gritty details, have made him a unique national resource. For example, early in 1959, the Eisenhower administration was preparing to open negotiations with the Russians toward cessation of nuclear weapons tests. Jim Killian, then science advisor to President Eisenhower, was relying on the President's Science Advisory Committee (PSAC) for the necessary technical studies on the means available to detect weapons tests. There were unresolved technical issues, and he turned to Pief, in particular, to head up a technical working group to deal with methods of detection of nuclear explosions in space. The issue at that time was the possibility of hiding nuclear explosions. Could exotic tests be concealed by exploding nuclear devices at very high altitudes or in outer space—even concealing tests behind the moon or the sun, as suggested by some scientists, such as Edward Teller? If you think we particle physicists are clever in our particle creations these days, you should compare them with some of the nuclear-test exotica one had to face then.

As Dr. Killian wrote in his memoirs, President Eisenhower opened a diplomatic negotiation with the Russians that year that included the methods and instrumentation for space detection that were recommended by the technical committee chaired by Pief. Subsequently, the negotiators with the U.S. delegation chaired by Pief reached an agreement based on the correct technical assessment of limitations and potentials for detecting and identifying high-altitude explosions. Pief himself played a prominent role in that negotiation, which was a basic step toward the subsequent signing and ratification of an atmospheric test ban treaty several years later during the Kennedy administration.

The fact that background radiation from atmospheric tests has decreased by two orders of magnitude in the past 20 years (since the end of above-ground testing of nuclear bombs by the United States and the Soviet Union) and the environment in which we live has been so cleaned up from threatening nuclear fall-out in no small measure derives from the success of that technical effort. Our gratitude to Pief, for his contributions to the achievement of the atmospheric test ban treaty is enormous. Had logic been able to win out over politics at that time, we might also now have a comprehensive test-ban treaty banning underground, as well as above-ground, nuclear-weapons tests, and many of the subsequent failures at arms control, as well as the current threat of space weapons, could have been avoided.

In his diary, George Kistiakowsky, who had succeeded Killian as science adviser, describes a meeting of PSAC with President Eisenhower at the Newport Naval Base in July 1960, at which he charged Pief with responsibility to present to the President the case for the cessation of nuclear tests. Pief must have done so convincingly and with characteristic forcefulness, because Kistiakowsky wrote ten days later in his diary, while at a Camp David meeting with Pief and others in preparation for a meeting of PSAC with the National Security Council, as follows:

> I succeeded in presenting myself as having been put into grave jeopardy by that briefing paper on the test ban given to the President at the Newport PSAC meeting. Could see that Panofsky was thoroughly uncomfortable and [I] thoroughly enjoyed it.

By the way, in a very humorous and revealing comment recorded by Kistiakowsky in his diary, we can also learn what an incredible lobbyist Pief was against an impressive array of East Coast opposition in his battle to create SLAC. Sometimes, in some battles, the odds can be insurmountable—even for Pief. Of course, Pief won this battle. But I suspect that, in spite of his indefatigability and persuasiveness as a lobbyist, Pief might not have won that titanic struggle against the effort to kill the SLAC project had it not been for the simple fact that his vision of the full beauty and power of high-energy electron beams was not yet widely shared in that distant past 25 years ago. I'll bet that at that time some thought it was even worth $114 million to send Pief off to his electron follies and get him and his merry band out of their hair, far away to the West across the Hudson River, not to mention across the Mississippi.

After Pief gained White House support for SLAC, his struggles were far from over—monumental political barriers and self-imposed barriers of principle remained. The political one is local legend— remember the Woodside powerline controversy that made Pete Mc-Closkey famous and led to his becoming our long-time Congressman. That controversy also brought great joy to the Palo Alto medical community, who, until we inherited their mantle, were the chief villains of the area because of their plans to expand the Palo Alto Clinic and build an associated hospital for it, which would have dislocated some downtown residents. The battle of principle, less widely known, was waged by Pief when he rejected the insistence by the Atomic Energy Commission (or AEC, as the earlier incarnation of the Department of Energy was known) that the contract for SLAC agree, on an open-ended basis, to any regulations imposed unilaterally by the Government on the basis of security requirements. Against strong outside advice, and rejecting a precedent already set by other academic labs in earlier AEC contracts, and with $114 million sitting right out there on the table, Pief and his fellow negotiators made this a "do-or-die issue." That provision was indeed struck from the contract. Stanford won, we all won, by that display of courage. If that isn't an example of staying true to principle—shoving $114 million in 1962 dollars back across the table after five years of hard work to get it— then I don't know what is.

One could go on and on describing Pief's Washington campaigns. At the time of the last great debate on ballistic-missile defenses, starting in 1969, Pief once again was out front with great effectiveness in the national debate and in private government councils leading up the ABM Treaty of 1972. And his contributions in that area have never ended. He's out there once again, now that the ABM battle has once more been joined. His active role in arms control is known today not only in Washington but just as well to hundreds of students and many colleagues here on the Stanford University campus, where Pief was one of the founding members of what has now grown into the Stanford Center for International Security and Arms Control. Both the Stanford Center and the cause of arms control are at the head of the line for more of Pief's attention when he hands over the SLAC directorship to Burt Richter's very capable hands next month.

To those of us privileged to work closely with him and who have followed his path to Washington, Pief has been a constant inspiration. He was our teacher and a model we have tried our best to emulate. The word used by our close colleague and friend Dick Garwin (himself no less valuable and no less rare a national resource) is that Pief has been to us a hero—in this age with so few heroes. He set new standards for all of us to follow, and he will no doubt continue to do so, both in the effort to reduce the threat of nuclear weapons and in supporting wise science policy.

Last year, for the most recent of his many honors, Pief received an honorary doctorate from his alma mater, Princeton University, with this citation:

> He has led our quest for the ultimate constituents of inanimate nature, using the resources of modern technology to open the realm of high-energy elementary particle physics and to catch glimpses of a fleeting world of "color," "charm," and "strangeness." Knowing intimately the awesome power of the atom, he has counseled us in the arena of nuclear arms, soberly reminding us of the mutually assured destruction that is the most likely outcome of their use.

As appropriate as that citation is, I remember a better one, a short and perfect tribute by Abraham Pais dating back to 1951—the summer we both first got to know Pief. That was a wonderful summer, with both Bram Pais and George Uhlenbeck visiting and lecturing at Stanford. I was their most appreciative student. To digress a moment, I remember Uhlenbeck telling a story about Stanford that appears in the memoirs of Boltzmann. After his retirement, Boltzmann spent a spring visiting Berkeley. This was shortly after Stanford was founded, near the end of the nineteenth century. Boltzmann tells,* in his memoirs of his visit to the Golden West, of what a strange country America is. In Europe, he said, the nobility live off the sweat and blood of the poor and with their wealth and power build castles for self-engrandizement. But here in this strange new world, Boltzmann recounted, you have people like Senator Stanford and his colleagues—

---

*This is a very loose translation of his remarks.

the four so-called "Robber Barons," who built our first transcontinental railway and got rich on the backs and the blood and sweat of the workers—and then, lo and behold, what did Stanford do with his wealth? He created a university. As Boltzmann said, "Who knows, some day you may even hear of it."

Pief, of course—and his creations—are a major reason that Stanford is, indeed, now heard of so far and wide. But, returning to Pais, and one evening as we sat musing and drinking at a watering hole down on El Camino (at that time, bars and bistros could be no closer than one and half or two miles from campus), I remember Pais saying: "That Panofsky, what a beautiful person."

Pais's tribute is as perfect today as it was in 1951. This, too, is one of the invariance principles of Pief Panofsky.

T.D. Lee

In 1956, at about the time of the downfall of parity, or should I say its elevation to the more fundamental but only approximate symmetry of CP, the great American novelist and playwright Thorton Wilder turned 60. On that occasion, Supreme Court Justice Felix Frankfurter sent him a wire with the following message: "Welcome to the great decades." Today I also say, "Welcome, T.D., to the great decades! Having beaten you there by two months, I can report that—at least so far—it's O.K. And there are some special advantages to look forward to. In a few years we can go to the movies at a cut rate and ride the buses and subways at half fare."

There are two very special pleasures of being a physicist: first of all, we enjoy sailing on one of the great adventure voyages of the human mind as we seek to discover what we are made of and what holds us together. And, secondly, we sail on this great adventure in the company of such wonderful friends, such marvelous people as the community here today; and it is a special pleasure to count Tsung Dao and Jeannette Lee as one's close friends.

Occasions like today have elements of fun as well as of seriousness. They provide great opportunities and wonderful excuses for reminiscing—which I will now proceed to do.

For scientific reminiscing, let me remind you of what the world was made of—or so we thought, when T.D. and others of us were graduate students 40 years ago. The basic nuclear glue was known. Sometimes we called it mesons and sometimes mesotrons. And I recall sitting in the University of Illinois Union for afternoon coffee with my two professors, Sid Dancoff and Arnold Nordsieck, the day the news arrived that the nuclear and cosmic-ray mesons, the π and μ, were different—which led Nordsieck to suggest that we view this new development with great caution because one of those two presumed elementary particles would surely go away in short order—otherwise things would be too complicated!

Our understanding of elementary particles and processes has advanced enormously since then by any measure, but we have yet to match the masterful description of the world as presented early in the 1950s by Amos and Andy. I was reminded of their theory several weeks ago by a retrospective on their once-popular radio and television series that was shown on public television very late one evening out in California. Back in those times—when T.D. was studying viscosity, turbulence, statistical theories of equations of state and phase transitions, and the motion of slow electrons in polar crystals—Kingfish was explaining to Amos that the world was really made of protons, neutrons, fig newtons, and morons! That was back around 1951—of course, long before one had learned about fig newtinos, smorons, and all those other Zuminos! (that is, particles predicted by theories incorporating supersymmetry, as pioneered by Bruno Zumino).

As one looks over the broad landscape of physics, it is truly very hard to find a region or a territory that has not been touched by T.D.'s incisive and enduring contributions, by his technical strength and virtuosity, or by his physical insights. But let me remind you that the many dimensions of T.D.'s contributions as a teacher and statesman of physics are almost as impressive as his research achievements. First, as all of us who have enjoyed and learned from his lectures and seminars know, he excels in the art of classroom teaching and in giving theoretical seminars, conference talks, and lecture series at summer institutes. He has been a superb teacher of us all. Additionally, T.D. has been more than the inspiration—he has been a personal teacher of an entire generation of young Chinese scientists, as he has provided exceptional leadership and energy in order to help China recover from the damage to their science wrought by the Cultural Revolution. In 1979, he lectured to some 1200 young Chinese physicists who assembled in Beijing to hear him hold forth on all modern physics—particle physics and statistical mechanics. This led to his classic book *Particle Physics and Introduction to Field Theory*, which was published in 1981. Therein you can find all of modern particle physics, circa 1981, assembled in 850 or so clear and concisely written pages, including symmetry theory, QCD and gauge theory, quark confinement, chiral theory, quark models and high energy processes, weak-electromagnetic unification, and the like.

T.D., the teacher and educator, has also made it possible for more than 700 of China's brightest young physicists to come to our universities for their graduate education under what he calls the CUSPEA program (whatever that stands for), but we know them as "Lee scholars." This is a program to give these scholars a superb modern training in physics while the education system in China is still being rebuilt, so that, upon returning home, they can themselves be the professors for their succeeding generation of students. Does anyone doubt the tremendous importance of that investment in developing the latent talent and skills of such a great pool of brainpower for the future of human culture and of the civilization of our planet, as well as for our understanding of nature? Without a doubt, I rate that program, dollar for dollar, as one of the most valuable investments a nation can make in its future.

And there is yet a fourth dimension to T.D.'s teaching activities. He has been the personal tutor of China's maximal leaders in helping them lead China to take great strides back to the scientific frontiers. Let me describe to you T.D.'s simple, sensible, and successful explanation to Deng Xiaoping of the need for postdoctoral research support and fellowships for the Lee scholars when they return home to China. As he described it to Deng, when teaching students in college, professors must pose the problems to them and also provide the correct answers. When students advance to the stage of writing a Ph.D. thesis, it is the task of the professor to pose the question and provide the problem— but not to know the answer ahead of time. That is to be determined by student's own research. What is important for the postdoctoral training is for young scientists to develop the capacity to pose problems on their own, as well as to find their own answers. Deng Xiaoping apparently understood that explanation very well, and China has now started a program to make it possible for their young postdoctoral fellows to develop their own new research programs in physics.

But let me go back a decade earlier and describe a 1974 meeting of Tsung Dao with then Chairman Mao Zedong, which marked a very early important step in the commitment of the Chinese government to the education of bright young scientists.

In the prologue to the book containing his Danz Lectures, being published this year [1986] by the University of Washington Press, T.D. describes how he answered Chairman Mao's question and explained to him why the concept of symmetry was so important. In Chinese, as described by T.D., the word "symmetry" carries the meaning of a static concept—that is, "the beauty of form arising from balanced proportions." But, in Mao's view, as recounted by Tsung Dao, the entire evolution of human societies is based on dynamic change. Dynamics is the only important element, not statics. Mao felt strongly that it also had to be true in nature. Therefore, he was quite puzzled that symmetry should be elevated to such an exalted place in physics.

To illustrate the deeper dynamical meaning of symmetry to Mao, as he sat talking to him in his residence inside the Imperial Palace, T.D. put a pencil on a pad of paper resting on the end table that was placed between their two chairs. Let me quote T.D.'s description of his demonstration:

> I put a pencil on the pad and tipped the pad toward Mao and then back toward me. The pencil rolled one way and then the other. I pointed out that at no instant was the motion static, yet as a whole the dynamic process had a symmetry. The concept is by no means static; it is far more general than its common meaning and applicable to all natural phenomena from the creation of our universe to every microscopic subnuclear reaction.

T.D. recounts that Mao appreciated the simple demonstration and then asked more questions about the deep meaning of symmetry and also about other physics topics, expressing regret that he had not had the time to study science. In the end of the conversation, Mao accepted T.D.'s proposal that the education of at least the very brilliant young students should be maintained, continued, and strengthened. This led, with the strong support of Zhou Enlai, to the elite "youth class," a special intensive education program for talented students from the early teens through college. It was established first at the University of Science and Technology in Anhui and later, because of its success, also at other Chinese universities.

Let me turn next to the many dimensions of T.D.'s research achievements. The numerous major honors T.D. has received are evidence enough of his enormous contributions. His mark can be found in just about every area of physics. In statistical mechanics, we look to the work of T.D., Yang, and collaborators for understanding the nature of phase changes, the theory of cluster expansions and the low-temperature behavior of hard-sphere boson systems, and for the analysis of the general many-body problem in quantum statistical mechanics. In the area of weak interactions, one need only mention parity violation and all its ramifications, including high-energy neutrino processes, experimental tests of CP, or T, invariance as well as various aspects of the heavy intermediate vector bosons. Most theorists have used the Lee model as a sandbox for some idea or other. T.D. has also made elegant studies of coherent states, or solitons, exploring bag models and abnormal vacuum states and their implications for high-energy heavy-ion collisions. He has undertaken a major research program in lattice-field theory, including the effects of gravity; in particular, he has developed a random lattice theory designed with a very elegant mathematical formalism to restore rotational symmetry properties to the lattice.

The day before I left Stanford last week to come East, I received a package of four new papers by T.D. and collaborators that describe new possibilities for configurations of cold stellar matter based on soliton solutions in general relativity. They found coherent quantum states with masses up to as much as 10^{15} solar masses.

There isn't enough time today to describe all of T.D.'s contributions to physics—even if I could do it so I won't try. Happy birthday, T.D.

Victor F. Weisskopf

My first meeting with Viki—Victor F. Weisskopf—occurred 40 years ago this fall, and it was a daunting occasion for me. It was my debut. I was scheduled to give my first ten-minute talk at an American Physical Society meeting in Chicago immediately following Viki, who was presenting the correct relativistic finite calculation of the Lamb Shift. My talk was about internal conversion—sometimes called "infernal confusion"—and had to do with the importance of magnetic multipole radiation of high order in nuclear isomeric transitions.

Adding up all the years since then, I realize that Viki will have known me more than half of his life, and it comes close to two-thirds of mine that I will have had the pleasure of knowing him as scientist, humanist, accompanist, and friend.

Viki, the physicist—what more need one say? His many achievements over so broad a range of topics and extending over so long a creative period have been widely recognized and honored, and are known to all physicists: Pauli–Weisskopf quantum-field theory for spin-zero particles; Weisskopf–Wigner line-breadth theory; the self-energy of the electron in pair theory and the correct interpretation and calculation of the Lamb shift as a radiative correction in quantum electrodynamics; understanding nuclear reactions and the cloudy crystal ball developed with Herman Feshbach; helping formulate bag models of the nucleon and parton wave functions. Viki has always moved forward to new frontiers as they have opened up. Often, it was his own contributions that were pivotal in opening those frontiers and in leading to a deeper understanding. With his deep intuitive insights and his creative approach, he never fell into the trap that Wolfgang Pauli cautioned against when he said: "Don't become an expert for two reasons: You become a virtuoso of formalism and forget real nature, and if you become an expert you risk that you are not working for anything interesting anymore." In any event, we, of course, would never accuse Viki of having been trapped into becoming a virtuoso of formalism, even within factors of 4π. And I am sure that Viki does not like the label "expert." In fact, he likes to call himself an amateur—as he described himself in his tribute to Eduardo Amaldi on the occasion of Amaldi's sixtieth birthday almost 20 years ago, using the definition of an amateur as a person who does something for the pleasure of it.

In my Washington life, I judge officials in government by a very useful ratio: the ratio of arrogance to ability. I have seen that ratio on occasion rise to very high levels and require renormalization lest it go off scale and threaten to diverge. I won't name my all-time champion on that ratio—his name still crops up occasionally, and it is not the first one that comes to mind. In physics, there is a ratio that it is as complimentary to excel in as it is uncomplimentary to excel in that arrogance ratio, and this is the ratio of physics understanding to obfuscating mathematical formalism. Viki stands very high on the peak of the latter. I am reminded of the very first summer school organized by Antonino Zichichi, now Head of the World Laboratory, in Erice, Sicily in 1963, 25 years ago. It was devoted to weak interactions. Sam Berman, now at Lawrence Berkeley Laboratory, worked out everything then known in the standard four-component formalism; Valentino Telegdi then showed us how to understand what all the spins were doing in a two-component formalism; and Viki completed the job by explaining everything Sam and Valentino had said with zero components!

I first experienced personally the Viki style and atmosphere of doing physics when I arrived at MIT in the fall of 1952 at the same time as Amos de Shalit. We were Viki's new research associates that year, and it was one tremendous experience. One way to describe it is to adapt a 1977 quote by Viki in the *American Journal of Physics*, in which he described working for Pauli. Viki wrote: "It was absolutely marvelous working for Pauli. You could ask him anything. There was no worry that he would think a particular question was stupid since he thought all questions were stupid." Viki, of course, was the anti-Pauli because he accepted all questions not as stupid but as interesting and as a challenge to probe to deeper levels of understanding. The resulting discussions—always cherished by those of us fortunate to participate—searched for new ways of developing a deeper physical and intuitive description of what the photon, or phonon, or quark (then we thought of mesons), or scattering phase was telling us.

The great school of physics that Viki created at MIT starting in the 1950s, where physics was exhilarating, exciting, demanding, and fun, was the model for my own efforts since then at Stanford. There was a secret bonus in Viki's methods that has served me well throughout the years. I learned from Viki to ask all the naive—you might even say dumb—questions in seminars. This taught junior colleagues and students to overcome their inhibitions and to be bold and to ask such questions, and thus to learn from the discussion generated by them. I soon found that, as a result of asking a lot of simple, naive questions, I was being credited unduly. It was simply assumed that I was asking such questions as a stimulant to discussion, even though I, of course, already knew the answers. The truth of the matter was, far more often than not, I asked them because I was confused. Whether the same is true of Viki or not, he will have to confess himself.

Viki's continued productivity in physics for more than 50 years belies the poetry of Paul Dirac. When Dirac was a student at Cambridge and participated in student drama productions, he wrote a ditty that is a dirge for most theoretical physicists:

> Age is of course a fever chill
> That every physicist doth fear.
> He's better dead than living still
> When once he's past his thirtieth year.

Now I am not sure whether theoretical physics and mathematics are the most unforgiving of all when it comes to age. I am sure Viki well recalls the Marschallin's lament in *Der Rosenkavalier* as she observes the new lines and creases in her face and, at the advanced age of "not more than 32" (according to the Hugo von Hofmannstahl libretto), she realizes that she is over the hill and faces the imminent prospect of losing her youthful 17-year-old lover, Octavian. But Viki seems immune to age and is still going very strong. Whereas many of us learned nuclear physics from Blatt and Weisskopf 36 years ago—that big, well-worn blue book—our students, grandstudents, and greatgrandstudents are now teaching particle physics from two new books by Gottfried and Weisskopf.

Throughout his career, Viki has made very major contributions, not only to research and teaching but also to administration, as CERN knows better than anyone else. Furthermore, Viki's contributions to the health and development of American high-energy physics—not

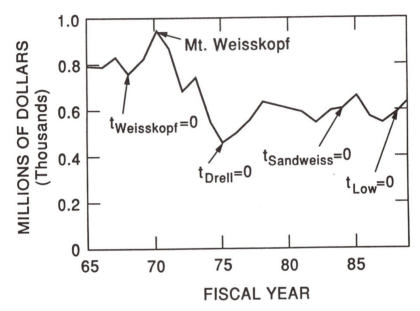

FIGURE 1. *Total high energy physics and SSC funding (Budget Authority in Fiscal Year 1989 dollars).*

just to European particle physics, which we see flourishing so well at CERN, at the German Electron-Synchrotron Laboratory (DESY) in Hamburg, and elsewhere—were so great that a mountain was named in his honor. It is a paper mountain—a theoretical one, of course, for high-energy physics funding by the Department of Energy through the years, as shown in Figure 1. I know it is ungracious to point this out at an occasion such as this, but I cannot resist noting how the funding actually decreased in constant dollars during Viki's stewardship of HEPAP (the High Energy Physics Advisory Panel of the U.S. Department of Energy, then the AEC) from 1967 through 1974, leaving me to restore it, at least in part, through 1983. Jack Sandweiss held it even until last year, and now we are counting on Francis Low to build a peak of Weisskopfian proportions and bring home the superconducting supercollider (SSC).

I turn next to Viki the humanist. Hans Bethe said it best, writing the foreword to Viki's 1972 classic collection of wonderful essays, *Physics in the Twentieth Century*: "All his life he has sought and contributed to knowledge, and all his life he has shown compassion." In his characteristic manner, Hans Bethe, with very few words, captured the essence of the Viki we know and love so well. I would add just one word to what Bethe said: Commitment—Viki's total commitment to deeds, as well as to knowledge.

One very major theme throughout Viki's life has been his devotion to international cooperation in science. He has worked ceaselessly to break down national barriers through international cooperation, and CERN is the living testimonial to his success. His guiding principle has been the same one stated by the great Russian playwright Anton Chekhov, as I just recently learned. My wife and I flew here via London, where we spent several days at the theater, and, in rummaging through books and references in preparing to see *Uncle Vanya*, I ran into this testament by Chekhov: "There is no national science just as there is no national multiplication table; what is national is no longer science." Viki himself has written and spoken very eloquently on this theme. The following is from a speech he gave in Warsaw in 1967 honoring Marie Curie:

> The significance of scientific collaboration far exceeds the narrow aim of a more efficient prosecution of our scientific endeavors. It stresses a common bond among all human beings. Scientists, wherever they come from, adhere to a common way of thinking; they have a common system of values that guides their activities, at least within their own profession. New approaches in bringing nations together can perhaps be discussed with more ease within this community, some political misunderstandings can be cleared up, and dangerous tensions reduced. As an example, we recall that the agreement to stop the testing of nuclear bombs above ground stemmed in part from prior meetings among scientists.
>
> We must keep the doors of our laboratories wide open and foster the spirit of supranationality and human contact, of which the world is so much in need. It is our duty to stick together, in spite of mounting tension and threatening war in the world today. The present deterioration in the political world is a reason stronger than ever for closer scientific collaboration. The relations among scientists must remain

beyond the tensions and the conflicts of the day, even if these
conflicts are as serious and frustrating as they are today. The
world community of scientists must remain undivided,
whatever actions are taken, or whatever views are expressed
in the societies in which they live. We need this unity as an
example for collaboration and understanding, as an intellectual bridge between the divided parts of mankind, and as a
spearhead toward a better world.

At this time of *glasnost* in the East and with seeds of new thinking
in international cooperation in political and strategic issues taking root
around the world, we as scientists can and should work to expand and
extend scientific cooperation, welcoming those who bring talent and
commitment. It takes a conscious effort to preserve our open international style of cooperation, especially in high-energy physics, with few
experimental opportunities and with scarce resources organized into
larger (but smaller numbers of) empires. But it is a very important
obligation for our field to make—for our own health and success and
for training and developing new, young leaders, as well as for helping
to foster the idea of peaceful international cooperation in all fields of
human endeavor and in human relations. As Viki said, the significance
of this effort "far exceeds the narrow aim of a more efficient prosecu-
tion of our scientific endeavors." CERN, of course, has been, is, and
(we all hope) will in the future shine as a world leader in worldwide
scientific cooperation. We look to the future laboratories—the World
Laboratory and the SSC—to further extend scientific cooperation and
collaboration in our field.

In this era of grand unification in the ten-dimensional world of the
theoretical physicist, Viki, through his unflagging dedication to the
unity of science and scientists, is surely the grand unifier in the real
four-dimensional world in which we all live. To paraphrase Chekhov,
there is no national Viki. We all claim him!

Viki has also worked hard to raise the sensitivities of scientists and
world leaders—political and spiritual—to the consequences of science,
consequences that are particularly crucial to understand in an age of
nuclear weapons. His leadership in this effort is widely recognized.
This leadership was referred to in a speech by Father Bryan Hehir, the
Catholic priest who was the intellectual driving force behind the very
influential and important pastoral letter by the American Catholic
bishops on war and peace in the nuclear age. The letter discussed the
danger of nuclear weapons and the urgency to reduce that danger and

to cut the bloated nuclear arsenals. Father Hehir discussed the paradox that the source of our current nuclear dilemma is found in one of our best achievements—the unlocking of the secrets of the nucleus. He then referred to Viki as "One of the wisest and most morally sensitive participants" in creating that paradox and quoted the following passage from a recent speech Viki gave at Los Alamos:

> Thinking back to those eventful years at Los Alamos from 1943 to 1945 evokes two opposite feelings. On the one side, it was a heroic period of our lives, full of the most exciting problems and achievements. On the other side, we must be deeply aware of the result of our work, which was awesome enough at the time when we saw the explosion in the desert and murderous enough when it destroyed two Japanese cities. The bomb did end the cruel and destructive war with Japan, but since then it has developed into the greatest danger that humankind has ever faced. And it threatens more and more to destroy everything on Earth that we consider worth living for. The paradox is the problem we live with.

The paradox of which Viki and Father Hehir spoke—namely, as we unlocked the secrets of the nucleus in one of our best achievements, we also created the great danger of the atom bomb—is with us today more sharply than ever. In the past three exciting, wonderful decades, our knowledge of nature has made enormous strides in advancing our understanding of basic processes, forces, and particles. Whatever the fate of super strings, we have achieved major progress in developing a unified model—if not a theory—of weak, strong, and electromagnetic interactions. We have developed new concepts unimaginable 30 to 40 years ago. We have the first outlines, based on actual data, of the evolution and history of our universe following the big bang of 15 billion years ago. At the same time, our advancing knowledge during this period has also given us even more powerful and dangerous means of destruction—H-bombs thousands of times more devastating than the primitive A-bombs that destroyed Hiroshima and Nagasaki, not to mention bacteriological weapons and the environmental havoc we are creating. Thus, as our dreams of understanding nature have advanced, there looms ahead also the threat of a nightmare, for our advanced understanding has also given us awful means with the potential for destroying ourselves and—along with us—our dreams.

In the competition between our dreams and our nightmares, Viki has been an important and active participant, as well as one of the

most morally sensitive ones, in Father Hehir's words, pitching in to tilt
the competition in favor of the dreams as he has reached out in his
public efforts to educate leaders and people from popes to ordinary
citizens. I, for one, greatly value these efforts of his.

This year [1988] is a good one to reflect on the competition between
our dreams and our nightmares. Developments during the year provide cause for a measure of optimism that the threat of the nightmare
may be diminishing. Most importantly, the United States and the Soviet Union have signed, ratified, and entered into force the Intermediate Nuclear Forces (INF) Treaty, which eliminates, globally and totally, an entire class of weapons. More significantly, this treaty
introduces extensive cooperative means of verification, including on-
site inspection, that few would have dreamed possible as recently as a
year ago. In addition, negotiations at the Strategic Arms Reduction
Talks (START) to reduce intercontinental or strategic nuclear weapons have built a framework with a large number of agreed provisions
that will substantially cut the number of deployed warheads. Serious
problems still remain to be resolved, but progress thus far gives good
grounds for optimism that a START treaty can be completed during
the coming year. Furthermore, the East and West have begun the
process of discussing conventional weapons reductions in Europe.
There is extensive talk of implementing confidence-building measures
beyond the Stockholm Accords of 1986, including an exchange of data
on the numbers and kinds of conventional forces that can be verified by
on-site inspection. Progress here will have the important effect of reducing a major cause of insecurity in Europe that results from the
threat of short-warning attack, or blitzkrieg, posed by the massed
forces near the East–West frontier. Perhaps—just perhaps—in the
coming years we will take big steps away from the threat of our nightmares, steps comparable to those we have achieved toward realizing
our dreams of understanding the physical world around us. I cannot
think of a better eightieth birthday present for Viki than to mark 1988
as a real turning point toward achieving our dreams and dimming our
nightmares.

I turn next to Viki the accompanist. I cherish deeply the many
wonderful hours I have spent playing violin–piano sonatas with him.
(Notice how we violinists call the pianist our accompanist.) In fact, as
Viki tells it, it is due to music alone that I had the great good fortune
to become his assistant in 1952. Viki likes to describe a phone call from
Felix Bloch at Stanford, where I then was an instructor, trying to sell
me to Viki. Viki responded that I sounded pretty good as a physicist

but that all his funds were spent, until Felix informed him that I was a good enough violinist that he might enjoy playing sonatas with me. At that point, Viki said he told Felix, "Well, that's different," and he said he would find the money to hire me. The interesting thing about that story is how it has changed over time. On the many occasions that Viki has introduced me to talk in colloquia or seminars at MIT or elsewhere since the 1950s, he has always cited that conversation with Felix Bloch, but it has undergone a slow but steady transformation over time. Monotonically, my physics credentials for becoming his assistant have eroded in these introductions, while my purported musical talent has improved. Viki has now almost reached the point of claiming that he hired me in spite of my physics because he wanted someone with whom he could play Beethoven, Brahms, Mozart, and Schubert.

I think that gives me a license to describe Viki the pianist. I had my chance last year in my retiring speech as president of the American Physical Society. I used the occasion to demonstrate the correlation between the musical and physics styles of those of my accompanists through the years who were theoretical physicists. I show this in Figure 2, which, I emphasize, is a graph of constant quality. I will not pinpoint any of the five individuals on that graph, but I'll bet few if any physicists doubt where Viki would be on it. He certainly knows. Viki and I thought that perhaps we might serenade you on this festive occasion, but we're restrained by an unaccustomed burst of modesty.

More seriously, my musical association with Viki has been a source of very special personal pleasure for us. Music is an expressive art. Bruno Walter, the great orchestral conductor and, like Viki, a Viennese, once wrote: "Music is a good conductor of personality, just as metal is a good conductor of heat. Through music, man himself speaks."

Music serves as a tremendous balance to our physics. No doubt that is the reason it plays so important a role in the lives of many scientists. In physics, as in all science, it is nature that speaks, but in music it is we, ourselves, who speak. Physics is logical, rational; whereas music is emotional, irrational. But both music and physics show beauty, harmony, elegance, and style. In both activities it is equally true: You know those very rare occasions when you do it just right, and they give very great pleasure.

Finally, Viki as a friend—and also, along with Viki, the great lady, Ellen Weisskopf. With our families, we have had many wonderful occasions together that remain a rich part of our lives. In Europe they

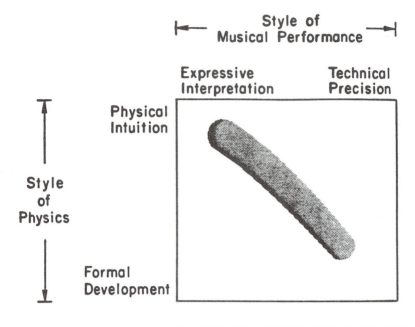

PLANE OF CONSTANT QUALITY

FIGURE 2. *Plane of constant quality. Input: F. Bloch, G. 't Hooft, F. Low, W. Thirring, and V. Weisskopf.*

include the summer schools in Erice; spring together in Vienna, 1972; visits in summer to the Weisskopfs' mountaintop home in Vesancy, France; meeting Sakharov in Moscow.

I would like to recount briefly Viki's and my meeting with Andrei Sakharov in Moscow in the summer of 1974. We were there for a small scientific seminar (dealing with bound-state models of the nucleon) organized by the Soviet Academy of Sciences. Sakharov also attended, and I take it as a great compliment that, upon meeting me for the first time, he felt confident to discuss human-rights problems with me and to detail the difficult circumstances of some of his colleagues. Andrei invited Viki and me to his modest Moscow apartment to join in his last supper before his first hunger strike. The time was July 1974, and our meeting coincided with the last of the Nixon–Brezhnev summits. Sakharov was using the presence of the world press in Moscow to bring to the attention of people around the world the plight of the ethnic minorities in the Soviet Union, who at that time had no rights at all to emigrate or join families in the West. Yelena Bonner came via taxi from the hospital, where she was being treated for severe glaucoma, to join us very briefly. It was altogether a very warm human experience. Andrei's telephone was ringing constantly with calls from capitals around the world, from the press, and from his Moscow friends expressing concern about his health. What I remember most vividly was Andrei telling us that, just minutes before our arrival, several policemen had come to his door with a letter written by his neighbors complaining that it was very difficult to live with the Sakharovs as neighbors because of their very noisy friends and visitors. What triggered that letter was a visit to their apartment on the preceding day by two lead singers from the La Scala Opera Company of Milan, which was in Moscow that week for performances at the Bolshoi Theatre. The two singers had obtained Sakharov's address and had come to his apartment to show their respect, affection, and support for him by the only means they could communicate to him—through music, by giving him a private recital. Andrei was very moved by this occasion, as were we to learn of it.

In 1966, Hendrik Casimir wrote an introduction to a collection of essays that were written to honor Viki when he ended his term as Director General at CERN. Casimir said: "It is Viki's unique achievement that he has carried over the devoted idealism and the enthusiasm of his early days into a new world of organized research and large-scale experiments." Those of us who know Viki have seen this same devoted idealism and enthusiasm in him in all walks of life: physics and science, humanism, music, and friendship.

Viki wrote not long ago: "Science has become adult. I am not sure whether scientists have." My concluding wish is this: Viki, I hope you never will become so adult that you lose any of that idealism and enthusiasm. Happy birthday!

Murray Gell-Mann

It is a pleasure to be here and join this distinguished group of Murray Gell-Mann's friends in wishing him, very warmly, greetings on his sixtieth birthday. Having reached this milestone myself two years ago, I can tell Murray that the air is good and the water is warm, so dive in and enjoy the next decade! Anyway, Murray, you have no choice.

As a fellow theoretical physicist who has learned much from Murray and his major research achievements since 1950, starting even before we had met, I consider it a mark of great distinction to be able to point to activities and experiences shared with him. Let me just mention two of them. One that has surely had a major influence on me for almost 30 years has been my membership in JASON, which was formed in 1960. Murray and I are charter members. JASON—the name has no special significance—is a group of academic scientists that the government supported to work part time on problems of national importance. It was created because it was recognized by the government, as well as the scientists themselves, that there was a strong need for independent and informed scientists who could and would do the analyses and help provide the necessary technical ingredients on which to base sound policy decisions, particularly on issues of national security. Scientists had made important contributions to winning WWII, and their counsel was sought and used in its aftermath. President Eisenhower, in particular, appreciated the importance of obtaining the best independent scientific advice when he created the full-time position of presidential science advisor and the President's Science Advisory Committee in 1958, after the Soviet launch of *Sputnik*. Scientists like Lee DuBridge, Bob Bacher, Pief Panofsky, and Hans Bethe, who had already contributed so much during the war and through the

1950s, as America entered the age of thermonuclear weapons and missiles into space, were the hard core of this effort. But they and their colleagues were no longer so young, and JASON was formed to train and to engage the following generations. Today, as in those earlier years, there still remains a crucial need to make the best technical support available to the government, and especially to the president. Presidential decisions are fundamentally and most importantly political ones, but they should also be realistic and solid on the technical issues defining the boundaries as to what is practical or even possible.

There are crucial technical ingredients when it comes to making policy decisions, to formulating verifiable arms-control treaties, and to developing military forces—particularly in the area of national security and defense planning. The president must be properly informed on the significance of the technical factors—even though he may not be expected to comprehend fully the technologies themselves—when he recommends a course of action for the nation. It was the conviction that we could contribute to sound policy through our technical analyses that motivated joining JASON—and that led to further governmental involvements, some of which Murray and I shared.

We also shared the experience of being attacked verbally as war criminals and having our physics lectures disrupted because we were involved with the U.S. government—and with the Department of Defense in particular—through JASON. Those incidents occurred in Europe in 1972 during days that were very painful to many Americans because of what we were doing in Vietnam, Cambodia, and Laos.

Looking back on my work for the government and my involvement in policy problems, I can think of few other activities in my life in which the ratio of output to input was so small and the results so frustrating. I don't know whether Murray's view of that effort is more or less positive than mine, but I do know that the gap between the realities of science and technology and the understanding of these realities by our government leaders is growing ever wider. There is a serious need to bridge that gap by reestablishing effective mechanisms of scientific advice to our leaders. The importance of bridging that gap was painfully illustrated when President Reagan, in 1983, called for the creation of a nationwide defensive umbrella. His vision of the Strategic Defense Initiative (SDI) came as a bolt out of the blue with no technical input. Based upon Hollywood fantasy and little else, it created false expectations; it has taken the country almost six years of a highly divisive, politicized, and often ill-informed debate on the important national policy issue of ballistic-missile defense to redirect SDI onto a sensible track. Or at least I hope so—anyway, that is my current optimistic assessment.

As a second instance of common activity with Murray, I recall our numerous intersections as a result of activities of the John D. and Catherine T. MacArthur Foundation. In this case, I have to cede an advantage to Murray, in accord with the Biblical maxim that "it is more blessed to give than to receive." Indeed, I do not begrudge him that blessed privilege at all. The MacArthur Foundation has been crucial to me in supporting as well as encouraging some of my efforts to contribute to peace and security through multidisciplinary research and training.

Working on these kinds of problems poses a number of very difficult challenges. First of all, one is working with very diverse cultures, studying behavioral, ethical, political, negotiating, and technical issues. Participants in all these activities must learn how to talk with one another, to communicate in a common language, and to show mutual respect for each other's work. That is not very easy. For example, the political types cannot coerce laws of nature to meet their grand strategy or political frameworks, no matter how appealing they may be. Scientists, likewise, cannot simply dismiss basic human insecurity or instinctive aspirations in attempting to base national planning solely on what seem to be perfectly logical conclusions from their analyses of technical issues or their calculations of bomb effects.

Secondly, there is a new challenge, for in a heavily armed nuclear world we are dealing with issues with no historical precedent. In some sense, we really have no history. We are making it for the first time. Before nuclear weapons were developed, war, though growing ever more terrible, was an accepted instrument of policy. But since then, with the development of nuclear and bacteriological weapons of such massive destructive potential, we have reached the point at which all-out war has become unthinkable. We have made a giant leap, by a factor of more than a million, in the destructive potential of thermonuclear bombs, pound for pound, relative to chemical bombs. Now, just one bomb on one missile or airplane can obliterate the totality of a major metropolis and its population. We have created a new condition, which President Eisenhower described in 1956 by saying "we are rapidly getting to the point that no war can be won." Pointing out that, with nuclear weapons, war would be no longer a battle to exhaustion and surrender of one of the adversaries, Eisenhower noted that the outlook had now come close to "destruction of the enemy and suicide."

Operating without a real history to learn from, our precarious situation is quite different from George Orwell's world of 1984. In *Nineteen Eighty-Four*, Big Brother found it useful and convenient to falsify history and to revise the record of the past in order to maintain the position of the Party. Our challenge in today's heavily armed nuclear world is quite different: It is to understand that we have lost history. In matters of nuclear weapons and war, history is no longer valid as a guide. Security can no longer be found either in greater strength or in defense, as it was before nuclear weapons. Nuclear war can no longer be regarded as an extension of diplomacy with other means, in von Clausewitz's frequently cited words. George Kennan saw and eloquently expressed his concerns about this new character of nuclear weapons of mass destruction in words written in 1949, the same year that *Nineteen Eighty-Four* was published:

> The weapons of mass destruction. . . . reach backward beyond the frontiers of western civilization, to the concepts of warfare which were once familiar to the Asiatic hordes. They cannot really be reconciled with a political purpose directed to shaping, rather than destroying, the lives of the adversary. They fail to take account of the ultimate responsibility of men for one another, and even for each other's errors and mistakes. They imply the admission that man not only can be, but is, his own worst and most terrible enemy.

Since we have lost history, we must give many words new meaning and change maxims derived from historical experience. Big Brother did this in *Nineteen Eighty-Four* as a cynical manipulation to consolidate power—writing in his Newspeak such famous slogans as "War Is Peace," "Freedom Is Slavery," and "Ignorance Is Strength."

At times it seems that we today have our own version of Newspeak, or "Nukespeak," such as, "To take the next step in arms control, we must build a new missile—but don't worry; it is only for bargaining leverage, and we'll call it the Peacekeeper."

And there is a third difficulty in this field: The traditional academic structures at many of our great universities are proving highly resistant to the creation of mechanisms for undertaking multidisciplinary work in policy studies in a serious and sustained way. One can generally round up a cadre of the usual suspects for a short-term look at a pressing problem. However, when it comes to mobilizing resources for a sustained commitment to scholarship and training in interdisciplinary policy fields, universities tend to be very conservative. This applies both to offering resources to support the work and to bestowing academic titles, which are the knighthood of the realm and are generally reserved for appointments in traditional departments on traditional subjects.

I believe strongly in a healthy conservatism in this area, in order to maintain rigorous academic standards and to avoid going overboard chasing the latest fashion in policy work. But there comes a point when the process of appointments is so rigid that innovation is stifled and the process gets in the way of achieving goals. Those of you who have followed recent experience at Stanford know precisely what I am referring to, and I bring it up here because, when we talk about violence and developing better ways of settling our disputes, resolving our conflicts, and keeping mankind from blowing itself up, we are dealing with a subject that will not go away or wither out of style in any foreseeable future. Now that we have knowledge of nuclear and biological weapons, the threat of unimaginable violence will remain with us as long as people inhabit the world.

It is appropriate for the universities to maintain the ivory tower from which to peer out over the landscape with widened horizons and a better perspective, the better to anticipate future changes and dangers. But this need not be their only role. Universities can also serve a constructive role in our society by coming down to Earth and entering into the fray of creative, multidisciplinary policy disputes about the issues challenging today's societies. It is here that forward-looking foundations—such as the great MacArthur Foundation, with leaders such as Murray Gell-Mann and Ruth Adams, the Carnegie Corporation of New York, and the Hewlett Foundation—have been very innovative and supportive catalysts. They have been the most important movers and shakers in the effort to bring more flexibility into the academic world for the study of policy-related, multidisciplinary issues. Murray, I believe, has coined the term "universities, academies, or centers without walls," in order creatively to study diverse and complex problems. I think this is an important concept to which universities will have to adapt in the future if they are going to remain important components of our society—in research, training, and teaching, and, specifically, in the area of national security.

To those who would suggest the basic problems of nuclear deterrence have been solved and there is no need to linger with the problem, and it is time to move on to new areas, let me say that it is surely not my perception that the field is played out. Indeed, we are in a period of very rapid and basic changes in issues of national security and arms control.

In little more than two years, two treaties with unprecedented measures of cooperative on-site inspection have been signed and ratified: The Intermediate Nuclear Force (or INF) Treaty of 1988 and the 1986 Stockholm Accord of the Conference on Security and Cooperation in Europe, which includes such confidence-building measures as advanced notification and close observation of large-scale military maneuvers. Good progress has also been made at the Strategic Arms Reduction Talks (START) toward a third treaty that would significantly reduce the numbers and megatonnage of the strategic, or intercontinental, nuclear forces. There is still a rough road ahead, but a few more steps like these and the superpowers' balance of terror and their relations with other nations will call for a serious reassessment.

The new Soviet leader calls not only for a domestic revolution in their system, but also for a fundamental change in the military framework of the relations between NATO and the Warsaw Pact countries. Mikhail Gorbachev has challenged the West with a promise of a unilateral reduction of conventional military forces and their restructuring from their present configuration, which raises concern about blitzkrieg, to one that meets the requirements of what he calls "defensive sufficiency." New technologies, such as space weapons and dual-purpose cruise missiles, looking identical but armed either with nuclear or conventional warheads, challenge many basic assumptions underlying the arms-control regime that has developed since the early 1960s. The knowledge of nuclear, as well as biological, weapons slowly but inexorably is spreading, and the capacity to build such weapons of mass destruction is proliferating ominously.

Thus, at this time—and looking ahead through what portends to be a long period of surprising, if not startling, changes—work on arms control and national security issues to reduce the threat of nuclear war presents new and difficult challenges of many dimensions. It requires synthesizing knowledge from many fields and networking the researchers. What is required is no less than a sustained interaction among (1) people who know the weaponry and its military uses; (2) people who understand technology and technical trends and their implications for the military; (3) people who know the Soviet Union; (4) people who know international relations broadly, particularly with respect to third-world nations; (5) people who know the processes of policy formation and implementation, including the political and economic dimensions; (6) people who understand human behavior, especially under stress; and (7) people with a deep understanding of the ethical dimensions. The task has grown more complex. The role of the Foundation as a "catalyst for change," in the felicitous MacArthur phrase, has grown even more important. In this and many other complex multidisciplinary issues—for example, the environment and understanding chaos—the contributions of creative individuals like Murray Gell-Mann are essential.

Amos de-Shalit

I first met Amos de-Shalit 37 years ago, in the fall of 1952, when he and I arrived at the Massachusetts Institute of Technology at the same time with the exceptionally good fortune to be research associates of Professor Victor Weisskopf. We and our families soon developed close bonds, and I learned to appreciate and love Amos as the gentlest, wisest, and most honorable friend and colleague I have ever known. I grew to respect him as a creative scientist of the highest achievements and standards, a patriot of inexhaustible energy and devotion to his country, a human of noble values, and, generally, a very beautiful person.

The first line of Stephen Spender's twenty-fourth Prelude reads: "I think continually of those who were truly great." The poem concludes with: "Born of the Sun they travelled a short while towards the Sun, / And left the vivid air signed with their honour." Those lines always come to mind when I think of Amos.

Amos and I were the same age—our birth dates were almost identical—and, although the world lines of our early lives were quite distant from one another, we arrived at MIT with a very similar compulsion to understand what the physical world was made of, to understand the nuclei of its atoms and the elementary particles and forces out of which nature has built the world around us. We shared the romantic vision—the deep religious belief, you might say—that there is a simple and beautiful and orderly nature that we might succeed in understanding if we worked at it hard enough. We also had many other common interests, particularly music—for Amos, a pianist, and I, a violinist, played sonatas together on occasion.

We also share a common heritage, the same roots. By happenchance, our parents followed different stars in their search for a better life, a life free of the strife and persecution that so frequently reared its ugly head in the pogroms of Eastern Europe, with the result that Amos was a Sabra and I a first-generation American. This meant that Amos had fought on the battlefield for Israel's independence, while I watched from across the Atlantic Ocean, participating only vicariously.

The Amos I met in the fall of 1952 in Cambridge, Massachusetts, exuded intense pride in the young state of Israel and had unbounded hopes for its future as a free, democratic society. It was more than a homeland at last for a people so brutally persecuted in the Holocaust. To him, Israel was also a beacon to the future as a truly democratic society based on knowledge, science, and cultural enlightenment.

We hear often these days of the dangers of nationalism and the disease of pride in a world armed with weapons of mass destruction that could do us all in. But when that pride propels a people to achieve noble aspirations of freedom and independence and to strive to realize the dream of applying scientific and democratic principles to build a more peaceful and a richer life, not only for oneself but also for one's neighbors, that is, indeed, a rich pride and a beautiful dream. That was Amos's dream—and he worked hard, all the years I knew him in his tragically brief life, to realize that dream and to justify that pride.

Amos and I were theoretical physicists, and we knew all too well that theoretical physics is a young person's field. Einstein published at the age of 25 his four great papers on special relativity, the photoelectric effect, the symmetrical statistics, and the Brownian motion. The history of twentieth-century physics tells us of great leaps of progress made by those with the unbound boldness of vision and intellectual optimism of youth—in their twenties and even up into their early thirties. These are the years when we urge our best students to concentrate on their studies, to sharpen their skills, to expand their intellectual horizons, and to give creative science their best effort. During those years, as Amos rose to the very top rank among nuclear physicists, he nevertheless found time—he seemed to create it—to help build and guide a great Weizmann Institute of Science, creating its outstanding department of nuclear science and its graduate school. Serving as scientific director, he travelled worldwide, raising the necessary funds to make possible the magnificent developments on its campus.

Nor did he shirk from advising Israel's leaders in their search for peace and cooperation in the Mideast and for better science education at all levels of schooling and across national boundaries.

The measure of the respect that Amos had already earned as a physicist can be seen in the tribute given by his colleagues at the time of his death. Together with two colleagues, Igal Talmi and Herman Feshbach of MIT, I wrote to a number of friends and colleagues of Amos's inviting them to contribute to a volume dedicated to his memory. Our invitation read as follows:

> We know you join us in the feeling of great loss at the recent death of Amos de-Shalit and in the desire to express the high regard and warm feelings we all had for him. There will be many memorials. But to his fellow physicists perhaps the most appropriate would be for each of us to dedicate one of our more significant papers to his memory. With this in mind a volume of the *Annals of Physics* dedicated to Amos de-Shalit and sponsored by the Weizmann Institute of Science has been set aside. We invite you to contribute to this volume. The volume will form a suitable memorial only if it consists of important contributions which will be referred to for many years. Such articles are not plentiful, but we hope that from Amos' wide circle of friends, a sufficient number will be forthcoming.

The response to our invitation was overwhelming. Instead of one volume, the tribute grew to two, big volumes containing 75 manuscripts contributed by more than 140 of the world's leading physicists. It was an immense tribute dedicated with deep personal sadness to the memory of a very distinguished scientific colleague and a close personal friend.

Much has been written in recent years about the responsibility of scientists to help mankind achieve a better life, to improve the human condition; to help avoid devastating plagues, diseases, and environmental catastrophes; and, especially, to prevent war, which, in the modern age—as a result of advances in chemistry, biology, and physics—has the potential for unimaginable destruction. In his play *Man and Superman*, George Bernard Shaw has the devil appear to Don Juan in the dream sequence in hell with the observation that, "in the arts of death [Man] outdoes nature herself. . . . When he goes out to slay, he carries a marvel of mechanism that lets loose at the touch of his finger all the hidden molecular energies, and leaves the javelin, the arrow, the blowpipe of his fathers far behind. In the arts of peace, Man is a bungler."

The cutting edge of scientific progress has a two-edged blade. As a result of the achievements of modern science, we look to the future with ever grander dreams to understand nature and to improve the human condition. At the same time we strive to realize these exhilarating dreams, we face the threatening nightmare that the understanding achieved by science has now made it possible to unleash forces of mass destruction of a magnitude to desolate our Earth and make it uninhabitable. What makes the challenge of this nightmare so pressing is that we recognize that we now possess the awesome power to do irreversible damage, spelling the end of the great civilization built by man's genius and sweat, if not the end of the human species, itself. We can no longer afford to make mistakes.

This means that the responsibility of scientists has never been greater to society. Never before has it been so important that scientists, who can best understand and explain the dangers that the applications of science pose, speak with reasoned, intelligent, and responsible voices in the halls of government. But those voices must not only be heard— they must be heeded, if they are to be at all effective.

This puts a special burden both on government and on the scientific community. Government leaders and their institutions must understand the folly and danger of thinking they can simply ignore or dispense with the voice of the scientist. This means they must be convinced of the value of that voice. And, the scientific community, as a whole, has the obligation to convince the government that our contribution to policy decisions is too valuable to ignore.

In the abstract, I would say that the universality of science and the fact that it cannot be avoided by policy makers is now broadly recognized. It is understood that scientists constitute one of the most important channels of communication among different countries in discussing the technical applications spawned by scientific advances. Moreover, there is growing recognition that many problems we now face can be addressed only regionally, if not internationally. These problems include health and disease, the environment, pollution, and conservation of scarce resources, as our hunger for energy and for food strains the limits of what we now know how to produce on this Earth, our finite spaceship.

From the very beginning of the state of Israel, and while he was still in his twenties, Amos was in the vanguard of scientists who recognized the importance of science—by its very nature, as a vehicle free of ideology and politics—for opening and extending constructive, peaceful relations among countries, particularly beneficial ones between the more advanced technical societies and the developing ones seeking to achieve a better life for their people.

As this understanding of the salient fact—that science knows no political or geographic boundaries and is truly a universal activity— has become more widely recognized, including by governments themselves, the importance of the scientist learning how to effectively provide advice to government has grown.

Amos didn't have to learn. He intrinsically had all the required ingredients to be listened to with trust and respect. He did the necessary hard work before speaking, and he applied the same rigorous standards in presenting his views that he always brought to bear in his professional, scientific life. In a word, he earned the trust of his government. His advice was valued, furthermore, because he had the good judgment to blend his vision and moral principles with a necessary measure of operational reality so as not to lose sight of the possible in pursuit of an ideal.

The world of scientists working effectively in public policy and with government leaders is a perilous one, fraught with the potential for pain, as both Andrei Sakharov and Robert Oppenheimer learned. For even raising the question of the morality of developing the hydrogen bomb, Oppenheimer was branded a security risk. Although he had brilliantly, energetically, and successfully led the effort to create the atom bomb during World War II, Oppenheimer was subjected to a very painful public persecution during the 1950s that questioned his loyalty. Consequently, he found himself twisting and turning in hostile political currents. The more recent saga of Sakharov, after years of threatening a total tragedy, seems now to have developed a happy ending as the Soviet Union of Mikhail Gorbachev pursues *perestroika* and *glasnost*. With his rehabilitation, Sakharov has been transformed from a persecuted dissident into an outspoken member of the Soviet government and, perhaps, the most popular and admired individual in the Soviet Union—but, as always, speaking out courageously against oppression, against prejudice, and for the implementation of democratic principles in his country and elsewhere around the world.

Both of these examples remind us that, as scientists, we are trained to study the fixed and rational laws of nature, but once we leave our laboratories to participate in matters of public policy and walk the halls of government, we enter into a vastly different world and must deal with shifting and often irrational laws of political and social interactions. Indeed, the scientist is entering a more complex and difficult world, for, as Einstein once said, "politics is much harder than physics." And it was this world that Amos entered so brilliantly, courageously, and effectively in his young life at the peak of his career in science.

The record of his past activities and the concrete evidence of his achievements at the Weizmann Institute give us some measure of Amos's work in this area.

From being close to Amos himself and, more recently, from discussions with my good friend Michael Feldman, I know a bit about Amos's efforts in the immediate aftermath of the Six-Day War. In early 1968, he formed and headed the so-called "Rehovot Group." This was a group of scientists and colleagues from the military, the government, and the financial world that met at the Weizmann Institute several times each month with the purpose of dealing with issues that the politicians, themselves, were not ready to touch. Their goal was to create plans and to prepare programs for meeting impending challenges so that the government would be ready to act constructively when the political leaders judged it was an appropriate time to deal with them. More than that, it was an effort to alert the government to problems coming down the road. Their first concern that I am aware of was that of addressing the very major problem of dealing with the Palestinian refugees. What the group had to contribute was the development of social and economic programs to help solve the refugee problem, which, as a result of the Six-Day War, had become a major social and political issue for Israel. One approach was to provide vocational training and small industrial programs that would permit refugees to move out of the camps and into constructive and dignified roles in society. To bring this plan into reality, financing was sought, and in some measure achieved, from outside Israel. Regrettably, events in the meantime have made clear that this vision of Rehovot outpaced and eventually diverged from political reality.

Science education is another area in which Amos developed productive dialogue between scientists and political leaders, leading to an important initiative. His nationwide program to reform science teaching has produced a rich harvest. Science teaching was a life-long interest of his. On previous visits to Israel, I have seen in the schools at all levels very impressive evidence of substantive improvements and successful innovation. When I look at science teaching in the public-school system in my own country—which, I must say with deep regrets, I consider to be a disaster area—I realize how valuable it can be when a committed, respected, and intelligent leader puts his energies and mind into so vital an area of his nation's development. Indeed, we can see the temple Amos created to accomplish his goal in science education in the Youth Science Center and the Science Teaching Department at the Weizmann Institute of Science.

Of course, in achieving lofty goals of this type, one also needs government leaders who are willing to listen and themselves be educated in the value and even the basic ideas of science. On my first visit to Israel, in 1959, I was witness to one of the great dialogues on science between a political leader and a scientist, which I shall never forget. I had just arrived at the Weizmann Institute to report on the first international particle-physics conference in the Soviet Union. At that time, no Israelis were invited to this meeting at Kiev. I came to report on the proceedings of the meeting and, by the way, also to report that never again would there be such a congress attended by a large percentage of scientists from the West if it did not also include Israeli scientists. During my visit, there was a reception at the Liberian embassy in celebration of the seventy-fifth anniversary of Liberia's independence. Amos took me to the reception with him, and there he entered into a spirited discussion with David Ben-Gurion, then Prime Minister of Israel, on the very nature of physical measurements and on the principle of complementarity in applying physical concepts to the description of atomic phenomena. It seems that the Prime Minister, on one of his retreats to his kibbutz, had been studying the writings of Niels Bohr on this subject. As I interpreted the discussion, it seemed to me that Ben-Gurion was resisting a conclusion that, in principle, neither he nor anyone else could carry out a coherent causal description of nature at the atomic level. This was evidently just one of a series of ongoing science discussions between Amos and Ben-Gurion. I am not sure Amos succeeded in convincing the Prime Minister that such a limit existed, in principle, on what he could know. But it was an extraordinary discussion, and it would have been wonderful if that fascinating dialogue between two fine minds could have been preserved in published literature.

What a privilege for a nation to have leaders with whom such a discussion is even possible! And how crucial it is also to have a scientific adviser, like Amos, whose voice can be trusted in the halls of government. It is all too easy to exploit one's scientific notoriety in order to promote personal or ideological goals—and we all have our lists of those who have succumbed to that temptation. This circumstance presents considerable danger to governments and leaders when they turn to scientists for help in formulating policies and making decisions on issues with important technical components calling for sound technical judgment, be they concerned with choices for national security, or for energy sources, or for technology development.

Treatises have been written and conferences convened on how to build a structure within government to ensure high-quality objective advice on scientific and technical issues. Past experiences have been analyzed to illustrate the danger of relying only on one scientist for advice that may be badly distorted as a result of the parallax in that scientist's vision of events in the political world. After all, there is no guarantee that clear vision and objectivity in the scientific laboratory will transfer successfully to the political world. Government committees are formed and offices are created to deal with such concerns on the theory that the technical and scientific components of various individuals' contributions add coherently to provide sound judgment, while the individual political biases are balanced out in a committee's deliberations. Such committees are important and generally work pretty well. I have served on many of them at all levels. Governments are well advised to use them—confidently and wisely even if, at times, they prove annoying because what they contribute may not be the desired or convenient (or even politically correct) advice. Their input is needed, and it can indeed be essential to protect governments from foolish or disastrous decisions. Unless you can count on having an Amos to rely on whenever needed, there is no alternative to an apolitical advisory-committee structure in place as a national resource.

One can only wonder what Amos might have contributed in present times with his wise and effective counsel, as around the world—and especially in this region—close neighbors are striving, and often conflicting, to achieve their aspirations for basic economic and political freedoms, on one hand, and, on the other, to meet their concerns about their basic security and very survival. We have yet to create new means of seeking changes and satisfying legitimate concerns without resorting to violence and stirring hatreds that mar the world today so tragically. The need to create such new means is an awesome challenge today in the Middle East between Israel and its Arab neighbors. I have no doubt that, were he alive, Amos would be in the vanguard of efforts to develop new approaches for meeting this challenge just as he was with the Rehovot Group in 1968. Such a commitment would be consistent with his demonstrated concept of scientific responsibility and patriotism.

I have described a very broad repertoire of achievements by Amos during his brief, but brilliant, career. He was recognized within the community of his colleagues as a scientist of extraordinary quality, integrity, and modesty; as a humanitarian committed to seeing the fruits of the tree of knowledge used for the betterment of mankind; and as a patriot dedicated to building, not destroying—to reason, not to force. It is difficult to overestimate the value of leaders such as Amos as role models, especially for students and young aspiring scientists. Their inspiration is very important in defining the character of a field of scientific inquiry such as physics. Throughout our careers, they inform our knowledge and shape our thinking. We honor them for far more than their scientific creativity. Reaching beyond their science, such giants as Albert Einstein and Niels Bohr used their science for the cause of humanity in searching for peace and social justice in an era marred by hate and persecution and threatened by nuclear devastation. Others followed in their wake—Oppenheimer, Sakharov, Rabi, Szilard, and Bethe, to name a few of the best known—who ventured out of the laboratory to apply their scientific knowledge and understanding of nature for the betterment of the human condition and to help the human race avoid nightmares of the sort we are now capable of triggering. Their character no less than their scientific brilliance has left indelible marks on modern physics. So did Amos, as all of us who were fortunate enough to have known him will always remember.

In his tragically brief life, he persistently strove to bridge the growing gulfs among different scientific disciplines, as also among different cultures and nations. His vision of a future in which knowledge would be shared by men and women of all nations, great and small, the developed and the still developing, is a vision that we still can all agree with and toward the realization of which we can all contribute, as he would certainly be doing were he still alive.

SAKHAROV

Tribute to Andrei Sakharov

Andrei, I always dared to hope—as did many of your friends and colleagues around the world—for this moment when you would be free to visit our shores and join us in our homes, our laboratories, our seminars, and in this great Academy—which, since your election in 1973 as a foreign associate, is yours as well as ours. Still, as I look back over the arduous and, at times, tortuous path you had to travel to get here, this occasion seems to me to be as close to a miracle as I ever expect to witness. The recent changes in your country that have made possible your visit and this occasion tonight offer the further hope that our two great nations will embrace common principles of human dignity and mutual respect. As they continue moving away from chilling confrontation toward constructive cooperation, the United States and the Soviet Union may better meet the challenges to the survival of humanity that you and your fellow board members of the International Foundation are addressing in your meetings this week.

Twenty years ago, Andrei Sakharov published his remarkable essay "Progress, Coexistence, and Intellectual Freedom." The two basic theses he developed in that essay are, first, that the division of mankind threatens it with destruction and, second, that intellectual freedom is essential to human society. His arguments in support of those theses remain as valid and compelling today as they were when he first presented them. That essay publicly marked Sakharov's emergence from the laboratory, where he had worked as a scientist—indeed, a great scientist. It was soon followed by further writings and speeches of great impact, and Andrei became recognized, not only as a scientific leader in search of nature's principles for the properties of matter, but also as a moral leader in search of ethical principles for a humanity striving for peace, progress, and basic human dignity.

From 1968 to the present, Andrei has continued to speak out—forcefully, courageously, persistently, and wisely on the main issues of our times: on problems of peace, the dangers of thermonuclear weapons, and the importance (and I quote from his 1975 book *My Country and the World*) "of disarmament talks, which offer a ray of hope in the dark world of suicidal nuclear madness." He risked everything and sacrificed much in his support of prisoners of conscience and his opposition to oppression wherever it occurs in the world. In his devotion to truth and human dignity and his defense of the freedom of the human spirit, Andrei has become, in the words of his 1975 Nobel Peace Prize citation, "the spokesman for the conscience of mankind."

Human history has been inspired and ennobled by the occasional emergence of figures of indomitable courage. Each of us has his or her own personal honor roll of those rare individuals whose lives have become morality plays with the dimensions of a historical epic, the theme of which is the struggle between conscience and principle on the one hand and raw political power on the other. Andrei stands tall in my honor roll of those giants who have been driven to do battle for principle in the manner described so eloquently by the young lawyer Gavin Stevens in William Faulkner's *Intruder in the Dust*:

> Some things you must always be unable to bear. Some things you must never stop refusing to bear. Injustice and outrage and dishonor and shame. No matter how young you are or how old you have got. Not for kudos and not for cash: your picture in the paper nor money in the bank either. Just refuse to bear them.

It is my great privilege to know Andrei Sakharov and his equally courageous and wonderful wife Yelena Bonner as close personal friends. This friendship dates back to our first meeting in Moscow 15 summers ago in June, 1974, when we were attending a working seminar on the substructure of elementary particles organized by the Soviet Academy of Sciences. But, beyond friendship, I also take personal pride in the fact that Andrei and I are members of the same scientific community. As theoretical physicists, we are fellow members of the crew on that great adventure voyage of the human mind searching to discover what we are made of. We share this passion to understand nature. What are the elementary building blocks on the submicroscopic scale of distances hundreds of millions to billions of times smaller than the size of the atom? What are the forces that glue together the building blocks—or elementary constituents—of nature into the protons and neutrons and other forms of matter that we actually see in the laboratory?

Andrei is most widely known for his courageous leadership in the defense of human principles that we hold dear and as the father of the Soviet hydrogen bomb. But you should also know that he is a great scientist whose brilliant career as a theoretical physicist is distinguished by seminal research contributions to fundamental physics, including the behavior of plasmas and the properties of elementary particles.

In 1950, Andrei, together with Academician Igor Tamm—an internationally honored and greatly admired former leader of Soviet physics, a Nobel laureate, and Andrei's teacher—wrote the pioneering paper in the controlled-fusion effort in the Soviet Union. In that paper, they introduced a confinement scheme for a hot plasma that is famous today under the name "tokamak." As a result of subsequent important work by other major figures in Soviet science—in particular, the late Academician Lev Artsimovich and including contributions by two of this evening's guests, Academicians Roald Sagdeev and Yevgeny Velikhov and their colleagues—this is one of the most promising methods now being pursued around the world, including right here in the United States, for developing fusion as a practical source of energy.

Andrei also made a contribution of crucial importance to our quest to understand the evolution of our universe following its physical beginnings in the "big bang" of 15 or so billion years ago. The problem he addressed is this: Physicists know that for each form of matter, there also occurs antimatter—for example, electrons and positrons; protons and antiprotons. Antimatter is a necessary consequence of joining the general principles of atomic theory—that is, the quantum theory—with Einstein's special theory of relativity—the theory on the basis of which we understand his famous equation $E = mc^2$. But we must wonder, then, what has happened to all the antimatter. Where did it go? In our universe—or all we can see of it, as we peer far out into space to receive signals just arriving from distant events that occurred ten or more billions of years ago—why are the massive systems of stars and galaxies made almost exclusively of matter and not antimatter? If the universe at the time of the big bang had no matter or antimatter—just energy—why do we now have this excess of matter over antimatter?

Andrei provided the clue for understanding this in 1968—the same

year he published "Progress, Coexistence, and Intellectual Freedom."
A leap of imagination allowed him to see that the absence of antimatter can be explained rather elegantly by joining a recent experimental
observation—that there is a very tiny difference between the behavior
of matter and of antimatter—with several general postulates that had
been made separately in other contexts. The most intriguing of these
postulates is that the proton, the nucleus of the hydrogen atom—long
believed to be a stable particle of nature—may, in fact, decay just like
other forms of subnuclear matter, albeit very, very slowly. This bold
hypothesis is currently being tested in laboratories around the world.
The experiments are very difficult and require massive equipment. No
one has yet seen a proton decay, so the hypothesis has yet to be
confirmed. But you can be sure that it is very comforting to know that
our universe lacks antimatter because, if we were to meet a galaxy, or
a star, or some other vast entity made of antimatter, we would all go
"poof." Collisions between little pieces of matter and antimatter would
make a nuclear explosion look, by comparison, like a popgun.

When the history books of the latter part of the twentieth century
are written, they will tell that this was a time when mankind was first
able to begin writing a history of the evolution of the universe following the big bang that is based on solid experimental data and theoretical concepts. And in that chapter of history, as in other chapters of
our times, Andrei's name will surely appear, this time as Andrei Sakharov, physicist.

Andrei's life in physics is clear evidence of the international character of science—true science. The "tokamak" idea of controlled fusion is of Russian parentage and is studied worldwide with a free and
eager exchange of new progress that is beneficial to all. Search for
evidence of proton decay is being pursued with international collabo-
rations on a worldwide basis in both hemispheres, East and West.
Science knows no boundaries, and efforts to create barriers—whether
to keep new ideas within or to prevent new ideas from entering from
the outside—have universally proved harmful to progress. The great
nineteenth-century Russian playwright, Anton Chekhov, said it best:
"There is no national science just as there is no national multiplication
table; what is national is no longer science." It is regrettable when, on
occasion, governments need to be reminded of this basic fact. It may
not be a law of nature, but it has proved to be a reliable rule of thumb,
that national interests and true security are better served by keeping
open the channels of communication of scientific achievements than by
erecting barriers to stem the transfer of knowledge.

And, just as good science knows no geographic or political boundaries, modern-day scientists have increasing difficulty in defining a boundary between work in the laboratory and a concerned involvement in the practical applications of scientific progress. Sakharov himself is one of the most important examples of this involvement and of the serious difficulties—and, on occasion, the painful disillusionment—that a scientist or a scholar may encounter when he or she reaches out of the private shell of the laboratory or the study and actively participates in society.

Sakharov has written (in an autobiographical essay published in 1974) that he "had no doubts as to the vital importance of creating a Soviet super-weapon—for our country and for the balance of power throughout the world," but tells of his concern for continuing bomb testing throughout the following decade and of his involvement in a military–industrial complex "blind to everything except their jobs" and of his coming "to reflect in general terms on the problems of peace and mankind and, in particular, on the problems of a thermonuclear war and its aftermath." The involvement of scientists in war and weapons—as in other major issues of importance to the human condition—is in itself nothing new. Its distinguished honor roll of olden days includes such luminaries as Archimedes, Leonardo da Vinci, and Michelangelo. But never before have scientists dealt with weapons of absolute destruction, with weapons whose use could mean the end of civilization as we know it, if not of mankind itself. And never before has the gulf been so great between the scientific arguments—even the very language of science—and the knowledge on these technical matters of the political leaders whose decisions will shape the future.

The new fact that the fruits of our learning threaten the existence of all mankind presents an acutely heightened ethical dilemma to scientists. Our predicament is precarious because we have so little—if any— margin of safety. As much as any scientist I know, Andrei Sakharov has understood the special obligation of the scientific community to alert society to the implications of the products of scientific advances and to assist society in shaping the applications of these advances in beneficial directions.

Scientists who enter the political realm and participate in the public debate on the implications of scientific advances bear a special responsibility to speak accurately and responsibly on the technical challenges to society. Once again, Sakharov is a model for us all. He has spoken out courageously, passionately, and with outrage, when appropriate, on issues of social injustice and oppression. But, when speaking as a scientist on technical and factual issues, he has maintained the same high standards that we demand in our professional scientific lives. It is our obligation to do likewise. Unless we do, we will compromise—and lose—any effectiveness and credibility we bring to the debate as scientists.

By his actions, Andrei has been an inspiration to all of us. Constant in purpose, clear in vision, modest, and unflinching in his courage to speak out in circumstances of great personal danger, he has inspired support, admiration, and devotion from people of all stations and nations. I shall never forget the first evidence of that devotion, which I saw when Andrei invited me to supper in his and Yelena's modest apartment in Moscow during our first meeting in July 1974. He reported that, less than an hour before my arrival, he had been visited by Moscow policemen bringing a protest from his neighbors about disturbing noises from his apartment. What had triggered this protest was an event that had occurred the previous day. The La Scala Opera of Milan was visiting Moscow that week for performances at the Bolshoi Theatre, and two of its lead singers had arrived at Andrei's door unannounced to show their admiration and affection for him, which they expressed the best way they could—that is, through song in a private operatic recital.

Andrei, I can't sing in tune and, have no fear, I won't try. Instead, I will close by asking all your friends here tonight to join me in a toast expressed in the words of your friend Lev Kopelev, author, compatriot, and known to many of us as the mathematician Rubin, who appears in Alexander Solzhenitsyn's great novel, *The First Circle*. Kopelev's beautiful tribute is: "The majesty of his spirit, the power of his intellect and the purity of his soul, his chivalrous courage and selfless kindness feed my faith in the future of Russia and mankind."

Andrei Dmitrievich Sakharov

WITH LEV OKUN

At the time of his death from a heart attack on 14 December 1989, Andrei Dmitrievich Sakharov was recognized both as a great scientist and as a persistent and uncompromising fighter for human rights and political freedom for all. He lived to see his Russian homeland start on the path toward implementing the principles of democracy to which he had devoted the last two decades of his life. His leadership in the struggle of conscience and principle against raw political power earned him worldwide accolades as the conscience of humanity. Gentle and modest in person, but of unconquerable persistence in his commitment to principle and opposition to injustice, he had become, in the memorial words of a Russian commentator, both "the saint and martyr of *perestroika*." With the end of his life, the curtain fell on a morality play with the dimensions of a historical epic.

Early Years

Sakharov was born in Moscow on 21 May 1921, into a family with the traditions of the Russian intelligentsia. His father was a physics teacher and was well known as the author of a physics textbook, which students still use. Andrei received his early schooling at home; in his autobiography, he writes of having difficulty relating to his own age group. He graduated from high school with honors in 1938 and enrolled in the physics department of Moscow University. In October 1941, when the German army was approaching Moscow, the university was transferred to Ashkhabad, where he graduated with honors in

1942. He tells of gaining his first vivid impression of the life of workers and peasants during the difficult summer of 1942.

Sakharov's fellow students recollect that his ability to think and to formulate and resolve science problems was remarkable. They also remember that he was the only person in their hostel who, in that time of deprivation and hunger, could give his own last piece of bread to someone who badly needed it.

After graduating from the university, Sakharov worked from 1942 till 1945 as an engineer at a large arms factory in Ulyanovsk on the Volga, where he developed several inventions to improve the plant's inspection procedures. Sakharov tells of writing several theoretical physics papers during this period and sending them back to Moscow for review. In Sakharov's judgment, those papers, which were never published, didn't really constitute original scientific work, but he wrote that "they gave me confidence in my powers, which is essential for a scientist."

During this period, in 1943, Sakharov married Klavdia Alekseyevna Vikhireva. They raised three children before her death in 1969.

Sakharov and Physics

In January 1945, Sakharov became a graduate student at the Lebedev Institute of Physics. His adviser, Igor Tamm, greatly influenced his future. Academician Tamm (1895–1971) was an outstanding theorist who in 1958 shared the Nobel Prize with academicians Ilya Frank and Pavel Čerenkov for developing in 1937 the theory of what is now commonly known as Čerenkov radiation. He was a man admired for his character, integrity, and warm personality. Outside of physics he is remembered in particular for his fearless fight against Trofim Lysenko and for his efforts to save and revive Soviet genetics.

Early Papers

Sakharov published his first research paper when he was 26 years old. He submitted it for publication in *Zhurnal Eksperimental'noi i Teoreticheskoi Fiziki (JETP)* in January 1947. (All 30 of Sakharov's scientific papers were originally published in Russian, most of them in *JETP* and *JETP Letters*; 24 of these papers appeared in English. See A. D. Sakharov, *Collected Scientific Works*, Marcel Dekker, New York, 1982.) The paper estimated the cross section for the production of mesons as the hard component of cosmic rays in a model proposed by Tamm. (In this model, now completely obsolete, the charged mesons are pseudoscalars, while the neutral one is a scalar). Sakharov considered meson production by photons and nucleons using the theoretical techniques developed in Walter Heitler's 1936 book *The Quantum Theory of Radiation*. To estimate the cross sections, he considered several of the many noncovariant diagrams. He also estimated meson production in nuclei, and found that, due to rather loose binding of nucleons, the effective threshold is close to $2\mu c^2$ rather than μc^2, where μ is the meson mass.

In November 1947, he successfully defended his Ph.D. thesis, "Theory of 0–0 Nuclear Transitions," and received the candidate degree. The main problem he discussed in the thesis was the ratio of the number of e^+e^- pairs to the number of single electrons knocked out of atomic shells (internal conversion electrons) in electromagnetic transition between two nuclear levels of the same parity, both having zero angular momentum. He considered two excited nuclei—RaC' (^{214}Po*) and ^{16}O*—for which controversial experimental and theoretical results existed at that time. His predecessors in this subject were J. Robert Oppenheimer, Julian Schwinger, Leonard Schiff (for ^{16}O*), Hans Bethe, Hideki Yukawa, and Shoichi Sakata (for RaC').

In his thesis, Sakharov also considered α decays of ^{12}C* into ^{8}Be* and ^{8}Be, and tried to explain the drastic difference between the probabilities of these decays—the branching ratio for the latter is only 2 percent. To this end, he introduced the notion of isotopic parity for a nucleus with equal numbers of protons and neutrons. Essentially what he meant was that the wavefunction of a system of nucleons had to be antisymmetric with respect to all degrees of freedom, including isotopic ones. For RaC', he also took into account the large Coulomb field of the nucleus. In the approximation that he considered, the Coulomb field of the nucleus did not change the total probability of pair emission, only the angular distribution of the electron and the positron.

The third part of his thesis was a calculation of the Coulomb attraction between an electron and a positron in pair production. This effect, as stressed in the thesis, becomes detectable only for the pairs in a very narrow kinematic region where the electron and the positron fly in the same direction—within, say, 1°—and their relative motion is nonrelativistic. The last part of the thesis was published in a modified form as a separate paper in *JETP* in 1948.

When you read Sakharov's thesis, which has 71 pages, you are impressed by how carefully all the steps are explained, all the intermediate formulas written down and numerical coefficients derived. He liked to write as clearly as possible. His friends recall that to handwrite formulas into a typed text was a pleasure for him.

In 1948, Sakharov also published a second paper in *JETP* and authored two reports of the Lebedev Institute. The *JETP* paper analyzed the optical method of measuring plasma temperature. When electrons are in thermodynamic equilibrium and deexcitation is negligible, the relative intensities of selected optical atomic lines are a measure of their temperature; otherwise these intensities give the so-called excitation temperature, which has no simple physical meaning. Sakharov also discussed molecular spectra, remarking that the linear relation between temperature and the logarithm of the intensity remains valid beyond the region where it is supposed to work. Many years later, he frequently would say that physical laws tend to be approximately valid far beyond the expected limits of their validity.

One of the two Lebedev reports mentioned above presents a calculation of the decrease in the intensity of a synchrotron's electron beam due to scattering on gas molecules in the initial period of acceleration, when the energy is under 1 MeV. The second report is much more interesting. Titled "Passive Mesons," it is a reaction to the discovery of the pion and the muon (he called the latter "passive meson 200") and to a paper by F. C. Frank. Frank considered exotic nuclear cold-fusion reactions catalyzed by the formation of "mesotronic hydrogen," which could give a free "shake-off mesotron" with an energy of 4 MeV. Frank tried to interpret in these terms the 4-MeV secondary particles (muons from pion decay) that were observed by Cesare M. G. Lattes, Giuseppe P. S. Occhialini, and Cecil F. Powell.

Sakharov's report contained the first explicit consideration of the muonic mesoatom and pioneered the idea of cold μ-catalyzed DD fusion. Sakharov's estimate of the Coulomb-barrier factor was more optimistic than Frank's by a factor of 10^3. But his conclusion was pessimistic: "With usual mesons 200 the meson catalysis reaction is impossible." Later work (including Sakharov's) has shown that the pessimistic verdict was premature. Today, muon-catalyzed fusion is a field of intense research with perhaps a promising future. Sakharov returned to the topic of μ-catalyzed fusion in his next open publication, coauthored with Yakov B. Zel'dovich, which appeared in *JETP* in 1957.

Plasma Physics

In July 1948, by a special government decision, Sakharov was enlisted in classified work on atomic weapons, as a member of Tamm's group.

He was one of the creators of the Soviet nuclear bomb and is often referred to as "the father of the Soviet hydrogen bomb" (more on this later). During the next eight years, Sakharov received the highest state honors for his important contributions: Hero of Socialist Labor, twice (in 1953 and 1956—he received it again in 1962), the Stalin prize (1953), and the Lenin prize (1956). He also received a doctor's (D.Sc.) degree (1953) and was elected to full membership in the Academy of Sciences of the USSR (1953). At 32 years of age, he was one of the youngest members ever elected.

The only paper by Sakharov during this period that has been declassified is his report, written in 1951 and published in 1958, entitled "Theory of the Magnetic Thermonuclear Reactor" (in fact, it was part II of a paper on this subject; parts I and III were written by Tamm). This was the opening and main paper in four volumes of declassified reports that the Soviet Academy published in Russian on the eve of the 1958 Geneva Conference on Peaceful Applications of Atomic Energy. The title of these volumes, as given in English translation in the proceedings of the conference, is *Plasma Physics and the Problem of Controlled Thermonuclear Reactions*. Although Sakharov's paper grew out of military research on high-intensity sources of neutrons, it opened new vistas in mankind's search for clean sources of energy for peaceful purposes. The first description of this plasma physics work was presented by Igor Kurchatov, head of the Soviet weapons project, in his talk at Harwell in 1956, when he came to the United Kingdom accompanying Nikita Khrushchev. The main idea was that of confining a hot plasma in a toroidal magnetic field. Sakharov's paper is the seed from which the tree of tokamaks and other, similar installations has grown.

Research on thermonuclear fusion is now being carried out in many countries. (The thirteenth international conference on nuclear fusion will be held this year in Washington.) Several large tokamaks are under construction in the Soviet Union, the United States, Western Europe, and Japan. It is expected that a deuterium–tritium reactor will start to produce energy early in the next century. Unfortunately, it will also produce a lot of radioactivity. A much cleaner deuterium–helium-3 reactor would be much more difficult to construct.

Sakharov published no scientific research papers between 1958 and 1965. This was a period when he grew increasingly concerned about the accelerating course of the arms race and the dangers of radioactive fallout from continued testing of nuclear weapons in the atmosphere. He published an analysis of the harmful consequences of radioactive

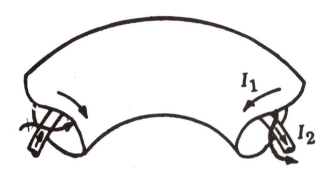

FIGURE 1. *Toroid diagram that Sakharov used to illustrate his scheme for a magnetic thermonuclear reactor. Currents I_1 in an external coil and I_2 in an axial ring produce magnetic lines of force that have a spiral shape. (From Proceedings of the 1957 Geneva Conference on Peaceful Applications of Atomic Energy, vol. 1, Pergamon, Elmsford, New York, 1961; reprinted by permission.)*

pollution in 1959 and was actively involved in initiatives in the Soviet Union leading to the Limited Test Ban Treaty of 1963 (a topic to which we shall return).

In 1965, Sakharov and eight coauthors published a short paper on the experimental development of magnetic cumulation, or compression. Sakharov had first put forward, in 1951, the idea of creating ultrastrong magnetic fields by converting the mechanical and thermal energy released in a chemical explosion. There were two types of magnetic cumulators: MK1 and MK2 (in Russian, the word 'cumulator' starts with k). In the MK1 scheme, the magnetic flux was compressed in a tube by coaxial implosion from outside; see Figure 1. In MK2, which was developed in the years 1952–1956 and reached much higher magnetic fields, the electric current in a solenoid was compressed by an explosion running inside the solenoid from one end to the other, and a magnetic field was ejected into a coaxial line and compressed there; see Figure 2. In this way, a 25-megagauss magnetic field was created in 1964. Subsequently, in 1966, Sakharov published a short review entitled "The Principles and Characteristics of Magnetoimplosive Generators." The prospects that this breakthrough opened have proved varied and bright. Ultrastrong magnetic fields are used in the study of electrical, optical, and elastic properties of various materials. They can be used for accelerating particles and projectiles. Regular international

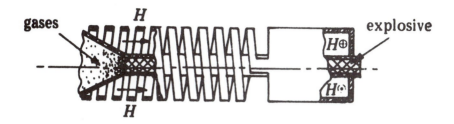

FIGURE 2. *The MK2 magnetic cumulation generator. The propagating explosion shorts and shortens the helix, decreasing its inductance. This increases the current in the helix and increases the magnetic energy. (From A. D. Sakharov et al., Dokl. Akad. Nauk SSSR* **165**, *65, 1965 [Sov. Phys. Dokl.* **10**, *1045, 1966].)*

conferences are devoted to the topic of megagauss fields. The most recent such conference, Megagauss V, was held in July 1989 in Novosibirsk.

Cosmology and Baryon Asymmetry

The papers on magnetic cumulation were a kind of farewell to the classified work of 1950s. In 1965, Sakharov entered a new field: He published his first paper on cosmology. The problem he dealt with was the formation of primordial astronomical objects from an initially homogeneous distribution of matter. He assumed that, at the beginning, the homogeneous matter was at zero temperature. The mechanism he considered was the gravitational instability of a uniform expanding universe. He generalized previous studies by taking into account quantum fluctuations. He also discussed later stages of evolution, when stars formed galaxies. This "cold" model was abandoned rather soon as a result of Arno Penzias' and Robert Wilson's 1965 discovery of the 3° K background radiation, but, even in 1980, commenting on this paper, Sakharov wrote, "It is still possible that the earliest stages in the development of the universe should still be described by the cold model."

In his next paper, written a year later, Sakharov already discussed the "hot" model of the universe known as the "big bang" and tried to consider the energy density of the hot photon gas at a number density higher than its Planck value.

His next publication—four pages in *JETP Letters* in 1967—is one of the boldest and most famous physics papers of the century. Its aim was to explain why the matter in the universe is built of protons, neutrons, and electrons, while antiprotons, antineutrons, and positrons are so rare that we can observe antimatter only when it is produced in high-energy collisions, mainly in particle accelerators. This particle–antiparticle disparity is usually referred to as the "baryon asymmetry of the universe," protons and neutrons being the lightest of all baryons. Sakharov made the elegant assumption that originally the universe was neutral and had no baryon asymmetry. He then had the brilliant insight to realize that an asymmetry would build up following the big bang, via nonstationary processes during the expansion of the early universe, if his novel idea of proton instability were combined with the violation of particle–antiparticle symmetry (*CP* symmetry), which James Cronin, Val Fitch, and their collaborators had discovered experimentally in 1964 in decays of kaons. According to Sakharov, some hypothetical processes violate baryon number conservation and *CP* symmetry on the Planck scale. Assuming the existence of several types of vector bosons with leptoquark quantum numbers whose emission transforms a quark into a muon, Sakharov introduced a trilinear non-renormalizable self-interaction of these leptoquarks that violates the conservation of the baryon and lepton numbers but conserves their difference.

Many features of this model became characteristic of grand unification models proposed in the 1970s, and the discovery of proton decay became, and remains today, the goal of several very-large-scale underground detectors. The estimate of the proton's lifetime given by Sakharov was about 10^{50} years. Grand unification models started with proton lifetimes of 10^{30} years but have been revised, as lower experimental limits now reach to 10^{32} years. It appears that it will take at least 10 years to add an additional factor of 10 to this limit. (The difference between the 10^{50}-year and 10^{30}-year lifetime estimates stems from the fact that Sakharov considered the processes to occur on the Planck scale; in modern grand unification theories, however, baryon nonconservation occurs at energies five orders of magnitude lower. The proton lifetime is proportional to the fourth power of this energy scale.)

The paper on baryon asymmetry was accompanied by a four-page letter containing a specific model of *CP* violation that fits the observed effect of *CP* violation in neutral-kaon decay and that can be used to compute the effect of *CP* violation in other processes. In contrast to grand unification models, in Sakharov's model the high-energy scale of baryon nonconservation was very high, but the mass of leptoquarks was low—on the order of the *W*-boson mass. Consequently, the leptoquarks would effectively induce the *CP* violation in $K \leftrightarrow \bar{K}$ transitions and cause some appreciable effects violating μ–e universality. Sakharov was disappointed when, shortly after his paper was published, experimental data were reported on the decay of K^0 into two neutral pions that purported to show a difference from this particle's decay into two charged pions. This was contrary to his predictions. Later, it would turn out that these neutral-pion data were wrong, but by that time Sakharov would be absorbed by other interests.

Sakharov continued to work on the baryonic asymmetry of the universe until the end of his life. "Baryonic Asymmetry of the Universe" served as the title of a *JETP* paper published in 1979 and of his last talk at a physics conference—the 1988 Alexander Friedmann Memorial Symposium in Leningrad. In 1979, he compared his approach with that of grand unification and worked out in detail the kinetics of baryon-nonconserving processes in the expanding universe. The main concerns of his Friedmann talk were the inflationary universe and the role of baryon nonconservation, and whether instanton-like transitions might wipe out the "grand" baryonic asymmetry at a later stage of the universe's evolution—namely, at the electroweak phase transition around 1 TeV. The talk demonstrates how closely he was watching recent developments in particle physics and cosmology.

Quark Model

For Sakharov, the years 1965–1967 were ones of extremely intense activity in several directions. In addition to his seminal work on the baryon asymmetry of the universe, he constructed (with Zel'dovich, in 1966) linear mass formulas for mesons and baryons in the framework of the naive quark model. Their main interest at the time was a model in which a baryon consists of four quarks and an antiquark (today $4q\bar{q}$ would be classified as a cryptoexotic meson). However, they also considered three-quark baryons.

Sakharov's interest in linear mass formulas persisted for many years. In 1975, he generalized them to predict the masses of charmed mesons and baryons, which were unknown at that time. In February 1980, at the beginning of his exile to Gorki, he reduced the number of phenomenological parameters in the formulas to six: three masses for the ordinary, strange, and charmed quarks; separate additive constants for mesons and baryons; and a common spin–spin coupling constant b, which in the case of baryons had a semiempirical factor of $\frac{1}{3}$ in front of it. With the new set of parameters, he succeeded in reproducing the observed patterns of meson and baryon masses. Moreover, in a second paper, received by *JETP* nine days later, by comparing the ratio of the respective mass differences between the vector and pseudoscalar particles caused by quark magnetic and chromomagnetic interactions, Sakharov determined, in the framework of his nonrelativistic quark model, the ratio of electric and gluonic charges.

The naive nonrelativistic quark model evidently does not address the most profound problems of modern physics. But Sakharov was not snobbish: He loved physics in every form. To think about a puzzle was fun for him.

The Book of the Universe

Returning to the mid-1960s, we find two papers by Sakharov devoted to the origin of the gravitational force. Here he considers this force as a "metric elasticity" of space. This elasticity is a reaction of space to its curving and is caused by quantum effects of vacuum polarization. In this approach, the Lagrangian of the gravitational field is assumed to be originally equal to zero; it becomes nonzero as an effective Lagrangian resulting from one-loop diagrams of virtual particle–antiparticle pairs. Zel'dovich applied a similar idea to the electromagnetic field. Sakharov himself returned to his original idea in 1970, 1974, and 1975, trying to overcome problems caused by quadratically divergent integrals (a cutoff at the Planck scale was assumed to provide the correct value of the Newtonian coupling constant). In 1974, Sakharov remarked that his approach was incompatible with the scalar–tensor modification of general relativity. In the 1980s, several theorists in the West—Stephen Adler and Anthony Zee, for example—continued this effort. From a pragmatic point of view, this "null Lagrangian" approach may be considered as a mathematical expression of a kind of composite model in which gravitons and photons are bound states of particles and antiparticles.

Starting from his first paper on the baryon asymmetry of the universe, Sakharov again and again returned to the tantalizing problem: What preceded the big bang? In 1965, he proposed the hypothesis of cosmological *CPT* invariance, considering a "pre-universe" that represents a *CPT* reflection of our universe with respect to the moment $t=0$.

In 1969, he considered this cosmological reflection in connection with the possible existence of stable neutral particles ten times heavier than protons; he assumed them to be more abundant than protons and to form what we now call "dark matter." In an article with the deceptive title "Antiquarks in the Universe," he proposed searching for these particles. In the same year, in a preprint titled "Multisheet Model of the Universe," he generalized the idea of a "pre-universe" by considering an infinite (or semi-infinite) series of collapsing and exploding universes. In 1972, he combined the cosmological *CPT* reflection with topological considerations concerning the possible origin of baryonic and leptonic quantum numbers.

Sakharov continued his physics research during the seven long years of his confinement in Gorki, a time of great stress and virtual isolation from his scientific colleagues. In three *JETP* papers (1980, 1982, 1984) he discussed various aspects of "multisheet" cosmology with and without cosmological *CPT* symmetry. In particular, in 1984, he discussed the possibility of quantum creation of an infinite number of universes, some of them possessing not one but several timelike coordinates. In all three papers, black holes attracted his attention. He discussed their role in smearing out inhomogeneities in density. In 1986, he wrote a special *JETP* letter on the evaporation of mini black holes, pointing out the role of evaporation of "shadow world" particles—that is, particles that interact with ordinary matter only gravitationally. He concluded his 1988 Friedmann Memorial talk by discussing the role of the false vacuum in the multisheet model of the universe.

Sakharov's cosmological views were an important part of his personality. Here is the end of his 1975 Nobel Peace Prize lecture:

> I support the cosmological hypothesis that states that the development of the universe is repeated in its basic characteristics an infinite number of times. Further, other civilizations, including more "successful" ones, should exist an infinite number of times on the "preceding" and the "subsequent" pages of the book of the universe. Nevertheless, this *weltanschauung* cannot in the least devalue our sacred aspirations in this world, into which, like a gleam in the darkness, we have appeared for an instant from the black

nothingness of the ever-unconscious matter, in order to
make good the demands of Reason and create a life worthy
of ourselves and of the Goal we only dimly perceive.

Sakharov and the Bomb

Just as Sakharov spoke from his brilliant mind as an uncommonly
creative scientist, so he also spoke and acted from his heart and conscience in his courageous and persistent battle for human rights, for
intellectual freedom, and for peace. He committed himself fearlessly
and relentlessly on both the individual and the global scale in his
opposition to human injustice and in his political and educational
efforts to reduce the threat of nuclear holocaust.

Evolution of Views

Sakharov wrote about how his social and political views evolved during the period from 1953 to 1968—the year he published his first
"nonphysics" paper, a remarkable and wide-ranging essay that was
printed first in the West, under the title "Reflections on Progress,
Peaceful Coexistence, and Intellectual Freedom." Following the publication of this and subsequent powerful writings and speeches, Sakharov became recognized worldwide as not only a great scientist but
also a moral leader of a humanity striving for peace, for progress, and
for basic human dignity.

Sakharov described his original satisfaction with having played so
prominent a role in the development of the Soviet H-bomb as stemming from a need to create, in the interest of peace, a balance to the
"capitalist bomb." He wrote:

> A few months after defending my dissertation for the degree
> of candidate of science, roughly equivalent to an American
> Ph.D., which occurred in the spring of 1948, I was included
> in a research group working on the problem of a thermonu-
> clear weapon. I had no doubts as to the vital importance of
> creating a Soviet super-weapon for our country and for the
> balance of power throughout the world. Carried away by the
> immensity of the tasks, I worked very strenuously and be-
> came the author or coauthor of several key ideas.

However, he also wrote of becoming increasingly involved during the
1950s with a military–industrial complex "blind to everything except
their jobs," and he told of coming "to reflect in general terms on the
problems of peace and mankind and, in particular, on the problems of

a thermonuclear war and its aftermath." Sakharov's concern about the harmful effects of radioactive fallout from atmospheric testing of nuclear bombs grew out of his involvement in the Soviet weapons program and led him to "an increased awareness of the moral problems engendered by such activities."

His first collision with the Soviet establishment can be traced back to 1955. After a nuclear test, he expressed the hope that such weapons would never be used, and in response Marshal Mitrofan Nedelyn, who headed the test, used a parable to tell him, in effect, that this was none of his business.

Sakharov convinced Kurchatov to try to persuade Khrushchev not to carry out a gigantic nuclear test. But the attempt failed. In 1961, Sakharov himself wrote to Khrushchev, insisting on the continuation of the nuclear test moratorium, and failed again. In 1962, he again addressed Khrushchev, this time to prevent a large-scale nuclear explosion in the atmosphere. Again his arguments were ignored. But finally the Soviet government approved his idea of a treaty banning nuclear tests in the atmosphere, outer space, and underwater. Sakharov wrote about his satisfaction that he was able to use his position to present to a key Soviet official an important idea that may have been instrumental in bringing about government support for such a treaty. This was his suggestion that the Soviet government set aside the controversial question of underground testing. The major nuclear powers signed the Limited Test Ban Treaty in 1963.

Nuclear Arms Control

During the 1970s and 1980s, Sakharov repeatedly spoke out strongly on the gravity of the threat of nuclear holocaust and on the most urgent need to control nuclear arms. In 1975, he wrote:

> The unchecked growth of thermonuclear arsenals and the buildup toward confrontation threaten mankind with the death of civilization and physical annihilation. The elimination of that threat takes unquestionable priority over all other problems in international relations. This is why disarmament talks, which offer a ray of hope in the dark world of suicidal nuclear madness, are so important.

Later, during the first year of his exile to Gorki, he wrote further, in *The New York Times Magazine* of 8 June 1980:

Despite all that has happened, I feel that the questions of war and peace and disarmament are so crucial that they must be given absolute priority even in the most difficult circumstances. It is imperative that all possible means be used to solve these questions and to lay the groundwork for further progress. Most urgent of all are steps to avert a nuclear war, which is the greatest peril confronting the modern world. The goals of all responsible people in the world coincide in this regard, including, I hope and believe, the Soviet leaders.

Both during his exile in Gorki and following his return to Moscow in 1987, Sakharov gave close attention to the strategic nuclear arms talks and stated carefully reasoned positions on the pressing issues. In particular, he frequently spoke out with concern about the U.S. Strategic Defense Initiative and its potential to destabilize the nuclear balance if deployed. He made one of his final comments on nuclear weapons during his first visit to the United States, in November and December 1988. In remarks at an occasion honoring Edward Teller, Sakharov drew parallels between his and Teller's "lifelines" and expressed his respect for Teller's guiding principles. He then commented, with respect to his work building the *H*-bomb:

I and the people who worked with me at the time were completely convinced that this work was essential, that it was vitally important. At that time our country had just come out of a very devastating war in which I personally had not had a chance to take direct part, but the work in which I became involved was also a kind of war. In the United States, independently, the same kind of work was being carried out. The American scientists in their work were guided by the same feelings of this work being vital for the interests of the country. But, while both sides felt that this kind of work was vital to maintain balance, I think that what we were doing at that time was a great tragedy. It was a tragedy that reflected the tragic state of the world that made it necessary, in order to maintain peace, to do such terrible things. We will never know whether it was really true that our work contributed at some period of time toward maintaining peace in the world, but at least at the time we were doing it, we were convinced this was the case.
The world has now entered a new era, and I am convinced

that a new approach has now become necessary. And I think in each case when a person makes a decision, he should base that decision on an absolute conviction of his rightness, and only under such circumstances can we ever find mutual understanding. And under such circumstances and in doing so, it is very important, and essential in fact, to find out all the points of difference as well as the points of coincidence and the points where the views are the same. There are certain issues on which Dr. Teller and I have views that coincide; for example, we are both concerned with how to insure the safety of thermonuclear energy. On the other hand, there are other spheres in which we disagree on matters of principle. One such issue is the issue of the space race, antiballistic missile defense. I consider the creation of such a system to be a grave error. I feel that it would destabilize the world situation. It is a system that would require enormous cost, both to establish and deploy such a system as well as to establish a system that would counteract it—the offensive system that would be able to counteract such a system.

Sakharov and Human Rights

During the 1960s, Sakharov became involved in an ever-expanding circle of issues of principle that took him beyond the debate over nuclear weapons policy. In 1964, as a young member of the Soviet Academy of Sciences, he opposed a political effort to let a mediocre assistant of Lysenko, the discredited charlatan of a biologist, into the academy. Election to the academy is by secret ballot. During the debate preceding the election, Sakharov protested against this new candidate, and indeed against Lysenko. This was no small step for him to take, as Lysenko, whom Stalin had made the "chief of biology" and who had destroyed genetics as a science in the Soviet Union, was close to and influential with Khrushchev, then the Soviet premier. At the end of the debate, which had been forced by Sakharov, the candidate was turned down for membership. It is reported that Khrushchev was so furious he threatened to abolish the academy. (This did not occur; Khrushchev was dismissed from office in October 1964.)

Beginning to Struggle

Sakharov's strong humanitarian convictions, his compassion for the persecuted, and his devotion to human dignity and freedom of the human spirit led to his first public appeals, in 1966, for victims of repression.

That year, he and 21 other prominent personalities signed an appeal to the twenty-third Communist Party Congress condemning attempts to rehabilitate Stalin. He also sent a telegram to the Supreme Soviet of the Russian Federation protesting a new clause in the criminal code dealing with "spreading deliberately false slanderous concoctions, defaming the Soviet state and social system." Sakharov saw that this clause gave the authorities a pretext for prosecuting people for their convictions. On 5 December, Constitution Day, he took part for the first time in the annual human rights demonstration in Pushkin Square.

In 1967, he wrote a letter to Leonid Brezhnev defending Alexander Ginzburg and three other human rights activists. He also talked to Brezhnev about Lake Baikal, in an effort to prevent industrial development on its shores, which would pollute this unique reservoir, the world's largest body of fresh water. The Soviet Academy did not support him in this effort, and the lake became badly polluted and is still being polluted today.

In 1968, as mentioned above, Sakharov published in the West his first "nonphysics" paper—his remarkable "Reflections on Progress, Peaceful Coexistence, and Intellectual Freedom." In this essay, he developed two basic themes: That the division of mankind threatens it with destruction, and that intellectual freedom is vital to human society. Sakharov repeated these two themes over and over during the next 21 years of his life. In his autobiography, Sakharov wrote:

> These same ideas were echoed seven years later in the title of my Nobel lecture: "Peace, Progress, and Human Rights." I consider the themes to be of fundamental importance and closely interconnected. My 1968 essay was a turning point in my life. . . . After my essay was published abroad in July 1968, I was barred from classified work and excommunicated from many privileges of the Soviet establishment.

In the Soviet Union, the essay was widely distributed through *samizdat*. About 18 million copies were printed throughout the world. (All Sakharov's political writings were originally published in the West, in English; only recently have they started appearing officially in the Soviet Union, in Russian.)

Sakharov commented frequently that, although his intellectual passion for physics remained as strong as ever, he realized that, as a result of the accident of his fame as the father of the Russian hydrogen bomb, he had acquired a moral obligation to use his notoriety—the fact that people listened and the press reported when he spoke—to act and speak out in defense of human rights, in which he believed so deeply. He said that he could not turn his back or walk away from helping those less famous or less fortunate. Thus, Sakharov wrote that "after 1970, the defense of human rights and of victims of political repression became my first concern."

In March 1970, he was joined by Roy Medvedev and Valentin Turchin in a letter to the Kremlin leadership analyzing many failures of the Soviet system "caused by the antidemocratic traditions and norms of public life" that had started with Stalin and were continuing. They pointed to pollution and environmental damage, censorship and imprisonment of writers, alcoholism, red tape, errors of policy, and technological backwardness. Their proposals for democratic reforms, including amnesty for political prisoners, the end of censorship, and an end to the labeling of citizens by nationality, went unanswered. Persisting in his cause, on 4 November 1970, Sakharov, together with Valery Chalidze and Andrei Tverdokhlebov, founded the Moscow Committee for Human Rights and focused more heavily on marshalling worldwide public opinion in the human-rights struggle.

Sakharov was joined in his campaign for human rights by Elena Bonner, whom he married in 1971. He met Bonner, a physician, during a rally with dissidents, and for the next 18 years she was constantly at his side as an equally courageous and determined battler. It was she who went to Oslo in November 1975 to accept the Nobel Peace Prize when Soviet authorities refused to grant Sakharov a visa.

Hunger Strikes and Gorki

The summer of 1974 marked the first of Sakharov's hunger strikes. During the period 1974–1985, Sakharov undertook four serious, health-threatening hunger strikes. In each instance, he used the hunger strike as a means of drawing attention to an injustice being suffered by others and mobilizing world opinion to bring pressure to right the wrong.

His first hunger strike was timed to coincide with the Moscow summit of President Richard Nixon and General Secretary Brezhnev in June 1974. With world press attention centered on the summit events in Moscow, Sakharov announced a hunger strike of finite duration (it lasted one week before it had to be ended because of its impact on his health) to call attention to the plight of the many minority groups in the Soviet Union whose members had no rights whatsoever to emigrate back to their native countries and rejoin their families. Although this strike received wide attention in the world press, it brought about no immediate change of policy. Sakharov emphasized its theme again in his 1975 Nobel Peace Prize address and on many subsequent occasions.

His second hunger strike occurred over a three-day period in May 1975 and was occasioned by Soviet refusal to permit Bonner to travel to Italy for a needed eye operation. Bonner's health problems were a constant concern to Sakharov during these years. Moved by the political impact triggered by this hunger strike, including selective boycotts by Western scientists, the Soviet authorities relented, and Bonner was permitted to travel to Italy, where the surgery was performed successfully. It was on this same trip to Italy that she continued on to Oslo to accept the Nobel Peace Prize for Sakharov.

Sakharov's third hunger strike was a severe ordeal that started in November 1981 and lasted for 17 days. By then, Sakharov had already been exiled to Gorki for almost two years for protesting the Soviet invasion of Afghanistan during Christmas week of 1979. The cause of this strike was the refusal of the Soviet authorities to permit Liza Alexseyeva to emigrate to the United States to join her fiancée, Alexei Semenov, who is Bonner's son and Sakharov's stepson. Sakharov was very deeply troubled by the suffering of this young couple, which he attributed to his own activities as a dissident and not to any fault of their own. News reports on the course of this hunger strike were fragmentary in the West. However, it soon became apparent from what was learned in the West, and from his personal appeals to several friends near the end of the strike, that his life was in grave danger. There was an enormous worldwide outpouring of support for him and of rage at his oppressors, who finally relented.

Sakharov's fourth and final series of hunger strikes started in May 1984, shortly after Bonner had also been sentenced to be confined in Gorki in a further effort to break off their communication with the outside world. The goal this time was to gain permission for her to travel to the West for urgently needed heart bypass surgery. These hunger strikes continued intermittently for 18 months, and the impact on Sakharov's health was life threatening. He was kept in a hospital facility for about 300 days. In October 1985, Sakharov once again achieved his goal, and a successful sixfold heart bypass operation was performed on Bonner in Boston in January 1986.

Sakharov's Legacy

It was Sakharov's remarkable achievement during the troubled decade of 1974–1985 to show to a world strained by violence, by hate, and by rigid ideologies that there is hope in the power of the human spirit and will. He moved governments and people alike and gave faith for the future through, in the beautiful words of his friend and compatriot Lev Kopelev, "the majesty of his spirit, the power of his intellect, and the purity of his soul, his chivalrous courage and selfless kindness."

When Mikhail Gorbachev came to power in 1985 with his new thinking, a convergence began to develop between the stated basic policy goals and aspirations of the Soviet government and the principles Sakharov had long espoused: free expression, democratic ideals, cooperative security arrangements with the West, and arms control. Sakharov's exile to Gorki as a dissident became an anachronism. By the end of 1986, the full rights of Soviet citizenship were restored to him, and he returned to Moscow and emerged as a citizen-hero and subsequently a member of the People's Congress. By the time of his death, he had become a leader in the newly revitalized movement for freedom and democracy in the Soviet Union. Just how powerful his voice had become as the conscience of the Soviet Union—and all mankind—was evident in the tremendous outpouring of respect and the deeply felt, sincere grief at his death.

Sakharov was an inspiration to all who knew him or knew of him. Constant in purpose, clear in vision, modest and unflinching in his courage to speak out in circumstances of great personal danger, he inspired support, admiration, and devotion from people of all nations.

Sakharov's voice is now sorely missed, but his spirit continues to energize and guide the quest he led for more than two decades—the quest for justice, human dignity, and freedom everywhere in this world.

Sakharov and Disarmament

Andrei Sakharov was admired and honored worldwide as a great scientist, an uncompromising fighter for human rights, and a leader in efforts to reduce the danger that nuclear weapons of mass destruction pose to all humanity. I was privileged to know Andrei as a personal friend and colleague. I knew and admired him as a gentle and modest man. The whole world was inspired by his unshakable commitment to principle and his courageous opposition to injustice wherever he found it.

Tragically, Sakharov is no longer with us. But his priceless legacy of wisdom, courage, and determination remains to guide all who honor the principles to which he devoted his life. Sakharov's crusade to reduce the danger of nuclear weapons and the threat of nuclear holocaust is an important part of that legacy. His efforts extended over three decades. At first he worked within official channels. Subsequently, at considerable personal risk and sacrifice, he moved out of the scientific laboratory and into the political process in order to make progress in his determination to reduce the dangers of these weapons of such enormous destructive potential. Even during his darkest hours of suffering he attached absolute priority to questions of war and peace and the effort to avert a nuclear war.

With his typical realism, Andrei combined his unwavering commitment to this goal with an appreciation of the practical steps required toward achieving it. This is how he expressed it in a message transmitted from Gorki to an international conference that we organized to celebrate his sixtieth birthday exactly ten years ago today in New York:

I consider disarmament necessary and possible only on the basis of strategic parity. Additional agreements covering all kinds of weapons of mass destruction are needed. After strategic parity in conventional arms has been achieved, a parity which takes account of all the political, psychological and geographical factors involved, and if totalitarian expansion is brought to an end, then agreements should be reached prohibiting the first use of nuclear weapons, and, later, banning such weapons.

In this short paragraph, Sakharov spells out both his ultimate goals and the necessary preconditions for achieving them through negotiated agreements. It was the combination of tactical realism with an unwavering commitment to his strategic goals that made Sakharov's voice so important and effective when he entered the political process.

His mix of pragmatism and principle played an important role in arriving at the Limited Test Ban Treaty that the major nuclear powers signed in 1963. The key here was to prevent further increases in dangerous radioactive fallout and environmental pollution. Sakharov urged that the controversial question of continued underground testing be set aside in order to achieve a ban on all nuclear bomb tests in the atmosphere, under water, and in outer space. He has described his personal satisfaction at being instrumental in moving the Soviet government to support such a treaty which remains in force today.

More recently, Sakharov argued that we should not delay important reductions in the bloated nuclear arsenals of the United States and the Soviet Union by insisting that, at the same time, we also had to solve all the problems created by the possibility of futuristic space-defense weapons. This issue threatened to block any progress in the Strategic Arms Reductions Talks (START) following President Reagan's speech in 1983 that launched the Strategic Defense Initiative (Star Wars). Sakharov reasoned that, although a Star Wars deployment would be a grave error and would destabilize the strategic balance, the technical limitations of such a system are so severe that they push any concerns about their potential effectiveness far into the future. He argued, therefore, that the negotiations at START to reduce the very large U.S. and Soviet strategic offensive forces should be unlinked from the more controversial issue of space-defense weapons. Sakharov's argument for unlinking has now been accepted. Both governments have also shown measured restraint on Star Wars work and, as a result,

Round I of START has progressed far and is seemingly close to successful completion.

What a great tribute it would be to the memory of Andrei Sakharov if the governments of the Soviet Union and the United States completed the current round of negotiations and ratified a START treaty during this year, the seventieth anniversary of his birth. Let us send out a message tonight: On Andrei Sakharov's seventieth birthday, we call on the leaders of the two nuclear superpowers to honor his memory by completing the START I Treaty this year. Its provisions will reduce strategic nuclear forces by almost 30 percent. As Presidents Bush and Gorbachev said in their Joint Summit Communique of June 1, 1990, the treaty also includes "the most thorough and innovative verification provisions ever negotiated." The reductions and the increased openness are important precedents. Furthermore, this treaty is a practical step based on realistic political foundations built, starting more than five years ago, by presidents Gorbachev and Reagan. We could then move on from the first round of START to START II and beyond.

Now that the Cold War has ended, we have the opportunity to reduce our nuclear arsenals to a much smaller force—a force still adequate to meet the one and only mission that Andrei Sakharov and I—and many others—accept for our nuclear forces. This is the mission to deter the use of nuclear weapons by a potential aggressor. As Andrei wrote in 1983 in his celebrated open letter to me entitled "The Danger of Thermonuclear War":

> I am convinced that the following basic tenet of yours is true: "Nuclear weapons only make sense as a means of deterring nuclear aggression by a potential enemy," i.e., a nuclear war cannot be planned with the aim of winning it. Nuclear weapons cannot be viewed as a means of restraining aggressions carried out by means of conventional weapons.

There will soon be a balance of conventional forces deployed in Europe at greatly reduced levels in accord with provisions of the treaty on Conventional Forces in Europe—the CFE treaty—signed in November 1990 by the 22 member states of the North Atlantic Treaty Organization and the Warsaw Treaty Organization. This new balance will remove concerns that led nations previously to rely on nuclear weapons to offset perceived threats of aggression by massed conventional forces. It will also remove any rational impediment to deep cuts in current nuclear arsenals when their only mission is—as Sakharov agreed—to deter nuclear aggression by a potential enemy. On this basis, we can strive for much deeper reductions of nuclear forces following START I.

Once the first round of START is completed, the United States and the Soviet Union should get back to the negotiating table for what I would like to call the Sakharov Round. The goal of the Sakharov Round should be to negotiate truly deep reductions. Several thousand remaining warheads in reliable, safe, and survivably based systems would be more than adequate for deterring nuclear aggression. Negotiating such a deep reduction in time to honor Andrei's eightieth birthday in the year 2001—or, better yet, to honor his seventy-fifth birthday in 1996—would be the finest tribute to his memory and the most important fulfillment of his principles I can think of. And, based on such success, who can say how far we might advance by the year 2021, the centennial of Sakharov's birth, toward an agreement "banning such weapons," the goal that Andrei identified for a radically changed world in his message from Gorki ten years ago.

Throughout his life, Andrei Sakharov sought to improve the world as he worked and fought against injustice and oppression as well as against the danger of nuclear war. The words Anatole France spoke to honor Emile Zola for his ultimately victorious quest for justice in the Dreyfus affair apply as an eloquent epitaph for Andrei Sakharov: "His destiny and his courage combine to endow him with the greatest of fates. He was a moment in the conscience of humanity."

COLD WAR YEARS

Arms Control: Is There Still Hope?

The pattern of recent events provides very little encouragement and few, if any, auspicious signals for the future of arms control. The second Strategic Arms Limitation Talks treaty (SALT II) has been derailed, at least temporarily; the mutual balanced-force reduction talks in Vienna remain stalled; little progress is reported from the negotiations for a comprehensive test-ban treaty or for limitations on antisatellite activities. Indeed, one hears more these days about rearming than about reducing arms.

Advances in weapons technologies are bringing with them prospects of a broader repertoire of missions for our nuclear armories, which continue to grow in numbers and improve in quality. More and more we hear of *usable* nuclear weapons and of fighting and winning nuclear wars. With these developments we have come once more to one of those perilous forks in the road from which several very different paths diverge. It is time for us to stop and ask as we enter a new decade: What are our goals? Where are we going? Do we even still remember what nuclear explosions do? Does the post-Hiroshima generation actually appreciate the horror of nuclear weapons and the dangers posed by the prospect of a nuclear conflict?

Thirty-five years have passed since the fireballs of the first atomic bombs over Alamagordo, Hiroshima, and Nagasaki lighted the dawn of the nuclear age, the age Winston Churchill called "the second coming in wrath." Their increase by a factor of 1000 in the scale of destructiveness was followed swiftly by yet another increase—again by a factor of 1000—in explosive power with the advent of the hydrogen bomb. Since then, the world has stockpiled some 40,000 nuclear bombs, about 99 percent of which belong to the United States and the Soviet Union. This growth of nuclear stockpiles has occurred at the same time as, and despite, frequent official statements affirming the nations' solemn commitments to control and reduce the nuclear threat; despite also the realization that we have accumulated so many nuclear weapons that the survival of civilization as we know it would be threatened were our nuclear stockpiles ever unleashed. Indeed, the number of nuclear warheads deployed by the United States and the Soviet Union on our long-range strategic systems has grown to more than 15,000, or by a factor of more than 2.5 since we began the intensive SALT negotiating efforts a little more than 10 years ago, with the primary purpose to limit these very same weapons. Not only have they increased in numbers, their prodigious technological improvements have created new difficulties for arms control, for verification, and for strategic stability at a faster pace than negotiations have progressed.

We may draw some comfort from the fact that during all this period our fear, revulsion, and respect for nuclear weapons have been effective in keeping us from using them—in spite of the fact that there have been numerous conflicts and opportunities. Indeed, deterrence has worked for more than three decades because we have recognized so far that the purpose of nuclear weapons is to deter nuclear war, and we have behaved accordingly. But how long will deterrence last? The latest advances in weapons technology, especially in missile accuracy and reliability, now threaten to erode the very doctrine of deterrence itself. In its place are offered visions of fighting and winning limited nuclear wars. I consider these visions to be phantoms, phantoms that are dangerous as well as technically false. Their emergence, however, emphasizes the urgent need for us to learn to do things differently. That need is even more urgent now than it was 20 years ago when Jerome Wiesner wrote so eloquently in the 1960 issue of *Daedalus* devoted to arms control: "Mankind's almost universal desire is to halt the frightening arms race and to provide, by rule of law, the security now sought so futilely from nuclear armaments and ballistic missiles. While the goal is clearly visible, the course is not."

Today we are still faced with a deadly dangerous dilemma. On one hand, we have no evidence from history to lead to the conclusion that war in the long run can be avoided. On the other hand, there is also no evidence from history to tell us what a nuclear war would mean. An all-out nuclear conflict would shatter the whole fabric of our society and of our civilization built over the centuries. Beyond that, the long-term worldwide effects of a major nuclear conflict on man and the environment, and on their future evolution, are largely unpredictable. This dilemma of our nuclear times could be resolved in principle by doing away with war—or by doing away with nuclear weapons. Although neither of these achievements is very likely in the coming decade, or in the foreseeable future, they stand as mankind's ultimate goals. They are, moreover, goals to be addressed with some determination and hope.

There is an old Navy saying to the effect that one always seeks to avoid disaster on one's own watch. In the past, the limited goal of avoiding disaster on one's watch has proved tolerable for national security policy. But now that we are sitting on a deadly nuclear powder keg, such a view is no longer good enough. We can no longer work simply to make it through our watch. Not only must we avoid a nuclear conflict in our time, we must also meet the challenge to reduce and, ultimately, to remove the threat of a nuclear holocaust. This is the greatest challenge of our generation as well as our obligation to future generations.

Andrei Sakharov has often expressed this same priority, most recently in a statement from his lonely exile in Gorki: "I consider that averting thermonuclear war has absolute priority over all other problems of our times." How, then, should we begin addressing the question of nuclear survival? The recent collapse of the SALT II ratification process reminds us forcefully that it is necessary to have momentum and hope in our broad political task of resolving conflicts and tensions while building toward a stable, just, and peaceful international order. In the narrower focus of efforts to control and reduce nuclear weapons and to avoid, or at least to minimize, the likelihood of nuclear conflict, we have, in practice, only two means available to us: formal negotiations and mutual restraint in new weapons programs. (A third means, unilateral disarmament, I do not believe can carry us very far.) These two means—negotiations and mutual restraint—need not and should not be mutually exclusive. Indeed, we need them both! The record of the past two decades shows that neither means alone will suffice if we are to make effective progress in controlling and reducing nuclear weapons. During this time, we have also experienced the difficulties that arise when negotiations have been allowed to stimulate antirestraint in the race to accumulate bargaining chips that, too often, like Pinocchio, take on lives of their own.

Neither the United States nor the Soviet Union has a laudable record of restraint. Two notable examples of missed opportunities are MIRVs (multiple independently targetable reentry vehicles) and the continuing ICBM (intercontinental ballistic missile) buildup following SALT I. Recall that the original justification for MIRVs was for penetrating ballistic-missile defenses by saturating their computers and radars and overwhelming their defensive firepower with an intense rain of many warheads. Nevertheless, U.S. MIRV programs proceeded full tilt after the SALT I treaty, which severely limited the deployment of ABM (antiballistic missile) defenses and thereby removed the purported rationale for MIRVs. Recall also that the consequence of the SALT I interim agreement on offensive systems was primarily to deflect the main focus of work from the restricted to unrestricted areas rather than to decrease its intensity. As a result, work proceeded full speed on missile improvements, leading to greater accuracy and reliability, and on more extensive MIRV deployments as the Soviets, in particular, built right up to the SALT limits.

Independent of this dismal record of failure in restraint, both the United States and the Soviet Union have recognized the importance of negotiations and have worked hard at them, at least until very recently. Our progress is modest; to many, the achievements after years of effort are disappointing. They are not, however, negligible. In particular, we have the all-important SALT I treaty limiting ballistic-missile defenses to a very low level of deployment. And, of course, we also have the limited atmospheric test ban treaty on the books since 1963. This is a major achievement. We, as will generations to come, value that treaty primarily for its contribution to protecting our environment from radioactive fallout. As an arms-control measure, perhaps its greatest value was in setting so important and successful a precedent of visible cooperation in the arena of nuclear weapons between the two major nuclear powers.

Nevertheless, independent of these achievements and of the eventual fate of the SALT II treaty, the bankruptcy of our approach to nuclear weapons is evident. These are weapons of mass destruction, and the possibility of ever using such weapons raises fundamental ethical and moral issues that should be faced at the center of our national and international discussions and negotiations of nuclear-weapons policy. Yet today these issues are muted in policy formulation as we continue to proliferate and diversify our nuclear stockpiles. How long can and will we continue to avoid the fundamental questions of using weapons of mass destruction? As Enrico Fermi and Isidor Rabi wrote in their addendum to the report by the General Advisory Committee of the

AEC in 1949 on the decision of whether or not to develop the so-called "super":

> It is clear that the use of such a weapon cannot be justified on any ethical ground which gives a human being a certain individuality and dignity even if he happens to be a resident of an enemy country.
>
> The fact that no limits exist to the destructiveness of this weapon makes its very existence and the knowledge of its construction a danger to humanity as a whole. It is necessarily an evil thing considered in any light.

At about this same time, George Kennan wrote a personal paper, as the counselor to Secretary of State Dean Acheson, expressing his concerns about the impact on U.S. policy of a growing reliance on atomic weapons of mass destruction in our arsenals. The occasion was his resignation as director of the State Department Planning Staff, and he summarized his concerns eloquently:

> The weapons of mass destruction ... reach backward beyond the frontiers of western civilization, to the concepts of warfare which were once familiar to the Asiatic hordes. They cannot really be reconciled with a political purpose directed to shaping, rather than destroying, the lives of the adversary. They fail to take account of the ultimate responsibility of men for one another, and even for each other's errors and mistakes. They imply the admission that man not only can be but is his own worst and most terrible enemy.

And now, 30 years and 40,000 nuclear weapons later, the question of whether the use of nuclear weapons can be justified on any ethical grounds is rarely heard in our national debates, and almost never in our formal negotiations. All attention is riveted on questions such as how to put a ceiling on the further growth in numbers of weapons by limiting the number of warheads to no more than 10 per ICBM or 14 per sea-launched ballistic missile! I am not suggesting that this is not also, in fact, an important question—as is our concern for maintaining a strategic stability based on our confidence that our nuclear weapons cannot be destroyed in a preemptive attack against them. But we seem to have so completely accepted the inevitability of a nuclear overarmed world that we are lost in the maze of such details *alone*. Enmeshed in these details, we seem to have lost view of the *scale* of the problem. We

have grown so relaxed about the threat and so accustomed to coexistence as mutual hostages under a nuclear sword of Damocles that all
our attention and effort is devoted to finely tuning a nuclear balance.

With regard to our vast nuclear armories, which are continually
being refined and polished and admired, I am reminded of lines from
Alexander Pope's *Essay on Man*:

> Vice is a monster of so frightful mien,
> As to be hated, needs but to be seen;
> Yet seen too oft, familiar with her face,
> We first endure, then pity, then embrace.

Recall how Pope continues:

> But where th' Extreme of Vice, was ne'er agreed,

and concludes:

> No creature owns it in the first degree,
> But thinks his neighbor further gone than he.

In a nutshell, that expresses our dilemma. Consumed by a detailed,
quantitative balancing of the nuclear vice that we have learned to
endure and now embrace, each country accuses the other of owning
more of what is evil than he himself possesses, and our nuclear debates
and discussions have become like those of the scholastics of the thirteenth century. To them, the fundamental ethical and moral issues of
religion had degenerated largely into questions of how many angels
can dance on the head of a pin. In his recent book *Endgame: The
Inside Story of Salt II*, Strobe Talbott has drawn the macabre parallel
of how, for us, the nuclear debate has similarly been reduced to how
many MIRVs can fit on the head of an ICBM. And, just as the desolation and devastation of the fourteenth century, with its hundred
years of wars, followed the thirteenth, are we destined to a similar or
a worse fate in the twenty-first? Will future historians, if there are any,
look back on the second half of the twentieth century as the golden age
of nuclear scholastics?

If modern civilization is to improve its chances for avoiding nuclear
holocaust in the long run, it is absolutely necessary to return to fundamental issues such as the one raised by Fermi and Rabi: "It is clear
that the use of such a weapon cannot be justified on any ethical ground
which gives a human being a certain individuality and dignity even if

he happens to be a resident of an enemy country." In today's world, with the initial conditions fixed by the existence of so many thousands of nuclear bombs and strategic rockets and bombers, we should not and cannot responsibly duck the same detailed issues that SALT has elevated to such exaggerated prominence. It will help us to "get by on this watch" if we can reach agreement on these specific issues—such as by negotiating verifiable limits on numbers of warheads per missile, or on the volume, total thrust, and total throw-weight of different missile or bomber types. But it is now abundantly clear that we cannot and will not get very far if *all* our concerns and efforts are focused very narrowly on such detailed issues. Furthermore, the rapidly advancing weapons technology and the growing repertoire of uses and targets for nuclear weapons are threatening to remove even the limited security we have sought through mutual deterrence.

Before unbridled technology leads to this, we had better identify some basic principles that we must adhere to if we are to keep control over what is happening. Perhaps then we may succeed in shaping the future directions in arms control. I identify six such major principles. If we can hold to them and insist that they define the context within which consistent negotiating policies and restraint measures will be pursued, we may have a chance. These principles are:

1. The sole purpose of nuclear weapons in today's world, and for as long as they are deployed, must be to *deter* nuclear war. No other purpose should be assigned them.

In singling out deterrence of nuclear attack among the missions of our strategic nuclear forces, I am emphasizing that there are no sensible alternatives to a policy of deterrence for the foreseeable future. Other missions for our strategic nuclear forces have frequently been proposed, ranging from political or military coercion to fighting and winning limited nuclear wars. However, you can't win if you don't survive. I am convinced that the overwhelmingly likely course of events of actually implementing any of these limited missions would be an escalation of hostilities to almost total mutual destruction. Furthermore, this is destruction against which, on technical grounds alone, there is no effective defense. Hence, I conclude that deterrence of nuclear attack is the proper mission of our nuclear forces. Weapons development and force structures must be planned toward this goal as the single overriding priority.

It has become stylish this year for revisionists to criticize as being immoral this view of deterrence as the U.S. strategic policy—it is frequently caricatured with the acronym MAD, for mutual assured destruction. We are told that the United States should not be targeting cities and planning the annihilation of tens to hundreds of millions of people but, with a higher morality, should target military and counterforce targets, sparing the innocent civilians. Frankly, I am puzzled as to why this straw man has been exhumed and is being flailed at this time, since it represents a circumstance with essentially no logical connection with today's weapons realities.

Assured destruction requires but a small percentage of our deployed warheads. Of our current total of well over 9000 nuclear warheads on our strategic bombers and missiles, only a few hundred are needed to obliterate the largest Soviet cities along with two-thirds of their total industrial base and close to 100 million residents—and this is due to immediate damage alone. Evidently, the United States has a sizable counterforce capacity in addition to its capacity for assured destruction. In fact, we have had a substantial counterforce capability since the early 1960s. At present, the characteristics as well as the large numbers of our rapidly retargetable, highly MIRVed forces present very extensive counterforce capabilities. They give us, in particular, the potential to respond in measure with the provocation—known as flexible response—against a broad spectrum of Soviet military targets, including naval bases, air bases, petroleum depots, assembly points, transshipment points, and so on. A broad repertoire of flexible response and counterforce is a reality of today's strategic forces—both for the United States and the Soviet Union. In fact, it has long been recognized that flexible response enhances deterrence by increasing the range of political options and maneuvers prior to conflict. Moreover, flexible response is still growing as a result of our technical virtuosity with nuclear weaponry. It is this very growth in the repertoire of counterforce missions, to include the capabilities to strike an opponent's missile forces in their hardened silos, that we now see posing a threat to deterrence. Today's debate in the United States on Minuteman vulnerability and the need for a new basing scheme for a large new MX missile with ten MIRVs is a reaction to the developing Soviet counterforce threat against the Minuteman silos.

The deployment of missiles that pose substantial and credible preemptive threats against major components of each other's arsenals of nuclear retaliatory forces conflicts with the goal of maintaining a stable strategic deterrence. A clear choice between these two alternatives must be made by both the Soviet Union and the United States. At this perilous fork in the road, both countries must effectively limit, as well as direct, the development of new weapons technology in order to maintain a deterrence based on survivable retaliatory forces. Such a stable deterrence is not an end in itself, but it can provide a base from which to work toward substantial reductions and, eventually, toward comprehensive disarmament.

2. No matter how small its yield, a nuclear weapon is fundamentally different from a nonnuclear one.

It has a long memory—a deadly radioactive memory. Furthermore, once the first nuclear weapon is used in anger, once the one-way bridge is crossed from nonnuclear to nuclear conflict, what will restrain the nations involved from escalating further when they believe their vital interests are at stake and they hold such vast stores of nuclear weapons in reserve? Will there be any effective limiting forces amidst the confusion and pressure of battle?

This assertion, that there is a fundamental difference between nuclear and nonnuclear weapons, was widely challenged several years ago during the extended debate about the so-called neutron bomb—the enhanced-radiation weapon that would be tailored to produce more radiation that is deadly to humans but less blast and heat. This weapon was proposed as a more usable nuclear weapon—particularly in the defense of highly developed and densely populated areas, such as Western Europe—because of the reduced collateral damage it would produce if delivered with precise accuracy. On this basis, it was argued that the improved warhead, by making the initial use of nuclear weapons in battle seem more credible, would enhance deterrence. However, there is another side to this coin. By the same token, it can be argued that this warhead also *increases* the likelihood that nuclear weapons would actually be used in combat. Once this or any other nuclear weapon has been used, the danger of further nuclear escalation is just as great. A decision to use the neutron bomb would be no less grave than a decision to use any other tactical nuclear weapons. I can think of no more dangerous folly than trying to fuzz the fundamental difference between nuclear and nonnuclear weapons.

3. Nuclear war would be so great an extrapolation of the scale of disaster in human experience, and so great a physical disturbance of our environment and ecosphere, that the unknowns of a nuclear conflict clearly far outweigh the knowns or predictables.

Yet there appear more and more detailed calculations that describe how hundreds of millions of people will behave in all-out conflict, when deadly radioactive rain will fall for many months. These calculations also predict casualty levels and recovery times with incredible precision. The fascination with these calculations reminds me of the exchange in George Bernard Shaw's *Major Barbara* between Lomax, a young man-about-town, and Andrew Undershaft, a millionaire munitions manufacturer. To Lomax's comment, "Well, the more destructive war becomes, the sooner it will be abolished, eh?" Undershaft retorts: "Not at all. The more destructive war becomes the more fascinating we find it."

Keep this in mind when you hear claims made on the basis of calculations about how much civil defense will contribute to the survival of how many people, and thereby to an ultimate victory, in a nuclear war for a nation that will suffer only 20 million fatalities while killing 60 million of their enemy! It is also well to keep in mind how rapidly individual units of society descend to chaos and fall apart at much lower levels of stress—just remember what happens during sudden blackouts. It makes you wonder how societies will react after just one thermonuclear weapon has hit—much less a hundred or several thousand.

Civil defense is, of course, a very important issue. It is also a very personal one, and at times an emotional one, because it touches the basic human instinct of survival. The potential for disaster is ever present in our society, and it hardly seems prudent to make no plans for survival or recovery in the event of a natural or a man-made disaster or accident, nuclear or otherwise. It is one thing, however, to view civil defense preparations as one does the lifeboats on an ocean linear, as insurance against unanticipated disasters. It would be quite a different matter to chart a course through ice fields and to risk running into icebergs because one plans to rely on the lifeboats for survival. The analogue of this reckless course would be to prepare to wage limited nuclear conflicts, relying on extensive civil defense preparations to reduce nationwide fatalities due to fallout to relatively low levels. Yet this is precisely what the Defense Department advocated, in late 1974, in its presentation to the Congress. Fortunately, many of the claims of civil-defense effectiveness and of prospects of "acceptably low" casualty levels were quickly shown to be false in a study organized by the Congressional Office of Technology Assessment, and the United States did not reorient its basic policy of deterrence toward one of preparing, on dubious technical and dangerous strategic grounds, for fighting limited nuclear war.

    4. In striving for progress in arms control, one needs bold steps that are timely and negotiable—and preferably simple.

In order to begin and to sustain such bold steps, there must exist a strong political will and commitment by our leaders. Otherwise, the experts become mired—at times hopelessly—in microscopic issues of technical balance, in insignificantly delicate details. The SALT II negotiations became an object lesson on this very point. There are *no* issues of nuclear survival that require the negotiation of a finely tuned balance. The crucial value of political will and decisiveness for progress was well illustrated early in 1972. After several years of almost stalemated haggling, both within the government and in the negotiations themselves, President Nixon provided an important impetus when he announced that we *would* have an ABM treaty that year. And, indeed, it was not long thereafter that the experts successfully negotiated an ABM treaty that remains our greatest arms-control achievement at this time. There is also a lesson in the failure of the comprehensive SALT II proposal of March 1977 by the Carter administration. This proposal called for substantial reductions in the deployment of strategic forces, along with restraints on missile tests that would have prevented, or at least greatly delayed, the weapons improvements that have created today's worries about ICBM vulnerability and the perceived need for the MX missile. Unfortunately, that most important part of the March comprehensive proposal was burdened by many detailed numerical provisions that were highly contentious; the proposal was presented publicly in a manner that diminished its negotiability; and eventually there was no alternative but to retreat from its bold and imaginative provisions. I hope the lesson learned from that failure will improve negotiating tactics in the future, but not scare either the United States or the Soviet Union from making bold proposals.

5. In our society, there is no substitute for, nor any power equal to that of, a responsible public constituency that is informed and aware of the basic issues of nuclear-weapons policy.

One need not master all technical details in the arms-control debate, but the question of *scale* must be comprehended. In "avoiding disaster on our watch" for the past 35 years, the searing, vivid memories of the holocaust of Hiroshima and Nagasaki have been important. I wish I knew an effective means to keep those memories from fading away. A world that retains such vast nuclear armories as we have today, but that loses its special fear and appreciation of their enormous scale of destructiveness, will be a more dangerous place to live. A nuclear overarmed world that has forgotten the horror that led five-year-old

Myeko in John Hersey's *Hiroshima* to ask, in the midst of the dust and debris of the devastated city, "Why is it night already?" is surely not safe.

6. Arms control is an important part of our national security.

Thus far, we have had no effective controls on offensive nuclear weaponry, and it is clear that each step forward in the arms race to more and improved weapons has *lessened* our security. If we are to reverse this trend, it will be necessary to understand the arms-control impact of new weapons before making a decision whether to deploy them. The importance of the arms-control factor was understood, and played an essential role, in the ABM debate of ten years ago. This also led to our negotiating the very valuable SALT I, treaty which severely limited ABM deployments. By way of contrast, we lost important opportunities for arms control by the decision to move ahead on MIRVs without first making a serious effort to avoid their extensive deployment. At this very time, we see the dollar costs and the strategic costs of that lost opportunity in the form of the MX program. The MX is designed to be the U.S. response to the growing threat to our land-based Minuteman force posed by the highly accurate and reliable MIRVed ICBMs now being deployed by the Soviet Union. It is a symbol of the failure of arms control.

The deployment of the MX is a very major decision now being faced by our country. Not only will it shape the U.S. nuclear deterrent through the rest of this century, it will also have a major effect on the future of arms control. For these reasons I want to describe it in some detail.

As currently proposed by the Carter administration, MX refers to a large new missile and to a new basing scheme. The missile is the largest one consistent with the provisions of SALT II. Its warhead is fractionated into ten MIRVs, which is also the largest number for an ICBM that is consistent with SALT II. The proposed MX deployment is in a land-based multiple-aimpoint system that relies extensively on secrecy and deception in order to maintain uncertainty about the location of the missile so that it cannot be targeted. Until a short time ago, this basing scheme took the form of 200 racetracks. The racetracks have since been straightened out into a linear grid pattern, but this change has very little impact on the operational complexities and deficiencies of the system. On each grid, there will be 23 hardened concrete shelters, one genuine MX missile, and 22 dummy missiles. The dummy missiles are there to protect the location uncertainty of the real one by simulating all the signatures of a real MX in each of the shelters or on the move between shelters.

The first question it is natural to ask about the MX is: Do we need it? The loss of the Minuteman force would not mean the loss of U.S. retaliatory capability. The other two legs of our strategic triad include approximately three-fourths of our deployed nuclear warheads. They are secure and are being strengthened, the strategic bombers with longer-range air-launched cruise missiles and the nuclear submarines with the modern new Trident boats, as well as the longer-range and more powerful Trident missiles. Therefore, it is natural to ask whether we need to respond at this time to the perceived growing threat to our land-based ICBMs in the fixed, hardened silos. Apparently, this question has already been answered in the affirmative by the country for a variety of reasons, in part political, in part strategic, and in part technical. It has been judged to be an unacceptable policy for the United States simply to accept, without a response, a substantial decrease in confidence in the invulnerability of a major component of our strategic retaliatory power, and we are now moving ahead with an MX program. The missile itself is being developed with initial flight tests scheduled in 1983. The basing scheme, however, is still being debated in the Congress.

Although I recognize that the Carter administration has made a serious effort to devise a basing mode that is consistent with the past record of the SALT negotiations and that will not impede prospects for future programs in arms control, I have serious problems with its proposal. I believe that a linear grid scheme—and, in fact, any land-based multiple-aimpoint scheme—is seriously flawed for contributing to our national security, and, furthermore, it presents serious problems for arms control. I consider the following to be its most serious problems:

- The requirement of maintaining confidence in secrecy, in deception, and in extensive simulation procedures in the midst of society.
- An acute sensitivity to the threat. It is necessary to be able to forecast accurately the number of warheads the Soviets will be deploying that could threaten the MX. In particular, the SALT II restraints on numbers of warheads per missile, as well as on total numbers of missiles, are required in order to plan the number of shelters and dummy missiles we will have to deploy. In the absence

of current or future SALT limits on the maximum number of threatening Soviet warheads, a multiple-aimpoint system has no assurance of catching up with the threat. It may lead to nothing more than an open-ended race between Soviet warheads and U.S. concrete shelters—hardly an attractive prospect. An alternative prospect of defending the MX with an antiballistic-missile system has also been discussed. This would require abrogating the ABM treaty of SALT I, an even less attractive prospect.

. The requirement of cooperative operational procedures to ensure that no more than the stipulated number of missiles are deployed in the guise of decoys; these procedures, which include barriers on access roads and removable plugs in ceilings of assembly buildings and shelters to allow periodic satellite viewing, will further stress the verification requirements of an enforceable arms-control treaty. This will be a particular problem if the Soviet Union follows our example by deploying a multiple-aimpoint system of their own as their response to the extensive countersilo threat against their ICBMs that will be posed by the 2000 very accurate MIRVs on our 200 MX missiles.

The United States should not now make the commitment to deploy the MX linear-grid system. It has flaws, and it creates difficulties. Moreover, it is not necessary for us to plunge ahead at this time, given the two other components of the strategic triad that are strong and secure and are currently being further strengthened by major modernization programs. It is precisely the strength of the triad that one can rely confidently on its two good legs while solving the vulnerabilities that threaten the third one. It is far more important that we make a wise decision than a quick one for the new MX deployment.

As a technical man, I realize that it is not always possible to come up with a good technical answer to every technical problem, but I am confident that we can do better than the MX linear-grid system, both for our national security and for arms-control prospects.

It is at discouraging moments like this—with both the United States and the Soviet Union moving toward decisions on major new weapons systems and with formal arms-control negotiations recessed for an indefinite period—that we must remind ourselves again why we cannot give up hope for arms control. We, meaning both the Soviet Union and the United States, must remind ourselves of the enormity of the destructive power of the nuclear weapons we are dealing with and of the scale of human tragedy and suffering if they were ever used. It is imperative that we reestablish an effective, aggressive, national—as well as international—forum for discussing the basic issues, such as addressed thirty years ago by those who questioned whether the use of nuclear weapons could *ever* be justified on *any* ethical grounds. It is not enough just to discuss and analyze the nuts and bolts of weapons technology. We must never lose sight of the change in the nature of war due to nuclear weapons. Shakespeare, in *Henry IV, Part Two*, wrote of the Archbishop of York, who could justify his path of insurrection by saying:

> I have in equal balance justly weighed
> What wrongs our arms may do, what wrongs we suffer,
> And find our griefs heavier than our offences.

In the nuclear era, the Archbishop of York has been replaced by Father Siemes, a Jesuit priest writing from the rubble of Hiroshima to the Holy See in Rome, as reported by John Hersey: "The crux of the matter is whether total war in its present form is justifiable, even when it serves a just purpose."

That question is today as inescapable as it is difficult. President Kennedy addressed it directly in his speech "Toward a Strategy of Peace," delivered at American University in 1963:

> I speak of peace because of the new face of war. Total war makes no sense in an age when great powers can maintain large and relatively invulnerable nuclear forces and refuse to surrender without resort to these forces. It makes no sense in an age when a single nuclear weapon contains almost ten times the explosive force delivered by all of the Allied air-forces in the Second World War. It makes no sense in an age when the deadly poisons produced by a nuclear exchange would be carried by the wind and water and soil and seed to the far corners of the globe and to generations yet unborn. . . . Peace need not be impracticable, and war need not be inevitable.

Finally, we—and by this I mean, of course, the Soviet Union as well as the United States—must also not lose sight of the eventual goal of eradicating the vice of nuclear weapons as we parry and propagandize about who owns, in Alexander Pope's words, the "Extreme of Vice." Right now is the time when it is crucial that both sides adhere to rules of reasonable self-restraint until negotiations get back on track. It is

Restrictions on Weapon Tests

WITH THEODORE J. RALSTON

One of the most effective elements of successful arms-control agreements between the United States and the Soviet Union has been restraints on the testing of new or improved weapons. Focusing on the testing phase of the weapon-development process has (1) permitted the achievement of substantial restraint in the development of destabilizing antiballistic-missile technologies through the ABM Treaty; (2) retarded the development of destabilizing ballistic-missile capabilities, such as increased numbers of reentry vehicles, maneuvering reentry vehicles, fractional orbital bombardment systems, depressed trajectory systems, and more than one new type of ICBM through the SALT II definitions hinged to types of ICBMs *tested*; and (3) permitted an effective verification regime keyed to the most readily verifiable phase of the weapon-development cycle, the test phase. While it is frequently observed that an approach to controlling weapons development through restraints on testing promotes greater stability and increases the effectiveness of verification, an additional fundamental point is often overlooked—restrictions on weapon tests can contribute to building confidence necessary to maintain a balance in overall weapons capability. This latter point is a necessary requirement for deterrence. It is our intent to examine how restrictions on testing can build confidence.

Objectives

In examining this question, we first address the relevant elements of the testing phase of weapons development. Second, we set out the goals and principles underlying the utility of test restrictions as arms control. Third, we suggest the scope and type of restrictions that should be considered and set out the criteria by which to evaluate them. Fourth, we attempt to illustrate the value of flight-test restrictions for the case of hard-target, first-strike weapons by showing the effect a reduction in the number of permitted flight tests of ICBMs would have on the military planning requirement for high confidence in performance and reliability.

Test Stages

There are two reasons for testing programs. One is to develop new weapon systems and see how well they work. A second and important reason is to increase the performance and reliability of systems already deployed. The development of new systems typically incorporates three test stages. The first is laboratory testing, or what is called "R&D tests" or "design-bureau tests."[1] This stage can encompass a relatively broad range of tests, ranging from component or subsystem testing (such as static tests of new rocket motors and tests of new types of arming or fusing devices) to short-range flights of a full system. The second stage, called Initial Operational Test and Evaluation (IOT&E), can include a series of tests performed with early-production models of an aircraft or missile, the purpose of which is to evaluate the components before a commitment is made to full-scale production for deployment. The final stage of testing is called Field Operational Test and Evaluation (FOT&E), in which the purpose is to test the full system as it will be deployed. Anywhere from 5 to 10 percent of the total number of the weapon to be deployed typically are tested in order to achieve a statistically significant number for judging the system's reliability. In the case of aircraft and missiles, the FOT&E group of flight tests is usually followed by occasional tests of operational systems to permit continued confidence in their operational reliability.

In discussing potential negotiated restraints on weapon tests we shall not consider limits on the research or conceptual development work that goes on in the laboratory. Restraints on this phase of testing would be unverifiable—at least without exceedingly intrusive on-site inspection that would undoubtedly be unacceptable to all parties concerned. Furthermore, such restraints would leave each side more uncertain about new technological possibilities than they are currently, and thus increase their respective concern about the possibility of technological breakthroughs. The precedent of distinguishing component and conceptual development work, on the one hand, and field work on prototype systems, on the other, was established in the ABM Treaty of 1972. We shall consider in this paper only the impact of restraints on tests of full prototype systems.

Goals and Principles

It is important to set out the goals of arms control in order to specify the underlying purposes to which restrictions on testing activity can contribute. It is our view that there are three primary goals of arms control:

1. Improving stability
2. Maintaining deterrence at lower levels of destructive power
3. Saving money.

Restrictions on testing can contribute to each of these goals. Stability in the balance of forces can be enhanced through restrictions on the development of weapon capabilities that, if deployed, would give one side a significant advantage over the other—for example, a new generation of very accurate missiles with a large number of independently targetable warheads. One logical step is to restrict the development of such capabilities by slowing the rate at which these capabilities are tested, thereby slowing the rate at which they are eventually added to operational forces.

Similarly, restrictions on testing can contribute to maintaining deterrence in several ways. First, depending on the restrictions, the inability to test potentially destabilizing capabilities fully can retard confidence that the weapons will perform reliably or to their full potential. Under such circumstances, it is unlikely that prudent military planners would choose to deploy these systems. The effect would be to prevent further addition of greater numbers or greater destructive power to existing force levels. Second, in order for deterrence to work effectively, each side must believe it can respond appropriately and in sufficient time to any new weapons development by the other side. Testing restrictions that have the effect of stretching out the development time for weapons that are eventually deployed can provide this margin of time.

Lastly, restrictions on testing activity—either in scope, magnitude, or depth—can save money by reducing the extensive field and operational test programs that are an expensive part of the life cycle for deployed weapons. For those weapon capabilities that are ultimately not deployed, more money can be saved by eliminating the field and operational testing altogether.

Confidence-Building Steps

Having stated the broad arms-control goals, the principles on which testing restriction agreements would be based need to be set out. The basic question is how to build confidence between two essentially adversarial nations. One way is to take steps that would reduce their respective uncertainties concerning the future magnitude, characteristics, and missions of the other side's weapon programs. The United States, for example, was quite uncertain in 1984 about whether then-recent tests of what are reported to be two new Soviet ICBMs portended major changes in Soviet ICBM force posture and characteristics. U.S. uncertainty was further aggravated by the question of whether these tests violated the provisions of the 1979 SALT II Treaty permitting only one new type of ICBM. One can imagine similar uncertainties circulating within the Kremlin with respect to U.S. plans for the MX, "Midgetman," maneuvering reentry vehicles, or supersonic long-range cruise missiles.

Negotiated test restrictions can contribute to confidence-building by aiding assessments as to the purpose and mission of a new system. Provisions restricting the number of tests can reduce concerns about rapid breakout from negotiated restrictions on forces in arms-control treaties by prolonging the time it takes to achieve new operational capabilities. Provisions restricting test practices to only those consistent with an agreed-upon mission can help reduce uncertainty about secondary missions, which might put deterrent forces at risk, in two ways. First, an agreed mission consistent with deterrence would prescribe the permitted "test envelope"—those test performance criteria and specifications appropriate to the mission, deviation from which would clearly signal a different intent. For example, during the SALT II debate concern was frequently expressed in the United States over the possibility that the Soviet *Backfire* bomber might have an intercontinental mission rather than being restricted solely to roles in theater warfare, as claimed by Soviet spokesmen. The inclusion of a provision defining a test-performance profile in conjunction with a requirement to declare test ranges could have helped reduce the uncertainties. Were the *Backfire* to be tested in a profile inconsistent with an intermediate-range mission, such a change would be apparent. Second, because a deviation from the agreed mission profile would be evident, uncertainties related to verification would be reduced, contributing to increased confidence.

Another principle for building confidence successfully is a willingness to make fair trades, or balanced and reciprocal concessions in negotiations. This principle recognizes the asymmetries in the two nations' force postures and development processes while at the same time demonstrating a mutual intent toward restraint. The key questions are how to determine what would be equitable as well as what steps would lead to a more stable balance.

The third principle of confidence-building is dependable verification and compliance. This requirement would be relatively easy to satisfy with restraints on testing of systems because its violations in a test program would be readily detectable. Flight tests of missiles or aircraft, in the initial-test or field-test stage, are the most readily verifiable. Lingering doubts about problems associated with systems of variable ranges, such as cruise missiles, which can be tested over relatively short ranges in the interior part of either country, could be diminished by agreement to declare test ranges in advance. This approach would have the advantage of substantially easing the monitoring tasks. Detection and analysis of a new weapons capability that did not involve a full test program would be more difficult than for a full program. However, such a test program would most likely involve a sufficient number of tests at least to raise the level of concern and analytic attention. Further, the value of whatever results were obtained from a shortened test program would have to be weighed against the concomitant decrease in the military reliability and questionable performance of the new system. Again, adoption of an agreed testing profile linked to a mission would help focus and clarify monitoring by specifying expected performance characteristics.

Value of Flight-Test Restrictions

Several types of restrictions on weapons testing could be equitable, could reduce uncertainty on both sides, and would be verifiable. In the first instance, they are related to flight tests of ballistic and cruise missiles and aircraft. Negotiability is a key factor, and there must be some realistic basis on which to pin negotiations on these restrictions, such as a previous agreement or negotiating track record. Examples of such broad restrictions are the following:

1. Declared times during which tests may be conducted
2. Declared test ranges and facilities
3. Prior notification of test activity
4. Prohibitions on concealment, deception, interference, and denial of data (e.g., encryption), coupled with verification standards regulating the type, quantity, and quality of data to be made available
5. Joint observation of tests.

A negotiated requirement to provide notification of launches of more than one missile could reduce the risk of accidental nuclear war, or at least public perception of such risks. Such a provision was agreed to in SALT II for ICBMs and the Soviets even went as far as to announce the dual, simultaneous launch of an ICBM and SLBM after SALT II was signed. The provision in SALT II required an announcement of an impending launch through a "Notice to Mariners" closing a specified missile impact area at sea. The time and place of launch and the coordinates of the impact area had to be provided within the "Notice." A requirement to provide trajectory data would make this step even more reassuring. Such a requirement would make it easier for each side to observe the other's missile tests, thereby increasing their confidence in their assessment of the other's capabilities.

Restrictions on encryption or other means of denying telemetry from missile tests are generally recognized as a necessity for ensuring the verifiability of qualitative restrictions on missiles. What is sometimes overlooked in discussions of this issue, however, is that agreement to prohibit means of denying data reinforces the value each party places in its independent ability to verify compliance. An important degree of confidence derives from this independence because the tools each party uses to verify compliance are under their unilateral control, which reduces the chances that false or misleading data can be introduced into the verification process. Since encryption has no other purpose than to keep the data secret from unauthorized observers (hence denial), the willingness to prohibit encryption (or at least to restrict it sharply) can be seen as a confidence-building measure. This type of measure also has the advantage of having already once been negotiated in SALT II. A broader agreement, therefore, might also be negotiable.

In addition to these broad provisions, it would be necessary to have certain agreements that pertained only to particular types of weapon systems. One possibility would be "testing type rules" for such "dual capable" weapons as cruise missiles or bombers; these weapon systems can be used for nuclear missions, but also for missions utilizing only conventional ordnance. As with other "type rules," the idea is that, after testing of a system in a particular configuration or for a certain mission, that configuration or mission would define the system for the purposes of an agreement, regardless of actual deployment. This is not a perfect solution for verifying compliance with negotiated restrictions, but it does make circumvention somewhat more difficult.

Flight-Test Restrictions to Improve the Survivability of Retaliatory Forces

A principal arms-control objective is to improve confidence in the survivability of each side's retaliatory force. Improvements in the accuracy of ICBMs can threaten this objective. For example, improved accuracy leads to the ability to further fractionate payload by adding more and smaller reentry vehicles (either overtly or surreptitiously through simulation or extra weight). This would render hardened second-strike forces more vulnerable to a first strike. Testing restraints can help to alleviate this problem.

One possibility is to restrict maneuvers of a missile's postboost vehicle (PBV), the final stage of a missile equipped with multiple independently targetable warheads, which controls, targets, and releases the warheads (called reentry vehicles). An approach that has been successfully negotiated is contained in the Second Agreed Statement to paragraph 10 of Article 4 of the SALT II Treaty, which keys the number of "procedures for releasing" reentry vehicles on any new strategic ballistic missile during flight testing to the maximum number of reentry vehicles on corresponding missile types flight-tested before May 1, 1979. This provision defines the "procedures" to mean those maneuvers of the PBV associated with targeting (including changes in orientation, position, and velocity). It constrains the capability to simulate during flight tests the targeting and releasing of more reentry vehicles than permitted. The arms-control effect of the provision is to restrain the ability to test a greater number of highly accurate reentry vehicles than currently carried (and currently accounted for in target survivability plans), and it therefore limits the capability to deploy more reentry vehicles than would threaten missiles in hardened targets.

Another possible approach would be to establish through negotiation a normalized test-flight staging profile for missiles by agreeing to general parameters for thrust, boost, and (where appropriate) PBV burn times, normalized to parameters consistent with a second-strike retaliatory mission. By setting constraints on these parameters during flight testing, it would be possible to control the type of delivery mission—for example, second strike as opposed to hard target. Combined with flight-test restraints on PBV maneuvers, a normalized staging profile could effectively restrain further development of destabilizing missions, depending, of course, on the parameters of the staging profile chosen as the standard.

Test Restrictions as a Means of Controlling R&D

Restrictions on weapon tests would represent a first step toward a comprehensive regime for establishing control over the pace of development of operational technology. These measures could (1) limit the pace of development and deployment of new systems, (2) lower the confidence of either side in its ability to carry out a successful surprise first strike, and (3) make verification easier by formulating monitoring tasks in terms of a "yes/no" decision as opposed to the more difficult "how much" decision.[2]

Another important advantage of these test restrictions is to draw a distinct line between R&D testing and field testing. New ideas can be researched in the lab (thereby maintaining a technological hedge), while full-scale tests of complete operational systems would be restricted with respect to which characteristics would be continued beyond R&D tests into the applied development phase preceding IOT&E and how fast they would be pursued.

Such a distinction between R&D testing and field testing is a necessary step in order to introduce arms control considerations into the weapons planning process. As it has been practiced to date, arms-control concerns are most often taken into account only after a particular capability has substantially reached the applied-development or field-testing stage. The effect has often been twofold—first, the changes in specifications required by arms control have come at a phase in the weapons program in which it is expensive to redesign or retool major subsystems or components; and second, it is counterproductive for

TABLE 1. Summary of U.S. Missile Flight Tests, 1964–1979

Year	64	65	66	67	68	69	70	71	72	73	74	75	76	77	78	79	Total
Minuteman II																	
R&D	4	11	11	17	8	10		3	1	2	2						69
Basic Training		3		5	2												10
Operational tests						13	26	17	7	5	5	2	7	3	3		88
Total	4	11	14	17	13	25	26	17	10	6	7	4	7	3	3		167
Minuteman III																	
R&D					2	13	14	4	3	4	5	4	4	4	3	1	61
Basic Training							3	3									6
Operational tests								10	11	6	6	7	7	9	7	2	65
Total					2	13	17	17	14	10	11	11	11	13	10	3	132

Source: Hussein Farooq, "The Impact of Weapons Test Restrictions," Adelphi Paper No. 165 (London: IISS, Spring 1981); see also M. Einhorn, G. Kane, and M. Nincic, "Strategic Arms Control Through Test Restraints," in *International Security* 8, No. 3 (1983):108.

both arms control and weapons effectiveness since the "fix" is usually an unhappy compromise that is neither good arms control (not verifiable, does not constrain capability) nor good weapons design (erodes performance, reinforces bad engineering).

Permitting R&D testing is essential in order to avoid surprises from new technological breakthroughs and to add to basic knowledge. Basic knowledge about how new weapon technologies function is necessary in order to assess similar developments by other parties, and as part of the knowledge necessary for sound and durable arms-control restraints. Particularly under the reality of increasingly complex and sophisticated systems, without such knowledge the chances of developing arms-control proposals that effectively restrain destabilizing capabilities are lowered.

A real constraint on development programs would be to negotiate sharp reductions on the number and type of permitted flight tests (for example, by 50 percent or more). Historically, both Soviet and U.S. missile-test programs have been tending to rely on test-flight programs consisting of fewer tests per year than previous years (see Tables 1 and 2).

By further reducing the number of flight tests, one could also reduce the confidence of military commanders that the designated system would perform as designed or planned. In the case of hard-target,

TABLE 2. U.S. SLBM Flight Tests

	Successes	*Failures*	*Total*
Polaris A1, A2, A3			
Flat-pad launches (1961–1963)	34	8	42
DASO (1963–1967)			
A1	21	15	36
A2	38	5	43
A3	44	2	46
Operational tests	(Initially 20 per year, from 1974 about 5 per year.)		
Poseidon C-3			
Flat-pad launches (1968–1970)	14	6	20
DASO (1971–1972)	23	5	28
Operational tests (1972–1980)	10	14	24
	(Tests continue at about 20 per year.)		
Trident C-4			
Flat-pad launches (1977–1979)	14	4	18
RV flight series (1974–1977)	4	0	4
DASO (1979–1980)	6	1	7
Operational tests (1979–1980)	15	2	17

Source: Hussein Farooq, "The Impact of Weapons Test Restrictions," Adelphi Paper No. 165 (London: IISS, Spring 1981); see also M. Einhorn, G. Kane, and M. Nincic, "Strategic Arms Control Through Test Restraints," in *International Security* 8, No. 3 (1983):108.

first-strike weapons, the reduction in the number of permitted flight tests would have two results:

1. Stretch out the time required to deploy a system that is considered operationally reliable in order to allow the other side to have greater confidence that it would have ample time to develop a similar system or appropriate countermeasures.
2. Retard confidence in the system's performance and reliability at

the level needed for such missions, which is much higher than for retaliation against countervalue or soft military targets.

The combined effect would be a return to confidence in second-strike weapons, a firmer basis for ensuring peaceful intent than hard-target, first-strike weapons.

We can illustrate simply how a limit on flight tests might stretch out the time before achieving a required confidence level in performance. Flight tests determine, among such other important quantities as reliability, the accuracy of a missile in hitting its target. Accuracy is frequently expressed in terms of the missile's circular error probable, or CEP, which is a statistical measure of ballistic missile accuracy. The CEP measures the distance from a chosen target within which, on average, one-half the total number of launched warheads will impact. Another very important quantity to planners is their *confidence* in achieving a certain accuracy or CEP. Confidence in achieving a measured value of the CEP for a given missile system improves with increasing numbers of tests, N, but the *rate* at which it improves increases relatively slowly with the square root of the number of tests; or, more accurately, as $1/(N-1)^{1/2}$. We can illustrate this effect by computing the estimated CEP in which we have 90 percent confidence—defined here as the upper-bound CEP—and comparing it to the actual measured CEP for different numbers of test shots. Their ratio is illustrated in Figure 1, for which the numerical values are computed on the basis of the following specific assumptions: (1) each coordinate of the miss distance is distributed normally, and (2) the mean and standard deviation remain constant throughout the test series. (The specific distribution for missile CEP estimates resulting from a finite number of tests depends on the characteristics of the missile tested. The one shown involves a single RV system with the miss distribution assumed to be circular [in order to give equal weight to both cross-range and down-range components]. The upper-bound CEP would be greater if the distribution of miss distances were elliptic, with a larger down-range component. It may be lower for a given number of missile test firings for MIRVs, since more RVs would be measured per firing. On the other hand, this statistical improvement may be countered by new systematic effects arising from dispensing of the MIRVs.)

Based on this curve showing how the 90 percent confidence upper-bound CEP decreases with the number of tests, it is possible to calculate how much delay an annual testing limit would have on achieving a given hard-target capability and the corresponding confidence deg-

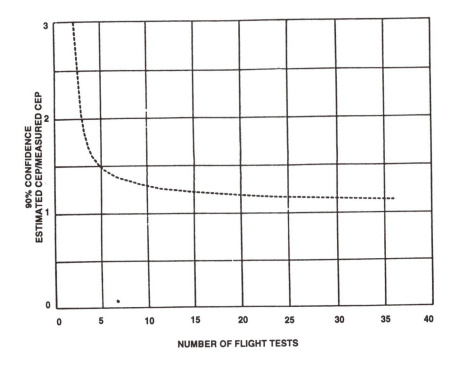

FIGURE 1.

radation. For example, twelve tests per year represent current typical practice for a missile system in development. The figure shows that twelve tests bring the 90 percent confidence bound to within 30 percent of the measured CEP—that is, the upper bound is about 30 percent more than the measured CEP. A test limit of six flights per year would delay reaching such a goal in a new system by one year. A fixed annual ICBM test quota of six ICBM flights a year would clearly cause a very substantial delay. Furthermore, changes in equipment or manufacturing procedures over a several-year period could mean that the necessary high confidence in the measured CEP would not, in practice, ever be achieved.

Conclusion

A partial regime of test-flight restrictions has already been negotiated successfully in SALT II. The provisions concerning the definition of new types of ICBMs restrict the *number* of flight tests allowed to the one new type of ICBM (twenty-five, the first twelve of which define the system, the final thirteen define the parameters of the system as those of the one new type). SALT II also took some tentative steps toward restrictions on the *type* of tests through constraints on PBV maneuvers in addition to constraints on growth greater than 10 percent variance in SALT parameters—that is, launch weight, throw weight, length, and diameter, and a requirement for prior notification of tests.

In the final analysis, confidence is built by assuring each party that its forces are maintained and developed in a manner that guarantees it will be able to retaliate effectively, while at the same time permitting the maintenance of an R&D capability to avoid technological surprise. The measures described would contribute to the maintenance of this deterrent, and it is primarily in this role that they can be called confidence-building measures.

Notes

[1] In the United States, this stage actually consists of three phases: (1) *basic research* in fields relevant to the technology (physics, chemistry, mathematics, electronics, etc.)—referred to in DOD budget parlance as "6.1 money" (package six, R&D Category 1, research); (2) exploratory development—application of basic science to potential applications (6.2); and (3) advanced development—implementation of the concepts worked out in 6.2

[2] A "yes/no" decision is a determination that a particular prohibited activity has or has not taken place. It is considered to be easier to detect the fact of the activity than it is to measure "how much" a particular prohibition on a performance parameter had been exceeded. Needless to say, there are cases when both can be difficult.

Civil Defense and
The U.S.–Soviet Strategic
Balance

The subject of civil defense is important because it touches the basic human instinct of survival. Is there anyone among us who can stand up and responsibly advocate that we and our society should ignore the ever-present potential of disaster, that we should make no plans and preparations for survival and recovery in the event of a nuclear attack or accident, or even for natural disasters?

At issue is not *whether* to do something. At issue is *what* we should be doing that could make a realistic contribution to avoiding nuclear war and to recovery, should deterrence fail and nuclear war occur.

Civil defense has entered with episodic prominence into our national-security debates for more than 20 years. In no other national-security issue have there been sharper reversals or more confusing contradictions than in our civil-defense policy. Our civil-defense activities have shifted between low and high intensity, and the focus of civil defense has shifted from blast shelters to fallout shelters, from community shelters to individual backyard shelters, from in-place shelters to population relocation or evacuation planning, and from preparing for nuclear attack to preparing for civil disasters. These changes are indicative of the fact that each new administration, and even new leaders within the same administration, have felt a need to do something. However, after further analysis and mature reflection, the country has found no feasible alternative to just going on pretty much with the same low-priority level of effort, justified by concerns about recovery from both nuclear attack and civil disaster.

Recent History of Civil Defense

Following the Berlin crisis in 1961, President Kennedy initiated an extensive and accelerated nationwide fallout-shelter program under Defense Department auspices. In assigning civil defense as a responsibility of the secretary of defense, he separated it from peacetime disaster-relief functions, which were assigned to the cognizant government departments and coordinated in the Office of Emergency Preparedness in the Executive Office of the President.

However, just as abruptly as it was created, this civil-defense plan was reduced drastically in scope two years later. Indeed, the shelter program didn't progress very much beyond the surveying, marking, and stocking of shelters in existing structures to the construction of new shelters, either in large buildings or of the backyard variety. There were two reasons for this. First, it was argued that our civil-defense posture should develop hand-in-hand with strategic-force structure and policy. But, commencing with 1963, the United States abandoned, as both futile and potentially provocative, a strategy based on counterforce, city-avoiding attacks. We opted instead for assured destruction, de-emphasizing passive defenses, or civil defense. Second, further analysis showed that an effective shelter program against nuclear attack would be exceedingly expensive and disruptive of our society, requiring a high degree of civilian organization, participation, and regimentation in exercises.

This shelter-marking program continued with low priority and low profile through the 1960s. It broadened in scope in 1971–1972, but it did not increase its budget, to consider peacetime hazards as well as nuclear attacks. This dual purpose of civil-defense planning relied on the cooperation of local, state, and federal governments and was emphasized by then Secretary of Defense Elliot Richardson in his *Department of Defense Posture Statement for Fiscal Year 1974.*

A third abrupt turn in the emphasis on civil defense, with an implication of future funding increases that has not, in fact, been implemented, was advocated the following year by the next secretary of defense, James Schlesinger, as an adjunct of a flexible-response doctrine that included options for limited counterforce against hard targets, such as fixed ICBMs in their underground silos. This doctrine justified civil defense as necessary to improve the credibility of our limited-nuclear-war posture by evacuating, relocating, and protecting the civilian population from the effects of limited Soviet nuclear attacks. Originally, the Defense Department claimed[1] that, with extensive civil defense available, we "could reduce nationwide fatalities due to fallout from a limited Soviet counterforce attack to relatively low levels—well under 1 million." This led to the conclusion[2] that "the likelihood of limited nuclear attacks cannot be challenged on the assumption that massive civilian fatalities and injuries would result," and, therefore, we were obliged to prepare for such conflict. At about this same time, the realization of a continuing robust civil-defense program by the Soviet Union led to claims of a developing civil-defense gap between the Soviet Union and the United States. This "gap" provided the basis of warnings that the United States would face a crisis instability if we were not able to provide comparably effective survival protection to our population. As a consequence of the added emphasis given to civil defense and its reorientation as an adjunct to flexible response, preparedness for nuclear attack was given priority over preparedness for peacetime emergencies.

These proposed changes in national civil-defense policy and strategic policy triggered extensive congressional discussions during 1975 and 1976—for the first time since 1963. In particular, members of the Senate Committee on Foreign Relations expressed great surprise at the low casualty figures in the Defense Department presentations and questioned the assumptions on which they were based. Subsequent detailed analyses by the Department of Defense and by the Congressional Office of Technology Assessment[3] in response to these questions showed those figures to be, in fact, grossly misleading. Furthermore, the existence of a civil-defense "gap" between the United States and the Soviet Union was widely challenged because of the lack of any evidence of the Soviet's achieving, or even showing any prospects of achieving, an effective defense of either their population or their industrial base against a massive nuclear attack.

The new rationale for civil defense provoked some intense public

---

[1]*Annual Defense Department Report for Fiscal Year 1976*, page II-55.

[2]"Briefing by Secretary James R. Schlesinger on Counterforce Attacks," hearings held before the Senate Foreign Relations Committee. Subcommittee on Arms Control, International Law and Organization, Sept. 11, 1974. See also *Analyses of Effects of Limited Nuclear Warfare*, prepared by the Congressional Office of Technology Assessment for the Senate Committee on Foreign Relations, Subcommittee on Arms Control, International Organizations and Security Agreements, Sept. 1975.

[3]In *Analyses of Effects of Limited Nuclear Warfare, ibid.*

debate during 1975 and 1976, but it had not yet impacted on the spending for civil defense when the Carter administration came to office just two years ago [in 1977]. At the outset, it appeared as if civil defense would remain quietly on the back burner. President Carter had expressed grave doubts about the concept of limited nuclear war during his campaign. Harold Brown, in an interview that appeared in the *Los Angeles Times* on December 26, 1976, shortly after he was designated to be secretary of defense, commented that there was little reason to believe that the Soviet shelter program would in fact confer a significant advantage in the event of a nuclear war, adding that "the way to counter a relatively ineffective system is not to replicate it on the other side."

The New Proposal for Civil Defense

Now we seem to be witnessing yet another new twist in civil-defense policy. Within the past two months, the Carter administration has expressed its intention to revitalize civil defense and to augment it by increasing its budget in fiscal year 1980 reportedly to $140 million, up by about $50 million, or slightly more than 50 percent from fiscal year 1979. The administration's plan emphasizes crisis relocation of the urban population. Yet another reorganization of civil defense is also proposed, this time pulling civil defense back out of the Pentagon and reunifying the planning for nuclear attack once again with civil-disaster planning in a new Federal Emergency Management Agency.

Until the overall scale and scope of these new plans are revealed, we can only speculate about their implications for the future. A $50 million add-on for fiscal year 1980 won't by itself accomplish very much; it would barely suffice to buy a road map for each evacuee. Evidently, this sum is no more than the first installment of a more substantial expenditure. At the other extreme, there is no evidence to suggest that these new plans are the start of a national multi-billion-dollar effort to match the Soviet investment in civil defense. A possible scale of plans and spending is suggested by a recent study, "Candidate U.S. Civil Defense Programs," which was prepared for the Defense Civil Preparedness Agency by the Systems Planning Corporation.[4] Their analysis estimated that a five-year investment cost of roughly $2 billion and some $200 million annual operating costs are required to develop the components of a credible nationwide population-relocation organiza-

---

[4]R. J. Sullivan, W. M. Heller, E. C. Aldridge, Jr. Technical Report 342 (March 1978).

tion and plan that could be implemented in a surge period extending at least one week during a crisis build-up. The envisaged actions during the surge period would include evacuating some 110 million people, or 80 percent of the population, from the metropolitan and other risk areas around the country; reconfiguring the normal peacetime wholesale/retail food-distribution patterns in the rural host areas; upgrading the available fallout protection for the evacuees; providing some in-place sheltering as a hedge, in the event that a full evacuation is impossible; training some 600,000 shelter managers; and stocking the shelters with basic supplies, which, for reasons of economy, would not be provided in peacetime.

As the Congress and the nation receive, analyze, and debate the new civil-defense proposal of the Carter administration, we must address two vital questions:

1. What impact will the proposal have on the national security of the United States? In particular, does the new emphasis on civil defense signify a fundamental revision of the strategic policy of the United States?
2. What realistic estimates can be made of the effectiveness and life-saving potential of civil defense in the event of nuclear attack?

Answers to these questions are required for guiding any new commitment to upgrade civil defenses. Surely they are not less important than the maps and plans that are to be provided for guiding population evacuation.

The Impact of Expanded Civil-Defense Programs on U.S. National Security

The national security policy of the United States recognizes that it is physically impossible to defend our vital national interests against a major nuclear attack. We have, therefore, given a heavy policy emphasis to international negotiations aimed at reducing the likelihood of military confrontation and have based our national security on a policy of deterrence of nuclear attack. Fundamental to deterrence is the requirement of having an assured destruction capability to devastate any nation that has initiated nuclear attack against us. In addition, we have designed our weapons programs and deployments to meet the requirements of flexible response—that is, the capacity to respond in measure according to the provocation—and of strategic stability. Central among the requirements for stability is the existence of strategic forces that cannot be destroyed by preemptive attack—that is, they should be survivable. This criterion lies at the heart of much of the current national-security debate within this country, with particular reference to SALT II. There is, quite properly, a serious concern about whether our Minutemen ICBMs will be vulnerable to a preemptive strike in the 1980s, owing to improved accuracy of the Soviet strategic missiles and extensive MIRVing of their ICBMs. This is, in my judgment, a serious issue to which the United States should respond, and is responding, with its military programs. The provisions of the draft treaty at SALT II have been designed to be compatible with such programs. However, within the context of a policy of deterrence and stability, civil defense plays a relatively minor role.

Additional missions, beyond deterrence based on assured destruction, have on occasion been proposed for our strategic forces. These missions range from political or military coercion to fighting and "winning" limited of nuclear wars. It is in the context of scenarios for fighting limited nuclear wars that civil defense is frequently viewed as having an enhanced importance. In this connection, recall the 1975 Defense Department claims of low casualty levels to a sheltered population in a limited nuclear counterforce attack that I referred to and criticized earlier. The important and immediate question raised by the renewed emphasis on civil defense proposed by the Carter administration is whether or not this is a part of a reorientation of our national-security policy toward a greater emphasis on fighting limited nuclear wars as opposed to deterrence based on assured destruction.

The ability to target and strike an opponent's nuclear forces—the strategic missiles and bombers plus the command and control centers—is a central requirement in a posture for fighting a limited nuclear war. However, such a capability—frequently referred to as hard-target counterforce—conflicts directly with a central criterion for strategic stability that applies to both the United States and the Soviet Union—that is, the existence of survivable strategic forces. It is here that a choice must be made. You can't have it both ways. This choice implies different weapons programs and deployments, as well as different arms-control positions.

I am not discussing here a choice of whether or not the United States should have flexible alternatives to massive retaliation. It has long been recognized, in defining the requirements of deterrence, that nuclear weapons might be launched with less than maximum force by either side. This requirement of "flexible response" can be implemented by our present forces. With our extensive and recently modernized retargeting capabilities, the president presently has many alternatives to the intentional and almost certainly suicidal massive retaliation against civilian populations. Flexible response, however, can create serious difficulties for stable deterrence if it is extended too broadly to include extensive hard-target counterforce and when the deployed forces are technically capable of implementing it.[5] Nor am I discussing here the relatively straightforward issue of maintaining a capacity for assured destruction. That will be assured for the foreseeable future by our Poseidon/Trident SLBM force moving quietly and invisibly under the ocean's surface and by our ready-alert SAC bomber force, which can be launched and flown out, given the warning that we can expect of an actual attack. In fact, the megatonnage on just one-tenth of these two alert and survivable components of our strategic forces could devastate the 200 largest Soviet cities by delivering, on the average, some ten times as much effective megatonnage per city as was delivered to Hiroshima and Nagasaki. Since more than 60 percent of the Soviet industrial base and more than 30 percent of their population (or 90 million people) are located in these 200 cities, this is presumably a magnitude of vulnerability to destruction that is of considerable significance to the Soviet leaders.

For an extensive and detailed analysis of the impact of civil defense on the assured-destruction capability of the United States, I refer to a recently completed study by the U.S. Arms Control and Disarmament Agency (ACDA).[6] The unclassified summary of this study, "An Analysis of Civil Defense in Nuclear War," was issued last month and presented to this Committee at these hearings. This study looks ahead to the mid-1980s, projecting the U.S. and Soviet strategic forces under the proposed SALT II agreement, and considers various civil-defense postures as well. In all the cases analyzed in this study, the United States is assumed to be retaliating after a Soviet first strike that has destroyed most of its ICBM force as well as the submarines in port and those bombers not on alert. The U.S. retaliatory strike is thus assumed to be delivered mainly by the alert bomber force and the fraction of the SLBMs at sea. The size of this surviving SLBM/bomber force depends

---

[5]For further discussion of this point, see testimony by S. D. Drell before the Senate Committee on Foreign Relations (January 19, 1977) [appearing in "Hearings on United States/Soviet Strategic Options"].

[6]U.S. Arms Control and Disarmament Agency, "An Analysis of Civil Defense in Nuclear War" Washington D.C. December 1978.

on whether the U.S. forces are on a normal day-to-day alert—that is, nongenerated—or are assumed to be fully generated—that is, on full alert—as would presumably be the case during a period of crisis if, for example, the Soviet Union were to evacuate its cities. The megatonnage delivered in these strikes is computed on the basis of the currently projected mix of U.S. warheads—including Trident missiles and air-launched cruise missiles—for the mid-1980s. The U.S. retaliatory strike is assumed to be directed primarily against Soviet counterforce and other military targets as well as their key national production capacity. Except where explicitly stated otherwise, the United States is assumed to hold back, from the retaliatory strike, a reserve force of 10–15 percent of its surviving warheads. Analogous targetting assumptions are made in calculating U.S. fatalities caused by a Soviet strike.

Life-Saving Potential of Civil Defense

The ACDA analysis concludes that such a retaliatory second strike by the surviving U.S. forces, assuming they were nongenerated, would destroy more than 600 of the largest Soviet cities and wipe out 65–70 percent of their industrial base. In fact, however, 80 percent of all Soviet cities and towns with populations of 25,000 or more would be attacked by at least one nuclear weapon. Furthermore, even if the urban population is assumed to utilize fully the best available in-place shelter capacity, this analysis finds that there will be more than 60 million civilian fatalities due to prompt and near-term fallout effects alone. Moreover, due to radioactive fallout generated by those weapons exploded at or near the ground, an interval of two months or longer would be required before workers could effectively start the task of rebuilding.

Were the Soviets to initiate a nationwide evacuation out of the cities, the natural and prudent reaction by the United States would be to put our forces on a fully generated alert so that a very high percentage of our SLBMs and strategic bombers would survive a Soviet preemptive strike. The casualty figures in this case, as shown in Table 1, reveal how limited is the predictable effectiveness of civil defense in the context of a policy of assured destruction. Even if the Soviets are successful in completing the evacuation of 80 percent of the urban population, providing them with expedient sheltering in the countryside and with the remaining 20 percent receiving the best available in-place sheltering, the total number of Soviet fatalities would remain very high.

TABLE 1. Near-Term Fatalities from Attack on Counterforce, Other Military Targets, and Industry (millions)

	U.S. fatalities		Soviet fatalities	
	Generated	Nongen.	Generated	Nongen.
No civil defense	N/A	105–131	N/A	81–94
In-place protection, no evacuation	107–126	76–85	80–88	60–64
In-place protection with urban evacuation	69–91	N/A	23–34	N/A
In-place protection, with urban evacuation (direct population attack)	87–109	N/A	54–65	N/A
In-place protection, with urban evacuation (direct population attack) and ground bursts			70–85	N/A

N/A = not applicable.

In particular, if the United States launches its reserve force of some 10–15 percent of the surviving warheads that were not included in the calculation above and targets them against the population, the Soviet fatality figures increase to 60 million. The fatalities would be even higher—in the range of 70–85 million—and the resulting industrial damage would be only slightly reduced if all the U.S. warheads were burst at ground level in order to generate maximum fallout against the population.

It is clear from the ACDA results in Table 1 that one can draw similar conclusions about the effectiveness of civil defense for reducing U.S. casualties in the event of a major Soviet (third) strike in response to our retaliation.

A very different picture of the life-saving potential of civil defense is often painted by considering a predetermined attack and comparing the casualty and fatality levels for a sheltered versus an unsheltered population, or an evacuated versus an unevacuated urban population. However, conclusions from these comparisons can be very misleading. As we have seen, the predicted effectiveness of civil defense in saving lives is very sensitive to parameters controlled by the attacker. In particular, in response to a nationwide urban evacuation that would be observed over a period of at least several days, an opponent would presumably and rationally place his forces on a fully generated alert, as well as retargetting some of them. This would largely neutralize any presumed life-saving potential of the evacuation.

It is on the basis of such considerations, and the numbers in Table 1, that I conclude that civil defense plays only a minor role in contributing to deterrence in the context of assured destruction. However, just as one cannot claim that civil defense will save a great many lives under all circumstances, one also cannot claim that it will not save substantial numbers of lives under some circumstances. Therefore, it would not be prudent to ignore or abandon civil defense and its life-saving and recovery possibilities. On the other hand, we should also not be deluded into thinking that civil defense would effectively alter the strategic balance even if supported at the current Soviet level of activity, which, in terms of the U.S. equivalent, is judged to cost roughly $2 billion annually.

Whatever the current geopolitical circumstances or recent historical experiences that lead the Soviet Union to continue its traditional emphasis on defense, it is apparent from our discussion that it has gained little if any strategic military value from its investment. I see no valid reason for the United States to imitate a comparable level of activity in civil defense. I fear that the net effect of our initiating such a massive effort would be to escalate the U.S.–Soviet arms competition and tension. This competition would be intensified by the same arguments that lead some U.S. observers to view the continuing robust Soviet civil-defense effort with alarm, in spite of its limited projected effectiveness; in spite of the fact that the Soviets have never tested their system with a large-scale city evacuation; and in spite of the fact that there is evidence that this program has experienced bureaucratic difficulties and apathy on the part of a large segment of the population.[7]

Civil Defense in Limited War

The case for civil defense as a vital component of a strategy for fighting a limited nuclear war depends on the very speculative and dangerous assumption that a limited nuclear exchange would *remain* limited and confined to military targets only, without escalating to an all-out ex-

---

[7]This assessment is also given by the Director of Central Intelligence in the unclassified summary of the CIA analysis "Soviet Civil Defense" (NI 78-10003, July 1978).

change. Nonetheless, a limited nuclear-counterforce strike is a possibility that is not altogether unthinkable.

There will always exist some lucrative and inviting counterforce targets, no matter how much we emphasize the importance to strategic stability of deploying and maintaining secure and invulnerable strategic forces. Some fixed land-based ICBMs will presumably be retained for quite some time in the strategic forces of the United States and the Soviet Union, in spite of their growing vulnerability to preemptive attack. I say this because of their robust and flexible command-and-control features and because of the enormous investment in ICBMs—particularly by the Soviet Union, which has concentrated more than 75 percent of its nuclear punch in its ICBMs. Additional counterforce targets include the naval bases providing berthing and support for the SLBMs and the air bases for the strategic bomber forces. There also exist redundant components of the command, control, communication, and intelligence infrastructure for these forces in hardened shelters; and there are, of course, many "other military targets," from supply depots and staging areas to transportation choke-points and military installations.

In the event of a limited counterforce strike, a moderate civil-defense program could save lives and help with recovery after a nuclear attack. It is generally agreed that it makes good sense, both in terms of the life-saving potential and cost-effectiveness, to emphasize developing the plans and organization for population relocation during a crisis surge period. I also believe that it makes good sense for this planning to be meshed together with civilian disaster recovery. Such coordinated planning should command greater public interest and hence be more effective. On this score, I strongly endorse the administration proposal to reunify the crisis-relocation planning for nuclear attack with civil-disaster planning in a new Federal Emergency Management Agency. Before endorsing any specific budget request, however, we should know much more about what the plans of the administration actually are. What is the ultimate goal and extent of this revitalized civil-defense program? Is it only contingency planning, or is it just the first step in a much more ambitious program associated with a revision of strategic policy oriented more toward fighting nuclear war?

If it is only contingency planning, then the public statements and arguments justifying the proposal as well as its basic contents should make this explicitly and unambiguously clear. Its support should not be built on the delusion that it makes nuclear war more credible because we are more likely to limit it, survive it, or win it. It is reason enough to view civil defense as a prudent and limited investment in one's contingency planning, whether against nuclear attack or civil disasters.

If, however, the administration's civil-defense plans are companion to a reorientation in our nuclear strategy toward greater emphasis on fighting a limited nuclear war, they should be rejected, along with such a change in policy, as harmful to strategic stability, potentially provocative, and therefore counter to our national-security interests. The argument for putting severe limitations on such preparations was stated clearly and persuasively in 1975 by the present secretary of defense, Harold Brown:[8]

> I am convinced that by far the least probable outcome is a nuclear exchange confined in any effective way to military targets. Providing that no one is deceived into thinking that the existence of forces, options and plans for a strategic counter-military exchange makes survival of either the United States or the Soviet Union in a nuclear war at all likely, or into forgetting that the fatal and almost certain outcome is the explosion on the cities of both countries of nuclear weapons, the existence of such plans and the development of such forces is an acceptable idea. However, to the extent that it erodes deterrence, this contingency planning could increase the likelihood of catastrophe. For that reason, it ought to be severely limited.

Is There a Civil-Defense Gap?

There are two arguments that one frequently hears in support of civil defense that I do not find at all persuasive. The first is that there is a civil-defense gap between the United States and the Soviet Union that threatens the credibility, if not the very existence, of the U.S. deterrent. In view of this, it is argued, we must build up our civil defenses to narrow the gap. Such an allegation is, in fact, not supported by further analysis. A Soviet effort to reduce casualties by fully and successfully implementing their civil-defense preparations and protection can be

---

[8]H. Brown, speech before Institute of U.S. and Canadian Studies of the Soviet Academy of Sciences in Moscow (March 1975); submitted for the record on Hearings on Civil Preparedness and Limited Nuclear War held before the Joint Committee on Defense Production, April 28, 1976, p. 130.

largely offset by placing the U.S. forces at a high level of readiness. In this event, many more SLBM and bomber warheads would survive the presumed Soviet first strike and be available for retaliation. The fatality estimates shown in Table 1 would be even higher if an attack were targetted primarily against the population instead of primarily against military and industrial targets, or if the attack were against an evacuation that was still in progress or only partially successful. There is currently no evidence to lead one to conclude that the Soviets would *effectively* implement a nationwide crisis evacuation. In particular, the Soviet Union has never tested a large-scale city evacuation, and there is no evidence that the Soviets *can* successfully execute nationwide crisis relocation. What the Soviets are known to have done is to build shelters for part of the work force and leadership and to have created a program for the training of civil-defense workers. Analysis of the Soviet population distribution and of the proximity of their population to industry shows that their urban density is greater than that of the United States, that their rural density and industrial concentration is similar to ours, and that their population collocation with industry is greater. On these grounds, they clearly have no inherent advantage over the United States.

Nor can one base an allegation that there exists a civil-defense gap on the grounds of Soviet hardening or dispersal of their key industrial capacity. Although we are familiar with published plans for protecting their industry, there is little evidence of industrial dispersal or hardening by the Soviet Union. This perhaps reflects the very great cost of such measures as well as Soviet realization of their limited effectiveness; if targeted, even buried facilities cannot survive.

The ACDA analysis of civil defense in nuclear war considered industrial damage as well as fatalities. Industrial facilities were assumed to be destroyed if they were subjected to overpressures of 10 psi (pounds per square inch) or more, which is equivalent to a wind blast of 600 miles per hour or more. This is an offense-conservative standard of damage, when compared with pictures of the mangled wreckage of the machine shop at the Mitsubishi Steel and Arms Plant in Nagasaki, which was subjected to an overpressure of 6 psi.[9] A summary of the ACDA findings is that the representative U.S. retaliatory strikes caused:

---

[9]ACDA report; also pictures in *The Effects of Nuclear Weapons*, edited by S. Glasstone (U.S. Atomic Energy Commission, rev. ed. 1964), see especially pp. 220–221.

- 65 to 70 percent destruction of key Soviet production capacity from U.S. forces in normal day-to-day alert status;
- 85 to 90 percent destruction of key Soviet production capacity from a generated U.S. force status;
- 60 percent collateral damage to untargeted Soviet production capacity from normal alert; and
- 80 percent collateral damage to untargeted Soviet production capacity from generated alert.

As also noted in the ACDA analysis, any attempt to harden above-ground industrial facilities could be easily overcome by detonating weapons at lower altitudes near ground with only a minor reduction in the area subjected to 10 psi overpressures.

A similar conclusion is found in the analysis of Soviet Civil Defense issued by the Director of Central Intelligence:[10] "Soviet measures to protect the economy could not prevent massive industrial damage. The Soviet program for dispersal of industry appears to be offset by a contrary tendency for investments in new facilities to be inside or near previously existing installations." These conclusions fully support those stated in the Report on Industrial Defense and Nuclear Attack, which is Part II of the Civil Preparedness Review issued in April 1977 by the Joint Committee on Defense Production of the U.S. Congress.

To summarize, an allegation that there exists an effective civil-defense gap between the United States and the Soviet Union cannot be sustained, either on grounds of life-saving potential or of industrial survival. In view of these findings, as well as an appreciation of the many uncertainties attendant to a nuclear exchange, the CIA analysis of Soviet civil defense stated as a key conclusion: "We do not believe that the Soviets' present civil defenses would embolden them deliberately to expose the USSR to a higher risk of nuclear attack." I concur.

Civil Defense As a Crisis-Management Tool

A second argument that I do not find at all persuasive for implementing a crisis-relocation civil-defense plan is that it would serve as an effective crisis-management tool. Crisis relocation of people on a large scale would cause a tremendous domestic and economic upheaval. Thus, it should be executed only in the ultimate extreme circumstances; probably it could be done no more than once. For an effective

---

[10]Op. cit.

flexible and repeatable crisis measure, we can readily raise the alert status of our military forces.

One possibility in the event of a crisis raising U.S. fears of an impending Soviet pre-emptive attack would be to evacuate only the population near our counterforce targets. This would involve moving a relatively small number of people out of a high-risk area to join a larger number who are presumably at lower risk. A limited relocation of this type would be interpretable unambiguously as a defensive move and would be much easier to accomplish than a full-scale relocation of the massive population concentrations in the urban areas of California and the Northeast into a relatively sparsely populated countryside. Civil-defense planning should include preparations for such a contingency. This would also help us to understand the difficulties and practical limits in implementing a full-scale nationwide crisis relocation of the population.

What Realistic Estimates Can Be Placed on the Effectiveness of Civil Defense in the Event of Nuclear Attack?

So far, we have emphasized physical parameters and calculable components of civil defense. There are, in addition, very important aspects that cannot be predicted or calculated in an analysis of the effectiveness of civil defense because they depend on human behavior under unparalleled conditions of stress and devastation. Honest and reasonable people can disagree on how important these human factors will be in setting the scale of the disaster. It is clear, however, that estimates of fatalities that ignore such imponderable factors are, at best, highly fragile minimum levels of expected fatalities.

A confident estimate of the effectiveness of a nationwide civil-defense system can never be given by either country, no matter how detailed the calculations and how quantitative the claims, because of the vastness of the unknowns: What are the prevailing winds and weather patterns? How much prior warning is available? How will the population behave during the evacuation and in the crowded shelters during and after a nuclear attack for a period perhaps extending over several months, or long enough for the deadly radioactivity to decrease to tolerable levels?

Beyond the immediate fatalities, there are the additional deaths, illnesses, and injuries from burns, fire, flying debris, exposure, radiation poisoning, panic, and the breakdown of law and order. Epidemic diseases, such as cholera and typhoid, are almost certain to break out because of inadequate sanitation, the inability to bury the dead, contamination and shortages of food, and the availability of only limited medical care and facilities; within the crowded shelters (with, at best, only about one square meter of floor space per sheltered person) will be many of the roughly 30 to 50 million injured people requiring medical care.

For massive nuclear attacks, the uncertainties are even greater, especially with respect to the long-term ecological effects and the problems of reestablishing a society in the midst of devastation on an unparalleled scale. The study *Long-Term Worldwide Effects of Multiple Nuclear Weapons Detonations*, issued by the National Academy of Sciences in 1975, is revealing in its emphasis on just how extensive are the physical unknowns that will determine the scale of the disaster resulting from a major nuclear conflict and how little can be predicted with confidence concerning, for example, depletion of the ozone layer or disruption of the food supplies in the Northern Hemisphere as a result of a major U.S.–Soviet nuclear conflict. In view of these large-scale environmental uncertainties and in view of the destruction of nationwide economic systems and the questionable continuity of governmental structures after such a conflict, there is little that can be said about the prospects for long-term postattack recovery, with or without civil defense.

Summary

- Civil defense should not be viewed as substantially increasing the likelihood of survival or of recovery in a major nuclear war. Retargeting by the attacker can offset most of the life-saving potential of civil defense. With or without civil defense, the urban/industrial base—including most of the cities and key national production facilities—will be destroyed in a major attack.
- A civil-defense program that is part of a reorientation in our nuclear strategy toward greater emphasis on fighting limited nuclear war should be rejected along with such a change in policy as harmful to strategic stability and potentially provocative, and therefore counter to our national security interests. Civil defense should not be used to create and support the dangerous illusion that there is a likelihood of waging and surviving a nuclear war that is limited and confined to military targets only.
- A massive nationwide relocation of the urban population is not an effective crisis-management tool.

- There are very great uncertainties in any estimate of the effectiveness of civil defense no matter how detailed the calculations. Civil defense does not offer a realistic escape from the current nuclear "balance of terror."
- I strongly favor the proposed reorganization of civil defense into a new Federal Emergency Management Agency that will be responsible for joint planning for both nuclear attack and civil disasters. However, a clear and substantive statement by the administration of the goals, extent, and ultimate cost of their newly proposed civil-defense plans should precede action on their new funding request.
- The maintenance of highly survivable strategic forces and progress in the negotiations at the Strategic Arms Limitation Talks (SALT) are both of great importance to the national security of the United States.

Current U.S. weapons programs are responding to the growing vulnerability of our Minuteman ICBMs, owing to improved accuracy of the Soviet strategic missiles and the extensive MIRVing of Soviet ICBMs. At the same time, we are making slow but steady negotiating progress at SALT. Based on what is known about the draft treaty at SALT II, I believe it will be an important step that I will strongly endorse in the interest of U.S. national security. Although its accomplishments are likely to fall short of my hopes and goals for real arms control, SALT II will be important for a number of reasons. It will establish an agreed numerical measure of overall equivalence, incorporating minor but real numerical reductions, that can serve as a solid basis for continuing negotiations in SALT III and beyond for more substantial reductions and more significant agreements. It will also put some modest limits on force modernization. This beginning of qualitative limits on weapons is important because the pace of military technological progress—when funded, as at present, with high budgetary priority—is so fast that it has been outstripping diplomatic success and creating new obstacles to progress in arms control. Now that we have formalized deterrence with the Soviet Union as a result of the ABM treaty of SALT I and are in the process (I hope) of formalizing overall equivalence in SALT II, I look to the next round of SALT for those measures of qualitative restraint that are required for maintaining strategic stability.

In view of the terrifying scale of destruction of which the current strategic arsenals of the United States and the Soviet Union are capable, I believe that the challenge to control nuclear weapons and to avert nuclear holocaust is the problem of overriding importance facing our generation. If nuclear war were ever to occur, civil defense could do little to improve our prospects of survival, much less of victory.

The Global Effects of a Nuclear War

As a scientist, I know that data and experiments are the most important ingredients in the study of physical phenomena. Everything we learn in science—the very core of our understanding—comes from our observations and our data. But my subject today is the consequences of a major nuclear war, and I am happy to say that we have no data in terms of which to describe these consequences. Therefore, there is little for me to offer by way of definite conclusions or predictions. What I can do best as a scientist is to set the scale and describe the unprecedented destructive potential of a nuclear holocaust. I can list the great uncertainty, the vast imponderables, and the overall helplessness of society to escape to the sidelines or avoid devastation if nuclear war were to occur.

The picture I will present was summarized very well in the preamble of the resolution on nuclear war and arms control that was passed overwhelmingly by the members of the National Academy of Sciences at its annual meeting last April [1982]. It said simply:

- Nuclear war is an unprecedented threat to humanity;
- A general nuclear war could kill hundreds of millions and destroy civilization as we know it;
- Any use of nuclear weapons, including use in so-called "limited wars," would very likely escalate to general nuclear war; and
- Science offers no prospect of effective defense against nuclear war and mutual destruction.

I have appended to my prepared statement for entry into the record a copy of this resolution, which calls on the U.S. Congress, the president, and other world leaders "to intensify substantially, without preconditions and with a sense of urgency," efforts to reduce nuclear weapons and reduce the threat of nuclear war.

Casualty Levels

Recall the enormous destructive potential in existing nuclear arsenals. The sum total of munitions expended over a period of six years in World War II added up to approximately 6 megatons (Mt). That is less than the megatonnage of *one* of the large nuclear warheads now deployed. Hiroshima and Nagasaki were devastated by "relatively small" bombs whose yields were roughly 15 kilotons. The totals today exceed 10,000 Mt!

About 90 percent of this unprecedented level of explosive energy would be released in intense heat and blast waves that would cause immediate devastation in the target areas. I wouldn't advise anyone to be within 10 miles of one megaton. Official estimates are that a combined total of more than 200 million U.S. and Soviet citizens would be killed outright in a major nuclear exchange that was designed to kill civilians. The "initial" survivors, a very large number of whom would be seriously injured, would face the longer-term, more subtle, but nonetheless hideous effects of radioactive fallout and infectious diseases (such as cholera and dysentery) due to poor sanitation. This is a prospect they would face without anything resembling adequate medical support.[1]

Radioactive Fallout

The dosage of fallout will be particularly large and threatening on a global scale if the nuclear bombs are detonated on the Earth's surface or at low altitudes. In this case, vast quantities of soil and rocks will be vaporized by the heat pulses, along with the radioactive bomb debris. Mixed together, they will rise with the fireball and form the characteristic mushroom cloud before settling back to Earth. The heavier

---

[1]A recent study published in *AMBIO*, the international journal of the Royal Swedish Academy of Sciences (vol. XI, no. 2–3, 1982, p. 114), estimates that 750 million people would be killed outright by the effects of blast alone if all the 1124 major cities of the Northern Hemisphere were targeted by approximately 2000 Mt on 5000 nuclear warheads. In addition, 340 million more would be seriously injured. This would leave roughly 200 million people, or about 15 percent of the urban population in the Northern Hemisphere, initially unharmed.

particles start settling within several hours as fine, deadly radioactive ash. For each megaton detonated, this ash, driven by the wind, will typically make 1000 square miles of the Earth's surface uninhabitable to unsheltered humans for several or more weeks. The lighter particles rise into the stratosphere, circulating the Earth for months and even years before returning to ground as worldwide fallout.

The medical consequences of the ionizing radiation following a global nuclear war can be estimated using actual data from the Hiroshima and Nagasaki explosions. The Japanese experience was the first extensive experience with sublethal and lethal effects of total body exposure in humans, and it permits conservative estimates to be made of the subsequent incidence of fatal cancers, genetic defects in children of survivors, and sterility. (Medical specialists will discuss the seriousness of this massive insult to the human gene pool in testimony to this committee following mine.) In addition, the fallout will cause devastation to natural plant and animal communities, thereby entering the human diet, as well as disrupting agricultural growth.

Surprises and Chance Discoveries

The effect of deadly, widespread fallout was discovered in the 1954 Bikini test of a 15 Mt bomb, contaminating the Japanese fishing boat *Lucky Dragon* 90 miles downwind and the Rongelap Atoll 100 miles from the burst point. This was the most dramatic illustration of the potential for large-scale nuclear war to kill and to maim on a worldwide scale far beyond the local effects of blast and fire alone. Other chance discoveries were also made during the testing of large nuclear weapons in the atmosphere in the decade before such testing was banned by the Limited Test Ban Treaty of 1963. They include the discovery following high-altitude bursts of a widespread electromagnetic pulse, or EMP, that can wreck electrical command, control, and communication equipment; of the blackout of high-frequency radio communications; and of the production of an artificial Van Allen belt temporarily enhancing the number of charged particles trapped in the Earth's magnetic field.

In a 1976 pamphlet (*Worldwide Effects of Nuclear War—Some Perspectives*), the U.S. Arms Control and Disarmament Agency (ACDA) emphasized the fact that much of our knowledge was gained by chance and went on to say that this "should imbue us with humility as we contemplate the remaining uncertainties (as well as the certainties) about nuclear warfare." At that time, Dr. Fred Iklé, currently under secretary of defense for policy, was the director of ACDA. In the foreword he wrote to this pamphlet, he observed:

> Uncertainty is one of the major conclusions in our studies, as the haphazard and unpredicted derivation of many of our discoveries emphasizes. Moreover, it now appears that a massive attack with many large-scale nuclear detonations could cause such widespread and long-lasting environmental damage that the aggressor country might suffer serious physiological, economic, and environmental effects even without a nuclear response by the country attacked.

Atmospheric Changes

Beyond the radioactive fallout, there are other sources of widespread, long-lasting, and potentially catastrophic environmental damage. One effect that is believed to be of major importance and has been discussed extensively is the disturbance of ozone in the stratosphere. In particular, if there is a massive exchange of high-yield weapons of one or more megatons, there will be a substantial injection of nitric oxide (NO) into the stratosphere with subsequent depletion of its ozone layer for a period extending several years. If the ozone shield in the stratosphere is reduced, an increased flux of ultraviolet radiation from the Sun will reach the Earth's surface. The resulting adverse consequences include increased incidence of skin cancer in fair-skinned people and decreased crop yields. Damage to different species of biological and plant organisms will vary considerably depending on their physical characteristics. As will be discussed later in today's hearings, there is uncertainty about the actual level of ozone depletion and also about the sensitivity of this effect to the mix of low- and high-yield nuclear weapons that are detonated.

Another possible result of a major nuclear war is the igniting of tremendous fires that may burn for weeks in forest, cropland, and urban and industrial areas. The small particulates, or aerosol, produced by the fires and forming the thick smoke layer will drastically reduce the amount of sunlight reaching ground. The actual reduction of the sunlight at the Earth's surface can be very different, depending on unknown factors, such as the total area that is burning, but recently published analyses indicate that this effect could be very serious.[2] It is estimated that the sunlight could be reduced by a factor as large as 150

---

[2]P. Crutzen and J. Birks, AMBIO *ibid.*

(that is, more than 99 percent would be absorbed before reaching ground). The fires could persist for months and completely disrupt, if not totally eliminate, agricultural production in the Northern Hemisphere if they occurred during the growing season. From this follow other consequences of social and economic disruption, not to mention the psychological strain of such a massive trauma to all the survivors.

There are evidently great uncertainties in our ability to predict the death and devastation, the disruption of the ecosphere, and the pattern—or even the possibility—of postattack recovery after a nuclear holocaust. We are still learning of new effects, such as the importance of the darkening of sunlight due to massive fires, that should increase our "humility as we contemplate the remaining uncertainties (as well as certainties) about nuclear warfare."

It is both numbing and frightening to realize that there exists even the possibility that vast forest fires triggered by nuclear war could reduce sunlight reaching ground in the Northern Hemisphere by a comparable factor to that which, according to recent theory, may have led to the extinction of the larger terrestrial vertebrates, including the dinosaurs, 65 million years ago in the aftermath of an impact by a large extraterrestrial body.[3]

Prospects for Limited War and Protection

One can, to be sure, speculate about very different nuclear-war scenarios with "limited" counterforce strikes, effective operation of antiballistic missile (ABM) defenses, and widespread availability and extensive use of civil-defense shelters. Are these, in fact, likely, or even real possibilities? Again, one cannot be sure. In the absence of data, we know no more about how a nuclear war might begin or end than we do about its overall consequences. There are, however, some important considerations to keep in mind when contemplating such propositions as limited and survivable nuclear conflict.

There is great danger that, once the vital interests of the United States and the Soviet Union are engaged to the point that either initiates a nuclear attack, both countries will dig even deeper into their vast arsenals of more than 50,000 nuclear weapons. Neither past experience and precedent nor war-gaming gives cause for much hope that the nuclear exchange and resulting devastation would remain limited and aimed exclusively at counterforce and direct military tar-

---

[3]L. Alvarez, W. Alvarez, F. Asaro, and H. Michel, Science, **208** (1980).

gets. In addition, there is no technical basis for any confidence that it will be possible to control the escalation of a limited nuclear conflict. There are too many opportunities during combat for confusion and error. Once the nuclear threshold is crossed, there will inevitably be a broad delegation down the line of authority for nuclear release. This will be required by the very short missile flight times and by the potential vulnerabilities of any conceivable worldwide command, control, and communication system from a national command center to the broadly dispersed military units with thousands of nuclear weapons. For these reasons—both human and technical—a limited nuclear war seems a most improbable event.

There is no effective defense against nuclear retaliation. This was recognized ten years ago when we signed the SALT I treaty, which severely limits ABM deployments. During the past decade, improved radar, interceptor, and computer technologies have enhanced the capabilities of terminal ABM for hard targets. This is particularly true for low-value targets, so that the defense can be effective even if there is a significant leakage. However, on technical grounds, I see no prospect of deploying—on ground or in space—an effective defense of the nation's people and industry.

I cannot conceive of a civil-defense system that could protect either the Soviet society or the American society from unprecedented and unacceptable disaster and devastation in all-out nuclear war. Calculations that are cited to illustrate the effectiveness of civil defense in saving lives differ in detail and draw widely different conclusions as to fatality levels. However, they all have one feature in common—namely, that their conclusions are critically dependent on a number of assumptions:

- Are all targets strictly military or industrial, or are cities directly targeted also?
- What is the total megatonnage delivered?
- Are the bombs air-burst, or are they ground-burst to produce maximum fallout?
- What are the wind patterns and weather conditions?
- Is the attack retargeted against the relocated population?
- Does the attack occur during evacuation, when masses of people are out in the open with no shelter?
- How long will people actually remain in their expedient shelters while the deadly levels of radioactivity gradually decline over a period of weeks?

For the life of me, I cannot understand how anyone can say, in the face of all the unknowns about the consequences of nuclear war and all the uncertainties in the effectiveness of civil defense, that with adequate civil defense preparations, the United States would be able to recover from an all-out nuclear war in two to four years. That, however, was the message of T. K. Jones, deputy under secretary of defense for strategic and theatre nuclear forces, as reported in the *Los Angeles Times* last January. In the same paper, the agency responsible for civil defense, the Federal Emergency Management Agency, is quoted as saying that, ". . . with reasonable protective measures the United States could survive nuclear attack and go on to recovery in a relatively few years."

It is a good antidote to such outrageous claims to quote a finding of the sobering study *The Effects of Nuclear War*, published in 1979 by the Congressional Office of Technology Assessment:

> The effects of a nuclear war that cannot be calculated are at least as important as those for which calculations are attempted. Moreover even these limited calculations are subject to very large uncertainties. . . . This is particularly true for indirect effects such as deaths resulting from injuries and the unavailability of medical care, or for economic damage resulting from disruption and disorganization rather than direct destruction.

Summary

I stress again that the problem with all precise nuclear-war scenarios, with their neat assumptions and predictions, is that we fortunately have no data! In real wars—the nonnuclear conflicts of past experience—we have learned to appreciate that the course of events is determined by such vitally important factors as surprise, individual bravery, motivation, and luck. These do not appear in theoretical scenarios! Perhaps that is why there are so few detailed calculations and claims about such real conflicts. The imaginary scenarios and computer printouts of casualty levels seem to proliferate only when there are neither data nor experience to test them against.

Appendix
Resolution: Nuclear War and Arms Control

—Whereas nuclear war is an unprecedented threat to humanity;

—Whereas a general nuclear war could kill hundreds of millions and destroy civilization as we know it;

—Whereas any use of nuclear weapons, including use in so-called "limited wars," would very likely escalate to general nuclear war;

—Whereas science offers no prospect of effective defense against nuclear war and mutual destruction;

—Whereas the proliferation of nuclear weapons to additional countries with unstable governments in areas of high tension would substantially increase the risk of nuclear war;

—Whereas there has been no progress for over two years toward achieving limitations and reductions in strategic arms, either through ratification of SALT II or the resumption of negotiation on strategic nuclear arms;

Be it therefore resolved that the National Academy of Sciences calls on the President and the Congress of the United States, and their counterparts in the Soviet Union and other countries which have a similar stake in these vital matters;

—To intensify substantially, without preconditions and with a sense of urgency, efforts to achieve an equitable and verifiable agreement between the United States and the Soviet Union to limit strategic nuclear arms and to reduce significantly the numbers of nuclear weapons and delivery systems;

—To take all practical actions that could reduce the risk of nuclear war by accident or miscalculation;

—To take all practical measures to inhibit the further proliferation of nuclear weapons to additional countries;

—To continue to observe all existing arms control agreements, including SALT II; and

—To avoid military doctrines that treat nuclear explosives as ordinary weapons of war.

DETERRENCE
AND ARMS
CONTROL

The Impact of a Public Constituency

It has often been said that war is too important to be left to the generals and that peace is too vital to be left to the politicians. So, too, are matters of nuclear weapons and policy too important to be left to the nuclear-strategy "experts." In reality, there are no experts on nuclear war. We have never had a nuclear war, and any scientist knows that you must have data before you can become an expert. We do not know how a nuclear war would start, be waged, or finally stopped. No one, including nuclear-strategy "experts," knows what would be left after such a "war."

What this means is that the public must inform and involve itself actively in the formulation of policy on these issues. This requires public outreach, public education, and active dialogue with our public officials. The record we will explore in this article shows that an informed and active public constituency can have a significant effect in shaping sound policy in highly technical areas that determine our very survival.

In the United States, there was no public debate at the time of the fateful decision by President Truman in 1950 to develop the second generation of nuclear weapons—that is, the *H*-bomb or hydrogen bomb. This was early in the cold-war period, and secrecy was applied broadly. As a result, the public played no role in the decision to move ahead to the megaton-scale *H*-bomb.

The debate within government on whether, and then how, to proceed with work on the *H*-bomb in response to the first Soviet *A*-bomb explosion in late summer of 1949 was carried on almost completely under a thick cloak of secrecy. We have no idea whether, in those strained times, an effort to negotiate with the Soviet Union to head off the development of the *H*-bomb might have succeeded, but we didn't even try. It was nine years later before a serious initiative on peaceful uses of nuclear energy was made, in 1958, but, by then, it was too late. The genie was out of the bottle, and there was no way to deny the basic scientific reality of the hydrogen bomb.

By the early 1960s, the design and building of hydrogen bombs had advanced to a mature technology. The scientists in the nuclear-weapons laboratories had become what Lord Zuckerman calls "the alchemists of our time, working in secret ways that cannot be divulged, casting spells which embrace us all."

Testing of *H*-bombs in the atmosphere continued at a rapid pace through most of the decade of the 1950s, leading to a substantial, worldwide build-up in the level of radioactivity. By 1960, an active and vigorous public constituency around the world had become concerned about this radioactive fallout and its effects on the health of their families and friends. They joined many scientists who understood the weapons in detail to protest continued testing. Scientists could bring a highly informed judgment to bear on the question of how the cessation of nuclear tests in the atmosphere would affect our national security.

This was the first important issue of nuclear weapons in which the public in the United States played a major role. Around the same time, some scientists in the USSR, and, in particular, Andrei Sakharov, were also advocating a ban on testing. In the Western world, concerned citizens by the hundreds of thousands applied strong political leverage, while the technical case in support of an atmospheric test ban treaty was presented by concerned scientists. These forces inside and outside of government enhanced one another. Working together, they helped accomplish what may well have been beyond the power of either alone: the Limited Test Ban Treaty signed in 1963 by President Kennedy and General Secretary Khrushchev.

By the end of the 1960s, scientists had developed important new weapons technologies that could potentially alter, in a fundamental way, the nuclear forces of the United States and the USSR. One new development was antiballistic missile (ABM) systems, using advanced computers, very high acceleration interceptor missiles, special nuclear warheads, and phased-array radars.

The original proposal to deploy ABM systems near large population centers in the United States stirred a major public debate, primarily because many people did not want nuclear-tipped missiles located, figuratively, "in their own backyards." Triggered by these public concerns, the ABM decision became an opportunity for extensive public debate. The halls of Congress and the media became vital educational forums for careful and informed technical analysis of the effectiveness and arms-control implications of the proposed ABM system.

Through this unprecedented public debate on a weapons system, Congress came to understand that the proposed ABM system was not going to do what was promised. By 1970, it was clear, on the basis of technical facts alone, that offensive missiles could respond with relative ease to any practical ABM system. Technical arguments for deployment collapsed, and the ABM debate boiled down to its value solely as political leverage for the arms-control talks—its value as a bargaining chip for the Strategic Arms Limitation Talks (SALT).

The outcome of this was the successful negotiation with the Soviet Union at SALT I of the ABM Treaty severely limiting deployment of ABM systems. That treaty is currently in force. I consider it to be our most important arms-control achievement to date.

At the same time as the ABM debate, however, the United States moved ahead rapidly with the development and deployment of multiple independently targetable reentry vehicles (MIRVs). The original American justification for MIRVs was that they would penetrate ballistic-missile defenses by overwhelming their defensive firepower with an intense rain of many warheads. They were offered as an insurance policy against Soviet ABM deployments, which had then begun around Moscow. However, when the SALT I treaty of 1972 prohibited the deployment of nationwide ABM defenses, American MIRV programs proceeded full tilt. The new rationale for MIRVs became our alleged need for counterforce—the need to threaten a wide repertoire of Soviet military targets, including their retaliatory forces.

MIRVs did not lead to an increase in the visible presence of nuclear weapons. Therefore, in contrast to ABMs, they did not cause a reaction from citizens who wanted no nuclear weapons nearby. In such circumstances, we deployed MIRVs with very little public attention or concern, the USSR responded with its own major buildup of MIRVed forces, and arms control suffered a setback. It is not that there was no opportunity for serious public debate about the pros and cons of MIRVs and their impact on the arms race and our national security. It was simply that there was no specific issue to bring the MIRV decision home to the man in the street and arouse public reaction. Therefore, no U.S. public constituency was created to nurture the cause of arms control in opposition to the MIRV. Moreover, the country was becoming increasingly concerned first with Vietnam and then with Watergate.

There was also little expressed public interest in the SALT II treaty when it came up for ratification by the United States Senate in 1979. The arms-control advocates and a few politicians pitched in and argued mightily. However, there was no public outcry, as there had been at the time of the ABM debate that set the stage for SALT I. The Senate debate on SALT II dragged on with little public pressure for ratification. Debate was eventually terminated as a result of the Soviet armies entering Afghanistan and the reaction of the American public to it, making it politically impossible to obtain ratification in the United States. In a reverse way, Afghanistan mobilized public opinion in the West against arms control, which again demonstrates the essential power of public opinion.

The original rationale for the United States developing the MX missile was to respond to the buildup of highly MIRVed Soviet ICBMs and to decrease the vulnerability of our land-based missile force, thereby improving deterrence. We sought to base the new ICBM so that it could not be attacked and destroyed. However, the debate in the United States, which was covered in the media much more thoroughly than the original MIRV decision, revealed deep differences of opinion on counterforce versus deterrence, on the effectiveness of the proposed basing scheme, and on its environmental impact.

The MX basing plan, as it was originally perceived, is no longer with us. Claims of the survivability and effectiveness of "Densepack," "Bigbird," and "Racetrack"—the three schemes with, at one time or another, administration backing—just did not stand up under close technical scrutiny. Today we are deploying only fifty MX missiles, and they have little to do with our security or with deterrence. They are not a major arms-control issue.

I see a pattern in this mixed record of the past. The atmospheric test ban treaty and the ABM debate that culminated in SALT I are two major successes in American nuclear-weapons policy. Further, the MX program has been restructured and sharply cut back from the original plans. It is notable that these results were achieved with vigorous and constructive public participation and support.

By contrast, the development of the *H*-bomb and of MIRVs greatly increased the devastating potential and the threat posed by our nuclear weapons. As such, they may be considered failures of our nuclear-weapons policy. Although there may have been no feasible alternative to developing the *H*-bomb, we didn't try to head it off. I find it significant that these technical escalations were undertaken without public involvement or debate, and also without a serious effort at negotiating them away. Another serious setback, after years of negotiating, was the Senate's failure to ratify the SALT II treaty because of a similar lack of an involved public constituency.

On March 23, 1983, President Reagan described to the nation his vision of the future in which we are protected against nuclear weapons by a space-age defense, popularly labelled "Star Wars," and no longer have to live in a balance of terror. We are, therefore, encountering once again major decisions that will determine the course of our nuclear-weapons policy until the end of the century and beyond. These decisions present challenges and opportunities to our citizens, scientists, and government.

The good news is that this issue is itself not shrouded in secrecy or ignored in the shadows of apathy—to the contrary. In the press, in the churches, in civic organizations, in universities, and in the political arena, a process of education about deterrence has begun in earnest, and nuclear weapons policy is commanding priority attention at this time. There now exists an active and concerned arms-control constituency ready to participate in a national debate that we all should welcome—scientists, government, and citizens alike. As a result of this public-inspired debate, Star Wars is still undergoing tough, critical scrutiny, including in particular its technical prospects and its impact on arms-control progress. And certainly the president, when he gave his speech in 1983, did not expect to find himself in 1987 with only half the money he wanted to get.

The public arms-control constituency created during the past few years must continue to grow and prove that it is enduring, informed, constructive, and energetic and that it has a broad political base.

To endure, it must have a clear and understandable goal. This means going beyond a freeze, which was an important goal in building a constituency but was inadequate to sustain it.

The public must also be informed. It must have a realistic sense that there are no easy, absolute solutions—not in the short term. We must keep working at the issue to make it become part of the public agenda through public education, public outreach, and meetings with our elected officials. We can make sure that public officials know that this is one of the issues on which they are going to be elected or not elected.

It is effective to choose a few issues and to be very well informed about them, so that one does not get caught out or discredited as a result of using shallow overgeneralizations, and then to hold to those positions like a bulldog. And one should avoid spending all of one's time in talking with like-minded friends. It is important to spend time reasoning with those who hold opposing views.

The public constituency must also be constructive. The attitude must be one that takes other people's arguments seriously, recognizes that opponents feel deeply about what they believe, and engages in civilized, constructive debate.

The public arms-control constituency must be energetic. Every citizen has his or her talents. Consequently, different people are going to be effective in different ways: in the electoral process, through public outreach, or through active research on the issues.

Finally, it is important to seek a broad political base—that is, not simply from the left or the right. Support will be required from a broad spectrum of the public.

Public involvement in arms-control issues is not only useful, it is essential. We have had no progress without it. Stimulated by the involvement of the public, we negotiated and ratified SALT I. Without it, we ended up with MIRVs and failed to ratify SALT II.

The Moral Issue and
Deterrence

The unprecedented scale of destruction and devastation of which nuclear weapons are capable presents us with fundamental issues—moral as well as practical.

As a scientist, it is natural for me to approach the issues of war and peace with a technical orientation. That is my strength and experience as I work to understand the physical realities of nuclear weapons and I study how these physical realities impose limitations on the available alternatives for national policy. These are important issues. But I am also a human being, and I understand that the challenge of nuclear weapons is ultimately a moral challenge, for these are weapons of mass destruction.

Today we recognize that the vast arsenals of these weapons of mass destruction that we have already accumulated could shatter the civilization created by human genius and inspiration over our entire recorded history of some thirty centuries. What right has man to cause—or even threaten—such a devastating insult to the Earth, the ecosphere, the very condition of human existence? If modern civilization is to improve its chances for avoiding nuclear holocaust in the long run, I believe it is absolutely necessary to return the nuclear debate to such fundamental issues.

In addition to the moral issue, we face a practical issue resulting from the enormity of the devastating potential of nuclear weapons. Simply, it is a fact that any nation initiating a nuclear war may be, literally, committing suicide. This fact is based on a technical reality that is almost universally recognized: There is no effective defense against nuclear retaliation. There is no technology known today, or on the technological horizon reaching into the future to the end of this century, that is capable of repelling an attack against our nation by thousands of nuclear warheads in their intercontinental missile paths that span distances of 6000 miles in less than a 30-minute flight time.

This physical reality was recognized in 1972 when we and the Soviet Union agreed to sign the SALT I treaty, which severely limits the deployment of antiballistic missile defenses, or ABM systems. That treaty is of unlimited duration and is in force today. During the past decade since that treaty went into effect, there have been technical advances: advances in radar, missile, and computer technologies for both offensive and defensive systems. However, on technical grounds, I still see no prospect whatsoever of deploying—on the ground or in space, with missiles or with lasers—an effective defense of the nation's people and cities.

On March 23, 1983, President Reagan called for a defensive umbrella over the United States against nuclear attack. The President's plans and his goals notwithstanding, there remains a physical reality of nature: Owing to the very great destructive power of nuclear weapons, the offense has—and can maintain—a predominance over the defense. The situation differs greatly from World War II, when the Royal Air Force won the Battle of Britain by destroying one in ten German planes per attack. The German air force could not endure such losses, and, even though nine out of ten planes got through the defenses, London survived its extinguishable fires. Contrast this with the nuclear era today. No matter how effective the defense, if it is less than perfect, it fails, for it takes but one medium-size bomb on target to extinguish Seattle. If only one out of twenty—or 5 percent—of the Soviet missiles were to arrive at American cities, our *immediate* casualties would very likely number in the many tens of millions, or more, and our industry and our major cities would be reduced to radioactive rubble.

I also cannot conceive of a civil-defense system that could protect our society—or the Soviet society—from the unprecedented disaster and devastation of a nuclear war.

The basic technical realities of nuclear weapons as I have described them present a stark picture for us all to recognize. Defenseless against these nuclear weapons of mass destruction, we live in a balance of terror as mutual hostages in today's world. This is a situation unprecedented in history. In the past, tribes, nations, and alliances have organized to protect their vital interests—their people, their cities and industry, their trade. They have done this by preparing to destroy an opponent's military forces in combat. This is no longer possible. There will, indeed, be no winners in a nuclear war. Therefore, the sole purpose of nuclear weapons is, and must remain for as long as they are deployed, to deter nuclear war.

Deterrence is the key concept of the nuclear age. It requires of us a new common sense. Although it has stood the test of time for more than two decades since both powers have had the ability to destroy each other, it is under siege from a chorus of critics with many voices. A clear understanding of what deterrence means must underpin any discussion or explanation of nuclear policy and weapons. Deterrence has three essential ingredients: one is a state of mind expressing a national will. A second is the military capability to retaliate with assured destruction. A policy of deterrence must make clear to anyone who contemplates starting a nuclear war against the United States and its allies that he would be putting his own society—his people, his cities, and his industry—at risk for an intolerable level of devastation. Rational behavior by governments and their leaders is the third essential ingredient of deterrence. Once they recognize the risks of starting a nuclear war, they must act accordingly and thus be deterred. Except for the fact that it has worked for the past two decades, there isn't very much that is attractive about nuclear deterrence. It is of questionable morality, of unquestioned danger, and—as a child of the nuclear revolution—devoid of historical pedigree. Despite these blemishes, it is the only game in town, and this fact must be understood.

Some critics challenge deterrence as immoral for threatening hundreds of millions of helpless citizens with annihilation, and they criticize it as based on a logical paradox for making threats that would be suicidal to implement. Such criticism is pretty strong and on target. Nevertheless, unless—or until—the human species makes that next great evolutionary advance by learning to resolve its differences peacefully and, as a result, removes the scourge of weapons and war from the face of this planet, I see—on technical grounds alone—no escape from the mutual hostage relationship and no choice but to make deterrence work. This is our immediate task in the decade ahead.

The pastoral letter "The Challenge of Peace," which was adopted on May 3, 1983, by the National Conference of Catholic Bishops on War and Peace, is a remarkable document—powerful as well as important—that probes the moral dilemma of deterrence. It asks important questions; it analyzes them skillfully; it is written clearly. And, I would add, it comes to the correct conclusions. After grappling with the basic issue of the immorality of threatening massive slaughter of the innocents, it arrives at the judgment that "deterrence cannot be accepted as 'an end in itself' " but points out that, since it offers the best promise of avoiding nuclear war, "deterrence may still be judged as morally acceptable provided it is used as a step toward progressive disarmament." To me, this is precisely the new common sense of nuclear weapons expressed simply and clearly.* There is no Pentagonese in these words.

Other critics challenge deterrence as a policy that violates the old common sense—the traditional wisdom—that nations must have military forces capable of attacking and destroying an aggressor's military strength, thereby reducing the damage they themselves will suffer if attacked. In today's jargon, this military capability is known as "counterforce." This requirement for counterforce is above and beyond what is often referred to as "flexible response." Flexible response means the ability to respond in measure with the provocation, and it is a reality of today's nuclear forces; they can be launched selectively or massively against an extensive repertoire of targets. But counterforce weapons, if deployed in large numbers, directly threaten to destroy significant parts of an opponent's retaliatory forces. This threat to his deterrent raises a major problem. On one hand, it is infeasible, on technical grounds alone, to disarm an opponent. On the other hand, as each country faces a growing counterforce threat to its retaliatory forces, it will simply build more—and we'll witness an open-ended arms race. A clear choice must be made: either to expand threats to one another's retaliatory forces or to give emphasis to maintaining the security of these forces.

Advocates of counterforce have recently been advertising their policy as meriting a seal of superior morality by emphasizing that it targets limited or controlled strikes against military and counterforce targets as opposed to an attack in full force against cities and hundreds of millions of people. Given the nuclear realities, how realistic, in fact, are such speculations and planning for "limited" fighting of nuclear wars? How would, or could, the conflict be managed—and terminated—without escalation to all-out destruction?

---

*The words quoted above are taken from the Second Draft of the pastoral letter. The third (and final) draft, as adopted overwhelmingly by the bishops' conference, quotes Pope John Paul II's judgment that "deterrence may still be judged morally acceptable, 'certainly not as an end in itself but as a step on the way toward progressive disarmament.' " The draft adds further: "Progress toward a world free of dependence on deterrence must be carefully carried out. But it must not be delayed."

Neither past experience nor war-gaming gives cause for much hope that the nuclear exchange and resulting devastation would remain limited and aimed exclusively at military targets. There is a great danger that, once the vital interests of the United States and the Soviet Union are engaged to the point that either initiates a nuclear attack, both countries will dig ever deeper into their vast arsenals of more than 50,000 nuclear weapons. In addition, there is no *technical* basis for any confidence that it will be possible to control the escalation of a limited nuclear conflict. Once the nuclear threshold is crossed, there will inevitably be a broad delegation of authority down the line for nuclear release. This is required by the very short missile flight times and by the potential vulnerabilities of any conceivable worldwide command, control, and communication system from a national command center to the broadly dispersed military units with thousands of nuclear weapons.

We are all familiar with the theoreticians and strategists heavily armed with computer printouts describing scenarios of limited nuclear conflicts with low casualties followed by rapid recovery. Given the lack of relevant data for input, it is amazing how many analyses of this kind one sees and how greatly exaggerated are the claims that are based on them.

Our extensive history of real wars—the nonnuclear conflicts of the past—has taught us to appreciate how vitally sensitive the course of events is to such factors as surprise, determination, luck, and individual acts of bravery and leadership. Perhaps that is why there are so few detailed calculations and claims for such conflicts. The data available from real wars—the nonnuclear conflicts we know only too well—have generated a healthy measure of humility, and they call to mind a remark by Rebecca West: "Before a war, military science seems like a real science, like astronomy; but after a war, it seems more like astrology."

When you hear claims made by individuals on the basis of their studies and calculations—but almost no data—as to how much civil defense will contribute to our survival, and thereby to an ultimate victory in a nuclear war, keep in mind how rapidly individual units of society descend to chaos and fall apart at much lower levels of stress—remember what happens during sudden blackouts. It makes you wonder how societies will react after just one thermonuclear weapon has hit, much less a hundred or several thousand.

On this score of limited nuclear war, I more highly value the experience and wisdom of General David C. Jones, former chairman of the

Newspeak and Nukespeak

The images that George Orwell's *Nineteen Eighty-Four* commonly brings to mind are "Big Brother," "doublethink," thought control, "Victory gin," and "two plus two equals five." I recalled them all upon rereading *Nineteen Eighty-Four*, but my great surprise was the essential accuracy of Orwell's predictions about nuclear weapons and nuclear conflict. I found it remarkable that Orwell wrote his scenario just three years after Hiroshima, in the dawn of the nuclear age. There were then none of the intercontinental missiles that today are poised many thousands of miles, but less than 30-minutes' flight time, away from our homeland, their thousands of nuclear warheads threatening total devastation. There were no hydrogen, or fusion, bombs—for which the primitive atom, or fission, bombs of the type that obliterated Hiroshima and Nagasaki are mere triggers. Nevertheless, although he was incorrect in many details, Orwell's prophecy—or was it a warning?—accurately foresaw the basic elements of the world's present nuclear stalemate.

We learn of the nuclear politics of Orwell's world along with Winston Smith as he surreptitiously reads Chapter 3, "War Is Peace," of the banned book *The Theory and Practice of Oligarchical Collectivism* by that shadowy and subversive object of Hate Week, Emmanuel Goldstein:

> What is more remarkable is that all three powers already possess, in the atomic bomb, a weapon far more powerful than any that their present researches are likely to discover. Although the Party, according to its habit, claims the invention for itself, atomic bombs first appeared as early as the

Nineteen-forties, and were first used on a large scale about
ten years later. At that time some hundreds of bombs were
dropped on industrial centers, chiefly in European Russia,
Western Europe, and North America. The effect was to convince the ruling groups of all countries that a few more
atomic bombs would mean the end of organized society, and
hence of their own power. Thereafter, although no formal
agreement was ever made or hinted at, no more bombs were
dropped. All three powers merely continue to produce
atomic bombs and store them up against the decisive opportunity which they all believe will come sooner or later. . . .
None of the three superstates ever attempts any maneuver
which involves the risk of serious defeat.

Orwell erred in not foreseeing the great jump in destructive energy,
by factors of 100 to 1000, that came with the development of hydrogen
bombs. He also erred in anticipating that a major war would be waged
between industrial powers in the middle of the 1950s, with atomic
weapons dropping on their cities, and that "the ravages of the atomic
war of the Nineteen-fifties have never been fully repaired." But Orwell
is right on target in prophesying—or warning—that atomic war would
become an incalcuable risk that "would mean the end of organized
society"; or, as he also remarked, "no decisive victory is possible."
That is an accurate description of our world today—our real-life 1984.
We label the nuclear stand-off anticipated by Orwell as nuclear deterrence. We recognize that any nation initiating a nuclear war may be
literally committing suicide. The fact that U.S. and Soviet citizens are
mutual hostages in a world heavily armed with nuclear weapons is a
physical reality, whether we like it or not. There is simply no technology that can defend our society against nuclear annihilation. Today's
nuclear stand-off has no precedent in history; it is a consequence of the
enormously destructive power of nuclear warheads. Furthermore, the
stand-off grows increasingly perilous as more and more countries develop the capability to build nuclear bombs.

Many find our present policy of deterrence morally repugnant,
based as it is on the threat to annihilate hundreds of millions of innocent people in retaliation against nuclear aggression. Many more are
confused by the logic of building and threatening to use weapons of
suicide. However, it is generally recognized that, short of doing away
with all or almost all of our present nuclear arsenals, we have no better
alternative to deterrence. Our task is to make deterrence work and to

avoid nuclear war, as Orwell's three great powers in *Nineteen Eighty-Four* managed to do by common consent.

The limited military utility of nuclear weapons has been recognized by our most senior, thoughtful, and battle-tested military leaders from the time of the first hydrogen bombs. As long ago as 1956, President Eisenhower took a leaf from *Nineteen Eighty-Four*, when he recognized that there would be no winners in a nuclear war, and wrote, "We are rapidly getting to the point that no war can be won." Maintaining that with nuclear weapons war would be no longer a battle to exhaustion and surrender, Eisenhower noted that the outlook had now come close to "destruction of the enemy and suicide."

The military uselessness of nuclear weapons was expressed directly, convincingly, and simply by Lord Louis Mountbatten in his last writings before his tragic assassination in 1979:

> As a military man who has given half a century of active service I say in all sincerity that the nuclear arms race has no military purpose. Wars cannot be fought with nuclear weapons. Their existence only adds to our perils because of the illusions which they have generated.

In summary, our predicament today is not all that different from that foreseen by Orwell. He foresaw no more nuclear wars in *Nineteen Eighty-Four*—not even limited ones that are occasionally described to us today as survivable and winnable. Orwell suffered no such illusions. His continual state of war was waged with conventional weapons only. Our own pattern of conventional strife differs from the scenario painted by Orwell. He wrote of intermittent bombs dropping on major industrial cities causing but few casualties, together with combat on peripheral battlefields that "involves very small numbers of people, mostly highly trained specialists, and causes comparatively few casualties." In our combat, the bombs have not rained on our cities; they have been confined to the battle areas, where they have wrought vast civilian death and destruction. But as to the nuclear dimension, and war on the scale of megadeaths and megatons, a nuclear stalemate has lasted for thirty-eight years, and Orwell's prophecy—or warning—has come true.

In *Nineteen Eighty-Four*, Big Brother found it useful and convenient to falsify history in order to maintain the position of the Party. Our challenge in today's heavily armed nuclear world is quite different: It is to understand that we have lost history. History is no longer valid as a guide in matters of nuclear weapons and war. Security can no longer be found either in greater strength or in defense, as it could before nuclear weapons. Nuclear war can no longer be regarded as "a continuation of state policy with other means," in Karl von Clausewitz's frequently cited words.

Since we have lost history, we must give many words new meanings and change maxims derived from historical experience. Big Brother did this in *Nineteen Eighty-Four* as a cynical manipulation to consolidate power—writing in his Newspeak such famous slogans as "War is Peace," "Freedom is Slavery," and "Ignorance is Strength." At times it seems that we today have our own version of Newspeak (or Nukespeak), such as "New nuclear weapons are bargaining chips," "A new missile [MX, SS-24, or many others] is arms control," and "We must build up in order to build down."

Nuclear weapons have also caused other basic changes in the meanings of words. These changes seem just as contradictory as the famous three maxims of Big Brother, but they are, in fact, central to our security. The lesson we learned in prenuclear times was that we must arm to defend our vital interests and to enhance our security. Today, however, we are, as President Eisenhower emphasized, dealing with weapons of suicide, weapons against which there is no defense. The old common sense based on history must, therefore, be replaced with a new common sense that recognizes as fact, rather than as a cynical manipulation of words, that we do *not* improve our security as we further increase the destructive power of our nuclear arsenals. On the contrary, as new weapons threaten deterrence, our security decreases; and, in this sense, we must understand that "more weapons mean less security." In addition, we have come to understand that "defense is provocative," a maxim that is at once the most challenging to our credulity, the most contentious to many, yet the most helpful for explaining the concept of deterrence.

The idea that defense is provocative is expressed in the preamble to the first formal strategic arms limitation treaty (SALT I), signed by the United States and the Soviet Union, which limits the deployment of defenses against ballistic missiles (that is, of antiballistic missile—ABM—systems). Signed by Richard Nixon and Leonid Brezhnev on May 26, 1972, it is of unlimited duration and is in effect today. In its preamble we find this statement of common purpose:

- Proceeding from the premise that nuclear war would have devastating consequences for all mankind,
- Considering that effective measures to limit anti-ballistic missile systems would be a substantial factor in curbing the race in strategic offensive arms and would lead to a decrease in the risk of outbreak of war involving nuclear weapons,
- Proceeding from the premise that the limitation of anti-ballistic missile systems, as well as certain agreed upon measures with respect to the limitation of strategic offensive arms, would contribute to the creation of more favorable conditions for further negotiations on limiting strategic arms. . . .

This treaty recognizes the technical infeasibility of a nuclear defense of one's nation—the people, the cities, the industry—as well as the fact that a major undertaking to develop and construct such a defense will very likely stimulate further buildup of offensive nuclear weapons. This is precisely what occurred prior to the SALT I treaty limiting the ABM.

During the 1960s, the United States observed initial construction of a rather primitive Soviet ABM system around Moscow, as well as similar activity at Leningrad. In response, we simply multiplied the size of our nuclear force. We did this by putting many warheads on each missile (the MIRVs, or multiple independently targetable reentry vehicles) in order to overpower and defeat whatever limited, partial effectiveness one could conceivably ascribe to the Soviet defenses. Furthermore, we went ahead with the development and deployment of thousands of MIRVs even after SALT I prohibited the deployment of the nationwide ABM defenses that were the original justification for the MIRV program. Predictably, the Soviets followed our course, four to five years later, with bigger, more menacing ICBMs and MIRVs.

The end result of the effort to develop nuclear defenses was simply to provoke a further major buildup in the offensive nuclear forces of both the United States and the Soviet Union. Offenses were enhanced in order to maintain a policy of deterrence based on a sure ability to retaliate effectively against nuclear aggression by an opponent. Defenses were at the same time negotiated away as technically ineffective.

The issue of defense against nuclear attack has been raised once again in 1983, but I believe offense predominates over defense just as strongly now as it did in 1972. This time the proposal is for a space-based "Star Wars" defense with exotic directed-energy weapons, such as high-powered lasers, x-ray lasers driven by nuclear explosions, and particle beams. There have, indeed, been very impressive technological advances in recent years—but I think it is likely that the new systems will remain vulnerable, just as the ABM systems of a decade ago were, to relatively simple and inexpensive countermeasures by the offense.

The fundamental problem with defense in the nuclear age is simply that it must be very close to 100 percent perfect or it fails. The offense has a great advantage simply because nuclear bombs are so enormously destructive. Thus it takes but one medium-sized warhead of the more than 8000 in the current strategic missile and bomber forces of the Soviet Union (the U.S. total exceeds 9000) to obliterate a major metropolitan area the size of San Francisco, causing roughly a million immediate casualties. I know of no current or planned technology that will lead to a defensive system that can operate effectively amidst many nuclear explosions and that can react to technically available countermeasures by the opponent's offensive forces with anything approaching 100 percent success.

Even if a defense were 95 percent perfect—so that only 5 percent, or 400, of the existing Soviet strategic nuclear warheads exploded on the United States, or vice versa—what good would it be? Immediate casualties would still be well above 100 million, and the devastation beyond comprehension! Orwell seems to have implicitly recognized this fact by his neglect of the possibility of defense against atomic attack. His fictional great powers, having learned their lesson from an "actual" atomic war in the 1950s, well understood the unacceptability of nuclear conflict and, by tacit agreement, avoided their use. They practiced nuclear deterrence.

There is, of course, no theorem that says it is impossible for us to do better than deterrence in the future. Perhaps with the help of new technologies—together with progress in arms control and even some evolution in human behavior and political structure—we can change the maxim from "Defense is provocative" to "Nuclear weapons are unnecessary." It is my judgment, however, that we cannot escape the nuclear threat with technology alone. The United States maintains a strong research-and-development effort in many weapons-related areas, including defense, to guard against technological surprise, and this is as it ought to be. Fortunately, our overall scientific effort bears very little resemblance to Orwell's scenario:

> The search for new weapons continues unceasingly, and is
> one of the very few remaining activities in which the inven-

tive or speculative type of mind can find any outlet. In Oceania at the present day, Science, in the old sense, has almost ceased to exist.

That is not to say that there is no cause for concern that so large a fraction of our most advanced technology and our best young university-trained minds are engaged in the military-industrial complex about which President Eisenhower cautioned in 1960. Weapons production and research do constitute a drain on the world's important resources, and we must ask how long it will be healthy or wise to divert those intellectual resources (not to mention the financial resources) from more productive pursuits. This problem is just one more important argument in support of arms control, a subject not even mentioned by Orwell. Beyond reducing the risks of nuclear war, the levels of destructive power in the nuclear arsenals, and the waste of material resources to the arms competition, effective arms control could also help in redirecting our most precious intellectual resources into more creative channels. General Omar Bradley, the great "American GIs' general" of World War II, addressed this very issue in 1957:

> The central problem of our time—as I view it—is how to employ human intelligence for the salvation of mankind. It is a problem we have put upon ourselves. For we have defiled our intellect by the creation of such scientific instruments of destruction that we are now in desperate danger of destroying ourselves. Our plight is critical and with each effort we have made to relieve it by further scientific advance, we have succeeded only in aggravating our peril.
> If I am sometimes discouraged, it is not by the magnitude of the problem, but by our colossal indifference to it. I am unable to understand why . . . we do not make greater, more diligent and more imaginative use of reason and human intelligence in seeking an accord and compromise which will make it possible for mankind to control the atom and banish it as an instrument of war.

With General Bradley, I believe that we must look to arms control if we are to work our way out from under the nuclear threat. Technology can contribute, but to imply that technology alone can lead the way, under the banner of "Star Wars" or by another name, is to retreat from physical realities. If we are to make serious progress, our record at arms control during the decade ahead will have to be better than it has been in the decade just ended—which saw a *tripling* of the number of nuclear warheads on the intercontinental missiles and bombers of the United States and the Soviet Union despite all our negotiating efforts to reduce precisely these forces. Our record pretty much matches Orwell's account: "All three powers merely continue to produce atomic bombs and store them up against the decisive opportunity which they all believe will come sooner or later."

Although our nuclear arsenals are still growing, it is by no means a commonly held view today that a "decisive opportunity" for a nuclear war threatens us in the future. In Orwell's world of escalating nuclear forces, there were no formal agreements or arms negotiations, and it is very sobering to think that we have managed to show little, if any, advantage relative to Orwell's *Nineteen Eighty-Four* in spite of years of intense arms-control negotiations with the Soviet Union and national effort at the highest levels of government.

For the present, our major challenge is to make deterrence work and to avoid a nuclear holocaust. Should we fail, Orwell's most famous maxim, "War is Peace," will come true—in the literal sense first introduced nineteen centuries ago by Tacitus. Writing about the campaigns in Britain of the great Roman leader Agricola, Tacitus tells of how Calgacus, the leader of the beleaguered defenders, tried to rally his troops by describing the devastation caused by the Roman legions with the words "Ubi solitudinem faciunt, pacem appelant" ("They create a desolation and call it a peace").

The basic theme of *Nineteen Eighty-Four* is the perpetuation of power by a clique—the Party and Big Brother—by whatever means available. It is a tale of cynical use and abuse of power in which nuclear weapons are almost incidental. Having learned from their atomic devastation in the 1950s, Orwell's major powers simply withhold nuclear weapons from the wars they continuously wage with one another. There can be no independent voice or expression of concern among the people of Oceania about the moral issues raised by the possible or threatened use of nuclear weapons of mass destruction. Big Brother would of course not allow it.

Fortunately, that is not our circumstance. Indeed, as we enter our 1984, the moral issues are being discussed with increasing emphasis, and the moral power of people concerned about the nuclear danger is gaining importance as a factor to be reckoned with in the formulation of policy. In the West, this development has been accompanied by the growth of a public constituency for arms control. In part, this growth has been spurred by the collapse of formal arms-control negotiations between 1979 and 1982, which awakened many to the fact that it was unwise to abandon such a vitally important (if also complex) issue to the attention of professionals. In part, this awareness was triggered by disturbing rhetoric about "winnable" and "survivable" nuclear wars. In part, it stemmed from growing concern with the seemingly incessant deployments of new generations of nuclear missiles.

We now have, for the first time, a major arms-control constituency in the West (if it exists in the East, it is necessarily stealthy), impatient for progress and demanding persuasive evidence of a strong commitment to nuclear arms control by our leaders. How enduring, how politically effective, how constructive this public movement will eventually prove is a subject for speculation, but it offers the prospect of one of the most significant differences between our 1984 and that of Orwell in the realm of weapons and arms control.

Our 1984 comes 36 years after Orwell wrote his classic. Let us look ahead another 36 years to 2020. What is our 2020 vision without the benefit of hindsight?

I think that what 2020 will be like depends on the further development of the two factors I have been discussing: the moral pressure of a concerned citizenry and the impact of new technologies on deterrence. If the newly created public arms-control constituency continues to grow and if it restores the moral dimension to the formulation of nuclear policy, there is good cause for optimism.

As new technologies are developed, however, and as new weapons are designed and tested, the policy of deterrence will come increasingly under attack, particularly from the would-be fighters of nuclear wars, with their talk of limited and winnable nuclear wars. If we go to space with Star Wars, will we accomplish anything beyond the addition of yet another dimension to the arms competition as the race between technological countermeasures intensifies? What will this competition do to such existing arms-control achievements as the SALT I treaty limiting ballistic-missile defenses? SALT I stipulates, "Each party undertakes not to develop, test, or deploy ABM systems or components which are sea-based, air-based, space-based, or mobile land-based." Will this, our major arms-control achievement to date, have to be weakened or sacrificed as we pursue a futile technological escape from deterrence?

My vision of 2020 is that of an optimist, based on my hope that the force of reason and arms control will prevail. I also suspect that, after several years of serious effort, we will come to the same conclusion with respect to Star Wars defenses that we did in 1972 with respect to the last generation of defensive technologies; namely, that defense is an impossible challenge and that there is no technical alternative to deterrence. I think there is a finite chance that this time we will have learned a lesson and that, in contrast to the decade following the SALT I treaties, we will make serious progress in reducing nuclear armaments and in stabilizing deterrence at a lower level of weaponry.

The sooner this happens, the better, for time in which the superpowers can make this progress is running out. In nuclear (as well as political) matters, the world of 2020 can be expected to look very different from Orwell's model. We face the almost certain prospect of a world with many nuclear-armed nations in 2020, and, as nuclear weapons proliferate around the world, the dangers to peace and survival will multiply.

Shortly after the first atomic explosion, Albert Einstein warned, "The unleashed power of the atom has changed everything save our modes of thinking; we thus drift toward unparalleled catastrophe." We are still drifting as the tides grow increasingly perilous. The year 2020 will require not just a clear vision but a strong commitment, wisdom, and patience in charting a new course.

STAR WARS
AND SCIENTISTS

Star Wars and Arms Control

I feel a certain sadness to be addressing this annual celebration of science on a topic that is almost totally devoid of any of the hope, the optimism, or the beauty of science. It is that hope, optimism, and beauty that spur us on to probe nature's secrets. Of course, the spur of fame is also present. As Milton wrote in *Lycidas*:

> Fame is the spur that the clear spirit doth raise
> (That last infirmity of noble minds)
> To scorn delights and live laborious days.

But far more important than fame in driving us on in our great voyage of exploration is our consuming passion as scientists to understand nature's secrets and our confidence that there is a simple, elegant, and understandable nature to be discovered. We are fortunate to be participating in one of the greatest adventures of the human mind.

None of this excitement or beauty can be found in the subject of nuclear weapons, Star Wars, and the technology of mass destruction. Nor is the problem we face one amenable exclusively, if at all, to the great power that science brings to bear in the study of nature. Instead, we confront deadly dangers created by man.

And the challenge we face of avoiding a nuclear holocaust is one that pits the forces of nature against man. This is indeed a problem of immense importance. In the powerful words spoken by Andrei Sakharov from his lonely exile in Gorki, it must be given "absolute priority over all other problems of our times." It is our moral obligation to generations yet unborn that we avoid a holocaust that could shatter the whole fabric of our civilization, a holocaust that might even spell the end of the human species as the result of a prolonged nuclear winter.

It is also fitting and proper—and there is an element of justice in it—for us to be considering the nuclear threat at a major scientific congress such as this, because it was science and technology that presented mankind with this challenge to our survival. We scientists do bring important physical insights and understanding that may help in the effort to reduce the danger nuclear weapons pose. Equally important, we can clarify the limits to the promise of technological fixes as potential cures for nuclear dangers.

Shortly after the atom bombs were dropped on Hiroshima and Nagasaki, within days of Japan's capitulation, Robert Oppenheimer addressed this question of the limits of science and technology in his letter transmitting to Secretary of War Henry Stimson a report on the scope and program of future work in the field of atomic energy. Writing for the Scientific Panel of what was known as the "Interim Committee," which he chaired, Oppenheimer said:

> We have been unable to devise or propose effective military countermeasures for atomic weapons. Although we realize that future work may reveal possibilities at present obscure to us, it is our firm opinion that no military countermeasures will be found which will be adequately effective in preventing delivery of atomic weapons.

Oppenheimer and his scientific colleagues immediately grasped how profoundly atomic weapons had transformed the nature of modern warfare. In view of the staggering destructive potential of even those primitive fission bombs, they realized that effective defenses would now have to meet a very much higher standard of performance than at any other time in the history of warfare.

This prospect led Oppenheimer to write, in his letter to Secretary Stimson:

> We believe that the safety of this nation—as opposed to its ability to inflict damage on an enemy power—cannot lie wholly, or even primarily, in its scientific or technical prowess. It can be based only on making future wars impossible. It is our unanimous and urgent recommendation to you that, despite the present incomplete exploitation of technical

possibilities in this field, all steps be taken, all necessary international arrangements be made, to this one end.

A decade later, in the 1950s, the thermonuclear age dawned, in which the fission bombs of Hiroshima and Nagasaki became merely the triggers of weapons of much greater destructiveness. One of America's greatest military leaders of World War II, President Eisenhower, added urgency to Oppenheimer's caution against looking to science and technology for the fix to escape from the nuclear menace. In his 1953 "Atoms for Peace" speech at the United Nations, President Eisenhower warned:

> Let no one think that expenditure of vast sums for systems and weapons of defense can guarantee absolute safety. The awful arithmetic of the atom bomb does not permit any such easy solution. Even against the most powerful defense, an aggressor in possession of the effective minimum number of atomic bombs for a surprise attack could place a sufficient number of his bombs on the chosen targets to cause hideous damage.

As the technology of bombs and missiles pressed forward through the 1960s, these warnings were almost swept aside and forgotten. Defensive shields against ballistic missiles were prophesied and promised as a cure for the cancer of nuclear weapons. But with a necessary dose of critical analysis, both inside and outside of government, ballistic missile defenses were soon recognized to be little more than quack medicine. The technical limitations of defenses against ballistic missiles, and the political problems created by the effort to deploy them, were eventually appreciated after lengthy debate. This led President Nixon to conclude two things:

- First, that the effort to build an effective nationwide ABM defense was futile. In a heavily armed nuclear world, the technical realities precluded the possibility of developing an effective nationwide defense against nuclear weapons, particularly against long-range ballistic missiles.
- Second, the effort to develop such a nationwide ABM shield could be destabilizing. It would accelerate the arms race as both the United States and the Soviet Union developed and deployed not

only competing ABM systems but also offsetting offensive forces to overpower, evade, or attack and disable the opposing ABM system.

Furthermore, each side would fear the purpose or capabilities of the other's defensive system. An ABM that could be effective in blunting a first strike by an enemy could be seen as equally, if not more, effective as an adjunct to our capability to mount a first strike against that enemy, designed to blunt his retaliatory second strike. In a crisis, such fears could bring mounting pressures for striking first and would thus contribute to crisis instability.

It was just such concerns that President Nixon emphasized in March 1969, in explaining his reluctant decision to forgo a broad nationwide defense:

> Although every instinct motivates me to provide the American people with complete protection against a major nuclear attack, it is not now within our power to do so. The heaviest defense system we considered, one designed to protect our major cities, still could not prevent a catastrophic level of U.S. fatalities from a deliberate all-out Soviet attack. And it might look to an opponent like the prelude to offensive strategy threatening the Soviet deterrent.

Despite these earlier conclusions, once again in the 1980s the call has gone out to science and technology to shield us from the threat of nuclear annihilation. In his "Star Wars" speech of March 23, 1983, President Reagan held out hope for a world free of the threat of nuclear retaliation and challenged the nuclear scientists "who gave us nuclear weapons" to "give us the means of rendering these nuclear weapons impotent and obsolete." We were told by the ardent Star Wars supporters, including the President, how much more moral it would be to replace deterrence based on the threat of nuclear retaliation with defense against nuclear annihilation.

But the attractiveness of the President's goal—or vision—must not obscure the physical realities of nuclear weapons. In today's heavily armed nuclear world there are more than 50,000 nuclear bombs, upwards of 20,000 of which are deployed at the ready on bombers and missiles of intercontinental range by the United States and the Soviet Union. Each single one of these is a weapon of mass destruction. What is the prospect of building a totally effective nationwide defense against all of them?

Is the answer in 1985 any different from what it was in 1972, when the United States and the Soviet Union negotiated and ratified the ABM Treaty, severely limiting the deployment of defensive systems? What has changed since then? Do the technical advances of the past 13 years, as prodigious as they have been, offer us new and better choices for dealing with the nuclear threat in 1985?

There have indeed been tremendous advances in recent years in the technology pertinent to this problem that have removed some of the shortcomings of previous defense concepts. These include, in particular:

- sensors for finding, identifying, and following targets;
- the means of producing directed energy beams of high power that travel as accurate bullets at the speed of light; and
- the ability to gather promptly, process rapidly, and transmit reliably enormous quantities of data for the purpose of battle management.

While these developments may represent advances in specific technologies pertinent to strategic defense, the challenge to build an effective *nationwide* defense involves much more than the solution of individual technical problems. Even if the very ambitious and costly research-and-development program recently proposed by the Administration achieves all of its major technical goals, far beyond presently demonstrated technologies, great *operational* difficulties will still remain in deploying a nationwide system.

It is difficult for a responsible scientist to say flatly that a task is impossible to achieve by technical means without being accused of being a "naysayer." Indeed, many instances can be cited in which prominent scientists have concluded that a task is impossible, only to be proved wrong by future discoveries. One should recognize, however, that the deployment of an effective nationwide defense is not a single technical achievement, but the evolution of an extensive and exceedingly complex *system*. It is a system, moreover, that must face countermeasures by an opponent determined to bypass it, overcome it, attack it, and destroy it.

Protection against ballistic missiles requires many links in a defensive chain, all of which are crucial. There must be sensors to provide early warning of an attack. There must be a command structure with the authority to make decisions on committing the defensive forces on exceedingly short notice and then to implement those decisions efficiently. This raises the grave problem of whether this chain of command, from warning to decision, must be totally automated or may contain human links. The defensive system must also have sensors that acquire and track the enemy missiles and warheads and then aim and fire the defensive devices, be they material interceptors, such as chemical rockets or hypervelocity guns, or directed-energy devices. Sensors must also determine which of the attacking missiles and warheads have been destroyed in order to allow military commanders to be successful in fighting secondary or tertiary engagements.

Furthermore, this system must work reliably in a hostile environment against a determined and uncooperative opponent who is dedicated to defeating it. We must be able to have high confidence in the system, although it can never be tested under realistic conditions, such as in an environment disturbed by nuclear explosions.

One cannot compare these awesome requirements with those faced by the Apollo program to put a man on the moon—an analogy that has been drawn to point to other great challenges that have been met by science and technology. Putting a man on the moon was solely a technical challenge. The moon couldn't shoot back, or run away, or dispense moon decoys, or turn off its lights. Even so, recall how many lengthy holds we witnessed during the countdowns for the moon shots—or, for that matter, for the space-shuttle flights. Such holds will not do for a defensive system that has barely seconds to spare and no privilege of saying, "Hold your attack. I'm not ready. Please wait a few minutes—or a few hours!"

In order to surmount these difficulties and attain a highly effective nationwide defense, the Strategic Defense Initiative is proposing to deploy a multilayered system. Up until now, we have thought of defense in terms of intercepting the many attackers—warheads and cruise missiles—as they arrive near their targets. In contrast with previous concepts of terminal defense, the crucial and necessary new characteristic of Star Wars will be the first of its three or four layers of defense that is to be designed to destroy most of the missiles over the enemy's own territory within seconds after they are launched—that is, during their *boost phase*, while their engines are still accelerating them into space. In the language of football, this corresponds to tackling the quarterback before he releases the pass rather than preventing the pass from being completed by covering the receivers.

Suffice it to say that, as interesting or intriguing as the concept of boost-phase interception may be, its prospects, whatever they may be, lie well in the future, orders of magnitude beyond today's technology and sensitive to countermeasures available to the offense. In particular, a boost-phase defense must complete its mission in seconds. At most, a few minutes are available to engage today's missiles during their boost phase, but the technology to shorten the total burn time to less than one minute already exists. This means that the interceptors will have to be predeployed in space—or they will have to get there very, very quickly.

If they are predeployed in space, their numbers must necessarily be very large, since only a small fraction of them will be within range of Soviet launch areas at any one time. And they themselves will be more vulnerable than the missiles that are their targets, as they move in predictable orbits like ducks in a shooting gallery.

These disadvantages of space basing have suggested that we look at the possibility of basing the interceptors on the ground, poised to pop up into space upon notification of an enemy launch. The only practical device that is compact and light enough for that is the x-ray laser pumped by a nuclear explosive. There is no law of physics that says this cannot be done, but, at present, our physical understanding of the potential of such devices is much too primitive to allow us to draw any conclusions about their practicality.

Moreover, we should remember that the laws of physics are not secret. They cannot be classified, and the possibilities of such lasers are well recognized by Soviet scientists. They have discussed these concepts in their literature, just as American scientists have in ours. As we well know from experience, they will build such devices if we do, probably not very long after we start, and surely long before we have a fully operational system of our own.

Will we have gained anything by this effort? Almost certainly not, since, by virtue of his x-ray lasers, the attacker will have tactical advantages over the defender. He shoots first, determining where the battle starts. Moreover, he can launch his own x-ray lasers against the defenders, and his lasers will be better shielded against the defender's owing to atmospheric absorption of x-rays.

It is ironic, but not surprising, that this widely heralded technology, which first triggered so much interest in Star Wars, is now being de-emphasized by the Administration's stated goal of developing a nonnuclear defensive system. In fact, its most practical application could well be as an antisatellite weapon against an opponent's Star Wars defenses, should we go ahead. Other schemes for accomplishing boost-phase interception have been proposed, but all share one or both of the difficulties of having vulnerable components—namely, large orbiting mirrors or particle accelerators—based in space or having very little, if any, time for accomplishing their interception.

In the face of such severe difficulties with the multilayered defense, I see no prospect of building an effective nationwide defense now or of achieving one in the foreseeable future, *unless the offensive threat is first tightly constrained technically and greatly reduced numerically as a result of major progress in arms control.*

Although one occasionally hears excessive claims to the contrary, I know of no informed analysts who differ from the conclusion that we must have constraints on the offensive nuclear forces, if defensive deployments can hope to be effective. I agree with Dr. Richard DeLauer, undersecretary of defense for research and engineering during the first Reagan administration, who said, "With unconstrained proliferation, no defensive system will work." It follows that we *must* achieve some success in the arms-control negotiations before any defensive system can become workable.

The challenge of Star Wars, then, is not only a technical one, nor even an awesome operational one, as I have discussed. It is also, perhaps foremost, a *political* challenge to succeed in limiting offensive forces while simultaneously developing defenses to stop them. But, is this possible or likely? Will the United States or the Soviet Union be willing to do this in a Star Wars environment? Would we be willing to accept limits or to consider reductions in the U.S. retaliatory capability, if we face the growing Soviet deployment of missile defenses that is sure to follow our own program? On the contrary, we can expect a buildup of offensive weapons on each side as a counter to the other nations' Star Wars efforts, much as the United States undertook a major buildup of our offensive forces in response to the initial limited deployment of Soviet antiballistic missile systems in the 1960s. We developed and deployed MIRVs, missiles with multiple, precisely aimed warheads, to overcome Soviet defenses.

The United States also reacted in a similar manner to the very expensive and extensive nationwide Soviet air-defense system, which now consists of more than 10,000 interceptors and thousands of radars. In response, we neither reduced nor abandoned our strategic bombers. Rather, we strengthened them. The United States has stayed well ahead of Soviet defenses by cost-effective and survivable countermeasures, especially the air-launched cruise missiles, which are soon to number several thousand, and looking to the future with "stealth" technology. With both their missile and air-defense efforts, the Soviets have merely succeeded in increasing the U.S. offensive threat. Why should we expect the USSR to react to our defensive programs any differently than we have reacted to theirs?

Facing the prospect of having to penetrate a defensive system, won't the Soviets, for instance, be reluctant to reduce the very large throw weight of their ICBMs? That throw-weight will be of even greater value to them against a missile defense, since they can add many more warheads and "penetration aids" to their present missile force without any construction of new missiles.

Enough said about the difficulties of Star Wars. There is no technological quick fix to remove us from nuclear danger. Former Secretary of Defense James Schlesinger summarized the realities very clearly and very strongly in a speech this past winter:

> There is no serious likelihood of removing the nuclear threat from our cities in our lifetime—or in the lifetime of our children. If those cities are going to be protected, they will be protected whether through effective deterrence or through the forbearance of those on the other side. And it is for that reason that cries of the immorality of deterrence are both premature and pernicious.

I concur. Evidently the administration now does also, because the Strategic Defense Initiative is described today, in 1985, solely as a research program to develop the means to strengthen deterrence, not to replace it. In its 1985 report to the Congress issued this spring, the Pentagon Strategic Defense Initiative office wrote: "In pursuing strategic defenses, the U.S. goal has never been to eventually give up the policy of deterrence. With defenses, the U.S. seeks not to replace deterrence, but to enhance it."

With this clarification, the argument for strategic defense has undergone a profound and dramatic change since the original proposal by the president and his most senior aides. I also hope we have come to the end of a period of excessively loose rhetoric about what such a system could do, invoking magic in a fashion reminiscent of the claim by Glendower, in Shakespeare's *Henry IV, Part I*, "I can call spirits from the vasty deep," to which Hotspur responds, "Why, so can I, or so can any man; but will they come when you do call for them?"

The prospect that imprudent pursuit of strategic defense will spur the offensive arms competition, and thus undercut both the effectiveness of the defense itself and the stability of the nuclear balance, raises the important practical question of what we should now be doing in strategic defense and arms control to improve deterrence and to reduce the risk of nuclear war. More specifically, what actions should the United States be taking now and during the coming decade to enhance our security and to reinforce stability, given the current state of U.S.–Soviet competition and the current state of their nuclear arsenals, and the trends that are likely to effect them? I recommend the following six actions that would meet our national-security needs, including improving our prospects for success in arms negotiations.

1.   Reaffirm our commitment to the ABM Treaty of 1972 and agree to continue to join the Soviet Union in not undercutting existing treaty commitments, including SALT II. Meanwhile, work jointly with the Soviets through the Standing Consultative Commission to resolve compliance disputes that have arisen with regard to both agreements. The ABM Treaty defines the common premises of the U.S.–Soviet effort to avoid nuclear war and to achieve arms reductions. It is a recognition of the reality that nations and people can be protected from the catastrophic effects of a nuclear war only by avoiding or actively preventing one from occurring and not by defending against missile attack. In this context, the Treaty has continuing value for structuring U.S. and Soviet offensive forces on a stable deterrence basis.

We are also at a point of decision with regard to the future of the SALT II Treaty, which the United States chose not to ratify in 1979, as well as for expanding the competition in weapons in space. When the newest U.S. Trident submarine, the USS *Alaska*, puts out for its sea trials this fall, we will have to deactivate a Poseidon submarine with its 16 missiles, or a comparable number of MIRVed Minuteman III missiles, to stay under the SALT II subceiling of 1200 MIRVed ballistic missiles. The moment of truth is imminently upon us for the decision of whether or not to comply. Likewise, Soviet compliance is at issue as they move ahead with tests of *two* new ICBMs, even though SALT II sets a limit of *one* new type of ICBM.

Thus, the issue of both sides' promises not to undercut existing arms agreements is already confronting us. Last year [1984], the U.S. Senate adopted, by a vote of 82 to 17, a resolution urging the president to maintain a no-undercut policy on a mutual basis, at least until the end of 1985. This resolution was included in the Defense Authorization Act signed by the president. A similar resolution now sits before the Senate, cosponsored by Senators Bumpers, Chafee, Heinz, and Leahy, calling on President Reagan to continue the no-undercut policy on a mutual basis through the end of 1986.

The United States must also decide this year whether to preserve the principle of no weapons in space through a ban—or continued moratorium—on antisatellite weapons. Continued development of the SDI systems will clearly preclude any possibility of avoiding the further development of space weapons.

2. Organize and support a prudent, deliberate, and high-quality research program on defensive technology, within ABM Treaty limits. The availability of such technology, together with the real possibility of American countermeasures, can contribute to discouraging the Soviets from deploying defensive systems in violation of the Treaty, minimizing the adverse effects of such a potential Soviet "breakout," if it should occur, and protecting us against technological surprises by the USSR. We had such a program before the president's Star Wars speech first raised the prospect of transforming it from a hedge against future developments into one preparing for breakout from the ABM Treaty.

3. Avoid large-scale technology demonstrations. It is now far too early for any program in strategic defense to consider technology demonstrations of types that could raise serious issues of compliance with the ABM Treaty. This was the explicit conclusion of a recent workshop* at the Stanford Center for International Security and Arms Control, as endorsed by signatories that include supporters, as well as opponents, of the Strategic Defense Initiative.

Such demonstrations would be politically mischievous with regard to ABM Treaty compliance. They are also technologically unwarranted—the technology has very, very far to go before it can meet minimum systems criteria—and very likely will lead to cost overruns and to an emphasis on engineering design that would be far from optimal.

4. Form a strong "red team"—that is, a team of devil's advocates to continually challenge the defense program concepts against potential Soviet countermeasures. Any deployed defensive system will have to be effective against a determined opponent who can resort to a wide variety of countermeasures to defeat, deny, evade, destroy, or other-

---

*"Strategic Missile Defense: Necessities, Prospects and Dangers in the Near Term" (Sidney D. Drell and Thomas Johnson, co-Chairmen; John A. Ernest, Philip A. Farley, John S. Foster, Jr., Richard L. Garwin, Sidney N. Graybeal, John W. Lewis, Wolfgang K. H. Panofsky, Theodore A. Postol, Condoleezza Rice, Malvin A. Ruderman, and George C. Smith) April 1985

wise overpower the system. It will also have to be cost-effective in defeating the offense. The importance of these two demanding criteria were emphasized by Ambassador Paul Nitze in his address to the World Affairs Council in Philadelphia on February 20, 1985, in which he said:

> The technologies must produce defensive systems that are survivable; if not, the defenses would themselves be tempting targets for a first strike. This would decrease, rather than enhance, stability.
>
> New defensive systems must also be cost-effective at the margin; that is, they must be cheap enough to add additional defensive capability so that the other side has no incentive to add additional offensive capability to overcome the defense. If this criterion is not met, the defensive systems could encourage a proliferation of countermeasures and additional offensive weapons to overcome deployed defenses, instead of a redirection of effort from offense to defense.

If we go ahead with development and deployment of a Star Wars defense that fails to satisfy these two requirements, we will be guilty not only of folly but of a dangerous folly. Wasting money is bad enough; wasting human talent and technological muscle is worse. But decreasing stability and intensifying the arms build-up should be totally unthinkable. In view of the nature and importance of its task, the "red team" should have a charter independent of the management of the defensive weapons research-and-development effort.

 5. *Enact legislation in Congress with the explicit provision that the research-and-technology program must proceed by means that are fully consistent with the ABM Treaty.* An appropriation of roughly $2 billion per year—up from the current level of $1.4 billion this year [1985], but well below the $3.7 billion requested by the administration for next year—is fully adequate for a strong program that makes appropriate choices among priorities in developing new technologies. In addition to avoiding the unwise and expensive large-scale technology demonstrations, the Stanford Workshop report I mentioned earlier makes the following recommendations for the SDI program:

 a) Improve the quality and survivability of sensors for early warning and surveillance. This should proceed regardless of R&D on strategic defenses.

 b) Conduct a strong research program to try to solve the problem of midcourse discrimination. This problem of distinguishing warheads from decoys and sensor and background noise has plagued defense concepts since the 1950s. We know of several reasonable means for destroying warheads, but no one has yet solved the problem of identifying them uniquely.

c) Eliminate infrared chemical lasers from consideration as weapons for ballistic missile defense.

d) Conduct a robust treaty-consistent research program directed toward understanding what performance levels are actually achievable with x-ray lasers pumped by nuclear explosions. There is no valid reason to impose a nonnuclear political bias on a treaty-consistent research program into defensive technologies.

6. *Form a senior-level, independent oversight panel that would examine the work on defensive R&D and report at the highest levels of government, to the Congress as well as to the Administration.* This panel of experts and former public officials in defense and arms control should maintain a sufficiently detailed knowledge of the technical and programmatic status of the work to advise the government on the setting of priorities. It should also conduct periodic program reviews to ensure that the work remains in close harmony with our overall military, security, and arms control goals and our strategic policy.

I emphasize the importance of Congress acting soon on this last recommendation to create an oversight panel. The Administration and the Pentagon SDI office have stated their intentions to conduct the R&D on defensive weapons "in a manner fully consistent with all U.S. Treaty obligations." However, the 1985 Report on SDI submitted to Congress in April 1985 has the strong flavor of what SALT I negotiator Ambassador Gerard Smith has called "an anticipatory breach of contract."

The 1985 Report documents an attempt to exploit every verbal ambiguity in the 1972 Treaty to pursue the new technologies. For example, Article V of the Treaty forbids development, testing, or deployment of "ABM systems or components" which are space-based or air-based. In the 1972 ratification hearings before the Senate Armed Services Committee, Ambassador Smith defined the prohibitions on development as starting when "field testing is initiated on either a prototype or [a] breadboard model." At issue is how far one can go in disaggregating components into subcomponents in order to claim compliance. Is it acceptable for an airborne or space-based sensor to be tested against a warhead, so long as it lacks a direct communication link to the ground? Is it legal for an airborne or spaceborne missile interceptor to be tested against a satellite, just not against an ICBM warhead? Or may it be tested against a warhead, so long as it doesn't carry its own target-tracking system?

The answers to these and many other similar questions will soon be required. Congress must make certain that the answers it gets can be defended in the court of world opinion, as well in the Standing Consultative Commission, where issues of treaty compliance are addressed and must be resolved. The Pentagon report gives no confidence that satisfactory answers to these questions will be provided by this administration in its rush toward strategic defense.

The importance of this and related compliance issues is apparent as one looks ahead toward possible deployments of defensive systems. As Paul Nitze remarked in his Philadelphia speech, if the Star Wars research program of the administration is fully successful in developing new technologies that satisfy his two criteria of survivability and cost-effectiveness, then, a decade or more from now, we can look forward to entering a transition period during which defensive weapons will begin to be deployed in conjunction with offensive forces. This, he said, would be a "tricky" enterprise: "We would see the transition period as a cooperative endeavor with the Soviets. Arms control would play a critical role." Granting Ambassador Nitze's optimism about the viability of the defense system, we will require an arms-control regime in order to get anywhere with our defensive deployments. Thus, the Star Wars program in the coming decade must not contribute to dismantling our current treaty achievements.

To summarize, a deliberately paced U.S. research effort on strategic defense, organized and pursued with clearly stated goals and means, abiding by the ABM Treaty, and in accord with the six recommended actions given here, should serve our security well at reasonable cost—not very different from what we have been spending in the recent past. It should also give the Soviet Union—itself engaged in R&D on strategic defenses—no real reason to feel the need for additional offensive or defensive forces in response. A U.S. effort with better planning, explanation, and diplomacy might moderate Soviet concerns and perceptions, which now include seeing the U.S. program as threatening their deterrent capability, menacing strategic stability, and defeating the prospects for arms control.

The impact of such clearly defined and constrained activities on the ABM Treaty should be nil, in the near and middle terms. Genuine success in creating a new approach to effective nationwide strategic defense would indeed present a challenge to the ABM Treaty. If this should occur, it would do so well into the future, and regardless of which side would succeed in developing the defensive system. In such an eventuality, the United States would need to conceive and negotiate a new arms-control regime that would successfully integrate offensive and defensive forces.

But, above all, we must step back and view the threat of nuclear weapons in the proper perspective. This threat is not solely or even primarily a technical problem. The difficulty is much deeper and the solution much more radical than what can be achieved by continually calling on the next stage of technology to provide a new Maginot Line.

In my own field of physics, the advent of quantum mechanics presented not just a technical problem of matrix algebra to physicists 60 years ago; it demanded a whole new way of thinking. And physicists who couldn't master it sank in the wake of rapidly advancing progress. The advent of nuclear weapons of mass destruction—fission bombs 40 years ago and thermonuclear weapons 30 years ago—presents all mankind with more than a technical problem of rescaling warfare. It demands that we develop new means for resolving our differences and conflicts. A nuclear war would be nothing short of suicide. History reminds us of how grave the danger is, for over the full span of human records there have been wars, and in them human beings have used every means available at the time to kill and overpower one another. We are witness to tragic and brutal conflicts at this very time.

Our challenge is thus not to make a better laser or computer. For the United States and the Soviet Union, above all, as possessors of close to 99 percent of the world's nuclear weapons, the challenge is to get serious—really serious—and committed to improving our political, diplomatic, and human relations. We must face the common danger: not each other, but nuclear weapons—ours, theirs, and those of an increasing number of nuclear-weapons-capable nations.

The path to a safer world cannot be paved by technology alone. The way will have to be paved initially, and for a large part of the way, by progress in diplomacy and arms control. Is there hope? I don't know. This is not a time for optimism. The arms talks have just resumed in Geneva under a heavy cloud of pessimism. But, as scientists, we are not altogether unfamiliar with surprises in our work. More to the point, there is strong evidence that we can make a great difference by involving ourselves in the process of seeking a safer world, not only as scientists and experts but as informed citizens helping to shape an informed public constituency.

Let me remind you of our two most notable successes in our nuclear weapons policy: the Limited Test Ban Treaty of 1963 and the ABM Treaty of 1972. In both cases, vigorous and constructive public participation and support proved to be vital ingredients in pushing the political process to these achievements.

The Limited Test Ban Treaty, which forbids above-ground nuclear weapons tests, was negotiated following a strong public outcry against health hazards caused by radioactive fallout from nuclear explosions in the atmosphere. The original 1967 proposal to deploy ABM systems in the United States near large population centers stirred a major public debate because many people objected to nuclear weapons being introduced, figuratively speaking, "into their own backyards." These two examples provide persuasive evidence of the value of constructive public involvement. The challenge and the opportunity call!

The Case Against Strategic Defense

WITH WOLFGANG K.H. PANOFSKY

In his address to the nation on March 23, 1983, President Reagan advocated that the United States "embark on a program to counter the awesome Soviet missile threat with measures that are defensive." He called upon the American scientific community, "those who gave us nuclear weapons, to turn their great talents now to the cause of mankind and world peace, to give us the means of rendering these nuclear weapons impotent and obsolete." These words have rekindled the debate about defense against nuclear weapons—a subject that had been relatively dormant since the antiballistic missile (ABM) debates of 1969 and the ratification hearings for the ABM Treaty of 1972.

Throughout history, military analysts have grappled with the role of offense versus defense. Many examples can be cited in which offensive or defensive measures have proved decisive to the outcome of combat. In considering defenses against nuclear weapons, however, one must recognize that the enormous increase in the explosive power of nuclear bombs has wrought a fundamental discontinuity in the relative effectiveness of offensive and defensive measures. We must now recognize that a *single* relatively small nuclear bomb is a weapon of mass destruction. A modern nuclear warhead weighing perhaps 100 pounds can pack an explosive power equivalent to 100 kilotons or 200 million pounds of a "conventional" explosive such as TNT. This increase by a factor of 2 million stems directly from the physical fact that chemical energies are measured in electron volts while nuclear energies are measured in millions of electron volts. In nuclear explosives, we are dealing with the forces that energize the sun and stars and fuel the cosmos.

Given the staggering destructive potential of nuclear bombs, effective defenses must meet a much higher standard of performance today than at any other time in the history of warfare. Historical arguments in the discussion of offense versus defense in the nuclear age can be, and often are, misleading.

In this article, we describe the current strategic relationship of offense dominance, the potential roles for strategic defense, and the technical promise of ballistic missile defenses. We conclude by balancing the values and the risks associated with the new research-and-development program, the Strategic Defense Initiative.

The strategic relationship between the United States and the Soviet Union currently rests upon the balance of offensive forces, a situation known as "offense dominance." If either superpower launches a nuclear attack, it faces the risk of a nuclear retaliatory strike that can endanger its very existence. While neither the United States nor the Soviet Union has made the destruction of enemy populations in response to enemy attack an explicit policy objective, both recognize that, should a large fraction of the superpowers' arsenals be used—under any doctrine, any choice of pattern of attack, or for any purpose—then the threat to the survival of the two societies is very grave indeed.

Before the president's speech, it was also widely accepted that, without drastic quantitative reductions and qualitative restrictions of the level of nuclear arms, it was not feasible to build a defensive shield that could effectively blunt, much less deny, a nuclear retaliatory strike.

The key element of the president's speech was a challenge to escape from this grim reliance on the threat of retaliation to deter aggression and nuclear war. "What if free people could live secure in the knowledge that their security did not rest upon the threat of instant U.S. retaliation to deter Soviet attack, that we could intercept and destroy strategic ballistic missiles before they reached our soil or that of our allies?" he asked. In expressing this hope, the president touched upon sentiments felt deeply by many citizens of the United States, the Soviet Union, and their neighboring nations, who seek a better peace than the present one, in which they are mutual hostages to annihilation. Many find this situation morally repugnant; moreover, it cannot be expected to prevent nuclear war for all time. Unhappily, however, we see no technical alternative to the mutual hostage relationship—the state of Mutual Assured Destruction (MAD)—as long as nuclear armaments remain anywhere near the levels now stockpiled or continue to grow as they are today.

We are emphasizing this point here because MAD is frequently represented as a doctrine promulgated by some misguided policymakers willing to gamble with the survival of their country. Nothing could be further from the truth. The history of the nuclear weapons competition is replete with attempts by policymakers in both the United States and the Soviet Union to avoid the mutual hostage situation. Each time, however, they concluded that technology simply does not permit such an escape, unless the total level of nuclear arms in the world can be drastically lowered.

Recall President Nixon's statement[1] in 1969: "Although every instinct motivates me to provide the American people with complete protection against major nuclear attack, it is not now within our power to do so." Going back even further, we find that, in the early days of the Kennedy administration, Secretary of Defense Robert McNamara attempted to adopt a nuclear policy of "city avoidance," in which the United States and, it was hoped, the Soviet Union would not target the opponent's cities. When combined with extensive civil-defense measures, this policy would greatly reduce the risk to the people of the United States, he thought. Yet, as the technical realities emerged, McNamara became persuaded that such measures would not prevent major population casualties. He concluded that a posture in which the vulnerability of population and industry did not play a dominant role was impossible.

The situation is similar on the Soviet side. In 1967 Soviet Premier Kosygin said, "I think a defensive system which prevents attack is not a cause of the arms race . . . its purpose is not to kill people but to save human lives." Yet, in the subsequent years, the recognition of mutual vulnerability has become central to the Soviet perception of the Soviet–American relationship. Leonid Brezhnev, for example, told the Twenty-sixth Party Congress in 1981 that "the military and strategic equilibrium between the Soviet Union and the United States . . . is objectively a safeguard of world peace." In September 1983, Marshal Ogarkov, chief of the General Staff, wrote that, "with the modern development and dispersion of nuclear arms in the world, the defending side would always retain such a quantity of nuclear means as will be capable of inflicting 'unacceptable damage' . . . on the aggressor in a retaliatory strike."

Clearly, public remarks by military and civilian leaders in the United States and the Soviet Union are fallible indicators of national policy and military capability. Yet these quotations, and the changes in thought they imply, also make it clear that there is worldwide recognition that the current military balance is "offense dominated," however repugnant the notion of a mutual hostage relationship might be.

In this situation of mutual vulnerability, maintaining the stability of the military balance is the principal tool for avoiding nuclear war. The United States and the Soviet Union should do their utmost to avoid a situation in which either would be tempted in time of crisis to use nuclear weapons first on the assumption that launching a preemptive strike would be preferable to facing a likely attack by the other. In other words, "crisis stability" calls for minimizing the perceived advantage to the party attacking first.

Much has already been done in the attempt to enhance crisis stability. Essential ingredients for ensuring stability are a reliable—and survivable—command-and-control system, the ability of each side's retaliatory forces to survive an attack, and the demonstrable ability of retaliatory forces to reach their targets. Efforts must also be made to minimize the likelihood that unauthorized, accidental, or third-party nuclear explosions might lead to all-out nuclear war.

In addition to the unilateral measures that each country can take to improve crisis stability, arms-control measures can also be negotiated, based on the recognition that enhancement of stability is a matter of mutual interest to the Soviet Union and the United States. In the latter category, the ABM Treaty signed in 1972 and supplemented by a protocol in 1974 remains a key step, as we will discuss later in detail. In addition, the agreement in 1963 to establish a "hot line" between Washington and Moscow, and the subsequent steps taken in 1971 and 1984 to improve that facility, is a noteworthy attempt to avoid nuclear war through miscalculation or misinformation.

While these measures can enhance the stability of the current offensive balance, they cannot guarantee it. In the long run, the primary thrust for relieving the situation must be political; the evolution of U.S.–Chinese relations during the past 20 years shows what can be done. The current mutual hostage relationship between the Soviet Union and the United States cannot be expected to endure forever. Insofar as technical means can contribute to relieving this relationship, we conclude that the only tool available is a *drastic* reduction of the world's nuclear arsenals. Extending the hope that, at the current levels of these arsenals, the mutual hostage relationship can be avoided through changes in doctrine or by technical measures will detract from efforts to attack the problem at its source: the existence of vastly excessive nuclear stockpiles worldwide.

In his speech, President Reagan proposed nothing less than a defensive system sufficiently comprehensive and impenetrable to make the American people immune to nuclear attack. His contention was that, once such a shield was erected, the nuclear-weapons states could be persuaded that these weapons served no useful purpose and could therefore be abolished.

Prior proponents of strategic defense have generally advocated roles short of the exceedingly ambitious goal proposed by the president. Similarly, some subsequent administration spokespersons have also stepped back from the president's "vision" and have supported considerably less ambitious missions for the administration's new research-and-technology effort, the Strategic Defense Initiative.

Most recent arguments in support of the Strategic Defense Initiative have emphasized the objective of "enhanced deterrence" against aggression. Indeed, this phrase was used in the Defense Department's five-year program for the new initiative submitted to Congress in March 1984. Some advocates include in this mission the protection of elements of the U.S. retaliatory forces. Other advocates have said that the Strategic Defense Initiative is intended as a useful tool in furthering the arms-control process with the Soviet Union. Finally, all advocates of the Strategic Defense Initiative continue to emphasize that research-and-technology programs on defense remain essential to keep pace with Soviet developments, thereby avoiding "technological surprise" should a Soviet system evolve on a short time scale. Let us examine in turn these potential roles of strategic defense.

Making Nuclear Weapons Obsolete. A defense meeting the president's vision would require near perfection in performance. If only 1 percent of the approximately 8000 nuclear strategic warheads in the current Soviet force penetrated a defensive shield and landed on urban targets in the United States, it would cause one of the greatest disasters in recorded history.

To attain such a level of protection, *all* means of delivery of such weapons to the United States must be interdicted with near 100 percent efficiency. This would entail not only defenses against intercontinental and submarine-launched ballistic missiles, but also against strategic aircraft and cruise missiles from air, land, or sea. Even the introduction of "suitcase bombs" would have to be prevented. Yet the

Strategic Defense Initiative specifically deals with only the ballistic-missile threat.

There is general consensus that U.S. air defenses, largely ignored in recent years, are incapable of dealing with any massive attack from the Soviet strategic air force. This is true even though the Soviet air force is currently much less capable than the U.S. strategic bomber force, which is now being outfitted with long-range, nuclear-tipped cruise missiles. U.S. air defenses were downgraded in the 1960s when it became clear not only that modernization and maintenance of an effective air defense would be vastly expensive and of dubious technical success but also that expansion of these air defenses would be a futile gesture against the delivery systems for nuclear weapons then evolving—the intercontinental and submarine-launched ballistic missiles.

By contrast, Soviet air defenses are much more extensive. Several rings of air defenses are emplaced around Moscow, and extensive networks of surface-to-air missiles are deployed throughout the Soviet Union. Soviet air defenses have gone through a number of evolutionary stages, with the new SA-12 being the most capable system. Nonetheless, the U.S. Air Force continues to believe that its manned bombers, the modernized B-52s, would be able to penetrate Soviet air defenses using such diverse penetration tactics as electronic countermeasures and a precursor ballistic-missile attack to destroy Soviet surface-to-air missiles prior to the air attack. In addition, cruise missiles can be delivered in the "stand-off" mode—that is, launched from aircraft outside the range of Soviet surface-to-air missiles and beyond the range of most Soviet fighters, a tactic that appears certain to extend the bomber threat against the Soviet Union for the foreseeable future. Moreover, the "stealth" technology being pursued in the United States, which involves measures to reduce the radar cross section of penetrating bombers and of cruise missiles, makes the future air-defense task exceedingly, if not prohibitively, difficult.

Conversely, it is indeed hard to imagine that, starting from the minimal system deployed to date, the United States could develop an effective air defense against an opponent determined to counter it. Nor has the administration proposed that such a program be initiated. Yet nuclear weapons could hardly be made "obsolete" unless the air strike "window of vulnerability" is closed.

Potential Soviet cruise missiles pose an even greater threat to the United States. Following the U.S. lead, the Soviets are now acquiring long-range cruise-missile technology. During the coming decades, we can anticipate that cruise missiles will be deployed on aircraft, on land, and on ships and submarines, unless, of course, such deployments are ruled out by arms-control treaties. The technology for defense against cruise missiles is similar in principle to that used against aircraft. However, cruise missiles have smaller radar cross sections and can follow terrain at lower altitudes, which makes them much more difficult to detect and then to destroy. In addition, there is a geographical asymmetry between the United States and the Soviet Union that heightens the danger to the United States: a much larger share of our society is built up near our coastlines, within easier range of cruise missiles launched from enemy submarines and aircraft. Finally, the introduction of nuclear explosives into the United States by clandestine transport cannot be prevented by technical means, as has been demonstrated by numerous studies. Although major powers, in particular the Soviet Union, are unlikely to adopt such a tactic, it remains a potential terrorist threat.

Even ignoring these other threats, we view the possibility of erecting an impenetrable shield against ballistic missiles as very remote indeed for many decades to come. Such a shield requires nothing less than the evolution of an extensive and exceedingly complex *system* that must work reliably in a hostile environment. Furthermore, one must have continued high confidence in the defense system, although it can never be tested under realistic conditions—especially against an offense that can adopt a broad repertoire of countermeasures against it.

Protection against ballistic missiles requires many links in a defensive chain, all of which are crucial. There must be sensors to provide early warning of an attack; a command structure with authority to make decisions on committing the defensive forces on exceedingly short notice and then to implement those decisions efficiently; sensors that acquire and track the enemy missiles and then aim and fire the defensive devices; and sensors that must also determine which of the attacking missiles have been destroyed in order to fight secondary or tertiary engagements successfully.

Even the most optimistic protagonist for defensive systems agrees that no single layer of defense could possibly be effective. Thus the Strategic Defense Initiative describes its goal as a multilayered defense of extensive scope, capable of attacking ballistic missiles during boost phase as they are lifted into space, then during the midcourse of their flight, and, finally, during their reentry over their targets.

We strongly emphasize that the issue is not whether a specific technology for the interception of incoming ballistic missiles can be demonstrated. We fully agree that a single reentry vehicle from a ballistic missile can be destroyed by nuclear explosives lofted by interceptors, as was shown to be feasible in earlier developments, or by nonnuclear, high-velocity projectiles (demonstrated by the U.S. Air Force in June 1984). We also believe that a demonstration can be staged in which an ascending ICBM boost vehicle can be damaged by airborne or space-borne laser beams. However, such demonstrations of the interception of cooperating targets hardly have bearing on the feasibility of the overall system or the solution of operational problems.

We will briefly discuss, in the next section, the technical options for a defense system. Here we simply state that the goal of a truly impenetrable shield against delivery of nuclear weapons of all kinds over the United States is, in our view, impossible to attain—to the extent that the word "impossible" can be associated with practical human undertakings. We agree with Undersecretary of Defense for Research and Engineering Richard DeLauer that, "with unconstrained proliferation, no defensive system can work."

Enhanced Deterrence. When submitting the five-year program for the Strategic Defense Initiative in March 1984, DeLauer testified before the House Committee on Armed Services that Defense Department studies have "concluded that advanced defensive technologies could offer the potential to enhance deterrence and help prevent nuclear war by reducing significantly the military utility of Soviet preemptive attacks and by undermining an aggressor's confidence of a successful attack against the United States or our allies." Program advocates claim that this mission can be met by even a less-than-perfect area defense of population and industry.

It is indeed true that, if a potential attacker faces the prospect of attrition of his forces by a defense, in addition to the expected retaliatory strike, his confidence in the success of his planned attack would decrease and the complexity of planning such a move would increase. If one could correctly anticipate that this would be the *only* Soviet reaction to an expanded Strategic Defense Initiative, one might consider this to be a sufficient reason to move ahead toward deployment of a nationwide defense against ballistic missiles. However, the much more likely Soviet response would be to initiate a variety of programs to counteract the effectiveness of such defenses to retain full confidence in their deterrent. More than likely, they would also move ahead with intensified defense programs of their own. The net result of these moves and countermoves would be the addition of yet another component to the arms competition between the superpowers, in both offensive and defensive forces, and the end of the ABM Treaty of 1972, which explicitly prohibits the development and deployment of nation-wide ballistic-missile defenses. In consequence, the security of the United States would be diminished, not increased.

In contrast to "enhancing deterrence," the combination of our offensive strength and the damage-limiting potential of our defenses could be seen as giving us more flexibility to use nuclear weapons to punish, or threaten to punish, Soviet actions we consider unacceptable. In other words, the threshold at which we would consider the use of nuclear weapons could be lowered.

The Soviets may see our defensive programs, accompanied by our ongoing intensive effort to modernize and improve our offensive forces, as evidence of preparations for a first strike—a first strike that would leave them with a weakened retaliatory force against which our defenses, although imperfect, would be relatively more effective. Of course, the same would be true if the roles of the Soviet Union and the United States were interchanged.

The argument that it is acceptable for the United States—but not the Soviet Union—to strengthen our deterrent with ballistic-missile defenses while disregarding the implied first-strike threat can only be sustained by invoking an asymmetry in the moral stance of the two societies. It implies that the United States should be protected from a Soviet first strike under all circumstances, while the Soviets would not have to fear such an attack from the United States. It can be argued that, during the 1950s, the United States did have a first-strike potential against the Soviet Union and did not exercise it. The Soviets would find this reasoning less than persuasive, as would most other nations.

Surely, the United States would feel highly threatened if the Soviets proclaimed a policy of developing nationwide missile defenses to "enhance deterrence" and then initiated an intensified program toward that goal. In fact, Secretary of Defense Casper Weinberger explicitly stated, in December 1983, that the Soviet development of an effective missile defense "would be one of the most frightening prospects I could imagine."

We find the argument that the evolution of ballistic-missile defense can serve a deterrent mission extremely difficult to support. *Prima facie*, it simply adds another component to the arms competition, and a relatively inefficient and potentially destabilizing component at that. It is well to keep in mind the precedent of MIRVs, or multiple independently targetable reentry vehicles, each carrying a warhead. MIRV technology was originally stimulated by the initial, limited deployment—and anticipated expansion—of ballistic-missile defenses around Moscow. By substantially increasing the firepower of the offense—measured in the number of warheads and damage expectancy, not megatonnage—MIRVs were designed to overpower these defenses. Yet MIRVs have not made us more secure; they themselves have become the focus of instability by their growing threat to land-based U.S. and Soviet intercontinental ballistic missiles (ICBMs).

To some extent, the issue is one of relative cost. Because the purpose of an area defense is to limit damage to U.S. population and industry at a certain cost, then one must consider how much additional cost the Soviet offense would have to incur to restore the damage expectancy to the same value it had before defenses were deployed. Such a ratio of offense to defense cost, called the exchange ratio, has been calculated in the past and has always been found to be highly unfavorable to the defense. It appears unlikely that new technologies will upset this earlier economic conclusion. In addition, cost estimates for systems based on technologies in the early research stages have often proved to be notorious underestimates.

Protection of the Offensive Deterrent. Another distinct objective of ballistic-missile defense, known as hard-site defense, is the protection of elements of the U.S. strategic retaliatory forces—in particular, hardened missile silos and hardened command centers. Technically, this job is easier than the broader area defense of population and industry described above because only selected targets have to be protected. Moreover, hardened targets can be damaged only by a direct hit or a hit within the immediate vicinity. Consequently, there is a narrow "threat tube," or region through which the attacking missiles must pass, to destroy a hardened target. Furthermore, protection of the retaliatory forces does not require a high standard of effectiveness: if a reasonable fraction of the retaliatory forces survive, the attacker can expect assured retaliation with an unacceptable level of damage.

The strategic mission of protecting retaliatory forces with a hard-site defense is very different from that of complete area defense for population protection envisaged by the president. The president's goal was to shift the burden for maintaining a strategic balance from offensive to defensive weapons. By contrast, protection of the retaliatory forces maintains the dominant role of offensive weapons on which the current strategic military balance is based: it enhances offense dominance by preserving the survival of offensive missiles and ensuring their capability to retaliate against the opponent.

The distinction between area and hard-site defense has played an important role in the history of U.S. missile defense efforts. During the 1960s, the United States developed a series of systems largely intended for area defense. While Secretary McNamara recognized the ineffectiveness of those ABM systems as a shield against substantial Soviet attacks, he proposed that a limited area defense, called the Sentinel system, be deployed to offer some protection against accidental or unauthorized launches and against attacks from minor nuclear powers. Subsequently, the Nixon administration recognized that even limited area defenses using then available technology were not desirable for U.S. security. These limited defenses would not effectively protect society. Moreover, because the Soviets could interpret them as the beginning of a nationwide system threatening to their retaliatory capabilities, these defenses could reduce stability. On the other hand, defense of hardened ICBM silos, if technically feasible, was judged desirable by the administration because it would provide protection from preemptive attack. As such, a hard-site defense would contribute to the stability of deterrence based on offense dominance.

This reasoning led to the proposal to deploy the Safeguard system designed to protect Minuteman sites. Unfortunately, Safeguard used the same hardware—large radars and long-range interceptor missiles—that had been developed for the earlier Sentinel area defense concept and was not technically effective as a hard-site defense. It had limited firepower, and its radars were few and vulnerable to blinding and to direct attack. In addition, its commonality of hardware with Sentinel raised the concern that it could be interpreted by the Soviets as a base for a future area defense, with its implied escalatory impact.

The stabilizing role of defenses specifically designed to defend hardened missile sites was recognized by the United States during the SALT I negotiations, but it proved impossible to formulate objective criteria to distinguish hard-site defense from area defense. Accordingly, the ABM Treaty of 1972 and its 1974 protocol allow both nations to deploy a missile defense system of no more than 100 interceptors either to protect the national capital or a single complex of ICBM silos. The Soviets opted for the former. They have deployed around Moscow the only operational, albeit limited, ballistic-missile defense system today. The United States chose the latter and began building a defense of the missile fields at Grand Forks, North Dakota; the defense was soon abandoned because of its cost-ineffectiveness.

In principle, hard-site defense could be made much more cost-effective than the old Safeguard system, and hardware could be designed specifically for this mission as distinct from area defense. The question of whether such a development should be pursued is raised whenever the survivability of the land-based deterrent is examined. Dedicated hard-site defense systems were extensively studied in connection with the protection of the current Minute-man fields, the *MX* "Racetrack" proposed in the Carter administration, and the Dense-Pack *MX* deployment proposed in this administration. In each case, the option was not pursued further, largely because its cost was considered excessive in relation to its projected effectiveness.

This history must be kept in mind when it is suggested that protection of the deterrent might be a useful by-product of the Strategic Defense Initiative, whose primary stated goal is a nationwide area defense. Although such a by-product might be of some value in stabilizing the offensive balance, it is important to remember that, in the past, even a fully dedicated hard-site defense has been judged of insufficient merit. Furthermore, a technology development program for hard-site defense would have major differences from one directed toward realizing the president's vision of rendering "nuclear weapons impotent and obsolete."

Keeping Pace with Soviet Technology. It has frequently been suggested that the United States should place greater emphasis on ballistic-missile defense because the Soviets are undertaking an active program in this area. Yet if the United States concluded that the Soviet effort gave them a significant military edge or threatened strategic stability or U.S. security, the logical U.S. response should be to counter the Soviet threat, not to emulate it. Historically, the Soviet Union has dedicated a much larger fraction of its strategic military effort to defensive programs—motivated in part by the Russian tradition of "protecting the homeland." Yet there is little, if any, disagreement among military analysts that neither the Soviet's extensive air defense nor the Moscow missile defense offers effective protection against U.S. retaliatory forces.

The Soviets are modernizing, within the bounds imposed by the ABM Treaty, the missile defense around Moscow. Specifically, they are replacing the exoatmospheric interceptors deployed since 1970 with a combination of endoatmospheric and exoatmospheric missiles of higher performance. In this respect, the Moscow system is acquiring a capability similar to the old U.S. Sentinel and Safeguard systems. One cannot, of course, dismiss the possibility that the new Moscow deployment might form the base of a future nationwide defense. The Soviets have developed modular tracking and missile guidance radars. Coupled with the Moscow system interceptors, these might result in a deployable nationwide defense system. There is no persuasive evidence, however, that the Soviets are, in fact, preparing for a nationwide deployment, which would constitute a "breakout" from the ABM Treaty. In any event, it would take many years before such a system could reach a level of deployment having potential for significant military effectiveness.

The Soviets have constructed large phased-array radars for early warning at three perimeter locations and have recently closed the remaining gap within this early-warning coverage by a further radar of similar design at Krasnoyarsk in Siberia. This radar has probably been under construction since before 1980 but is not yet operating. It has drawn specific attention and raised serious concern because its location—away from Soviet borders, in contrast to the other early-warning radars—constitutes a likely violation of the ABM Treaty. The Soviets state that this radar is designed for space tracking rather than early warning, but this is difficult to reconcile with its characteristics. Be this as it may, the military significance of this radar is minor, although its political significance is important if it does indeed constitute a violation of the treaty.

The Soviet Union has also been pursuing significant research-and-technology programs for ballistic-missile defense, including research on the use of directed-energy weapons for this purpose. Although this Soviet effort has been proceeding steadily for well over a decade, many phases have remained essentially unchanged for some time. Soviet research differs in many details from that pursued by the United States, but its overall quality is comparable to the existing U.S. effort. One should recognize, however, that the Soviet Union lags the United States in many of the supporting technologies essential to a successful area defense. This is particularly true in computer hardware and software and in various sensor systems. In short, there is no need for the United States to match the Soviet ABM effort on the basis of its technical merit. Even if it were desirable for purely political reasons to keep pace with the Soviets, it would be difficult to justify an expansion of the current U.S. research-and-technology effort on that basis. The possibility that the Soviet program might result in new discoveries cannot be ignored, however. Therefore, a deliberate U.S. research-and-technology program can be justified to allow us to interpret Soviet progress and to prevent "technological surprise."

There is little controversy about whether deliberate research and technology programs on ballistic-missile defense should be continued, particularly given the desire to avoid technological surprise. However, the actual magnitude of such a program—and especially public statements referring to its purpose and promise—should be tempered by balancing realistic expectations for a technically functional ballistic-missile defense system against the risks of proceeding beyond the research-and-technology phase, should it appear feasible to do so. Above all, a realistic technical assessment of ballistic-missile defense must consider operational limitations, including those stemming from countermeasures by the offense, no matter how successful the technology programs may be. The risks of going forward with deployment include intensified arms competition, a decrease in stability, and abrogation or termination of the ABM Treaty of 1972.

For as long as there have been ballistic missiles, defenses against them have been studied. This paper can only touch upon some of the generic questions relating to the technical potential of the various defense concepts under consideration in the Strategic Defense Initiative.

Few of these technologies are genuinely new, although some have been considerably upgraded. Radars and high-performance missile interceptors, carrying both nuclear and nonnuclear warheads, high-power laser beams, particle beams—all these have been under investigation for many years. What might be considered new are the potential x-ray lasers pumped, or energized, by nuclear explosions; the use of active optics to correct dynamically the performance of mirrors used to focus beam weapons; and the great advances in the technology of handling vast amounts of information in a short time.

Ballistic-missile defense systems can be deployed on the ground, in space, or both. As mentioned earlier, the Strategic Defense Initiative is considering a multitiered defense against ballistic missiles based in space and on Earth, with intercept layers proposed during the boost and post boost (or bus) phase, during midcourse, and during warhead reentry. The purpose of such a multilayered defense is to achieve a very high level of overall system performance, beyond what is practical to achieve at each individual stage of intercept, and to attenuate the incoming force of warheads in successive steps.

Space-Based Interceptors. Basing interceptors in space has advantages and disadvantages. A major advantage is that, in space, there is no atmosphere to interfere with the propagation of the means of intercept—either such directed-energy weapons as light beams or particles, or more massive projectiles. A serious disadvantage is that space-based platforms are expensive and vulnerable—in fact, more vulnerable than ballistic missiles. Satellites in space move in precisely predictable orbits, which can be kept under observation for protracted periods. Thus, an attack on space-based defenses can be executed much more deliberately than can attacks on ballistic missiles. This vulnerability is so fundamental that many have doubted the practicality of space-based battle stations for a viable ballistic-missile defense.[2]

Inevitably, the basing of defensive systems in space would initiate a round of offense–defense competition in which the offense would seek to develop various options for attacking the space platforms (using a combination of antisatellite measures) while the defense would attempt to harden the space platforms and engage in evasive or otherwise protective tactics. Space-basing would not offer a simple way of deploying a defensive system. More likely it would stimulate further escalation of the arms race into space. Without more study and even in-depth experimentation, one cannot draw firm conclusions on the outcome of such competition—if there were a clear outcome. One can conclude, however, that escalation of such competition into space would be expensive and also dangerous to those space systems now used for surveillance, early warning, communication, navigation, and commerce.

Based on those facts now known, our judgment is that placing defensive systems on space platforms would constitute a highly undesirable escalation of the arms competition. It also appears quite unpromising on technical grounds. Under no circumstance should the remote possibility of using space for ballistic-missile defense purposes be accepted as a valid argument against proceeding in serious, good-faith negotiations with the Soviet Union toward banning weapons from space.

Boost-Phase Interception. The possibility of boost-phase interception is the principal new technical element in the ballistic-missile defense picture. "Boost phase" refers to the first several minutes of powered flight before the missile releases its multiple warheads. There are several advantages to boost-phase interception. The missile is much easier to locate and track while its engines are burning, and boosters are relatively "softer" and easier to destroy than the postboost vehicles and reentry vehicles they carry. Destruction of a booster would eliminate its entire payload, which may contain a substantial number of warheads plus many more decoys (perhaps in the hundreds). Booster interception would therefore reduce the difficulty of the task faced by the subsequent layers of defense.

Boost-phase interception, however, is a formidable task. The defense has very little time to commit its resources to intercept the booster. In addition, the booster spends a fair fraction of its active burn time shielded by the atmosphere from the interceptors, be they beam weapons or homing vehicles. Furthermore, it is possible for the offense to deploy "fast-burn" boosters, which spend essentially all of their shortened burn time in the atmosphere. Fast-burn boosters can be developed with available technology and with only a limited cost in missile efficiency as measured by its payload.

In principle, the booster can be attacked by space-based chemical lasers, space-based x-ray lasers, space-based neutral particle beams, and massive projectiles of very high speed—the so-called "kinetic-energy weapons." In addition, the booster can be attacked by "pop-up" systems—that is, directed-energy weapons carried aboard rockets launched into space after detection of an attack. Some of the key features of the various boost-phase weapon concepts will be discussed in turn.

Let us first consider satellite-based, high-powered lasers delivering an intense beam of infrared light against an ascending booster. Aside from the general issues associated with space-basing discussed above, we face the logistical difficulties associated with effective deployment of the entire system. If the space platforms are located in lower Earth orbit, then a large number must be deployed to keep within firing range all potential ICBM launch areas in the Soviet Union. The exact number required depends, of course, on the lethal range of the space-based lasers. This is also true for other intercept devices. Typical assumptions about what may be achieved technically with efficient, high-powered infrared lasers and large, high-quality optical systems for forming the laser beam lead to a requirement of several hundred laser battle stations against an ICBM threat of 1400 boosters, the size of the current Soviet force.[3] Moreover, if this boost-phase system is to be effective at all times, each of these battle stations must carry a power source of sufficient size so that the small fraction of lasers that are "on station" have enough fuel to be able to defend against a simultaneous attack of the entire Soviet missile force. To supply this fuel would require placing in orbit the equivalent of several hundred loads of the space shuttle.

Any specific numbers can be contested from either the optimistic or the pessimistic side. On the pessimistic side, one can maintain that, in the example above, the boosters might be hardened beyond our assumption, or they could be rotated to spread the area over which the energy is absorbed, or their burn time could be reduced, shortening the time available for the engagement. On the optimistic side, one can project even more powerful lasers with increased range, which would reduce the number of orbiting platforms required from many hundreds to dozens. We doubt that such differences in views can be reconciled soon through additional research and development. We are dealing with a dynamic situation in which both the offense and defense participate—the issues are operational as well as technical.

A second option for boost-phase interception is space-based neutral particle beams of high energy traveling close to half the speed of light. It has long been known that intense particle beams produced by accelerators will damage targets. The energy transfer of such a particle beam to a target is quite efficient and difficult to counteract. However, particle-beam devices face formidable technical and economic obstacles. In the atmosphere, these weapons have a short effective range, owing to interactions between particle beams and the atmosphere. If used in space, the particle beams would have to be neutral rather than charged to escape deflection and dispersion by magnetic fields. Such neutral particle beams, then, would have to be formed by neutralizing beams "born charged" when produced in accelerators. The neutralizing process can be quite efficient, and it introduces only a small additional divergence into the beam. However, the logistics and power numbers that go with such devices are similar to those discussed for chemical lasers, and the costs, if anything, are even less favorable. Because of these problems and the generic issues of space-basing, we do not attribute much promise to this approach.

A third option for boost-phase interception is x-ray lasers. It is now publicly known that nuclear explosions can be used to "pump," or supply energy to, laser devices that can generate beams in the x-ray region of the spectrum, thereby concentrating a fraction of the energy of a nuclear weapon into a narrow cone. Naturally, the narrower the cone and the higher the efficiency for converting bomb energy to laser output, the longer the interception range. There has been some analysis of the atomic processes for making x-ray lasers in the open U.S. and Soviet literature. Intense pulses of x rays damage the boost vehicle by "blowing off" the surface skin of the vehicle because the x rays are absorbed in an extremely thin layer of the vehicle. This is similar to the kill mechanism of the earlier Sentinel and Safeguard systems, in which the interceptor carried nondirectional nuclear warheads to intercept reentry vehicles in space.

The use of such x-ray devices for boost-phase interception is constrained by their very limited penetrating power, generally less than 1 millionth of the thickness of the atmosphere. Thus, if the offense chooses to shorten the burn of the booster—at some limited penalty in missile performance—so that the boost phase is completed in the atmosphere, such x-ray devices would become useless. In addition, it is clear that the source—a nuclear explosion—destroys itself once used. Although one can visualize multiple targets for a single explosion, any defense that requires a sequence of interceptions must involve separate nuclear explosions and thus separate platforms. Moreover, one has to consider offense tactics, such as nuclear bursts detonated in advance of the main attack, which might interfere with the sensors that guide the x-ray laser. These advance nuclear explosions can heat the top of the atmosphere, causing it to expand and to rise, thus shielding the booster for a longer portion of its flight.

For all of these reasons, space-basing of x-ray laser devices appears thoroughly unattractive. An alternative would be to deploy a pop-up system based on ground. In principle, an x-ray laser pumped by a nuclear explosion is sufficiently small to be launched by a missile on detection of an enemy attack. Such a system would have to be based quite near Soviet territory, offshore from the United States, in order to make it geometrically possible to achieve an interception. Moreover, like any other system for boost-phase interception, a pop-up system would have to operate on an automated basis, given the minimal time available between detection of booster launch and commitment of the interceptors. This raises profound policy questions about whether such nuclear devices should be prepositioned close to Soviet shores and launched without human intervention.

To avoid the problems associated with the boost-phase interception options discussed above, various hybrid systems have been proposed. The most prominent concept calls for large mirrors placed in space to focus laser beams onto enemy targets. The laser beams would be generated by a series of ground stations, widely dispersed to hedge against adverse weather conditions, or located on mountain tops above the weather. The beams from the ground would be focused to large relay mirrors in synchronous orbit, an altitude of 36,000 kilometers. To focus the beam would require active optics systems that could compensate for the atmospheric disturbances. The relay mirrors would also have to be aimed precisely and continuously at various mission mirrors in lower Earth orbit. These, in turn, would focus the beam onto the boost vehicles. In principle, this system might indeed direct damaging levels of energy at the boost vehicle, although the technical requirements are quite severe. However, relay and mission mirrors are subject to all the vulnerabilities for space-borne stations discussed previously. If some of the mission mirrors were launched into lower Earth orbit on detection of an attack, there would still be the problem of the short engagement time characteristic of all pop-up systems. The economics and practicality of this system cannot really be analyzed at this stage of development.

A boost-phase defense can also be designed that relies on direct impact by small homing rockets traveling at high speeds, comparable to those of the ICBMs themselves (about 5 to 7 kilometers per second). This is a well-developed technology, which could be deployed much sooner than the more exotic directed-energy beam weapons. However, it is also a much more limited technology that could be countered by the offense with relative ease. In particular, the interceptors are much too large and heavy to "pop-up" atop a single missile and instead would have to be launched from a constellation of space-based battle stations. Such a system thus inherits the many operational problems of all space-based systems: vulnerability to direct attack; ineffectiveness against fast-burn boosters; and the large number of space platforms—and enormous tonnage—required because each is "on station" only a small percentage of time. On balance, we consider kinetic-energy systems to be of limited potential and generally ineffective for boost-phase interception.

Midcourse Interception. Intercepting ICBMs during the midcourse of their flight has been proposed many times in the past. Midcourse lasts perhaps 20 to 25 minutes, much longer than boost phase. Although this longer engagement time is an advantage, other factors make midcourse defense exceedingly difficult and have discouraged missile defense designers in the past.

The potential targets in midcourse are both the postboost vehicle and the individual warheads. The postboost vehicles are, or can generally be designed to be, harder than the boosters, and their burn times can also be greatly shortened. The numerous individual warheads are even harder still. Decoys are readily deployed in midcourse because there is no atmospheric drag to affect their trajectories. In addition, the signal on which an interceptor can "home" is more difficult to generate in midcourse because there is no friction to heat up the vehicles and dissipate energy. Radar cross sections are generally small and infrared signatures weak. Background radiation can be enhanced by high-altitude nuclear explosions to confuse interceptor sensors.

The contest between midcourse interception by any means and a coordinated attack appears quite favorable to the offense because the number of targets—real and decoy—can be proliferated almost at will at relatively low cost. Candidates for midcourse interceptors include all the devices mentioned in connection with boost-phase interception, but in this phase the operational problems appear even more severe. To be effective, the interception system has to operate in a hostile environment for a protracted time. Therefore, in addition to increasing the number of targets to be engaged by the defense, the offense can adopt active tactics that threaten the defense. In short, midcourse interception remains an extremely difficult problem; the new technologies have done little to modify earlier pessimistic conclusions. In particular, even with a highly effective layer for boost-phase interception, the overall battle-management problem is severe in midcourse. Currently, there is no viable concept for a highly effective midcourse defense against a massive threat of thousands of warheads, postboost vehicles, and perhaps many tens of thousands of decoys.

Terminal Defense. Once individual reentry vehicles and decoys enter the atmosphere, lighter decoys become easily distinguishable, which greatly reduces the number of targets to be engaged by a terminal defense. Early developmental systems for terminal defense used nuclear explosives carried by high-performance ascending rockets as interceptors. Recent improvements in technology, in particular in guidance precision and in higher acceleration rockets, have made it possible to destroy an incoming warhead by nonnuclear means, as the Air Force demonstrated in June 1984.

Even with these advances, terminal defense on a nationwide basis is an enormously more difficult task than hard-site defense of selected targets. Urban industrial complexes are spread all over the nation, and they are much more vulnerable and valuable than missile emplacements. No serious claims have been made that terminal defense alone could offer significant protection of the U.S. population and industry against a massive Soviet ICBM attack. Only if boost- and midcourse-phase interceptions have eliminated all but a few percent of attacking warheads could any hope be extended for an effective terminal defense.

On the positive side, nationwide terminal defense can offer some protection against minor attacks, be they accidental or unauthorized launches or attacks by third powers using a small number of missiles. It is important to note, however, that ballistic missiles are hardly the most likely threat from minor powers, as their development and manufacture require a major technological effort. Moreover, an areawide terminal defense is exceedingly expensive, certainly amounting to tens if not hundreds of billions of dollars.

As noted earlier, an expanded ballistic-missile defense effort poses several strategic risks, including potential conflict with arms-control treaties and the risk of accelerating arms competition.

Danger of Confrontation with Arms Control Treaties. The administration has been careful to describe its current program as research, and the activities it proposes for the next fiscal year appear to be in compliance with obligations under existing treaties. However, if the Strategic Defense Initiative were to expand in the future from its current research-and-technology focus through prototype and systems testing to actual deployment, several arms-control treaties would be at risk. These are the 1972 ABM Treaty and its associated 1974 protocol, the 1963 Limited Test Ban Treaty, and the Outer Space Treaty of 1967.

The ABM Treaty explicitly prohibits regional and nationwide ballistic-missile defenses, permitting only a single deployment of limited firepower for the defense of the national capital or one designated ICBM complex. Although the treaty permits research and technology, it prohibits a number of new developments, including the development, testing, or deployment of mobile, land-based systems and those based in air, space, or sea. Ambassador Gerard Smith, chief U.S. negotiator of the ABM Treaty, defined the boundary between permitted and forbidden activities during the treaty-ratification hearings before the Senate Armed Services Committee in 1972 as follows:

> The obligation not to develop such systems, devices or warheads would be applicable only to the stage of development which follows laboratory development and testing. The prohibitions on development contained in the ABM Treaty would start at that part of the development process where field testing is initiated on either a prototype or breadboard model. It was understood by both sides that the prohibition on "development" applies to activities involved after a component moves from the laboratory development and testing stage to the field testing stage, wherever performed.

This interpretation would clearly prohibit prototype and systems testing as well as engineering development.

It has been suggested by some supporters of the Strategic Defense Initiative in and out of government that, if confrontations between expanded defense activities and the ABM Treaty were to occur, then the treaty could be renegotiated to accommodate the proposed activities. The ABM Treaty is of indefinite duration and is subject to review every five years. This review, however, does not imply renegotiation, which would be a separate matter. It also contains a provision for either party to abrogate the treaty, after suitable notification, invoking jeopardy to its "supreme interests."

The Strategic Defense Initiative would also violate the Limited Nuclear Test Ban Treaty and the Outer Space Treaty if it moved ahead with tests and operational deployment in space of x-ray lasers pumped by nuclear explosions. The Outer Space Treaty prohibits the placement of weapons of mass destruction, including nuclear weapons, in space. The 1963 Limited Test Ban Treaty prohibits nuclear explosions in the atmosphere, under water, and in outer space. Although this treaty in itself has had only minor impact on the bilateral U.S.–Soviet arms competition, it has reduced worldwide fallout by two orders of magnitude and has been a substantial moral force in the cause of nuclear nonproliferation.

For a number of reasons, neither renegotiation nor abrogation of the three treaties mentioned above can be taken lightly. First, these treaties have served U.S. national security well. Second, should outright abrogation occur, the concomitant political price would be heavy. Third, should renegotiation be initiated at the request of the United States, but with the Soviet Union disclaiming interest in such a move, the United States would have to pay a price in concessions to the Soviet Union to arrive at settlement.

The ABM Treaty, in particular, has been of great value to U.S. and NATO security. The treaty has helped limit competitive and escalatory growth of the strategic arsenals, which could well have exceeded current bounds. Furthermore, as documented in the 1972 Moscow summit, the ABM Treaty was enacted by both nations in recognition that peaceful coexistence was a matter of practical necessity. In that spirit, the ABM Treaty is a key step in the political approach to preventing nuclear war. It is much more than just a symbol of arms-control hopes. It is not based on idealism; instead, it accepts the mutual-hostage relationship between the United States and the Soviet Union as a present necessity and as an objective condition, not as an active threat. Although the Soviets have never accepted "deterrence" in precisely the same terms as those used by most U.S. analysts, they have frequently emphasized that, under current conditions, nuclear war would be tantamount to suicide for both sides. In this sense, deterrence is not based on mutual threats but on prudent reciprocal restraints, such as those embodied in the ABM Treaty, to avoid nuclear war.

The ABM Treaty has also helped to lift the veil of secrecy surrounding the Soviet Union by guaranteeing that satellites and other surveillance tools located outside of national boundaries—the so-called "National Technical Means" of verification—shall not be interfered with in peacetime. It also established the Standing Consultative Commission, a generally effective private forum for airing queries and resolving issues of treaty compliance by the United States and the Soviet Union.

In its final 1984 report, the President's Commission on Strategic Forces (the Scowcroft commission) observed, "Ballistic missile defense is a critical aspect of the strategic balance and therefore is central to arms control . . . no move in the direction of the deployment of active defense should be made without the most careful consideration of the possible strategic and arms control implications."

The Strategic Defense Initiative has not been greeted with expressions of support from the NATO alliance. This is not surprising, as the ABM Treaty is of great value to our nuclear-armed allies—especially the British and French—because it ensures the ability of their missiles to reach their targets. Were the treaty modified or abrogated, resulting in the expansion of Soviet missile defenses, the independent and much smaller deterrent forces of our allies would lose their effectiveness much sooner than would U.S. forces.

Clearly, careful consideration will have to be given to the future of the ABM Treaty, should the activities of the Strategic Defense Initiative provide promising results.

The Risk of Escalation. Whatever the long-range objective of the Strategic Defense Initiative—be it President Reagan's vision of complete protection against nuclear weapons or the more recently stated goal of enhanced deterrence—during the actual deployment of a ballistic-missile defense, we will face a protracted time during which the offense dominance of the strategic balance is still a reality. Even optimistic projections of the development and deployment of only a partially effective missile defense, ignoring any treaty obstacles, span a decade or more. In contemplating the wisdom of deployment, we must factor in the likely Soviet responses and their impact on stability and escalation of the arms race.

The Soviets may respond by emulating the U.S. defense initiative or by taking specific offensive countermeasures against the U.S. moves, or both. Whichever choice they make, the Soviets will react during the development time to U.S. official statements as well as to emerging technologies and their potential military effectiveness to judge whether the United States remains deterred from initiating nuclear war under all conceivable conditions. To Soviet leaders, a crucial question will be, "Does the U.S. leadership still recognize that it would be suicidal to start a nuclear exchange?"

This is a troublesome issue, because the president's speech and the subsequent, often inconsistent, justifications of the Strategic Defense Initiative have created a widespread impression of a drastic shift in U.S. strategic policy. In fact, little has happened yet, either in strategic posture or in technical development. The program planned for the next fiscal year constitutes only a modest increase over the total ballistic-missile defense activities of the Defense Department in prior years.

But what about the year after that, and beyond? The announced five-year Strategic Defense Initiative program is both ambitious and expensive, totaling $26 billion from fiscal year 1985 through 1989, as compared with a current spending rate of roughly $1 billion per year. Will this intensified program lead the Soviets to conclude, for example, that the president is really extending hope that the U.S. population can be shielded from the horrors of nuclear attack and is thereby accepting notions of fighting a limited nuclear war?

Soviet leaders have continued to emphasize that they will maintain the capacity to retaliate in the face of new U.S. strategic programs. This fact, combined with a "worst-case analysis" of the U.S. defense initiative, will surely lead the Soviet Union to drive for expanded offensive programs in addition to specific countermeasures to reduce the effectiveness of the emerging U.S. defenses. This risk is real, and it is futile to believe that economic pressures would coerce the Soviets to moderate their responsive deployments. Strategic nuclear forces are only a fraction, probably much less than one-quarter, of the total Soviet military burden. Moreover, the Soviet Union is now spending twice the portion of its gross national product on military programs than is the United States. The Soviet system is more capable of with-standing criticism of this economic drain than is the United States.

A further serious risk is that the effort to neutralize the effect of nuclear weapons by deploying nationwide missile defenses might make the use of such weapons appear to be more acceptable, thereby deflect-ing efforts to reduce the dangers and burdens of arms competition through negotiations.

On the positive side, *after* an effective arms-control regime has been established through negotiated treaties and unilateral restraint, and once the level of nuclear weaponry has been reduced drastically from today's levels of more than 50,000 warheads, we can see a stabilizing role for ballistic-missile defense. In particular, if the nuclear stockpiles were reduced to very low levels, a defense system would make the security of the United States and its allies less sensitive to the precise intelligence information on small numbers of weapons retained by an opponent or third parties.

In this context, the prospect of defense can add important support to negotiations leading to low levels of nuclear weaponry. However, missile-defense deployments cannot *precede* such a reduction of offensive forces or be intertwined with it without incurring all the risks of instability and escalation discussed above. Therefore, we still conclude that a reversal from the current offense-dominated balance to defense-dominated stability between the United States and the Soviet Union cannot occur—"We can't get there from here"—until offensive nuclear weapons have been reduced to extremely low levels worldwide through negotiation and prudent restraint.

In closing, we have grave doubts about the wisdom of expanding research and technology on ballistic-missile defense as a high-priority national program with a goal of deploying a nationwide defense. We see no practical prospect whatsoever of constructing a strategic defense that can—lacking prior *drastic* arms-control restraints and reductions—enhance deterrence, much less render nuclear weapons impotent and obsolete. Even if the Strategic Defense Initiative achieves all of its very ambitious technical goals, serious operational questions will still remain, in view of the staggering complexity of the system and of potential offensive countermeasures. We fear that pressure for expansion of this program beyond a deliberate research-and-technology effort will lead to a decrease in crisis stability, to confrontation with existing treaties, and to an incentive for expanded arms competition, resulting overall in a net decrease in national security. All these warnings relate at least as much to current oratory as to actual technical programs.

We believe that the focus and size of the Strategic Defense Initiative should be restricted to research into new technologies. Such a program would also provide a hedge against Soviet technological breakthroughs or defense developments. The United States should make clear by policy declaration the limited nature of its strategic defense program and should avoid activities leading to erosion of the provisions of the ABM Treaty. It should signal its determination to comply fully with the ABM Treaty and should insist that the Soviet Union join in adhering to the treaty's strict interpretation.

The revived interest in defensive technologies should in no way deflect the nations of the world from giving highest priority to efforts to diminish the risk of nuclear war, to terminate the offensive strategic-arms competition, and to reduce the world's nuclear arsenals.

Notes

[1] For full references to these and subsequent quotations, see S. D. Drell, P. J. Farley, and D. Holloway, *The Reagan Strategic Defense Initiative: A Technical, Political, and Arms Control Assessment* (Stanford Center for International Security and Arms Control, Stanford, CA, 1984). (Published by Ballinger Publishing Co., Cambridge, MA 1985).

[2] E. Teller, Popular Mechanics, July 1984, 84–122.

[3] If the capabilities of space-based lasers are extrapolated many orders of magnitude from present performance to a brightness of 4×10^{20} watts/steradian, corresponding, for example, to a power output of 100 MW as a feasible goal in the infrared region and to an optical system with a 4-meter diameter mirror operated at its diffraction limit, and if we assume that the fluence (i.e., energy/unit area) required to fatally damage the booster is 20 kilojoules per square centimeter, then approximately 300 laser battle stations in lower Earth orbit are required. See reference 1 for more details.

Thoughts of a Retiring APS President

As I review the 40 years since I joined the APS in 1947 as a first-year graduate student, I realize first and foremost what an enormous gig we have been on. We have made breathtaking progress on our voyage of discovery during the second half of the twentieth century. We are now dealing with concepts we could hardly imagine 40 years ago. In the same way that we look back on the seventeenth century and the time of Isaac Newton as a time of wonder at the discovery of the universality of nature's laws, laws that apply to the solar system as well as to phenomena on Earth, so will the inhabitants of the twenty-first century and beyond look back to this amazing era. They will see that enormous progress was made toward achieving a unified theory of nature's forces and building blocks. They will see the first bold strokes of a picture—of a theory rooted in data—of how our universe evolved from the Big Bang of some 15 or so billion years ago. They will also find momentous achievements of both basic and applied significance that are remaking the structure of the familiar world—high-temperature superconductivity being just the most recent.

But, just as we have dreamed of profound new understanding and progress, perhaps of a complete theory of everything, we also have created a nightmare with our scientific advances. The nightmare is simply this: Because modern science has given us weapons of such enormous destructive potential—bacteriological as well as nuclear—the dream may end in a holocaust of almost unimaginable proportions and consequences.

Humanity faces no greater challenge than to avoid such a holocaust. Toward the end of World War II, the United States Strategic Bombing Survey was established to conduct a study of the effects of our aerial attacks on Germany and Japan. After visiting Hiroshima and Nagasaki, the survey team wrote in, June 1946, at the conclusion to its report:

> No more forceful arguments for peace and for the international machinery of peace than the sight of the devastation of Hiroshima and Nagasaki have ever been devised. As the developer and exploiter of this ominous weapon, our nation has a responsibility, which no American should shirk, to lead in establishing and implementing the international guarantees and controls which will prevent its future use.

This remains a challenge to all Americans, but it also has a special significance for the international community of scientists who created the nuclear weapons that pose so grave a danger to our survival. Moreover, this challenge presents an especially difficult dilemma to scientists. We are trained to approach issues such as the danger from nuclear weapons as technical issues. We bring important physical insights to an understanding of the mechanisms of a nuclear explosion, the significance of its power, the reality of radioactive fallout, and its deadly human consequences. These facts are crucial and must be understood because they limit the range of practical policies for facing the nuclear danger and seeking to avoid conflict. Laws of nature cannot be coerced or ignored in setting policy goals. But we also face a very profound, fundamental moral issue in dealing with nuclear weapons of mass, indiscriminate destruction. And *this* is a realm to which the scientist brings no special expertise.

New Aspects of an Old Dilemma

It is, of course, not at all new for scientists to be involved in war and weapons of death. But in our time there is a new element that acutely heightens the scientist's dilemma. Never before have scientists dealt with weapons of absolute destruction, with weapons whose use could mean the end of civilization. Never before have we had so little margin for error. At the same time, the gulf between the responsibilities of our leaders and their understanding of the technological weaponry they command has grown to dangerous proportions. Former British Prime

Minister Harold Macmillan lamented this fact in his book *Pointing the Way* (Macmillan, London, 1972):

> In all these affairs prime ministers, ministers of defense and cabinets are under a great handicap. The technicalities and uncertainties of the sophisticated weapons which they have to authorize are out of the range of normal experience. There is today a far greater gap between their own knowledge and the expert advice which they receive than there has ever been in the history of war.

This is a dangerous gap, one we must try to close. Success in closing it will require efforts from both sides: from the scientists as well as from society's political leaders.

I do not view this effort as a moral obligation for every scientist. Each individual, scientist or not, must choose his or her path and goal in society. I do, however, believe that our scientific community as a whole has a special obligation to assist society, through its governments, to understand the implications of the products of our scientific advances and to shape the applications of those products in ways more beneficial than dangerous to the human condition.

It is in this spirit that The American Physical Society undertook the study of the science and technology of directed-energy weapons in 1985 (*Physics Today*, May, page S1).

This subject was thrust into the forefront of public interest by President Reagan's famous "Star Wars" speech of 23 March 1983, in which he called on the scientists "who gave us nuclear weapons to turn their great talents now to the cause of mankind and world peace, to give us the means of rendering these nuclear weapons impotent and obsolete." He held out hope of a world freed from the threat of nuclear retaliation by advanced defensive technologies that "could intercept and destroy strategic ballistic missiles before they reached our soil." In response to this call, the APS Council concluded that the society could and should make an important contribution to informed public debate on the desirability and dangers of such weapons systems by independently evaluating the physical basis, the technical feasibility, and the related implications of such weapons in an unclassified but thorough technical report.

The issue raised by the president is one of profound importance. What the president is calling for is nothing less than a fundamental change in the basic strategic relationship between the United States and the Soviet Union. Nor is he the first president to raise this issue in search of a safer world to be achieved by applying new technologies to strategic defense.

Every president since Eisenhower, upon entering the White House, has asked quite properly: Can't we defend ourselves? Can't science and technology provide a shield against the threat of nuclear annihilation? Can't we somehow do better than live as mutual hostages under the condition of mutual deterrence? Upon further analysis and after detailed study of the technical realities, each president until Reagan concluded that the answer was no. This conclusion led to the negotiation, during the first Strategic Arms Limitation Talks, of the ABM treaty, a treaty of unlimited duration that was ratified in 1972 and that remains in force today.

It was, of course, proper and vital for President Reagan to raise the question of missile defenses again in 1983, in view of the prodigious technical advances that had been made in the more than ten years since the SALT I accords were negotiated. Do these advances now offer us new and better prospects for dealing with the nuclear threat as we look ahead into the future?

I am very proud of The American Physical Society, for we have been able to produce a substantive and superb report on critical technical and scientific issues that have to be addressed in seeking to answer President Reagan's challenge.

Star Wars

I personally have been very heavily involved for many years in studying technical and arms-control implications of strategic defense. Since being elected to the presidential line of APS more than three years ago, I have judged it appropriate to refrain from expressing my views on SDI at society meetings or in society publications, though I have fully presented them elsewhere. Now that I have served my time, however, I feel free on this occasion to express my personal views on what the United States should be doing in strategic defense. These views are based on my best technical judgment and can be summarized in three points:

Support a strong research program that complies with the ABM treaty. A high-quality and balanced research-and-technology program in strategic defense that is consistent with the ABM treaty is in the security interests of the United States. Compliance with the treaty will impose no harmful technological burden on a properly structured U.S. program for the coming decade.

The gap between today's technology and an effective defensive system is so great that it is now far too early for any program in strategic defense to consider technology demonstrations of types that could interfere with the treaty.

Indeed, our SDI program will be superior and more likely to achieve its goals of determining what advanced technologies look promising and what systems concepts look practical if its research priorities are not distorted by premature emphasis—or politically motivated requirements—to stage early demonstrations. A considerable body of evidence has shown that early demonstrations of new technologies have two deleterious effects. First, they tend to freeze the technology being demonstrated before it is fully mature, thus guaranteeing less than full capability. Second, they tend to absorb money from the associated R&D program (because of cost overruns), thus eliminating the possibility of better solutions. A funding level of $2–2.5 billion per year is fully adequate to support a strong SDI program.

Do not deploy systems prematurely. A decision to begin premature deployment of a partial strategic defense system would, to put it politely, make no sense. It could not be justified technically and would not serve the security interests of the United States. We must still surmount major technical obstacles before we can consider systems testing, let alone deployment.

Consider, for example, the problem of boost-phase defense. This crucial first layer of a nationwide defense must destroy the enemy's salvo of attacking missiles during their boost phase, within minutes after they are launched and before they can deploy their many thousands of multiple warheads and their potentially hundreds of thousands of decoys.

The only technology available at present to accomplish that critical defensive mission must rely on space-based chemical rockets guided to impact by heat-seeking sensors. These are known as "kinetic-kill vehicles" or "smart rocks." For a boost-phase intercept mission, they must be based in space because there won't be enough time for them to reach their targets if they are launched from the ground.

With the currently available technology for sensors and guidance, the hit-to-kill interceptor rockets will weigh many hundreds of pounds. Thus, deployment of a satellite fleet carrying such weapons would require the United States to launch many millions of pounds into space—tens of millions, in fact. Recall that 10 million pounds is more than 160 shuttle loads. And, once in space, the satellites would be extremely vulnerable to direct attack as they circled the Earth like sitting ducks in a shooting gallery. The existing technology of ground-based interceptors with nuclear warheads—already deployed—would pose a particularly acute threat to such satellites.

In a competition of countermeasures and counter-countermeasures with a ground-based antisatellite threat, this kind of space-based defense would be at a serious disadvantage. To use a popular phrase, it might even be called fatally flawed.

First of all, a ground-based interceptor requires considerably less energy to raise one nuclear warhead weighing several hundred pounds to a given altitude than it would cost the defense to insert into orbit at the same altitude one interceptor of comparable weight.

Second, there is the problem of the absentee ratio. The attacking country need only punch a hole in a small fraction—perhaps no more than 10 percent—of the defensive constellation that is over its launch sites at the time of its attack. The defense, on the other hand, must equip the entire constellation to counter the ground-based antisatellite threat.

For these two reasons, a technology program would have to succeed in reducing the weight of the individual interceptor rockets from today's designs of many hundreds of pounds to no more than a few tens of pounds before this concept could conceivably be of any practical value. Even then, serious issues of systems effectiveness and countermeasures would still remain. In particular, the satellites in space must protect themselves against threats from the entire 4π solid angle around them, and they will be vulnerable for long periods of time. And, as the Soviets replace their present lumbering boosters with modern rockets with faster-burning solid-fuel engines that can lift warheads into space in little more than a minute or two, both the time and the space above the atmosphere available for interception will shrink virtually to zero.

I vigorously oppose the current early-deployment push, which seems to be largely politically motivated. The element of urgency is distorting the research effort by driving "proof of feasibility" experiments that are expensive and time consuming. Not only is it technically unjustified; it will almost certainly spell the demise of the ABM treaty. See Figure 1.

We have to be realistic in assessing the enormously difficult challenge of achieving not just one individual technological objective—such as a very light, high-acceleration rocket or a very high-powered laser—but rather an effective nationwide defensive system that would be faced with enemy countermeasures designed to defeat it.

This is not a matter of man versus nature, which is the character of a technical problem. It is much more difficult: It is man versus man. The system must remain effective against all efforts to defeat it by a determined opponent.

Enforce and clarify treaty provisions. There is a need to relate the provisions of the ABM treaty to what the treaty calls "other physical principles"—that is to say, new technologies—for strategic defense. The ABM treaty has provided the basis for U.S.–Soviet efforts to achieve stability, to seek reductions in nuclear armaments, and to avoid war. Although progress in achieving reductions in nuclear arms since the treaty was ratified has been disappointing, we certainly should continue to enforce it unless technical and political developments make it possible to supersede it by a superior peace-preserving regime. What is needed is an effort to strengthen the treaty in consultation with the Soviet Union by resolving outstanding issues of compliance and by clarifying its application to new technologies in strategic defense.

In particular, we need to relate the ABM treaty and clarify the terms of its application on a case-by-case basis to the new physical principles for strategic defense, including space-based battle stations; directed-energy beams; and sensors utilizing lasers, optics, and particle beams for threat detection, tracking, and transmittal of information to the battle stations.

Unrestrained testing, including testing in space, of the new technologies as advocated under the Administration's so-called broad interpretation of the ABM treaty is not in the strategic interests of the United States. The treaty, as it was interpreted prior to 1985, contains provisions that were designed liberally to allow the signatory nations to pursue strong research-and-technology programs in strategic defense, while at the same time preventing preparations for rapid deployment of a nationwide defense following sudden withdrawal of a party from the agreement.

It is in our interests to maintain these restraints on the extensive Soviet program in strategic defense. They too have their SDI program, which includes, like ours, the development of powerful lasers.

With regard to the Soviet effort, I hasten to add that I disagree with claims occasionally made that the Soviet program may soon pose a military threat to us. Particularly in the critical areas of battle management, which rely heavily on computers and software, their technology lags seriously behind ours.

An agreement to abide by the provisions of the ABM treaty as they have been enforced up to now will provide a strong impetus to the ongoing negotiation aimed at deep cuts in the offensive strategic arsenals of the United States and the Soviet Union. Achieving such deep cuts is a stated policy goal of both the United States and the Soviet Union. It is clearly a desirable goal in its own right. But, in addition, it will be important to the U.S. strategic-defense program. Unless the offensive threat is greatly reduced numerically and limited by appropriate technical constraints as a result of major progress in the U.S.– Soviet political dialogue, I see no prospect of building an effective nationwide defense now or of achieving one in the foreseeable future.

The strategic-defense program of the United States in the coming decade must not contribute to the dismantling of our current treaty achievements. While one may justly conclude that SDI played a constructive role in bringing the Soviet Union back to the arms-control negotiating table, it should not stand as a barrier to progress.

Science Advice

The current debate over Star Wars has sharply divided scientists into warring camps and has led to a deep schism between a large segment of the scientific community and our government. The fault for this schism may well be attributable to a failure of institutions in our government.

We are dealing here with an issue of fundamental strategic importance, and one that presents an extraordinarily difficult technical and operational challenge. Yet it burst upon the political agenda based on no prior technical analysis. As our distinguished colleague John Bardeen wrote on 13 September 1985:

> President Reagan prepared his speech with no prior consultation either with technical experts in the Pentagon concerned with research in the area or with his own science adviser, Jay Keyworth. I was a member of the White House Science Council at the time. Although we met only a few days before the speech was given and had a panel looking into some of the technology, we were not consulted.

I am convinced by this incident that effective use is not being made of scientific input into technical defense issues at the highest level. The government has a need here. It cannot dispense with scientists, and it must also bear its share of the burden of closing the gap between itself and scientists. Its obligation is to arrange for the best possible scientific analysis and advice before risking major decisions or raising impractical expectations. Furthermore, the scientific advice must be neutral and free of political and doctrinal biases. This is not easy to achieve.

President Eisenhower understood these issues well when he created, in 1957, the position of a full-time science adviser in the White House and also established the President's Science Advisory Committee (PSAC), which served the president and the nation well for more than a decade before it was disbanded in 1973. He also showed his wisdom when he dismissed the issue of the committee members' political affiliations by saying, according to his first science adviser, James Killian, that he liked scientists for their science and not for their politics.

Since the mid-1970s, after PSAC was abolished, numerous scientific groups and numerous individual scientists all have urged the Federal government to reestablish a PSAC-like entity in the executive branch. There is clear need for a preeminent science council with working panels, a degree of continuity and independence of action, functioning to give the president an accurate and informed view of the technical components of his basically political decisions. We have no such effective mechanisms at this time.

Sakharov

Looking back, I asked myself, what was my most satisfying experience in office? Without a doubt it was sending a telegram to Soviet General Secretary Mikhail Gorbachev on 19 December 1986—it was my last official communication as APS president—expressing my deep appreciation for his action in releasing Sakharov from internal exile in Gorki and permitting him to return to Moscow. Early in January 1986, the very first letter I signed as APS president was also addressed to Gorbachev. (These two documents are appended to this essay). Noting that 1986 had started auspiciously with concrete new arms-control initiatives between the United States and the Soviet Union following the Geneva summit conference of 1985, I expressed hopes for progress during the year in efforts to reduce the threat of a nuclear holocaust.

At the same time, I expressed my deep personal concern for the situation of Sakharov and asked if it was too much to hope that during 1986 we might see his return to the normal privileges of Soviet citizens in Moscow. I pointed out that many of the issues that the General

Appendix

January 23, 1986
General Secretary Mikhail Gorbachev
The Kremlin
Moscow, USSR

Dear Mr. General Secretary:

I write as a nuclear physicist who has been involved for many years in the analysis of weapons and efforts through arms control negotiations to reduce the dangers they pose.

I am pleased that 1986 has started with concrete new initiatives leading to raised hopes for progress in the mutual efforts of the Soviet Union and the United States to reduce the threat of nuclear holocaust. I welcome your important call for an end to all underground nuclear weapon tests based on verifiable procedures and for a major reduction in our current arsenals.

Recent proposals by you and by President Reagan, as well as your recent Summit meeting, have indeed raised the hopes of many people throughout our troubled world for the new year. To many, it is a source of great encouragement that the leaders of the world's two most powerful nations have declared their intentions to improve cooperation while working to reduce the threat of conflict between our societies. This hope is further fueled by anticipation of the follow-on summits of 1986 and 1987 with their promise of substantive achievements.

At the same time as I express my support and appreciation for these important initiatives, I wish to address another issue that is of deep personal concern to me and to many people of good will in many nations. My reason for writing a personal letter to you is to urge you to permit an improvement in the circumstances of my friend and scientific colleague, Academician Andrei Sakharov.

Is it too much to hope, Mr. General Secretary, that 1986 may also see the return of Sakharov, one of the Soviet Union's most distinguished citizens, to his home and the normal privileges of a Soviet citizen in Moscow? Recall the important—indeed crucial—contributions that Sakharov has made to the very issues you yourself have raised in presenting Soviet positions for pursuing peace. For many years he has emphasized—as both you and President Reagan have also warned—that "the questions of war and peace are so crucial, they must be given absolute priority even in the most difficult circumstances" and that:

> The unchecked growth of thermonuclear arsenals and the build-up toward confrontation threaten mankind with the death of civilization and physical annihilation. The elimination of that threat takes unquestionable priority over all other problems in international relations. This is why disarmament talks, which offer a ray of hope in the dark world of suicidal nuclear madness, are so important.

At the summit you and President Reagan encouraged expanded U.S.–Soviet cooperation in fusion research for producing energy. Soviet achievements and worldwide stature in this sophisticated scientific field are based on the pioneering work of Andrei Sakharov in developing the tokamak concept. Sakharov's own participation in an expanded cooperative program to harness fusion for peaceful purposes would do more than add his own considerable brainpower to this effort—many of his western colleagues would be strongly motivated to join in with him.

On August 6, 1985, the fortieth anniversary of the atomic bombing of Hiroshima, you announced a five-month moratorium on underground nuclear bomb tests by the Soviet Union and offered to extend it into 1986 on a mutual basis with the U.S. It will indeed be a great day when the U.S. and the Soviet Union achieve a comprehensive test ban treaty and ban once and for all further development of deadly nuclear weapons. The path toward such a goal is long and arduous; and prominent among the first footprints on that path are those Andrei Sakharov made almost thirty years ago. We honor his influential efforts within the Soviet Union which culminated in the Limited Test Ban Treaty of 1963, terminating above-ground testing of nuclear weapons and the buildup of radioactive poisons in the atmosphere. He said then that a complete "cessation of test explosions will preserve the lives of hundreds of thousands of people and will have a still greater indirect effect by helping to lessen international tension and to reduce the possibility of a nuclear war—the greatest danger of our age." Can we hope to hear his reasoned and eloquent public voice, now silenced in Gorki, once again addressing this issue in 1986?

Is it too much to hope that we may also benefit from Sakharov's contribution to the renewed debate on the problems, prospects, and dangers of intensified U.S.–Soviet rivalry in developing weapons in space? He was ahead of his time when, in a 1967 interview with Ernest Henry, he simply and correctly described the dangers of a world armed with both offensive nuclear missiles and defenses against them:

> As everyone knows, the United States and the Soviet Union possess enormous stockpiles of strategic missiles with thermonuclear warheads. The two countries are, speaking figuratively, armed with nuclear "swords." The construction of an antimissile defense system would mean adding a "shield" to the "sword." I think that such an expansion of nuclear missile armament would be very dangerous. This is why. Under the present political and technological conditions, a "shield" could create the illusion of invulnerability. For the "hawks" and "madmen," a shield would increase the lure of nuclear blackmail. It would strengthen their attraction to the idea of a "preventive" thermonuclear strike.

His technical judgment was also accurate, in my opinion, when he wrote to me from Gorki in 1983 in his last publicly available statement (*Foreign Affairs*, Summer 1983): "Much is written about the possibility of developing ABM systems using super-powerful lasers, accelerated particle beams, and so forth. But the creation of an effective defense against missiles along these lines seems highly doubtful to me." There is no doubt that his voice could make important contributions to the public debate on this issue which is so fundamental to future U.S.–Soviet policy planning and arms control prospects.

Finally, Mr. General Secretary, consider simply the human element. Sakharov is a great theoretical physicist, and it was as scientist to scientist that I first met him in Moscow at a working seminar organized by the Soviet Academy of Sciences. Soviet achievements in science are a source of great national pride, and Sakharov is one of your greatest theoretical physicists. How sad it is that he is now almost totally isolated from his scientific colleagues, their discussions, criticisms, and their latest results, which are so essential to a scientist's work. Is Soviet fear of his lone voice so great as to justify this destruction of a scientific giant?

The Soviet Union has gained deserved credit and praise for taking the step of compassion in permitting Andrei Sakharov's wife, Elena Bonner, to visit her family and seek much needed medical care here. I urge that you now take the second humane step of permitting Andrei Sakharov to return to Moscow to work for peace and for physics.

Respectfully yours,

Sidney D. Drell
Professor and Deputy Director
Stanford Linear Accelerator Center
President, American Physical Society

[Telegram sent December 19, 1986]

General Secretary Mikhail Gorbachev
The Kremlin
Moscow, USSR

Greatly appreciate important action by Soviet Government granting permission to the Sakharovs to return to Moscow and resume normal academic work. I expect this to contribute to improving scientific cooperation.

Sidney Drell, President
American Physical Society

PROGRESS

The INF Treaty

Thank you for this opportunity to testify in support of the "Treaty Between the United States of America and the Union of Soviet Socialist Republics on the elimination of their Intermediate-Range and Shorter-Range Missiles" (henceforth referred to as the INF Treaty). I strongly urge that the Senate recommend its ratification as negotiated and signed. In my testimony endorsing the INF Treaty, I draw on 28 years of experience as an advisor to the U.S. government on technical issues of national security and arms control. My statement to the committee represents my own personal views and not those of any organization.

I will develop three major arguments in favor of ratification of the INF Treaty:

1. The negotiated reductions in numbers of missiles are in our strategic interest.
2. The provisions for verifying these reductions are fully adequate and constitute valuable and unprecedented progress in instituting cooperative measures of verification.
3. Ratification of the treaty will give concrete evidence that the two superpowers, the United States and the Soviet Union, working together can resume progress toward reducing the threat of nuclear conflict.

1. The Negotiated Reductions in Numbers of Missiles Are in Our Strategic Interest

The final agreement to eliminate all ground-based missiles, deployed and nondeployed, of intermediate and shorter range, between 500 kilometers and 5500 kilometers, along with their launchers, support structures, and specified support equipment, is consistent with the U.S. position at the beginning of the negotiation. This marks a major concession by the Soviet Union, which will be removing almost four times as many deployed nuclear warheads and almost twice as many deployed missiles as will the United States. The treaty numbers are as follows: The Soviet Union will eliminate 857 deployed* and 895 nondeployed missiles, or a total of 1752 missiles, compared with 429 deployed and 430 nondeployed, or a total of 859 missiles, by the United States. In terms of deployed nuclear warheads, the Soviet Union will be eliminating missiles for delivering 1667 warheads, compared with the U.S. deployment of 429 (and a planned maximum of 572 in NATO). In accord with the U.S. position, the elimination of these missiles is global, removing thereby the Soviet SS-20 threat in the Far East as well as in Europe. It is also total, removing undeployed as well as deployed systems. Furthermore, it does not include third-country systems, thereby leaving the missile forces of the United Kingdom and France unrestricted, as well as those of the People's Republic of China.

Concern about these provisions, which are numerically lopsided in favor of the United States, has been expressed on two grounds:

1. They will lead to the decoupling of the U.S. nuclear guarantee to NATO.
2. They will lead to the denuclearization of the NATO deterrent against a massive Soviet supremacy in conventional armaments.

The facts do not support these claims, and appropriate U.S. and NATO military planning, doctrine, and resources will ensure that these expressed concerns do not materialize in the future.

Three years after the INF Treaty is ratified and its provisions have been fully implemented, according to the negotiated schedule, NATO will still retain close to 4000 nuclear weapons. In purely numerical terms, the INF Treaty is but a modest step. It removes less than 4 percent of the nuclear weapons in the world today. It reduces NATO's deployed nuclear arsenal only by roughly 10 percent. In fact, the Soviet Union will be removing more missiles that are potential targets for

---

*These include 405 deployed SS-20s, each capable of delivering three nuclear warheads; 65 single-warhead SS-4s; and 387 shorter-range missiles. Since the treaty was signed, there have been minor corrections to these numbers.

NATO than NATO will be decreasing its warheads with which to attack them, in the ratio of 857 deployed Soviet missiles to 429 U.S. nuclear warheads.

Another measure of the INF Treaty is this: in 1976, before the Soviets started deploying their SS-20s, they already had some 590 SS-4 and SS-5 intermediate-range missiles deployed with their nuclear warheads, and the United States had no such missiles deployed. Fifteen years later, in 1991 (if the treaty is ratified this year), both sides will have zero deployments of these forces. In the meantime, the United States has developed sea-launched cruise missiles to augment the nuclear arsenal available to NATO and has modernized and strengthened the forward-based aircraft capable of long-range delivery of nuclear weapons. These forces, plus the sea-launched ballistic missiles assigned to the Supreme Allied Commander for Europe, give NATO a strong, long-range nuclear punch. This hardly points to a denuclearization of the NATO deterrent. Substantial forces will remain for implementing the U.S. nuclear guarantee to NATO.

While it is a significant diplomatic achievement, the INF Treaty does not, by any means, solve NATO's security problems. What it does do is to remove one rung in the escalation ladder of nuclear war in NATO. It thereby increases the importance of NATO's implementing a strategy and maintaining a posture of conventional forces that are less reliant on early use of nuclear weapons. This is a limited, but important, step in the right direction.

The stability of our military position in Europe must rest on a deployment of forces that makes clear to a would-be aggressor that, based on any rational calculation, he cannot achieve success by striking first, no matter what his goal. The presence of large numbers of nuclear missiles with the combination of range, speed, and accuracy that are characteristic of the Pershing II and the SS-20 is disruptive of such stability. They present a credible counterforce threat with short warning times against vital military command, control, and communications centers deep behind the lines in Western Europe and the USSR, thereby enhancing a mutual insecurity that can be dangerously destabilizing in times of crisis or heightened tension.

The next stage of negotiations in the European theatre should focus on the need to establish an overall stable relationship of conventional forces. This task will be complicated by the fact that much more than bean counting must be considered—simple numbers of tanks, men in arms, or aircraft represent but a small part of the balance. Nothing can compare in importance to the quality, training, readiness, and motivation of the soldiers, sailors, and pilots and the technical quality and maintenance of their weapons. Far more than firepower, the ability to know what is going on in the battle area, with good and timely surveillance and communications, is of crucial importance. I see no reason for the Western democracies to shrink from competing in these areas as we seek to reduce military instabilities and establish a better balance of conventional forces, preferably at lower levels of deployment.

Establishing a force posture that does not expose NATO to a credible threat should be viewed as a prerequisite to agreeing to further reductions in short-range tactical nuclear weapons as part of NATO's deterrent. However, I do not view a change in the current conventional balance as a prerequisite to the INF Treaty, given the high level of nuclear firepower and the diverse means of long-range delivery that would remain available to NATO.

The report "Discriminate Deterrence," recently published by the Commission on Integrated Long-Term Strategy (dated January 1988), emphasizes the great importance for the United States to "strengthen our ability to respond to aggression with controlled, discriminate use of force." Among its recommendations are four programs that are responsive to this need and that are important to NATO security:

- "Low-observable" or "stealth" technology that, together with new operational concepts as appropriate, can make existing radar-based air defenses ineffective, as well as disrupt and blunt an invasion.
- Accurate, long-range smart munitions—or PGMs (for Precision-Guided Munitions)—capable of delivering heavy firepower directly to critical targets at the front of the attacking columns and on the airfields and depots deep in the rear.
- Extended and more capable battlefield air defenses.
- Capabilities to obtain and disseminate timely intelligence information, including information gathered from space, of preparations for attack, and of troop dispositions and movements in support of military operations.

These developments should be pursued with vigor, independent of the INF Treaty. They are far more important to NATO security than is the presence or absence of a class of nuclear weapons of terror.

As noted by Senator Helms, the INF Treaty also does not destroy nuclear warheads, just their delivery systems. But, even by itself, that is no minor achievement. The treaty removes more than 1600 nuclear warheads that currently are poised on deployed missiles and present genuine threats to our allies. I view the point raised by Senator Helms as a challenge to make future progress in reducing the amount of fissionable material available for fabricating nuclear weapons, not as a reason to reject this treaty. I hope that, as we reduce the sizes of the world's missile forces, we will also initiate negotiations toward verifiable reductions of the stockpiles of fissionable material for weapons as well. It is the present U.S. position that we need to increase our nuclear stockpile in order to meet the requirements for weapons we still plan to build. But if, as a result of further progress in strategic-arms reductions (as called for by President Reagan and General Secretary Gorbachev), our arsenals are reduced, so may our stockpiles be. As the appetite for these weapons shrinks, it is natural for their food supply to shrink also.

2. The Provisions for Verifying These Reductions Are Fully Adequate and Constitute Valuable and Unprecedented Progress in Instituting Cooperative Measures of Verification

The INF Treaty establishes the most comprehensive and intrusive verification regime for arms control ever agreed to by the United States and the Soviet Union. The provisions for verifying compliance give the United States everything it wants. They represent a breakthrough.

As one who has been closely associated with verification problems for many years, I am pleased—and, indeed, amazed—by the progress negotiated here.

Except for missile-production facilities, all facilities mentioned in the treaty are subject to some form of on-site inspection, both within U.S. and Soviet territories and within the territories of other countries where the missiles and support facilities are based. These on-site inspections will provide for establishing a base-line inventory (starting between 30 and 90 days after the treaty takes effect); for witnessing the actual destruction of missiles and launchers at designated elimination sites; and for confirming the elimination of facilities. In addition, each party has the treaty right to conduct short-notice "challenge" inspections of missile-operating bases and support facilities, and of former bases, too, for 13 years after the entry of the treaty into force (with a declining number of 20 such inspections per year to 10 per year during this period).

A permanent continuous monitoring system will be created at the portals of any facility of the other party at which there is final assembly of ground-launched ballistic missiles that use stages similar to one of the prohibited missiles or, lacking such a facility, at the portals of a former missile-production facility. This continuous monitoring right continues for up to 13 years, although it will terminate after the second year if no final assembly of the type described above is observed for 12 continuous months. The specific concern of the United States here is to ensure that prohibited activities and deployments—particularly of SS-20s—are not hidden at facilities where the strategic Soviet road-mobile SS-25 ICBMs are assembled. This provision removes concern about the possibility of a dangerously rapid break-out from the treaty.

This concern is also addressed by cooperative measures introduced by the INF Treaty to enhance the ability of National Technical Means—that is, surveillance systems in space or on the ground outside of Soviet borders—to ensure that missiles banned by the treaty are not hidden at SS-25 bases. In particular, for three years, or until a treaty limiting strategic forces is negotiated and ratified, either party may request that, within six hours, the other open the roofs of fixed garages for launchers, remove the missiles and launchers to display them openly for satellites passing overhead to see, and leave them in full view until twelve hours after the request was received. Each party has the right to make six such requests per calendar year for one deployment base at a time.

In order to resolve compliance questions, the treaty establishes the Special Verification Commission. Although separate and distinct from the Standing Consultative Commission established by SALT I in 1972, it provides a very similar mechanism. Its success in resolving disputes will depend on the willingness of the two countries to cooperate in problem-solving efforts.

I have outlined these provisions to emphasize how unprecedentedly comprehensive they are. They are of great value in their own right, but, more than that, they provide experience in the type of cooperative means of verification that will be required for future agreements to limit strategic offensive forces. It is very much in the interest of the United States to encourage this development of cooperative means and on-site inspection as valuable supplements to the National Technical Means that we have relied on thus far for verifying treaty compliance. Similar means are at the heart of the agreement signed by the 35 nations of the Conference on Security and Cooperation in Europe in 1986, and the INF Treaty greatly expands the coverage of such provisions. As we look ahead to the still more ambitious strategic-arms control arena, intrusive on-site measures of verification will be required if we are even to hope to restrict the deployment of small, widely deployed, and dual-purpose sea-launched cruise missiles.

During the INF ratification debate, concern has been expressed about the record of Soviet compliance with previous arms-control agreements. On such an issue as compliance there are, inevitably, ambiguities due to questions of interpretation of complex treaty provisions and due to uncertainties in the intelligence data. A central issue here is what the required standards of compliance are. Of primary importance in judging compliance is whether activities that are ambiguous, or that appear to be treaty violations, can constitute a threat to U.S. national security. This is a very difficult, multifaceted issue of intelligence gathering and analysis. My net assessment is that, so far, the Soviet Union has a satisfactory record of compliance with current treaty agreements, and this record provides a basis for continuing the negotiating process and for the United States' continuing to honor current treaty commitments. There are several compliance issues that should be resolved, but both countries have adhered to the vast majority of the constraints contained in the treaties they have signed.

There is one clear Soviet violation of the ABM Treaty, and there are several examples of ambiguities and of questionable compliance that, unfortunately, some present and former officials have publicly charged incorrectly to be violations. The one clear violation is an unfinished, large phased-array radar located near the town of Krasnoyarsk in Siberia. Even if completed, this radar will not pose a military threat, in view of its physical characteristics.* The United States has also expressed concern about the substantial increase in Soviet encryption of data during their missile test flights, but this alleged treaty violation has, in principle, been removed by the Joint Communique signed at the Washington Summit. In the Communique, the leaders agreed that a ban on telemetry encryption during missile flights should be part of an upcoming treaty reducing strategic offensive arms.

In addition to being able to assess the military and security significance of a potential Soviet violation, the United States must be prepared to take appropriate actions. Three principles should guide a U.S. response:

- First, confirmed violations should not simply be ignored or accepted. They should be resolved and corrected by persistent dis-

---

*The relatively low-frequency range in which this class of radars operates precludes them from effectively managing an ABM engagement, because they are susceptible to black-out. See Appendix to this testimony for a fuller discussion of this issue. In the summer of 1987, the Krasnoyarsk radar was visited by a U.S. delegation of Congressmen and scientists.

cussion through the appropriate forum that has been created for monitoring compliance of the treaty provisions. For the INF Treaty, this is the newly created Special Verification Commission. It is, of course, important to enter these discussions in a problem-solving mode, avoiding premature public accusations which invariably make the task more difficult.

. Second, if there is ambiguity as to whether or not a violation has been observed, it is useful to enter into direct discussion with the Soviet Union, maintaining an open and balanced view rather than making an immediate presumption of guilt. Again, a problem-solving approach is called for.

. Third, in response to a Soviet violation, the United States must, of course, protect its security interests, taking whatever measures are required. The appropriate response may not be either to abrogate a treaty or to imitate the Soviet violation.

During the INF ratification debate, concern has also been expressed about loopholes in this treaty. In particular, it has been suggested that the Soviet Union might deploy a new class of missiles to replace those being eliminated, and, furthermore, they can do this legally by testing them at a range in excess of 5500 kilometers. According to Article VII, paragraph 4, of the INF Treaty, such missiles do not come under the treaty restraints.

This example simply points up that, standing alone, the INF Treaty is but one step, a step that does not complete the journey toward a stable balance at lower force levels. In fact, there is no need for either country to build new strategic missiles—ICBMs or SLBMs—to replace the intermediate-range missiles being eliminated. Any of the existing strategic missiles in either country, with their many thousands of warheads, can be reprogrammed onto the same targets now assigned to the INF missiles. What we have in this example is not a loophole, but an argument for ratification so that we can move ahead to complete a treaty at the Strategic Arms Reduction Talks (START) that will make the INF Treaty more valuable, and vice versa.

The INF negotiations were separated from START at U.S. insistence in order to simplify the process and to enhance prospects for achieving progress toward a mutually desired goal. Although initially opposed to such unlinking of the two talks, the Soviet Union eventually agreed. In accord with the Summit Communique, both countries are committed to the effort to negotiate "at the earliest possible date" reductions in the strategic forces that would completely eliminate this concern. In the event that such talks should collapse and the level of strategic forces should once again start to grow substantially, the United States would, indeed, be faced with a new circumstance. If this circumstance were judged "as having jeopardized its supreme interests," the United States would then have the right to withdraw from the INF Treaty under Article XV. That is, of course, neither the assumption nor the intention of the parties entering the negotiations. In the meantime, this concern can be muted if the Soviet Union and the United States reaffirm their commitment to the restrictions of SALT II on the number of deployed strategic missiles. It was the United States that unilaterally abandoned those limits of SALT II in 1986. We should now declare our intention once again to comply and take the very minor corrective action required to bring our current forces under the negotiated ceilings.

A second concern about the provisions of the treaty has to do with the uncertainty in the total number of undeployed Soviet INF missiles. How confident are we that all the Soviet storage areas will be disclosed, and how can we confirm the elimination of all undeployed missiles?

This issue raises again the question of what are the required standards of compliance. In judging this issue, it is important to bear two factors in mind. First, the treaty stipulates that all such missile systems must be eliminated. Therefore, the challenge is not to count accurately the number remaining but, more simply, to determine if there remains even one such missile, or launcher, or support facility, which, by itself, would be prima facie evidence of a violation. Under this circumstance, the risk of exposure to a would-be cheater is much greater. In addition, any such missile system, if retained covertly, would be a wasting military asset, since neither the missiles nor their launchers could ever be test-fired or participate in troop-training exercises. It would also have no deterrent value whatsoever, if its existence were secret and its potential threat unknown. One can expect that, over time, with more operational experience and with follow-on strategic agreements broadening the scope of such cooperative measures, confidence will grow in the accuracy of U.S. knowledge of the database of Soviet missile systems. This knowledge will grow increasingly valuable and essential if still deeper reductions in the level of nuclear forces are to be negotiated and verified. Both the United States and the Soviet Union are committed to seeking such deep cuts.

The cooperative means negotiated in the INF Treaty are an important supplement to our national technical means for verification of treaty compliance. They provide the groundwork for progress toward a firmer base for verifying future treaties. They do so by finding that delicate balance that meets U.S. verification needs without exposing us to the danger of intelligence fishing expeditions by permitting "any place, any time" inspections, which we would find unacceptable. The negotiators deserve the highest praise for crafting these provisions, which, in their own right, argue strongly for ratifying the INF Treaty.

3. Ratification of This Treaty Will Give Concrete Evidence That the Two Superpowers, the United States and the Soviet Union, Working Together, Can Resume Progress Toward Reducing the Threat of Nuclear Conflict

Above and beyond the immediate and direct impact of its provisions, a treaty must be judged by the new prospects it creates for the future. Even a limited step in reducing nuclear weapons can assume much greater importance if it portends continuing interactions and dialogue between the parties to it and if the parties are led to anticipate and, thereby, to focus efforts on making subsequent progress toward still more valuable agreements.

Judged by this standard, the INF Treaty is unquestionably a major achievement. Failure to ratify it, after seven years of intense negotiating effort, would dim any hopes of progress for the foreseeable future and would constitute a serious blow to the effectiveness of U.S. leadership in the Western Alliance.

The communique signed by President Reagan and General Secretary Gorbachev at the conclusion of the Washington summit in December 1987 is encouraging evidence that the United States and the Soviet Union are now poised to move ahead from the INF Treaty to an even more substantial agreement—one that reduces the number of warheads on strategic (or intercontinental-range) launchers by as much as a factor of 2.

The broad framework of such a treaty has already been negotiated. It sets a limit of 4900 warheads on strategic ballistic missiles under a total ceiling of 6000, including nuclear weapons carried on strategic bombers. The limit on launchers, intercontinental bombers plus ballistic missiles, is 1600. The negotiators at START have also made considerable progress toward closure on a number of sublimits on individual weapons categories, although several significant issues remain to be resolved. At stake in negotiating these sublimits is how best to establish a stable balance of deterrent forces, such that each party can maintain high confidence in the survivability of its forces against the threat of a pre-emptive first strike. In this regard, it is notable that the Soviet Union has agreed to cut its heavy missile force of SS-18s in half and to reduce the aggregate throw-weight of its ICBMs and SLBMs to a level approximately 50 percent below the existing level.

The verification provisions outlined in the communique are even more comprehensive and intrusive than those in the INF Treaty, on which they build. In particular, they include "continuous on-site monitoring of the perimeter and portals" to confirm the output of critical production and support facilities; "short-notice on-site inspection" of various declared locations; and, "in accordance with agreed-upon procedures, short-notice inspections" at various locations where covert actions may be occurring.

Three outstanding issues apparently remain to be resolved before the START negotiators can join the INF team in the winners' circle:

1. Mobile ICBMs
2. Sea-launched cruise missiles (SLCMs)
3. SDI and the ABM Treaty.

1. Mobile ICBMs

Mobile basing of ICBMs is one way to maintain confidence in their survivability, now that ballistic missiles have demonstrated very high accuracy. Mobile ICBMs can thus contribute to a stable deterrent balance, and it would be in the interest of the United States to negotiate for the freedom to mix silo-based and mobile ICBMs within the sublimits agreed to at START. However, mobile ICBMs also create verification difficulties when it comes to counting the number deployed.

This suggests that it would be advantageous to restrict mobile deployments to single-warhead ICBMs only. This would ensure that our uncertainty in counting the number of deployed Soviet mobiles would not be multiplied, and amplified, by a large MIRV number.

Under such a treaty restriction, the Soviet Union could proceed with its SS-25 mobile deployments but could retain its MIRVed SS-24s only in fixed silos. Similarly, the United States could retain MX missiles in silos and would proceed with the development of a Midgetman missile capable of mobile deployment. If we conclude a START agreement with the limits outlined above, I would recommend—primarily on grounds of cost—that the United States seriously consider loading the initial deployment of the Midgetman in fixed silos. The point is that, in an arms-control regime with equal limits on warheads, a single-RV missile is not valuable enough to be vulnerable, even when it is sitting in a silo. The attacker would be required to expend more of his own warheads than he would be destroying.

2. SLCMs

In the Summit Communique, both sides "committed themselves to establish ceilings" on the deployment of long-range nuclear-armed SLCMs, above and beyond the 6000-warhead limit, and "to seek mutually acceptable and effective methods of verification of such limitations, which could include the employment of National Technical Means, cooperative measures and on-site inspection."

Of all the verification challenges, this is the most difficult. I cannot offer a complete solution to this problem. SLCMs are small. They do not require fancy launchers. They can be widely deployed on many ships. They are dual-purpose missiles: they can be deployed with short ranges (~ 600 kilometers), with heavy high-explosive warheads, or with long ranges (~ 2500 kilometers), with light nuclear warheads. At the same time, SLCMs do not pose the threat of a large pre-emptive strike. They take a long time to arrive at target, and long warning times should be available in the event of a massive attack. In view of the verification difficulties, it will be necessary to accept standards of verification for SLCMs that are somewhat lower than for ballistic missiles that do pose a pre-emptive threat. These standards, of course, should be militarily significant as well as realistic.

The most effective means of verification will involve continuous monitoring of production and assembly facilities, as proposed explicitly in the Summit Communique. They may also require challenge inspections to verify deployment restrictions, as well as special tagging to prevent covert conversion of short-range to long-range SLCMs by changes in fuel and warhead loadings.

There would be merit in the United States and the Soviet Union agreeing to maintain Functionally Related Observable Differences (FRODs) between long-range and short-range SLCMs. Such an agreement would require each country to make appropriate technical choices in missile design and would be akin to the agreement on FRODs for strategic aircraft modified to carry long-range air-launched cruise missiles. On the basis of such FRODs, together with cooperative measures as appropriate, it would be possible to consider a simple limit on the total number of long-range SLCMs, irrespective of how they are armed. The advantages of such an agreement include its relative simplicity together with its political value in removing the need to identify explicitly which ships in the U.S. Navy are armed with nuclear weapons.

We should move ahead with a START Treaty even as talks on cruise missiles continue and are allowed several extra years to work out the more demanding terms of verification. As noted earlier, SLCMs do not pose a threat of pre-emptive first strike, but the substantial reductions in strategic forces already agreed to are very much in our security interests.

3. SDI and the ABM Treaty

The issue here is not whether there should be a U.S. effort to pursue research and to develop technology in ballistic-missile defense. The question is, what program should the U.S. support, and how should the program be affected by the ABM Treaty of SALT I?

A high-quality, well-balanced research-and-technology program in strategic defense that is consistent with the ABM Treaty is in the security interests of the United States. Compliance with the treaty will pose no harmful technological burden on a properly structured U.S. program in strategic defense for the coming decade.

I strongly support Congressional action that restricts SDI funds for fiscal year 1988 to activities fully compliant with the ABM Treaty. The ABM Treaty has provided the basis for U.S.–Soviet efforts to achieve stability, to seek reductions in nuclear armaments, and to avoid war. We certainly should continue to enforce it unless technical and political developments make it possible to supersede it by a superior peace-preserving regime. What is needed is an effort to strengthen the treaty in consultation with the Soviet Union by resolving outstanding issues of compliance and by clarifying its application to new technologies in strategic defense.

Unrestrained testing, including testing in space, of the new technologies or the "other physical principles," as advocated under the administration's so-called "broad interpretation" of the ABM Treaty, is not in the strategic interests of the United States. The treaty, as it was interpreted prior to 1985, contains provisions that were designed liberally to allow the signatory nations to pursue strong research-and-technology programs in strategic defense, while at the same time preventing preparations for rapid deployment of nationwide defense following breakout from the ABM Treaty. It is in our interests to maintain these restraints on the extensive Soviet program in strategic defense. They too have their SDI program, which includes, like ours, the development of powerful lasers.

An agreement to abide by the provisions of the ABM Treaty as they have been complied with up to now will provide a strong impetus to the START negotiations. It is difficult to envision substantial reductions in strategic offensive forces being agreed to by the United States and the Soviet Union in the absence of the restraints of the ABM Treaty on developing and deploying defenses designed to defeat them.

The strategic-defense program of the United States in the coming decade must not contribute to the dismantling of our current treaty achievements, nor should it stand as a barrier to progress in arms control that serves our national security interests.

Conclusion

I strongly urge that the Senate recommend ratification of the INF Treaty as negotiated and signed. To quote from the December Summit Communique:

> This treaty is historic both for its objective—the complete elimination of an entire class of U.S. and Soviet nuclear arms—and for the innovative character and scope of its verification provisions. This mutual accomplishment makes a vital contribution to greater stability.

Beyond this treaty, there are many steps—and more difficult ones—on the journey to a safer world. Progress on this journey will require the best that sound national planning, diplomacy, technology, and arms control have to offer. We should ratify this treaty as an important step on that journey. We face no greater challenge than that of avoiding the unimaginable devastation of a nuclear holocaust and of building a safer world for our children, their children, and future generations.

Appendix

Soviet construction of a large phased-array radar (LPAR) at Abala-kovo, near the town of Krasnoyarsk, in Siberia violates the ABM Treaty, which stipulates in Article VI(b):

> Each party undertakes not to deploy in the future radars
> for early warning of strategic ballistic missile attack except
> at locations along the periphery of its national territory and
> oriented outward.

The purpose of this restriction on LPARs is primarily to prevent the preparations for rapid deployment of a nationwide defense following break-out from the ABM Treaty. It is designed to limit the long-lead-time elements necessary for a defense of missile sites or national territory. A network of LPARs deployed throughout a nation's territory would be a necessary component of an effective territorial defense system, requiring many years to build and eventually spanning the entire national territory. Once such an LPAR network were in place, other ABM components, such as interceptors and smaller engagement radars, could theoretically be rapidly deployed near the LPARs, protecting them from direct attack and preserving their contribution to an ABM defense. A further reason for this limitation is that LPARs on the periphery are considered to be so vulnerable to direct attack that they could not reliably contribute to an ABM system.

Consistent with the ABM Treaty provisions, the Soviet Union has been constructing a ring of seven other LPARs, of a type similar to that at Abalakovo, at peripheral sites near their borders and oriented outward. These will provide early warning in the event of missile attack. If and when it is completed, the Abalakovo radar will close the gap in this early-warning screen by covering the threat corridor for submarine-launched Trident missiles fired from the northern Pacific and Arctic oceans. It violates Article VI(b) of the treaty because it is not located on the periphery, looking outward. In fact, its beams will reach over nearly 3000 miles of Siberia to the border.

If and when it is completed, the Soviet LPAR at Abalakovo will, by itself, present no military threat to the deterrent capability of the United States. Early warning LPARs such as this operate at relatively low frequencies (a few hundred megahertz, corresponding to wavelengths of approximately one meter) as is appropriate for detecting objects, such as incoming warheads (RVs), at large distances. Such radars can be blinded easily by high-altitude nuclear explosions, which cause the radar beams to be bent or absorbed (due to the free electrons released by a large explosion ionizing the air), and thus cannot be relied on for accurately locating a threat and managing the battle to destroy it. Battle-management radars must be designed to operate at much higher frequencies in order to avoid these beam-distorting effects. In contrast to the Abalakovo radar, which is vulnerable as a large, soft target, they also must be defended and hardened against direct attack. They should also be better positioned to defend their targets than is the one at Abalakovo, relative to nearby Soviet missile fields.

Managing Strategic Weapons

WITH THOMAS H. JOHNSON

At the Washington summit in December 1987, the United States and the Soviet Union signed the Intermediate-range Nuclear Forces (INF) Treaty, eliminating all their intermediate-range and shorter-range missiles, and instructed their negotiators in Geneva to work toward a reduction of strategic offensive nuclear arms by approximately 50 percent. The two countries also agreed to sweeping new cooperative procedures for verifying treaty compliance. At the same time, however, charges and countercharges of treaty violations have been exchanged, efforts to resolve current issues of compliance at the Standing Consultative Commission have broken down, and the United States has formally abandoned all Strategic Arms Limitation Talks (SALT I and SALT II) limits on strategic offensive forces. The present period is thus characterized both by high hopes for new compromises and by antagonism on a variety of major issues.

No one can say what will emerge from this turbulent atmosphere in the long run. But, no matter what happens in the continuing negotiations, it is clear that, if lasting improvement in the superpowers' strategic relations is to be achieved during the next two decades, it must arise from a realistic assessment of contemporary U.S.–Soviet relations and of likely military and political developments.

One necessary element in charting a path toward a more stable relationship is a pragmatic judgment of technological trends and their military implications. These technological realities constitute the constraints or boundary conditions that the United States and the Soviet

Union will almost certainly have to cope with in setting defense priorities and in negotiating arms-control agreements during the next twenty years.

We begin by summarizing those technical realities and trends that can reasonably be foreseen over the next two decades. These provide the basis for formulating an approach to increasing both the security of the United States and the stability of the nuclear arms balance with the Soviet Union. This approach incorporates both very specific bilateral agreements and de facto arms control through judicious unilateral decisions about weapons development and deployment. Above all it is designed to point out a pragmatic path for the near-term future.

The land-based intercontinental ballistic missile (ICBM) forces of the United States and the Soviet Union are each capable enough to cause apprehension as to their potential for a devastating first-strike counterforce attack against the other superpower's fixed, land-based targets. A 50 percent reduction, such as may be negotiated in the Strategic Arms Reduction Talks (START), will not change this situation appreciably. In response to this threat, both nations will continue to develop, test, and deploy mobile ICBMs, unless limited by strict treaty provisions. As long as mobile missiles are allowed, their total number is not likely to be accurately verifiable. However, if a treaty were to allow only small mobile missiles armed with single warheads, the overall uncertainty about the number of warheads deployed and their leverage in threatening counterforce attacks would be correspondingly reduced.

Both countries will also continue to develop, test, and deploy in large numbers submarine-launched ballistic missile warheads with very high accuracy, comparable to that of the best ICBM warheads, which will be capable of delivering a prompt counterforce attack against such hard targets as missile silos, command posts, and communications centers. Unless otherwise constrained, the numbers and accuracy of the U.S. SLBM force, and possibly of the Soviet SLBM force, will come to cause the same apprehension that ICBMs now do. However, operational difficulties (such as launch coordination) rather than technical considerations will continue to make a devastating counterforce attack from SLBMs less credible than one from ICBMs.

Both technological and operational considerations will prevent gains in acoustical detection capabilities from threatening the security of deployed strategic submarine forces. Research in nonacoustic means of detection is very unlikely to alter this situation. With increasingly effective communications, strategic submarines will thus become more secure and more reliable. These same factors, plus a new generation of submarine-launched cruise missiles, will make attack submarines more effective, and will render the protection of surface battle groups and convoys more difficult, expensive, and problematic.

Furthermore, both the United States and the Soviet Union will develop and deploy very accurate cruise missiles, using "stealth" technology to attain very low radar cross sections. The Soviet Union will in all likelihood continue to expand and modernize its large air defense system. However, our judgment is that the ability of cruise missiles to penetrate defenses will continue to outstrip the capabilities of defenses against them. The United States will retain confidence in the ability of its air-breathing force of modern, long-range cruise missiles to deliver massively destructive ordnance.

Both countries will extend and vary their passive military use of space for intelligence, communications, navigation, early warning and threat assessment. They will also enhance the effectiveness of their conventional forces with improved surveillance and target identification.

Despite any expanded deployment of strategic defenses, societies will remain vulnerable to nuclear destruction. Technology capable of providing a limited but fairly effective defense of hardened military targets against light attacks will be developed and tested, but it is impossible to say now whether strategic defense will eventually provide an effective or preferred means to enhance the survivability of retaliatory forces. The progress of arms-control negotiations in achieving limits on offensive forces, together with further advances in technology, will be central to answering this question.

Assuming these to be the most significant strategic-arms trends over the next two decades, the task for the United States is to determine what force design and what arms-control measures are best suited to the attainment of a survivable deterrent force and stability in the overall balance of forces. This entails evaluating the contributions to strategic stability of the major weapons systems.

One of the principal engines of instability in the nuclear arms race is the preoccupation with strategic counterforce targeting. "Counterforce" refers in general to one's ability to attack and destroy the military strength of an opponent, thereby limiting the damage one will suffer if attacked. It is frequently argued that such a war-fighting capability strengthens deterrence, and that it would be needed in the event deterrence failed; in some quarters, counterforce targeting has also been presented as a "moral alternative" to targeting cities and many millions of innocent civilians. But counterforce weapons pose a dilemma: If deployed in large numbers, they threaten the destruction of a significant part of an opponent's strategic deterrent forces— namely, his command-and-control system, his fixed land-based ICBMs, his bomber force, and his submarines in port. This threat is sufficiently ominous as to have a tendency to undermine the basis of deterrence, especially when the counterforce weapons are high-technology ballistic missiles with short flight time, high reliability, and great accuracy. Over the past two decades, this threat has generated a preoccupation with securing strategic offensive forces against such massive first strikes.

In evaluating the counterforce threat, one must ask this question: Can a significant fraction of one's deterrent forces be placed at risk of effective elimination by the attacker at some cost he will find reasonable? One must ask this question about the components of one's strategic forces and their associated command-and-control facilities. The latter have been the object of much recent concern since, if they can be eliminated swiftly by direct attack, the effectiveness of one's entire deterrent force can be degraded. But, because effective attacks against specific command-and-control targets can be executed by small numbers of strategic-weapon systems, this problem cannot be solved by setting numerical limits on offensive forces alone.

Both the United States and the Soviet Union take extensive and various precautions to guarantee their ability to control their deterrent forces, even under attack. Coordinated attacks on missile-launching submarines are now, and will probably remain, impossible to execute because of limits to the capacity for antisubmarine warfare. Bombers, on the other hand, can be attacked with missile warheads that are individually very cost-effective (that is, a single ballistic reentry vehicle can eliminate one or more loaded bombers). But operational considerations of alert and warning, as well as of aircraft dispersal, make it difficult for an attacker to rely with great confidence on an ability to destroy preemptively a large fraction of the opponent's bombers. On the other hand, protection of the bombers against the threat of preemptive attack is expensive; the United States has so far sought to balance economy and security. In essence, the United States can resolve this dilemma unilaterally—for example, by providing more dispersal bases.

In sum, there are unilateral remedies to most of the threats of counterforce attack, although the remedies require extensive planning and are expensive. Broad efforts to secure command and control must continue, and modernization of airborne strategic forces must emphasize their survivability. This still leaves the peculiar fixation on the "window of vulnerability" imperiling land-based ICBMs, a case that epitomizes the logical dilemma of counterforce targeting.

ICBM vulnerability has arisen from two developments: multiple warheads (multiple independently targetable reentry vehicles, or MIRVs) and the high accuracy of counterforce weapons. Of these two, MIRVs are the critical factor. Without them, an attacker could not hope to do better than break even; the destruction of a single missile would require the expenditure of at least one attacking missile. In a world with only single-warhead ICBMs, and with a comparable number of launchers on both sides, even a high level of missile accuracy would not be very threatening; one would not then need to consider the difficult job of trying to constrain the evolution of technology.*

Thus, the objective of arms-control agreements seeking to enhance stability should be to provide incentives to both sides to shift toward single-warhead ICBMs, within an overall limit on the total number of warheads (ICBM plus SLBM) that each side could use for prompt first strikes. This should be a major objective of force development for both nations; neither side can do it alone. We believe this goal should have a higher priority than that of merely reducing the number of such vehicles.

To summarize, the desiderata arising from considerations of the problems of counterforce are: first, continued guaranteeing of the security of airborne and seaborne deterrents and of strategic command, control, communications, and intelligence; and, second, elimination of the risks inherent in counterforce targeting of ICBMs. The first requires judicious force development that secures deterrent forces against threats from new technologies and reduces the threat posed by short-warning attacks. There are three approaches to achieving the second objective: reducing the threatening nature of attacks, protecting the missiles themselves against possible attacks (including making them less attractive targets), or removing the ICBMs entirely.

---

*There are no practical means of preventing the continuing improvement in the accuracy of ballistic missiles. However, if a small annual quota of ICBM and SLBM test firings were negotiated, both countries would have lower confidence in both the reliability and accuracy of their missiles to execute counterforce strikes against hard targets. This lower confidence would be caused primarily by operational, rather than purely technological, considerations. The overall deterrence value of the forces would, nevertheless, remain strong.

We address the first approach by investigating force developments that reduce the threat to ICBMs, and we explore the terms of the second approach, which hinges on the problem of ICBM basing, a controversial problem of long standing. The third approach— removing ICBMs—we do not view as a practical objective during the next 20-year period.

The excellent command-and-control characteristics of ICBMs, their large throw weights (particularly useful for carrying penetration aids, such as decoys and jammers, to be used against defenses), their high reentry velocities, and their relatively low operating costs (below those of SLBMs on a cost-per-warhead basis) all continue to make ICBMs attractive as offensive weapons, even as their monopoly on high accuracy disappears. The costs of protecting them against counterforce attack will likely remove their operating-cost advantage during the next 20 years. But they will always retain advantages by virtue of their distributed deployment and their command-and-control properties. Militarily, they are the weapons of first choice to provide a credible capability for implementing limited nuclear options—that is, their ability to respond in measure to provocation at any level, which we consider a necessary component of deterrence. (This is both less than and distinct from "nuclear war-fighting.") Such ability, plus the obligation they impose on an offense to be complex enough to coordinate attacks against both ICBMs and alert bombers, makes the maintenance of at least some ICBMs advisable.

How large should the ICBM force be? How should it be based? These questions are not independent, and the question of basing does not yet have a clear answer.

The total number of high-velocity warheads (on both ICBMs and SLBMs) should be fixed by U.S.–Soviet agreement. With such an agreement, and with ICBMs based in a highly secure mode, only a small number of ICBM warheads—several hundred—would be needed. If, as at present, the United States relies on an uncertain survivability of its ICBMs in a massive counterforce attack, a thousand or more reentry vehicles on ICBMs would seem to be necessary to provide sufficient survivable warheads. Deploying ICBMs as single-warhead missiles reduces the probability of success of a counterforce attack by requiring the attacker to target and destroy more missiles.

But questions of numbers and of basing become coupled if the eventual choice for basing is mobile missiles. The possibility of either side's cheating in deployment of mobile missiles would place a high premium on guaranteeing that such ICBMs do not have multiple warheads, a guarantee that should be a high-priority goal of future arms-control efforts.

Confident delivery of a massive and simultaneous strike against a missile force based in hardened underground silos and numbering between many hundreds and more than a thousand would present awesome difficulties. Nevertheless, the possibility of such an attack cannot be dismissed. One must ask: How vulnerable is the U.S. ICBM force to actual execution of a disarming first strike? The most that can be said is that, whatever the chances of success of such a strike, those chances will increase during the next two decades in the absence of new constraints. It is therefore inevitable that resources will be devoted to the search for a more suitable ICBM basing mode, one that meets favorable cost-effectiveness criteria as well as force-structure, political, and strategic requirements.

There are five classes of options for secure land basing of ICBMs: deceptive basing, deep underground basing, mobile basing, deployment of an active defense, and hardened silos. We regard only the latter three as still being competitive options.

Mobile missiles would be preferable in the single-warhead mode, so that the numerical uncertainty arising from verification difficulties would not be a major concern. Detailed analyses on various mobile-basing schemes for the single-warhead Midgetman currently estimate system costs to be significantly greater than for fixed basing in silos. However, the United States continues to consider the mobile Midgetman deployment, in part because it is argued to be the most economical when costs are calculated in terms of the desired level of *surviving* warheads against the currently postulated Soviet threat. This conclusion, however, is sensitive to three considerations: a continued high level of deployment of ICBM warheads by the Soviets, the availability of a sufficient land area in the United States for basing mobiles, and the hardness of the missile-launcher–transporter system. The inferred cost advantages may no longer be valid, however, if the reductions in strategic-missile warheads discussed by Washington and Moscow are successfully negotiated.

Active defense (for example, defense by antiballistic missile, or ABM, systems) of land-based missiles is another option. It has three major problems. First, on the basis of technology available in the immediately foreseeable future, active defense of ICBMs will have to use interceptors carrying nuclear weapons, which would require a fundamental change from current U.S. insistence on nonnuclear strategic-defense systems. Second, before deploying an active defense, the United States would have to develop and test an entirely new system and show it to be cost-effective and capable against potential countermeasures. (Of course, success in developing such a system would mean that the United States could retain its current ICBMs and basing, with perhaps the addition of some new silos; and the system's cost would very likely be less than that of a new force of mobile ICBMs.) Third, fielding an active defense for silo-based ICBMs would certainly entail abrogating or, at a minimum, extensively revising, the ABM treaty. Even though radar and interceptor technologies are allowed by the treaty, provisions on numbers and basing would have to be changed.

Justification of active defense of silos requires a complex cost-effectiveness analysis—comparing proliferation of the offense and countermeasures with further improvements in the defense. One would have to develop a detailed engineering design of a system before one could determine if a criterion of cost-effectiveness might be satisfactorily met. Our judgment is that, so far, no option that would meet such a criterion has been clearly shown to exist. The difficulty of producing an active defense option is sensitive to the total number of threatening ballistic-missile warheads and to advances in technology, such as the development of warheads that can maneuver independently and maintain accuracy. The problem would be easier if the United States and the Soviet Union were successfully to negotiate reductions in the number of threatening warheads.

The final option is to deploy either MIRVed or small, single-warhead ICBMs in very hard silos. Existing Minuteman silos could be rendered substantially harder if they were refitted with smaller missiles. Deployment of single-warhead missiles in hard silos would be consistent with an arms-control regime that restricted the United States and Soviet Union to equal numbers of strategic-missile warheads. In a circumstance of symmetrical deployment of single-warhead ICBMs, individual missiles would not be sufficiently valuable to be lucrative targets; an attack would cost more warheads than could be destroyed. If only the attacking side retained MIRVs, after a first strike against single-warhead missiles, the total expenditure of warheads in an attack would still be greater, but the financial cost could easily be less, depending on the relative cost of the boosters for MIRVs and single warheads. Thus, silo basing also benefits strongly from well-verified limits on total deployments, to prevent the achievement of an advantage in cost-effectiveness through increased numbers of warheads. This option is the least expensive of the three considered. Its strategic attraction is that a greater vulnerability can be accepted for individual targets of lower value, particularly for ICBMs, which would become, by virtue of smaller relative numbers, a strategically less critical component of the deterrent force.

Reductions in the ICBM fraction of the deterrent force would make the sea-based forces, both ballistic missiles and cruise missiles, relatively more important to deterrence. The trends discussed above suggest that this will be an effective strategy.

Both the United States and the Soviet Union should be free to allocate warheads between ICBMs and SLBMs within an agreed total as they choose, according to their own technological, geographic, and bureaucratic priorities. Subsequently, this total could be lowered gradually without either side losing confidence in its deterrent. Strategic-arms agreements should permit continued modernization of allowed SLBM forces in the interim. Providing these missiles with penetration aids and extending their range to include a larger fraction of the oceans in their operating areas will increase confidence in their survivability.

Modernizing SLBMs would also lead to their improved accuracy and could cause concern about them as an emerging hard-target counterforce threat. If, however, the number of deployed SLBMs were limited, their modernization would not add significantly to the destabilizing nature of the perceived threat. Such deployments could increase the incentive to move away from a heavy reliance on highly MIRVed, fixed, land-based ICBMs toward a more stabilizing force mix. Once ICBMs were reduced to more stable sizes and types, SLBMs could be traded off for cruise missiles, through gradual lowering of the agreed total number of ballistic missile warheads; the threat of counterforce attacks would thereby be further reduced.

Cruise missiles occupy a unique place in strategic-weapons planning. First, quantitative limits on sea-launched cruise missiles cannot be accurately verified. Second, cruise missiles have very little, if any, potential for large-scale, prompt counterforce targeting because of their technical characteristics—their low velocity and their vulnerability as targets for various kinds of interceptors. Their low velocity means long flight times through variable atmospheric conditions that cannot be predicted well at the low altitude at which cruise missiles fly. Massive, highly coordinated strikes by cruise missiles against large, geographically diverse targets, such as ICBM fields, would be impractical because of the long warning times the missiles would afford were any of them detected. The likelihood is high (from the attacker's conservative point of view) that more than a few of the large number of cruise missiles in such an attack would be detected relatively early. Furthermore, if nuclear weapons were to start exploding in a target vicinity, cruise missiles arriving later might not survive; because they are not hardened against various nuclear weapon effects nearly as well as are ICBM reentry vehicles, attack coordination presents an even more worrisome problem for cruise missiles than it does for ICBMs. Finally, the slowness of cruise missiles precludes their use against targets that can reasonably be expected to move—for example, military units, mobile ICBMs, or command posts.

Individual hard targets can probably be protected against limited cruise-missile attack because the flight time of cruise missiles allows significant opportunity for detection by airborne early-warning and control systems (AWACS) on station near the targets, or by large arrays of tower-mounted radars. Moreover, once located and identified, cruise missiles are relatively easy to destroy. However, such a defense against cruise missiles could prove very expensive; the large number of airborne or tower-mounted sensors and extensive associated systems required for protection of each target preclude this defense from being practical for very large or soft targets and, in particular, for very numerous targets.

Three classes of appropriate targets for cruise missiles remain: cities, industrial facilities, and certain high-value military targets—such as submarine bases, airfields, large fuel depots, and proposed ground-based laser facilities. All are too large and too soft to protect with high confidence against attack by large numbers of cruise missiles.

In sum, although cruise missiles can inflict massive damage, they are far less threatening against an opponent's deterrent force than are accurate, reliable, and highly MIRVed ICBMs. Since any cruise-missile attack might be detected with significant warning time, the attack planner cannot rely on a doctrine that depends on minimal or no warning. The realistic prospect that there will be a long warning time of a large cruise-missile attack is an essential element in increasing the stability of deterrence, since it reduces the odds that decisions will be made impulsively on the basis of incomplete information. It also enhances the perceived survivability of most strategic military forces and support elements.

One can argue that cruise-missile forces have an important and undesirable defect: The fact that their precise numbers are not accurately verifiable rules out prospects for negotiating tight numerical limits on the levels of deployment, particularly for sea-launched cruise missiles. However, because nuclear-armed cruise missiles are inappropriate for executing large-scale prompt counterforce attacks, there is no strong incentive to enlarge a force centered on cruise missiles to anything like the extent of the currently deployed strategic ballistic-missile force.

By accepting the evident defect of an inability to count cruise missiles precisely, one could take advantage of these missiles' stabilizing characteristics, making it possible to accept an arms-control regime that would prescribe no limits on certain classes of cruise missiles and shift the emphasis of deterrence to a force structure with far fewer ballistic warheads. Within such an approach, one could continue to implement numerical limits, with satisfactory standards of verification, on air-launched cruise missiles and their carriers. The threats posed by ALCMs are relatively symmetric, assuming that long-range ALCMs will retain their ability to penetrate existing and prospective Soviet air defenses.

Sea-launched cruise-missile (SLCM) deployments can be diversified by basing them on surface ships as well as on submarines, a process that has already begun. Frequently expressed opposition to extending deployments of nuclear-armed SLCMs to surface ships has generally arisen from three sources: fear of further expanding the size of the nuclear arsenal in unverifiable ways; concern that major surface ships bearing nuclear-tipped SLCMs would be tempting and vulnerable targets; and concern for the physical security and control of the surface-deployed weapons themselves.

The first concern is largely moot, since some SLCMs have already been deployed. Removing them is an unrealistic solution within the near future, since the essentially unverifiable nature of the SLCMs will not be changed by wishing the situation were different. A total ban on SLCMs of all kinds—conventional as well as nuclear—on surface ships might change this reality, but such a ban seems a highly unlikely prospect. Furthermore, the importance of diversification of SLCM carriers will increase as SLCMs become a larger fraction of the deterrent forces.

With regard to the second concern, about the relative risks of SLCMs on ships, there is no reason to believe that, in general, they should be more attractive as targets than other classes of seagoing nuclear forces, particularly aircraft carriers. Concerning the third point, the physical security and control of the weapons can and should be greatly improved with permissive action links (safety devices that prevent the firing of a nuclear weapon without presidentially delegated authorization) like the ones currently employed in the U.S. bomber force.

One aspect of SLCM deployments tends to favor the Soviet Union: A large fraction of the American urban and industrial base, in contrast to that of the Soviets, lies relatively close to the seacoasts, and thus to potential launch areas for SLCMs. The significance of this asymmetry can be reduced, though not altogether removed, by developing longer-range SLCMs.

Once the total number of ballistic-missile warheads has been reduced to a mutually acceptable minimum, thus removing concern about a disarming counterforce attack, future reductions in nuclear weapons could proceed by eliminating the right for certain classes of ships to carry nuclear-armed SLCMs. The progress of such restrictions can be adjusted to guarantee a stable regime as verification capabilities evolve and as numbers of weapons decrease. Finally, if adequate SLCM-counting methods are developed, restrictions can accommodate U.S.–Soviet geopolitical asymmetries by providing freedom to allocate between ALCMs and SLCMs under an agreed total.

The critical practical issue surrounding strategic bombers continues to be the perceived necessity for the ability to penetrate all the way to the target. This is a problem for efficient force modernization, but one that bears little direct relation to strategic stability. We fail to see the necessity to carry pilots and large, expensive vehicles all the way to strategic targets.

The continued case for high-performance penetrating bombers seems to hinge on four major arguments: (1) the combination of bombers and ALCMs puts a great stress on air defenses, thus providing maximum penetration for both (and causing continued heavy Soviet investment in air defenses); (2) bombers can find mobile targets or be redirected to secondary targets, whereas ALCMs cannot; (3) bombers continue to be needed for other missions (as, for example, B-52s were used in Vietnam); and (4) because of the insufficient range of ALCMs, bombers must penetrate Soviet air defenses even to launch cruise missiles. In our view, none of these arguments makes a compelling case for continuing the development of new penetrating bombers. Extending the range of ALCMs beyond 2000 miles, a feasible option, would entirely dispose of the fourth argument.

The third argument—conventional use—is indeed a valid reason to keep some bombers in the force. But the requirements are different from those for a bomber force capable of penetrating the world's heaviest air defenses during a nuclear conflict. The military requirements of the United States for a new, highly versatile, large-payload bomber for combat support and long-range naval attacks do not appear to have been carefully analyzed apart from the assumption that the bomber must penetrate the airspace of the Soviet Union.

Furthermore, to locate a mobile target, a bomber pilot would have to be quite close indeed, about an order of magnitude closer than the distance at which radar can currently acquire airborne targets. Although a bomber may penetrate toward a target at high speed and low altitude, at a speed of several hundred miles an hour the ground close by is a complete blur for a pilot, who would have to slow down to see anything and gain altitude to increase his field of view. Both of these actions would vastly decrease the bomber's survivability, even if it were a stealth aircraft.

Arguments for the importance of placing stress on Soviet air defenses are highly sensitive to what one assumes to be the relative potential for successful penetration by bombers as compared to ALCMs, and to the additional costs the Soviets must bear to be able to intercept both. To support the argument quantitatively, one must assume either that bombers penetrate very much better than ALCMs do, or that Soviet expenditures to cope with the dual threat would be significantly larger. Neither has been shown to be true.

As is the case with SLCMs, expansion of the role of ALCMs as the airborne leg of the strategic triad will not come without cost. Airplanes designed or adapted for use as ALCM carriers would have attendant costs, although the costs certainly will not equal those necessary for a new generation of penetrating bombers. The savings from eliminating the penetration requirement for bombers could more appropriately be spent in increasing the survivability of ALCM carriers—for example, with more dispersal bases. The air-breathing leg of the triad is the most expensive per warhead, but its unique capability to be recalled, plus its excellent survivability and reliability, will continue to be valuable.

The scope and pace of strategic defense activities will depend on the future of the 1972 ABM treaty. If the treaty is modified or abandoned in order to allow the full, unrestrained development of new technologies, competition in defensive programs will increase and create new pressures for expanding offensive-missile forces and for improving their ability to penetrate any initial deployments of defenses. Advanced interceptors, such as the Soviet SA-12, might provide a partial defense against SLBMs, depending on their deployment mode (including extensive internetting with other systems, especially an expanded deployment of acquisition radars) and on their performance against offensive countermeasures (including radar suppression and trajectory changes). In this light, actual deployment of these weapons will have to be monitored carefully if the current ABM treaty regime is to be maintained.

The one strategic-defense technology with tested military capability—nuclear-armed interceptors—is not capable of a significantly more ambitious role than to defend hard points, preferably of dispersed target sets such as ICBMs. The United States must solve two problems in order to consider any significantly more capable defensive system: It must develop means of discrimination in midcourse between attacking reentry vehicles and their accompanying decoys; and, for a full nationwide defense, it must develop a reliable, survivable means of intercepting missiles in their boost phases. Even though other major issues will remain, if these two problems can be solved in the next decade or so, it will be possible to evaluate realistically the full military capability of various classes of ballistic-missile defense systems.

Meanwhile, the primary question remains the size and direction of research and technology development for strategic defense, including testing of functional prototypes.* Maximizing the eventual utility of defenses will require negotiating simultaneously to reduce offensive forces and to extend and strengthen cooperation in arms control with the Soviet Union. Such cooperation would play a critical role in determining any future deployment plans. For the coming decade, a research-and-development program consistent with the ABM treaty is sufficient to fill this need.

Strategic warning, photoreconnaissance, and communications satellites are among the most valuable of U.S. military assets. Guaranteeing their security and strengthening their capabilities by vigorously exploiting advancing technology should therefore be among the highest of U.S. defense priorities. The principal means for providing such protection are moving the satellites (except for photoreconnaissance satellites) to higher orbits, applying various kinds of stealth technology, using hardening measures (which would be particularly effective against directed-energy weapons and other forms of electromagnetic

---

*See the report of a workshop at the Stanford Center for International Security and Arms Control: "Strategic Missile Defense: Necessities, Prospects, and Dangers in the Near Term," April 1985.

attack), providing redundance of means for performing tasks, and maintaining ready spares (and attendant expendable launch vehicles) to replace lost assets. We remain skeptical about the real value of keep-out zones (a zone around a satellite that is not to be entered by the satellites of another country) and shoot-back defensive satellites, but further thought and research in all areas of satellite protection will be valuable.

If nothing is done to change the present course, we foresee a continued evolution of existing strategic nuclear systems toward higher capabilities and larger numbers that, taken as a whole and unconstrained, will pose a greater threat to the security of the superpowers and thus a greater threat to peace.

As for remedies, we are suspicious of proposals that attempt to transform or eliminate the source of insecurity with bans on single types of weapons or on new technology. Adaptations and constraints on the applications of a variety of technologies are likely to be more possible to achieve; their ramifications can be more confidently understood.

Therefore, we propose a conservative and evolutionary response to an evolving threat—specific bilateral agreements and judicious unilateral choices in force modernization. We recommend bilateral agreements to reduce drastically the total number of warheads on ICBMs and SLBMs; to limit mobile ICBMs to single-warhead missiles; to permit modernization of SLBM forces, with a primary emphasis on improved operational security and survivability; and to increase bomber survivability by providing more dispersal bases. We also favor expanding cooperative means of verification, particularly on-site inspection and presence; strengthening survivability and multiplicity of command-and-control systems; and protecting space assets by a variety of means, principally redundancy, ready spares, and higher altitudes.

Cruise missiles play a prominent role, in our view. We advocate reducing the role of both ICBMs and SLBMs, with the result that the bulk of the U.S. deterrent force should comprise two categories of cruise missiles, ALCMs and SLCMs. In addition, the air-breathing deterrent should move from a penetrating bomber force toward an advanced ALCM force.

Our approach is not to be interpreted as recommending an unlimited increase in numbers of SLCMs and their carriers. We believe that, in fact, the numbers will remain within reasonable limits and that the operational aspects of deployment can be made and kept strategically stable.

Unilateral actions by the United States to ensure a high survivability of the independent components of the American deterrent force are more important than seeking to negotiate rigorous equality in the numbers of warheads. We anticipate a political evolution toward deeper numerical reductions as both sides develop operational confidence in cooperative measures of verification, including such measures as challenge rights and on-site inspection.

None of our suggestions would stand in the way of the various current proposals for significant reductions in total deployed nuclear forces. Evolution toward force structures that simultaneously are inherently secure and give long warning time in the event of a massive attack will not only be stabilizing, but also will remain a source of stability as total numbers of weapons decrease. We believe that the limited proposals we make here for managing the strategic balance in the near term can provide a practical basis for subsequent steps toward smaller and more stable strategic forces.

PROSPECTS
AFTER THE COLD
WAR

Why Not Now?

WITH THEODORE B. TAYLOR

Go Cold Turkey
[by Theodore B. Taylor]

The resolution we are debating has two parts: The first calls for the abolition of nuclear weapons, which I take to mean the worldwide prohibition of the use, possession, production, and development of nuclear explosives and certain classes of means for their delivery, such as ballistic missiles. It includes the emplacement of means designed to enforce this prohibition, to the extent that it is possible. The second part concerns timing—that this objective should be accomplished within 11 years.

On January 15, 1986, Mikhail Gorbachev proposed that "a step-by-step, consistent process of ridding the Earth of nuclear weapons be implemented and completed within the next 15 years, before the end of this century." On June 9, 1988, Rajiv Gandhi proposed to the UN special session on disarmament an action plan with a "binding commitment by all nations to eliminating nuclear weapons, in stages, by the year 2010 at the latest."

These proposals have been largely ignored by government leaders and arms-control and disarmament professionals in the West. I have been unable to find a single published assessment of either of them. When they come up in discussions, they are most often summarily dismissed as unrealistic, utopian, and unworthy of further consideration.

The main reason for this widespread rejection has to do with the perceived risks of cheating. Under a global abolition agreement, if one country retained a few, or maybe not so few, illicit nuclear weapons, it might exercise intolerable and massive control over other countries. Since no verification system can absolutely assure that no one will cheat, it is then argued that the only way to avoid nuclear war for the foreseeable future is to maintain the capacity to destroy any country in retaliation for nuclear attack, or even for the threat of an attack.

But I see several troublesome problems with relying on nuclear deterrence for decades into the future:

- *It legitimizes possession of nuclear weapons.* This stimulates the spread of nuclear weapons to other countries, increasing the likelihood of nuclear war by misunderstanding or by design. The idea that nuclear weapons are legitimate for a few countries, but not for others, is simply unacceptable in much of the world.
- *Nuclear deterrence does not deter nuclear terrorists.* Its continued presence in the world is likely to stimulate some terrorists to go nuclear.
- *It does not necessarily deter irrational and desperate leaders from calling for suicidal attacks with nuclear weapons.* Isn't it conceivable that Adolph Hitler might have used any available nuclear weapons rather than surrendering, even if it meant certain destruction of all Germany?
- *It maintains conditions that might lead to accidental nuclear war.* How likely this is depends not only on the number of nuclear weapons but on complex command-and-control interactions.
- *Nuclear deterrence stimulates the high-technology arms race.* It maintains excuses for continuing intensive research and development, especially nuclear tests and missile flight tests, to assure the capacity to retaliate against any technological advances by the other side.
- *Nuclear deterrence preserves reliance on a capacity to commit, under certain conditions, an indiscriminate act of vengeance that can justly be called mass murder.*

Instead of maintaining nuclear deterrent forces at any level, consider what would happen if they were abolished. How would nuclear warheads be disposed of? (No current or imminent treaties call for destruction of warheads; they are to be returned to the owner countries without restriction.)

Verified elimination of nuclear warheads under future treaties has been the subject of detailed studies for several years. A joint project of the Federation of American Scientists and the Soviet Committee of Scientists for Peace, for example, concluded that nuclear warheads can be verifiably destroyed after they have been identified and made available for destruction, without revealing any sensitive information about their design. The proposal is to use the uranium from warheads as fuel for nuclear power plants, attenuated to such low concentrations of uranium 235 that it cannot be used to make nuclear weapons. Plutonium should be disposed of directly to avoid the danger that it might be used for making weapons. In this way, all the fissile material in the world's present stockpiles of about 60,000 nuclear warheads could be disposed of in less than five years.

But these studies do not indicate how to verify that no warheads have been hidden. I have reluctantly concluded that *technical* verification of absolute compliance with a ban on nuclear weapons is not now possible. Instead, we may have to look to nontechnical solutions. One possible strategy might be to establish and reinforce a worldwide popular taboo against acquiring nuclear weapons or the means for making them. This should include frequent, widely publicized articulation of the taboo by all government leaders, and at least annual pledges by all heads of state, that their governments have strictly adhered to the nuclear abolition. Upholding international law, leaders would urge any individuals who have evidence of cheating to report it to an appropriate United Nations authority—and ways to do so without fear of reprisal would be provided. Whistle-blowers would be greatly rewarded, and individual violators would be severely punished.

The threat of nuclear war is not the only threat to human survival. We are destroying the capacity of our habitat to support us, and nothing short of intensive, cooperative, constructive action to save our global homeland will suffice. We do not have 20 years to deal with the immediate threats of climate instabilities and environmental poisoning. The real enemy, as Walt Kelly's Pogo told us three decades ago, is not "them" but "us."

If we shift our attention away from ways to destroy each other we may, just in time, show that we are capable of the new ways of thinking that Albert Einstein called for more than 40 years ago.

Technically, we could eliminate all nuclear weapons before the end of the century. It took just three years of the Manhattan Project to bring about the revolutionary effects of atomic bombs on warfare, and less than five years of intensive peacetime action to shift the scale of those effects another thousandfold with the development of hydrogen bombs. If we spend the next 11 years doing everything we can to "make peace better instead of making war worse," as my friend Lewis Bohn put it, we can abolish not only nuclear weapons but all modern weapons of mass destruction before the end of the century.

Not So Fast
[by Sidney D. Drell]

We are debating the resolution that nuclear weapons should be abolished by the year 2000 because of the remarkable meeting at Reykjavik, Iceland, where Ronald Reagan and Mikhail Gorbachev apparently came to the brink of concluding that all nuclear-armed ballistic missiles and, perhaps, all nuclear weapons should be abolished by the end of the century. Those Reykjavik discussions, which made our European allies so nervous, are commonly ridiculed, but I do not share that view. I believe that Reykjavik made the subject of significantly reducing the number of nuclear weapons, not just limiting or controlling them, an issue for serious public discussion. Before that, such discussions were mostly confined to academic seminars or peace-group panels.

It is good to get back to basics: Can we get rid of nuclear weapons? Are they usable, or are they so destructive that civilized human beings cannot even think of "pushing the button"? Over the years, we have grown too accustomed to their face. Not only do we accept them but we have elevated them to the fine art of battle plans and scenarios for fighting nuclear wars. We need to be reminded of what President Dwight Eisenhower said in 1956: With these weapons of mass destruction, we are rapidly reaching a point where no all-out war can be won—because it is no longer a battle to exhaustion and surrender, but "destruction of the enemy and suicide."

The destructive potential of nuclear weapons is so great and their murderous impact so indiscriminate that leaders from all walks of life have concluded that they must never be used. If these weapons are not usable, if their existence may threaten our very existence and leaves little if any margin for error, then inevitably we ask, "Why not get rid of them—and the sooner the better?"

I fully endorse working toward an *eventual* goal of removing all nuclear weapons from the face of the Earth. That is an important goal because history has shown that every weapon ever invented has been used in war. Pope Innocent II, in the year 1139 A.D., declared the recently developed and deadly crossbow "hateful to God and unfit for

Christians" and forbade its use. Only a few years later, this edict of the Second Lateran Council was amended to permit use of the crossbow against Moslems. Shortly thereafter, this limitation also broke down, and the crossbow was used indiscriminately against one and all until more efficient means of killing superseded it. It is already a departure from the norm that, for 44 years, since Hiroshima and Nagasaki, no one has employed nuclear weapons in actual conflict, although their use has been contemplated on numerous occasions.

With that eventual goal in mind, we must address the physical facts and the practical problems of statesmanship. What can we do in the 11 years that remain before the year 2000?

Let me start with two technical observations about nuclear weapons and stockpiles:

- Even if all nuclear weapons are destroyed or rendered harmless and all weapons fuel (fissile material) attenuated for use in power reactors, knowledge of how to make such weapons cannot be eliminated. Given a future commitment or urgency to restart making nuclear bombs, for whatever reason, the experience of World War II shows we are never more than a few years away from a nuclear-weapons capability.
- There is no way to verify compliance with a total ban of nuclear weapons. Last year's debate over ratification of the INF (intermediate-range nuclear forces) Treaty shows how hard it is to develop confidence that one can actually verify its proscriptions against one class of weapons. We can see weapons being destroyed—and we could also weigh weapons fuel being contaminated if stockpile reductions were negotiated—but what about secret caches? Although we may be able to gain confidence that hundreds of weapons are not retained in a secret arsenal, I know of no way to get that number down to dozens in the near future.

Recognizing these two technical limitations, my argument is based on political realities: this is a world of nation-states, adversarial interests, fear and distrust between different economic and political systems, and intolerance grounded in religious beliefs. The removal of nuclear weapons must be tightly coupled to progress in reducing distrust, fear, and intolerance and in removing the image of the enemy between nations with adversarial relations. That is not to suggest that political and social progress must precede large reductions in our nuclear arsenals—or vice versa. Each can assist the other. Getting rid of nuclear weapons is much more difficult than a well-defined technical challenge. Albert Einstein once said, "Politics is much harder than physics."

But the process can be started, and now is as good an opportunity as we have ever had. In two years, the newly constructive dialogue between the United States and the Soviet Union achieved two notable results: the 1986 Stockholm accord on prenotification and observation of conventional military maneuvers and the Intermediate-Range Nuclear Forces Treaty.

One can hope that the pace will quicken as more constructive political relations and reduced fears lead to unilateral moves of good sense that need not await formal treaties and exquisitely balanced concessions. An auspicious example was Mikhail Gorbachev's December 7 announcement of substantial unilateral troop reductions. A Western response is now in order. General John Galvin, supreme allied commander, Europe, reportedly mentioned a very sensible one—reduction of NATO battlefield nuclear weapons. We are beginning to see the first benefit of new thinking calling for less threatening offensive-force postures. Political accommodations and sensible unilateral moves to reduce and reconfigure conventional military forces may further accelerate progress.

We must greatly reduce the risk of nuclear war by seeking a stable strategic balance at a much lower level of nuclear forces. We should first reaffirm their purpose—simply to deter any use of nuclear weapons by an opponent. To this end, survivably based nuclear forces—at a fraction of their present level—are adequate.

But a major change—a phase change—in the world political order will be required before we can abandon a policy of deterrence based on strategic offensive nuclear forces. The political shape of a disarmed world is beyond my hopes for my children's and grandchildren's generations. That is not a statement of despair. The young American republic of 1789, or again in 1812, could not very well have foreseen living in peace and fully sharing a *disarmed* 2500-mile border with a nation of the British Commonwealth, yet that was achieved within a century. I am on the negative side of this debate only because the year was set at 2000, and I cannot at present identify all the practical steps leading to zero nuclear weapons, any more than I can to no weapons of any kind.

I can, however, see some useful forward steps:

- Negotiate more confidence-building measures to remove the threat of blitzkrieg conventional attacks.
- Alter deployed conventional forces to defensive postures where East meets West. Define realistic and essential security objectives, and deploy and train forces to meet them without early reliance on nuclear weapons. In effect, make nuclear weapons less relevant.
- Strengthen international organizations, and cooperate and devote resources to removing sources of conflict and to solving the more pressing of the Earth's problems: hunger, ignorance, fear, disease, pollution, and overpopulation.
- As scientists, assist the current efforts to achieve and enforce a treaty prohibiting chemical weapons. There is no way to verify total compliance with such a ban, just as there is no way to verify total nuclear disarmament. But, through active support and full cooperation in the self-policing of such a ban, we can help realize this goal. We can commit ourselves to it in a statement of conscience—a new Hippocratic Oath.

In response to revelations about the Libyan chemical-weapons plant, West German Foreign Minister Hans-Dietrich Genscher recently urged the scientific community "to make their entire know-how available so that we can solve the still unsettled questions concerning a global ban on chemical weapons, especially the related verification issues."

Genscher's words were echoed by his Italian counterpart, Giulio Andreotti, who said that the problems posed by verification were difficult, but not impossible, to resolve: "Technical complexity cannot, and should not, be used as an alibi to delay the resolution of what is essentially a political problem, since it is based on the question of confidence between states," he said.

In this way, scientists—who have created the technology of unparalleled means of mass, indiscriminate destruction—would begin to participate as a community in supporting declared national goals to ban such weapons. This step could move us toward what some day may be a nuclear-free world.

Taylor: I'm puzzled. Sid Drell is pressing, without reservation, for abolition of chemical and biological weapons while saying that goal is impractical for nuclear weapons in the foreseeable future. I've asked some of my friends who agree with him about the basic inconsistency of their position. The answer is generally that nuclear weapons are absolute weapons, whereas biological and chemical weapons are not. How hard have they looked at genetic poisons that can potentially kill on a massive scale? Some kind of technological inertia that characterizes physics—as opposed to biology and chemistry—is assumed to apply to nuclear weapons but not to chemical and biological weapons.

Many people are now less worried about nuclear war beginning between the United States and the Soviet Union than about other countries initiating it. This worry is a direct consequence of nuclear proliferation. The policies of the two superpowers have encouraged this through the magnitude of their accumulation of weapons. To legitimize nuclear weapons for us, but then demand that countries forgo this route to "security"—we can do it, not the rest of you—is simply not going to fly. I have yet to speak to any Indian, Pakistani, Brazilian, Argentine, or Mexican who accepts that double standard. If there isn't a clear commitment by the superpowers to directly abolish nuclear weapons—if not by the year 2000, as soon as possible after that—the Non-Proliferation Treaty will begin to break down at the review conference next year. It will not be renewed in 1995, and we will all worry about the new phase of nuclear-war fears that will involve not one, not 13, but God knows how many countries because they'll all be hidden. The history of proliferation since the Chinese announced that they were a nuclear weapons state has been one of ambiguity and secrecy. Without abolition, the club will slowly but steadily enlarge.

Drell: I emphasized chemical weapons, first, because they are an immediate danger: They're being used. A million people were killed in the Iran–Iraq war, many through the indiscriminate use of chemical weapons. We've got to get rid of them quickly because the restraints have already broken down. A second reason has to do with the political aspects of the problem. Many countries have stated that they support banning chemical weapons. In that political framework, we can do something, and we should make it an example from which to move on to the next, the nuclear problem. There's no other fundamental difference. It's not a matter of chemistry versus physics. But let's admit that one reason there is a political consensus to move on chemical weapons is because some who would otherwise be unwilling to ban them know that they have a nuclear fallback. So getting rid of all the "weapons of indiscriminate destruction" will be very difficult, but we have a possibility to eliminate one, and we should take that opportunity.

Other nations have every reason to give us hell at the next nonproliferation review convention. The nuclear powers have failed to live up to their promises. Just read the prologue, the first part of both the Partial Test Ban Treaty and the Non-Proliferation Treaty. We promised to work to reduce our nuclear forces, and to stop testing nuclear weapons underground—and we have done neither. There is no reason for other countries to look to us for leadership and to sit there and accept our fascination with continually making more and more accurate weapons while we say, "Don't do it yourself." We have to make clear that we share the goals of working to stop underground nuclear-bomb testing at an appropriate time and working to reduce our arsenals to zero.

The difference is not with the goal but with the time scale. I am stuck in a phase similar to that of the American Catholic bishops in their landmark pastoral letter of 1983, reiterated last year: deterrence is not acceptable as an end in itself, but it is a morally acceptable policy, because it offers the best prospect of avoiding war now, so long as you're working toward gradual disarmament. I recognize all the inherent contradictions that people from Jonathan Schell to George Kennan and including the two of us have struggled with on the issue of deterrence. What sense does it make to threaten to use a weapon that you say no person of any humanity could conceivably use? Yet these weapons exist.

There are two time scales in this world. There's the practical time scale of what we can do during the next decade, which is to reduce the number of weapons and to make deterrence more stable by working so that better command and control and survivable forces exist. There's a longer-term time scale that's beyond my technical vision, beyond my vision of the politics of the world, that calls for getting rid of nuclear weapons in the long run. On that we do not differ.

Questions from the Audience

Eisenhower, Kennedy, Johnson, Nixon, Carter all considered the use of nuclear weapons at least once, whereas you said that leaders from all walks of life concluded that these weapons could never and should never be used. How do you explain that?

Drell: It's one thing to consider their use as part of a political strategy, as an effort to effect a foreign-policy result. It's another thing to consider their use by having your finger on the button ready to launch them. I think there's a big difference.

Has there not already been a forceful taboo on the use of nuclear weapons?

Taylor: There has been a taboo in some people's minds. It is by no means universal. There are still strong indications that it is the policy of the United States to use nuclear weapons in certain circumstances in which they have not been used against us. Many have raised the question of why we don't—as the Chinese have done formally—make a clear commitment that we will never be the first to use nuclear weapons. I don't know the answer.

If the Soviet Union were to unilaterally eliminate its nuclear weapons, would you still argue that the United States retain some nuclear weapons?

Drell: Someone would have to explain to me how I would know that the Soviet Union removed all their weapons. That is the heart of the problem.

Would you advocate "no first use" now?

Drell: I have stated that there should be no "early" first use. That means that we should define our security goals and organize our forces so that we can meet our obligations without having to rely on early use of nuclear weapons. That's different from our current policy in NATO. I do not go beyond that statement. It's part of deterrence to keep quiet on drawing lines like that.

I also think it is not useful to a nation's credibility to make statements that may not be operational when push comes to shove. No one can know whether the statement that "I promise not to use that weapon" has any meaning. What is meaningful is the way you train your forces, equip them, deploy them, and define your security objectives.

How can we prevent a future Hitler in his bunker from releasing a concealed nuclear weapon according to the nontechnical prescriptions that you have outlined?

Taylor: We do the best we can to reveal that a future Hitler has nuclear weapons. The starting point for that is to make possession of the fuel from which nuclear weapons are made illegal, with extremely severe penalties for violation of the agreement. I would fall back on a combination of the taboo and the encouragement of whistle-blowers worldwide to make it extremely difficult for a Hitler to do such a thing. We keep looking backward at the lessons of history, thinking in old ways, and never assessing the consequences of our actions—the impact of proliferation—as the potential threat that it is.

Do we need a world body with power to enforce the elimination of nuclear weapons? Who enforces if cheating is discovered?

Taylor: We need an international mechanism for enforcing the rules and more than that for legislating the rules. I would strongly argue for starting with the United Nations. It has been scorned and laughed at, but it has accomplished a great deal. The initial commission of the General Assembly passed a resolution supporting complete abolition of nuclear weapons, so that organization has given itself the right charter, and we should use it. It is not going to be easy. The problem up to now has been a lack of will and resources.

I have nothing but admiration for one aspect of Gorbachev's behavior. He has pointed directly and unambiguously to the United Nations as the starting point for eliminating nuclear weapons or enforcing verification procedures, or in fact making sure that we don't pursue a weapons race in space—nuclear or otherwise—by setting up an international space agency. I applaud that.

How harmful is the fact that the concept of deterrence has become part of our culture? Is the question as simple as which is more evil, the Soviet Union or nuclear weapons?

Drell: The image of evil that we have of the Soviet Union has had less to do with nuclear weapons than with policies that many of us have found repugnant. This includes both the human-rights issue and the way the Soviets trampled over neighboring peoples after World War II in their quest to define a secure belt around their country.

What's important today is that, for good reason, the image of the enemy and the image of the "evil empire" is being modified. Some people find it difficult to adjust to a world in which you don't have a readily identified enemy. It is a great unifying force and a great comfort to be able to say "we know who the bad guy is. Let's get him." But the world has become more hopeful for the future, and it's a little bit more difficult to define the best way to achieve our goals.

Nuclear weapons have not been the main cause of the changed atmosphere. We have always feared them. Every leader who's gone into the White House, and has had his hand on the button for the first time, has had to say to himself, "Could I ever push that button? Is that weapon really of any use to me at all?"

The argument is usually made the other way—that, because of nuclear weapons, this intense period of hatred and adversarial relations between the superpowers did not explode into war. History gives no parallel that I know of, because we both had a weapon we were both afraid of. We've been lucky. There can be accidents, miscalculations—proliferation is the great danger. We can't just be calm about it, we have to do something better.

History tells us that middle-aged and older men have sent younger men off to battle while remaining safe at home. Nuclear weapons put them all at risk. If we eliminate nuclear weapons, won't national leaders send young men off to battle again?

Taylor: I have no idea. This brings up the argument that, before nuclear weapons can be abolished, we have to establish a system of world government in which all aspects of national sovereignty are removed. I don't see the need for that. Diversity in almost every complicated set of processes, biological or otherwise, is stabilizing. I'm thankful that we have these diverse cultures and diverse countries. On certain fronts, the unifying mechanism, where it's necessary, can be through the United Nations.

I don't see a need to make sure that young people aren't sent off to war before we start getting serious about abolishing nuclear weapons. It may in fact happen that both occur simultaneously if we really devote our efforts to dealing with problems that threaten all of our lives and safety.

The U.S. nuclear-weapons plants are now shut down due to safety and environmental hazards. Can we negotiate a total global ban on nuclear-weapons production and let the radioactive decay of tritium set the pace for nuclear disarmament?

Drell: If we were to complete the negotiation of the START treaty, the reduction of warheads—which would be some 30 percent or so—would surely long delay the need for new tritium. I'm not aware of any need for new plutonium. The best way to address that question is to sign an arms-control treaty. The framework for this exists and is available to the Bush administration this year.

Taylor: I agree with Sid. I object to using the decay rate of tritium, 5.5 percent per year, as a way of pacing disarmament. That's only a factor of less than two by the year 2000. Now is an auspicious time to cut off production of plutonium and tritium because we're having problems at Savannah River, and Hanford, and all over the place. The Soviets are having their share of problems too. All these things make the world more dangerous. The facilities we use for making weapons materials in the United States are unsafe. Why don't we go to the Soviets right away and say, "Look, let's stop this"?

Wouldn't the international program for nuclear disarmament suggested by Dr. Taylor be in itself a way to build the kind of trust that Dr. Drell says is necessary?

Drell: It would be a component of what I think is necessary. There are deeper questions of hostility and enmity in this world. Removing political and economic causes of adversarial relations has to go hand in hand with progress in removing the nuclear threat. But it will take more than one decade to transform the world into a family of humanity that is free of bitter divisions and hatreds. All I can say is, The faster, the better.

Verification Triumphs

The START treaty represents an important step toward a safer twenty-first century. Four major accomplishments measure its value:

- It reduces the nuclear-attack potential. In particular, the number of the most threatening warheads on ballistic missiles is cut in half, and their aggregate throw weight is cut to 54 percent of the current Soviet total.
- It contains incentives for both nations to reduce preferentially the number of warheads carried on multiple-warhead ballistic missiles (MIRVs). It limits MIRVs to 10 warheads, and to a limited extent it permits downloading of warheads on already deployed missiles. In addition, START heavily discounts the numbers of gravity bombs and air-launched cruise missiles loaded on long-range strategic bombers. This will result in a more balanced mix of forces less capable of threatening a first strike—especially on the Soviet side.
- The treaty permits both nations to improve the survivability of their deterrent forces. Confidence in the survivability of these forces is a vital prerequisite for stability in the U.S.–Soviet strategic balance.
- It institutionalizes unprecedented cooperative verification measures. This may be the greatest achievement of the START treaty. Its carefully crafted provisions not only meet the requirements for verifying compliance with the treaty's numerical limits and operational restrictions, they also guard against using verification procedures as intelligence fishing expeditions.

Like the Intermediate-Range Nuclear Forces (INF) Treaty, START supplements verification by national technical means (satellite surveillance) with a number of measures that require cooperation. For example, the two countries will exchange telemetry tapes for every missile test flight, along with information to aid in interpreting the tapes. Information provided in this way can be validated independently by comparing it to information obtained unilaterally from national technical means—in particular, from our technical intelligence-gathering systems in space or outside of Russian borders. Furthermore, encryption of test data, as well as data denial using encapsulation techniques, is prohibited except for a few, strictly limited purposes such as the study of re-entry physics. The availability of all these measurements will both simplify and greatly enhance confidence in monitoring treaty provisions pertaining to the development of new missile types and to exercises violating numerical limits on warheads.

On-site inspections will be supplemented by continuous monitoring devices at key sites. Together they will provide strong assurance that covert activities on a scale that might affect the strategic balance will be discovered in a timely fashion. Fifteen inspections a year to update data—at any identified aircraft, submarine, or ballistic-missile base or deployment area for mobile ICBMs—will allow each side to verify compliance with limits on numbers and physical properties. Ten additional inspections per year will allow investigators to verify that the number of warheads deployed on a missile does not exceed the negotiated limit.

These 10 inspections will be done on short notice: Within nine hours of the time the inspectors arrive in the country, they are to be transported to the base they select. Upon arrival, they will designate the missile to be inspected, which must remain buttoned up until they can look at it—and the inspection must begin within eight hours. These "challenge" inspections add confidence that the provisions on warhead numbers and on downloading will be obeyed. They also guard against uploading warheads and swapping old types of missiles for new ones.

This kind of verification regime, of which I have given only a glimpse, greatly increases the transparency in the two sides' military activities. At their summit in Washington in June 1990, presidents Bush and Gorbachev issued a statement saying that START incorporated "the most thorough and innovative verification provisions ever negotiated." Based on 28 years of involvement in technical verification issues, I strongly endorse their claim that these measures "will not only provide for effective verification of the obligations of the treaty, but will also greatly increase the mutual confidence which is essential for a sound strategic relationship." I believe they insure that covert activities on a scale and of a nature that could threaten U.S. security will be discovered promptly.

START negotiators had to go far beyond the INF verification protocols to draw the line between what is required for verification and what might compromise intelligence information. Because INF eliminated total systems, any evidence of testing, or of a support system, or of activity at storage sites would indicate a violation. But START requires verification of specific numerical limits and operational restrictions on many systems that will still be deployed, maintained, and tested—and this is a much more difficult task.

The comprehensive verification structure START negotiators erected to meet this demanding task also provides a framework for progress in reducing strategic nuclear forces in the future. If both sides have the will to proceed—and if some kind of stable central government remains in Moscow—the START verification infrastructure can make further reductions relatively quick and easy. Nuclear-armed sea-launched cruise missiles and tactical naval nuclear weapons in general may pose new verification challenges. But the next stage will not require many years of negotiation and a new treaty of more than 700 pages.

In the post–Cold War world, we have an opportunity to implement much deeper reductions in strategic forces. The Warsaw Pact is gone, along with the massed conventional forces that threatened a short-warning attack—and many targets are being removed from the U.S. Single Integrated Operating Plan (the U.S. targeting plan for nuclear war). The new balance of conventional forces at lower levels, along with the recently demonstrated prowess of U.S. conventional military power, has eliminated the need for a large U.S. nuclear umbrella to protect our allies against conventional attack. U.S. nuclear forces can be reduced considerably below the START levels and still meet their only valid mission: to deter *nuclear* attack on our alliance partners as well as the United States.

The United States and the Soviet Union still have far to go in reducing the great excess of nuclear weapons in their arsenals. The reductions defined in START should be implemented because they are highly favorable to the security interests of the United States. But the treaty has also created an infrastructure and reduction formula that will greatly facilitate further progress, insofar as future political devel-

Science and National Security

My talk was given a prescient title by the organizers of this program. It has the virtue of allowing me to talk about pretty much anything on my mind. I am grateful for that because any more specific title that might have been proposed several months ago would very likely have been somewhat overtaken by events, particularly following the speech of President Bush on September 27 and the October 5 response by President Gorbachev.

Science and national security have been interwined throughout history. Science has not only given us new and potentially ever more devastating means of destruction, it has been important also to our learning the limits on what one can accomplish with weapons. This too is a key role, because it is as crucial to know what one cannot do as it is to know what one can do. We often dream of policy goals that we would love to achieve, but we mustn't forget that the laws of nature cannot be coerced to do what we want. This indeed was a major factor in the debate of the 1980s after President Reagan's Star Wars speech. In many quarters, the goal of an impenetrable astrodome defense for the United States against a massive ballistic-missile attack was heralded and promoted with assurance, although cool analysis of the technical facts made it clear that, against a determined opponent, it was not a realistic goal. Fortunately for setting policy in the 1990s, that fact is now very widely recognized.

The Star Wars debate—which often generated more heat than light—is a very good example of the importance of scientists and scientific input at the highest level when governments consider technical defense issues that are crucial to our national security.

But there is also a caution that it is appropriate to highlight here at a scientific conference. The prominence and the enormous destructive potential of the new weapons produced by science in the latter part of this century has occasionally led to a perception that we scientists have *the* key to finding the path to peace, and away from nuclear war and devastation. Yes, our role is significant. Technology has indeed made important contributions to "national technical means" of verifying compliance with arms-control agreements and providing early warning of potential missile attacks, as well as to the awesome battlefield superiority displayed in the Persian Gulf War. However, the events of the past few years have also made it abundantly clear that the path to peace will be paved not by technology alone, but primarily by constructive political developments, by negotiations, by moving from confrontation to cooperation, and by bold political steps.

It is here that we have seen the greatest progress in the last two years that has contributed enormously to improving our national security. We now have a constructive dialogue between the United States and the fragmented Soviet Union. The United Nations proved that it could play a constructive political role following Iraq's invasion of Kuwait, now that it is no longer split by Cold War confrontations between the East and the West. The START I treaty has been signed. And, best of all, we have the Bush and Gorbachev initiatives of September 27 and October 5, respectively. I consider those two speeches a turning point in the U.S.–Soviet nuclear confrontation—the best news on that front since we started living under the nuclear threat following Hiroshima.

They accomplished four big things. First, they dramatically reduced the role of the less-than-strategic weapons, giving promise that, in Europe, the reduced ground forces on all sides will be free of nuclear weapons, as will the worldwide naval forces for all but the strategic submarines with their ballistic missiles. The weapons being retired include the ones that have presented the largest difficulties in safety and in command and control. They are among the oldest, technically the most primitive and most accident prone in the arsenal, and they present the greatest dangers of unauthorized dispersion. The Soviets in particular have deployed many thousands of nuclear warheads in this short-range class throughout their republics. Their elimination will greatly relieve worldwide concerns that these weapons, with their deadly nuclear material, may fall into the hands of dissidents or terrorists or may actually be used in civil strife.

Second, both leaders reduced the alertness of strategic forces, moving further away from postures that presented the possibility of sudden attack. Along with this, they also accelerated reductions in the numbers mandated by the START treaty.

Third, by announcing unilateral steps, the leaders set a precedent for a new and more flexible process of arms control to serve as a companion to the increasingly cumbersome negotiations of formal treaties. Nothing remotely like President Bush's announcement would have been conceivable even three years earlier. The value of that announcement has, of course, been greatly increased by the rapidity and range of President Gorbachev's response. The differences of emphasis in the two statements are peripheral and much less important than the large degree of their overlap. They indeed reinforce each other. Both countries have now opened the path to arms reductions by reciprocal unilateral actions to join the more developed one of increasingly complex bilateral agreements. These new initiatives mark progress much larger than was expected by any one outside the circle of decision. Above anything else, this shows how much the old rules have changed for the good in the U.S.–Soviet basic nuclear relationship.

And fourth—and perhaps the most important of all as we look ahead—the courageous and broad decisions by both leaders reflect and reinforce in both countries a growing public judgment that our two countries, the Soviet Union and the United States, are and should be much less adversarial as we face our common problems in the twenty-first century.

Much, of course, remains to be done. A speech marks a turning point, not the end of the road. President Bush, for example, proposed an important new negotiating agenda, including a new initiative to enter into detailed technical discussions of cooperative measures to improve command and control of nuclear weapons and to enhance their physical security. Technical information that we share with the Soviets on improving command and control and weapons safety will enhance our safety since we are the most likely targets of an accidental or unauthorized missile launch from the Soviet Union or one of their submarines. The president's agenda also includes negotiating verifiable means of dismantling nuclear warheads as the United States and Soviet Union begin to actually reduce the number of warheads in our excessively large stockpiles. That, too, will be a most important first.

However, I want to focus on a different theme here, and that is, What can science do to contribute to better security during the coming years, in view of the new developments on the political scene?

The most threatening new development we face comes from the proliferation of the technology for building and delivering weapons of mass destruction. In particular, I refer to nuclear warheads on ballistic missiles. The recent discoveries of how extensive and advanced were the Iraqi programs toward building nuclear weapons provided a rude wake-up call on the imminence of the danger of nuclear proliferation. The challenge to counter or slow the pace of proliferation is one with many complex political dimensions, and it calls for devising the right mix of carrots and sticks—both economic and political—to provide incentives to discourage new countries from entering the nuclear club. Some will no doubt go nuclear for whatever regional or ideological reasons, but it will surely remain in the highest interest of the more developed and wealthier nations of the world to preserve the 46-year-old tradition of not using nuclear weapons. If that tradition goes, we will have the most to lose.

The very successful application of technology in the Persian Gulf War showed one valuable contribution of science and technology to strengthening this tradition of avoiding the use of nuclear weapons. The development of high-tech, precision-guided munitions, together with timely information and total awareness of events on the battle-field, served two important roles in this regard. First, there was no need for the greater fire power of even the smallest nuclear weapons that some would urge us to develop in order to make them "more usable." After all, against a localized hard military target, a factor of 10 in the improvement of accuracy is worth about a factor of 1000—from ton to kiloton—in bomb yield. But have no doubt about how great are the dangers of further escalation to higher yield, once the nuclear threshold has been crossed. And, second, although the U.S. nuclear arsenal failed to deter Saddam Hussein, the effectiveness of our conventional forces, enhanced so substantially by the high-technology sensors and precision guidance, should greatly raise the stakes for the next would-be agressor.

Our forces will continue to need the best that technology has to offer, so long as the world we inhabit remains peopled by nations that still see the image of an enemy in one another. Furthermore, the United States, with its global interest and responsibilities, will continue to require better sensors and communications to maintain an awareness of developments around the world, even as we reduce our reliance on overseas bases. This, by the way, is more than a technical challenge, because the product we seek is understanding—and that also requires good education, knowledge of languages, and familiarity with many cultures. One may hope that, in the future, with better global awareness, we shall be able to pick up earlier and more accurate signals of proliferation of weapons of mass destruction. Without question, it will require a strong scientific community and a technical R&D base to undergird these activities.

Let me turn to another challenge for science. In a world with new nuclear countries that may be less deterred by our nuclear weapons than was our Cold War adversary, we may find that a better case can be made for limited defenses against accidents or primitive missile attacks. To prepare for an informed policy choice, we must rely on the research-and-development community to learn the best possible opportunities for, as well as the realistic limitations on, ballistic-missile defense.

We can hope that this is what we will now learn from the new R&D program on ballistic-missile defense, which has changed from its initial unrealistic goal of a nationwide "astrodome defense" to a more achievable one of Global Protection Against Limited Strikes (GPALS). The United States and the Soviet Union understandably share a desire to improve their security against the threat posed by one or a few ballistic missiles, whether launched accidentally against each other's homeland or launched by another country with a newly emerging, relatively primitive system. How to do this—or even whether the potential threat warrants deploying an expensive system—has yet to be decided. Any decision must be based on a realistic assessment of the available technologies, as well as on the impact of such deployments on our security, on the stability of the nuclear-deterrent balance, and on prospects of further arms reductions. If these questions are addressed in the same spirit of cooperation and of shared mutual interests that set the tone of President Bush's speech on September 27, there is good reason to be optimistic about the prospects of making welcome progress on this issue.

A number of very different missions have been proposed for GPALS. They range from a theater defense of battlefield deployments of U.S. and allied military forces and of population centers from attack by low-tech, short-range ballistic missiles of Third World countries in regional conflicts to the defense of the U.S. homeland, either from unintentional or accidental launches of sophisticated Soviet strategic weapons or from attack by primitive weapons from newly emerging nuclear nations.

These threats present very different technical problems—advanced countermeasures and penetration aids, or none, or high versus low re-entry velocities—and a single unitary approach to all of them is not sensible. I believe that, at this time, we need better knowledge about potential ballistic-missile threats, as well as the technologies for countering them, before we start anew any deployments of ballistic-missile defenses and before we enter treaty negotiations with the Soviets. Different threats (a battlefield defense or regional city defense against Third World, relatively primitive, tactical ballistic missiles, in contrast to a nationwide defense against even a limited launch of advanced, long-range Soviet missiles) call for different defensive systems.

Furthermore, whatever actions the United States takes, it will be important that we do not disrupt the strategic balance, lead to abrogation of the ABM Treaty, or provoke Soviet countermeasures.

Very much has been written or said about both the requirements for, and the tensions between, deterrence and ballistic-missile defenses. I have nothing to add to that long record, but I would rather step back and take a deep plunge here, looking further ahead with the question whether the United States, the Soviet Union, and the world in toto might not now be ready for what President Reagan proposed at Reyjkavik five years ago, and that is to reduce all ballistic missiles— the "fast fliers"—to zero.

Removing the ballistic-missile force would not eliminate the capacity for nuclear offensive actions. Rather, it would put a greater burden on the strategic-bomber force, which has the dual advantages of being recallable in the event of accident or misunderstanding and of being many hours rather than minutes away from delivering its deadly devestation. With bombers, we would no longer be living a mere 20–30 minutes away from nuclear obliteration. Not only do the strategic bombers take many hours to reach their targets, they can be removed from an armed, alert posture—a step recently implemented by both President Bush and President Gorbachev—thereby further lengthening the time interval to catastrophe. Moreover, with modern technology that has already been developed and demonstrated, one can have the necessary confidence in the effectiveness of a long-range bomber with accurate and stealthy stand-off cruise missiles (ALCMs) armed with nuclear warheads.

A U.S. proposal to eliminate all offensive ballistic missiles was first presented by President Reagan at the Reyjavik Summit in October 1986. Embraced by President Gorbachev, it eventually foundered on the difference between the U.S. and Soviet positions on SDI— particularly the Soviet misguided insistance to limit all SDI research, development, and testing to the "laboratory." Speaking at the University of Chicago on November 17, 1986, Secretary of State George Shultz stated the argument for zero ballistic missiles forcefully:

> In such circumstances, both the United States and the Soviet
> Union would lose the capability provided by ballistic mis-
> siles to deliver large numbers of nuclear weapons on each
> others' homelands in less than 30 minutes time. But Western
> strategy is, in fact, defensive in nature, built upon the pledge
> that we will only use our weapons, nuclear and conven-
> tional, in self-defense. Therefore, the loss of this quick kill
> capability—so suited to preemptive attack—will ease fears
> of a disarming first strike.
> The nuclear forces remaining—aircraft and cruise missiles—
> would be far less useful for first-strike attacks but would be
> more appropriate for retaliation. They would be more flex-
> ible in use than ballistic missiles. The slower flying aircraft
> can be recalled after launch. They can be re-targeted in
> flight. They can be reused for several missions.

And he concluded that they "would be capable of fulfilling the requirements of the Western alliance's deterrent strategy."

Any consideration of total elimination of ballistic missiles—or even
of their deep reductions—has to start by answering the hard questions,
such as, What are our targeting requirements? What if any risks do
such reductions present? How do we get there from today's force
structure?

Our requirements and risks have been analyzed thoroughly in the
context of a U.S.–Soviet Cold War confrontation. The result is the
current triad of ICBMs, SLBMs, and strategic bombers—and the not
altogether comfortable acceptance of living less than 30 minutes from
oblivion. New factors emerging in the post–Cold War era may radically change that conclusion. A new analysis is called for that fully
incorporates the sweeping worldwide political changes of the past few
years.

Targeting requirements have diminished considerably with the demise of the Warsaw Pact and the Conventional Forces in Europe
negotiation of balanced limits on conventional forces at greatly reduced strengths. These developments have muted arguments for extended deterrence against a massive conventional attack, and, in fact,
we are now removing the battlefield nuclear weapons and have substantially reduced the number of targets in our Single Integrated Operating Plan. Correspondingly reduced is the need for "time-urgent
counterforce," which requires the capabilities of fast-flying, accurate
ballistic missiles in contrast to slow-flying, ALCM-loaded bombers.

Another factor is cost. At greatly reduced levels of deployment of the strategic offensive forces, the cost differential between missile and bomber forces will decrease in importance for two reasons. The first is that the total costs will be less; the second is that, as we continue to lower the degree of fractionation of the missile payload enroute to de-MIRVing the missiles, the difference in cost per deliverable warhead between bomber and missile payloads will also decrease, especially if we insist on mobility in order to retain invulnerability of land-based as well as sea-based missiles.

Moreover, it should be practical to maintain confidence in the safety, security, and survivability of a dispersed bomber force. In particular, no direct Soviet threat to such a force would exist with no ballistic missiles or nuclear-armed SLCMs, which Presidents Bush and Gorbachev also proposed to remove in their initiatives. Confidence in the bombers' survivability would be a most critical requirement before going this route, as would be the most careful technical and operational analysis for assessing risks to their survivability.

There would be no concerns about SDI deployments and their threat to stability if there were no offensive ballistic missiles. Any country could choose its own unilateral or cooperative path for deploying defenses against shorter-range ballistic missiles as insurance against hostile neighbors. Peaceful cooperation in space would become a reality.

I give great importance to building a world order that, if free of U.S.–Soviet confrontation, is also as free as possible of nations retaining any "quick-kill capability" for nuclear attack at long range. It is generally assumed that, early in the next century, a dozen or more countries will have the capability of delivering weapons of mass destruction over very long distances—up to intercontinental range. It is certainly in our interest to avoid such a threat to the U.S. homeland if at all possible. It is axiomatic that the ability to head off the deployment of such weapons *by political means* will be considerably enhanced if all nations are willing to forego them. Although recent experience with Iraq illustrates the difficulty in verifying how far a country can move covertly toward a nuclear capability, long-range ballistic missiles are large and their testing and deployment is impossible to hide from "national technical means" of detection.

It will undoubtedly be a very difficult challenge to remove all long-range ballistic missiles. Although this proposal seemed all too visionary when President Reagan first proposed it in 1986, it now seems to be more realistic in the aftermath of the Cold War—and also more compelling under the threat of proliferation. Such a proposal as this faces primarily political obstacles, but meanwhile science and technology should give a serious look at how to get us more than 20 to 30 minutes away from potential obliteration. It would require worldwide assurance of treaty compliance and of attack warning—capabilities we already demonstrate pretty well technically. More openness would also be important—such as open skies, the more-than-35-year-old Eisenhower proposal recently agreed to by the Russians—but, beyond that, more openness and less obsessive secrecy in all matters nuclear. Such secrecy does harm to the process of policy-making, and by now there are few real secrets to protect.

It may not be a near-term goal—but a world free of long-range, nuclear-armed ballistic missiles is surely an eminently worthwhile goal to strive for. It should serve for us as the distant star of Robert Frost, "to stay our minds on and be staid."

Testing of Nuclear Warheads

Viewed from a technical perspective, continued underground testing of nuclear weapons can contribute to improving the safety of the U.S. nuclear weapons stockpile. It is my view that increased safety is the main reason and indeed the only compelling one for continuing underground testing. Viewed from a political perspective, however, continued testing of nuclear weapons may hinder efforts to counter if not prevent the proliferation of nuclear weapons in the years ahead. We therefore face a difficult challenge of weighing technical judgments about the importance of continued testing for enhanced safety against political judgments about the importance of a Comprehensive Test Ban Treaty (CTBT) for strenghtening, or even preserving, the nonproliferation regime.

On the technical side, which I am more comfortable and capable to judge, I would emphasize that we can and should make important progress toward enhanced safety of the nuclear stockpile. A number of measures for improving safety do not require underground nuclear test explosions. They include:

- redirecting the weapons RDT&E program toward enhanced safety as its principal goal;
- performing laboratory experiments to develop a data base that is required for sound analyses of the risks of initiating a nuclear yield or of dispersing plutonium under a variety of abnormal circumstances for existing weapons;
- retiring older weapons from the stockpile that fail to meet modern safety design criteria;
- adapting existing warheads of compatible size that already incor-

porate the desired safety features to several different weapons systems that are designated to remain in the U.S. arsenal; and

. adopting operational procedures—such as limiting aerial overflight—to reduce handling and transporting risks.

However, to go further and design new warheads with safety-optimized designs, or just simply safer configurations, it will be necessary to perform underground nuclear tests.

In 1990 the House Armed Services Committee (HASC) formed a Nuclear Weapons Safety Panel to provide Congress with a technical analysis of the safety of the U.S. nuclear weapons as a basis for debating future policy decisions. I chaired that Panel* which did the first and only independent comprehensive review of the safety of the U.S. nuclear stockpile since World War II and its subsequent build-up to more than 20,000 warheads. This study was initiated because of concerns about the safety of several weapon systems in the U.S. arsenal. These systems have since been removed from the deployed forces.

It was a major conclusion of our study that "unintended nuclear detonations present a greater risk than previously estimated for some of the warheads in the stockpile." An important contribution to the understanding of these greater risks has come from advances in super-computers that make it possible to carry out more realistic, three-dimensional calculations to trace the hydrodynamic and neutronic development of nuclear detonations. We now appreciate—and underground tests have confirmed—how inadequate, and in some cases misleading, were the earlier two-dimensional calculations.† Noting that, today, the uncertainties in the safety of nuclear weapons are simply too large, the Panel concluded that it is important to "identify the potential sources of the largest safety risks and push ahead with searches for new technologies that do away with them and further enhance weapons safety"

I see three questions whose answers are central to arriving at a

---

*The other members are Drs. John S. Foster, Jr. and Charles H. Townes. In an addendum to this testimony to the Defense Nuclear Facilities Panel of the House Armed Services Committee I include relevant excerpts on nuclear warhead safety from the Panel Report dated December, 1990.

†For example we were wrong in assumptions about the location of the most sensitive point in the weapon at which a one-pint detonation of the high explosive could initiate a nuclear yield. We also know very little about the risk of multi-point insults—i.e., incidence of fragments nearly simultaneously—causing a nuclear detonation. This is important for understanding risks for highly MIRV'd weapons like the Trident and MX missiles.

decision whether the U.S. should continue testing or agree to a comprehensive test ban. These are:

1. What gains in safety can reasonably be achieved by continued testing?

2. How extensive a test program is required and how many years will it take to fully meet appropriately conservative safety criteria for the U.S. nuclear stockpile?

3. Are the gains in safety that would result from continued testing more important than the political value, real or perceived, of a CTBT for strengthening or even preserving a non-proliferation regime?

1). What gains in safety can reasonably be achieved by continued testing?

Important contributions to the safety of warheads result from equipping them with modern enhanced nuclear detonation safety systems (ENDS) and insensitive high explosives (IHE).[‡] ENDS have been introduced into the stockpile starting in 1977 in order to enhance electrical safety of nuclear weapons against premature detonations. Currently about 70% of the weapons in the U.S. nuclear arsenal are equipped with ENDS. On the basis of current plans, it is anticipated that all weapons without ENDS will be removed from the stockpile by the end of the decade. No nuclear testing is required to complete this important stockpile improvement program for enhanced safety.[§]

The fact that nuclear warheads contain radioactive material, and in particular plutonium, in combination with high explosives gives rise to major safety concerns. In most bombs the nuclear primary is surrounded by a shell of high explosives which, upon detonation, initiates an implosion to generate the nuclear yield. An accident or incident causing detonation of the high explosive would result in radioactive contamination of the surrounding area, and might possibly lead to a small nuclear yield as well. IHE has been developed to reduce this danger.

In contrast to conventional high explosives (HE), IHE possesses a unique insensitivity to extreme abnormal environments. The consequences of a violent accident such as an airplane fire or crash, or the drop of a missile while loading it into a launching tube, may be very

---

[‡]In dealing with safety of the complete weapons system, issues of choice of missile propellant and how the systems are handled are also of importance.

[§]Limited testing would be required if we were to choose to deploy the newest and still safer implementations of ENDS that could help make the weapons more terrorist proof.

different depending upon whether the high explosive is IHE or conventional. In contrast to its safety advantages, IHE contains, pound for pound, only about two-thirds of the energy of conventional HE and, therefore, is needed in greater weight and volume for initiating the detonation of a nuclear warhead.

It is generally agreed that replacing warheads designed with conventional HE by new ones with IHE is a very important step for improving safety of the weapons stockpile. The understanding[¶] between DOE and DOD in 1983 calls for the use of IHE in new weapons systems unless system design and operational requirements mandate use of the higher energy and, therefore, the smaller mass and volume of conventional HE. It was also "strongly recommended" by the Senate Armed Services Committee[*] in 1978, under Chairman John Stennis, that "IHE be applied to all future nuclear weapons, be they for strategic or theatre forces."

Although IHE was first introduced into the stockpile in 1979, as of this year less than 35% of the stockpile is equipped with IHE. I know of no plans or indications to suggest that the percentage of weapons in the stockpile with IHE will exceed approximately 55% by the end of the century. Even if we proceed with reductions such as proposed in President Bush's State of the Union message on January 28, 1992, the percentage will reach no more than 65%.

A program to make an important improvement in the safety in the U.S. arsenal by removing all conventional HE and replacing it by IHE in the stockpile for the 21st century would require only a modest and limited underground test program. The details of this program would depend upon whether existing warheads such as the W88 and the W76 in the Trident system are redesigned and tested with IHE, or whether existing warheads designed with IHE, such as the W89 warhead being

---

[¶]This is spelled out in two memoranda. The then Assistant to the Secretary of Defense for Atomic Energy [ATSD(AE)], Richard L. Wagner, wrote on April 28, 1983: "In most of the newer nuclear weapons we are using this insensitive high explosive, and, where appropriate, plan to retrofit older nuclear warheads in the stockpile with IHE." "...the DoD policy for new nuclear weapon development is that IHE will be used unless the Military Department responsible for the nuclear weapon development requests an exception from USDRE (Under Secretary of Defense for Research and Engineering) through the ATSD(AE). Such requests will be considered favorably where the military capability of the system clearly and significantly would be degraded by the incorporation of IHE." The then Director of Military Application in DOE, Major General William Hoover, wrote: "Based on this policy, we should expect IHE to be included in the draft Military Characteristics for new systems. It is our intention to support these requirements whenever feasible."

[*]Recommendation of the Senate Armed Services Committee presented on May 17, 1978, by Chairman John Stennis. (See Report No. 95-961; page 10)

developed as a technology demonstration of pit reuse, are adapted for the Trident missile of the future. In either case the requirements for testing would be limited and could probably be completed by the time of the 1995 crucial 5th review conference of the Non-Proliferation Treaty (NPT), if pursued actively starting now.

A third major step to remove the risk of plutonium dispersal by a detonating warhead would be to develop the technology of a fire resistant pit (FRP). Current FRPs, which can be thought of as vaults in which the fissile material of the nuclear primary is contained, are designed to contain molten plutonium against the roughly 1000 °C temperatures of an aircraft fuel fire that lasts for several hours. FRPs would fail in the event of detonation of the conventional HE and therefore should be used only in weapons equipped with IHE. It was a recommendation in the 1990 report of the Nuclear Weapons Safety Panel that all nuclear weapons loaded onto aircraft, both bombs and cruise missiles, be equipped with FRPs, together with IHE and ENDS. These are viewed as the three critical safety features for avoiding plutonium dispersal or a nuclear detonation in event of aircraft fires or crashes. Currently, no more than about 10% of the weapons in the U.S. stockpile are equipped with FRPs. This percentage will probably grow to about 20% if retirements of weapons that are anticipated, based on President Bush's initiatives, are implemented. I know of no plans to do more.

The technology of FRPs is well known. The requirements for underground testing to develop FRPs for U.S. warheads are limited depending upon whether existing warheads with FRPs are adapted to new systems or whether, because of design constraints imposed by existing missiles and their reentry vehicles, it proves necessary to develop new warheads. The test program may or may not extend beyond the 1995 date of the NPT review to fully incorporate the benefits of fire resistant pits.

The safety effectiveness of FRPs is limited to temperatures encountered in aircraft fires. They cannot assure containment if they are also crushed in an accident leading to a fire. Nor will they provide plutonium containment against the much higher temperatures created by burning missile propellant. For enhanced safety in such circumstances it is necessary to develop new and more advanced weapons design concepts. To give a specific example, a concept familiar in the world of binary chemical weapons would separate the very hardened plutonium capsule within the warhead from the high explosive prior to arming the weapon; or similarly it might separate the high explosive itself into two non-detonable components. I do not know whether such, or other, advanced design concepts will prove practical when measured against future military requirements, availability of resources, and budget constraints. However, as recommended by the Nuclear Weapons Safety Panel, "they should be studied aggressively. R&D is not cheap but the payoff can be very valuable in terms of higher confidence in enhanced weapons safety."

2). How extensive a test program is required and how many years will it take to fully meet appropriately conservative safety criteria for the U.S. nuclear stockpile?

Advanced concepts to make weapons as safe as reasonably achievable, such as the binary one discussed above, would take longer to develop and I cannot say *at this time* how many years it would take to develop. After initial tests it may become clearer how extensive the program should be or whether this is even a productive line to follow in search of a truly significant enhancement of safety. These and other advanced concepts have not yet been adequately explored, and their analysis and testing will certainly extend beyond the 1995 date of the NPT review. However, I believe that, with adequate resources, an underground test program directed to develop such advanced concepts that enhance safety, perhaps, as suggested, by requiring an arming action in order to physically collocate the missile and the high-explosive components, could be accomplished within a decade. The result of such a program would be a weapons stockpile that meets desired safety criteria and that can be relied on with confidence without requiring continued testing for reliability.*

3). Are the gains in safety that would result from continued testing more important than the political value, real or perceived, of a CTBT for strengthening or even preserving a non-proliferation regime?

The safety record of the U.S. nuclear establishment is very good. There have been a number of incidents, but never an accident leading to a nuclear yield. Nor have there been any accidents leading to plutonium dispersal since SAC bombers loaded with nuclear weapons were taken

---

*During the past decade most tests were planned primarily for the development of new warheads and the study of weapons effects. Current tests are emphasizing safety enhancement and pit reuse.

off airborne alert in 1968. Nevertheless, there is still room for substantial improvements in nuclear weapons safety, as the answers to the first two questions make clear. Some of these improvements can be achieved by retiring older weapons and modifying existing ones; some can be achieved by changes in the handling procedures. However, in order to implement further improvements, continued testing is required.

It is important to recognize that there is no clear answer to a question such as "How safe is safe enough?" What is required is judgment informed by careful analyses and adequate data on how far to push, or to relax, safety standards. Informed judgments on such issues must be based on a realistic assessment to avoid nuclear weapons accidents because of their potentially exceedingly harmful consequences, both physical and political. In particular the credibility of our entire nuclear weapons system could be severely damaged if even a minor accident were to occur involving a nuclear weapon and leading to a small detonation or the dispersal of plutonium. We have seen how accidents with civilian nuclear power reactors, and the resulting perceptions that governments were less than fully attentive to the possible health risks, have been so harmful to the debate on energy policy.

Against the importance of continuing underground tests, in order to meet the very demanding safety criteria for the U.S. arsenal, I have great difficulty in attempting to judge how important a CTBT would be at this time. I agree with Secretary of State James Baker when he said in Washington, D.C., on September 19, 1990, that "we cannot approach nuclear proliferation in a business-as-usual manner"; and further when he continued both in his name and in that of then Soviet Foreign Minister Shevardnadze, that "we both see proliferation as perhaps the greatest security challenge of 1990's... and we agree that stopping and countering proliferation must be a central part of our agenda."

If, or when, it is judged that agreeing to a comprehensive test ban would be an important aid to the non-proliferation effort, I recommend that the United States should agree to such as ban. Looking ahead to 1995 and beyond I presume that there will come a time when a CTBT will help strengthen the non-proliferation regime. Meanwhile, however, I support a testing program designed to advance the possibilities and understanding of enhanced safety, and thereby helping us prepare for the possibility of a comprehensive test ban.

In pursuing such a program I also recommend that the U.S. abandon its current* official position that we must continue to test as long as we have nuclear weapons. It should be replaced by a policy that limits underground tests to those that are required to insure that all the weapons constituting our future nuclear forces—i.e., warheads together with their delivery systems and their operational handling procedures—can be certified as meeting appropriately conservative criteria for nuclear weapons safety. This program would consist of several low yield tests per year. However, based on our 1990 review of nuclear weapons safety for this Committee, I cannot say *now*, nor do I believe the information is yet available to say now, how many tests or how many years of testing will be required to meet this safety goal. The government can and should emphasize in public discussion what are our safety criteria and the objectives of our tests, as well as the technologies we are developing in order to enhance safety. There would be no compromise of U.S. security to share many of these technologies with the Russians—or any sophisticated nuclear power—to help improve safety. On purely military grounds I see no strong reason to avoid an exchange of general information on test goals. By now there are few real secrets to protect. It is about time for more openness and less obsessive secrecy in all matters nuclear.

*NOTE ADDED:

As of this writing, the United States has joined Russia and France in a moratorium on all underground nuclear tests until July1, 1993. President Bush announced in July, 1992 that the U.S. would develop no new weapons. Subsequent U.S. legislation allows for a limited program of fifteen tests to be completed by October, 1996 and devoted to safety improvements only, except for a very few that can be justified as tests for reliability and for the British stockpile. After Oct. 1, 1996 the U.S. would perform no further tests unless any other nations continue testing. Assuming that deep reductions in the nuclear arsenals are implemented in accord with the Joint Understanding in June 1992 between Presidents Bush and Yeltsin, I believe that the most important safety goals can be achieved by the October 1996 cut-off date for testing enacted by Congress this year. We should be working toward the goal of a world-wide cessation of testing by that date.

Addendum on Nuclear Warhead Safety

The following is largely an extract from the report prepared by the Panel on Nuclear Weapons Safety of the HASC.

Concerns that have been raised recently about the safety of several of the nuclear-weapons systems in the U.S. arsenal have led the government to take immediate steps to reduce the risk of unintended, accidental detonations that could result in dispersing plutonium into the environment in potentially dangerous amounts, or even in generating a nuclear yield. These steps include temporarily removing the short-range air-to-ground attack missiles, SRAM-A, from the alert bombers of the Strategic Air Command (SAC) and modifying some of the Artillery-Fired Atomic Projectiles (AFAPs) deployed with U.S. forces. In addition, the Department of Defense and the Department of Energy, which hold dual responsibility for the surety of the U.S. stockpile of nuclear-weapons systems—that is, for their safety, their security, and their control—have initiated studies looking more broadly into safety issues.

This is a very important, as well as opportune, moment to undertake a safety review of nuclear weapons, for reasons that go well beyond the immediate concerns about several specific weapons. As we enter the last decade of the twentieth century, the world is in the midst of profound, and indeed revolutionary, changes in the strategic, political, and military dimensions of international security. These changes, together with the continuing rapid pace of technical advances, create an entirely new context for making choices in the development of our nuclear forces for the future. It is likely that, in the future, the U.S. nuclear-weapons complex will evolve into a new configuration—perhaps smaller and less diverse, and with lower operating expense, but with enhanced requirements for security and control.

During the Cold War build-up, military requirements emphasized the design of weapons to maximize yield-to-weight or yield-to-volume ratios so that the maximum number of warheads could be deployed at maximum ranges. The new challenge for the U.S. nuclear-weapons complex is to adapt the process better to meet the challenge of maximizing safety in appropriate balance with reasonable military requirements as we face reductions and design changes in our nuclear stockpile.

To summarize our recommendations very briefly, we propose organizational initiatives to strengthen and make more fully accountable the safety-assurance process, and we identify priority technical goals for enhancing safety in a timely fashion. We emphasize the need, as well as the importance, of developing the data bases and performing credible safety analyses to support the choices that are made concerning weapons design. We also affirm the importance of vigorous R&D efforts in the Department of Energy weapons laboratories in search of new technologies leading to significant advances in safety-optimized designs.

This is not a call for enlarging the nuclear weapons program. It is a call to reorient it to give higher priority and more of its resources to enhanced safety.

Because the consequences of a nuclear-weapons accident are potentially so harmful, both physically and politically, major efforts are made to protect nuclear-weapon systems from detonating or dispersing harmful radioactive material if exposed to abnormal environments, whether due to accidents or natural causes, or resulting from deliberate, unauthorized intent.

Safety requirements for nuclear-weapon systems apply both to the warheads themselves and to the entire weapon system. For the warheads, this implies design choices for the nuclear components, as well as for the electrical arming system, that meet the desired safety standards. For the weapon system—that is, the rocket motors and propellant to which the warhead is mated in a missile and the aircraft or transporter that serves as the launcher—safety implies, in addition to design choices, operational, handling, transportation, and use constraints or controls to meet the desired safety standards.

The official safety criteria for the nuclear stockpile that were adopted by the United States in 1968 state:

> 1) In the event of a detonation initiated at any one point in the high explosive system, the probability of achieving a nuclear yield greater than 4 pounds TNT equivalent shall not exceed one in one million [and that] one point safety shall be inherent in the nuclear design; that is, it shall be obtained without the use of a nuclear safing device;
> 2) The probability of a premature nuclear detonation of a warhead due to warhead component malfunctions . . . in the absence of any input signals except for specified signals (i.e. monitoring and control), shall not exceed: a) prior to receipt of prearm signal (launch) for the normal storage and operational environments described in the stockpile-to-target sequence (STS), 1 in 10^9 per warhead lifetime, b) prior to receipt of prearm signal (launch) for the abnormal environments described in the STS, 1 in 10^6 per warhead exposure or accident.

Technical advances have permitted great improvements in weapons safety since the 1970s. At the same time, technical advances have greatly increased the speed and memory capacity of the latest super-computers by factors of 100 and more. As a result, it has become possible, during the past three years, to carry out more realistic calculations in three dimensions to trace the hydrodynamic and neutronic development of a nuclear detonation. Earlier calculations were limited to two-dimensional models. The new results have shown how inadequate, and in some cases misleading, the two-dimensional models were in predicting how an actual explosion in the real three-dimensional world might be initiated, leading thereby to dispersal of harmful radioactivity, or even to nuclear yield. A major consequence of these results is a realization that unintended nuclear detonations present a greater risk than previously estimated (and believed) for some of the warheads in the stockpile.

These new findings are central to an assessment of nuclear safety and of the potential to improve stockpile safety. We turn now to a description of individual components that contribute to the overall safety of a nuclear-weapon system as a basis for evaluating how the design choices affect the safety of the weapon system.

Enhanced Nuclear Detonation Safety

The Enhanced Nuclear Detonation Safety System (ENDS) is designed to prevent premature arming of nuclear weapons subjected to abnormal environments. The basic idea of ENDS is the isolation of electrical elements critical to detonation of the warhead into an exclusion region, which is physically defined by structural cases and barriers that isolate the region from all sources of unintended energy. The only access point into the exclusion region for electrical power for normal arming and firing is through special devices called strong links, which cover small openings in the exclusion barrier. The strong links are designed so that there is an acceptably small probability that they will be activated by stimuli from an abnormal environment. Detailed analyses and tests give confidence over a very broad range of abnormal environments that a single strong link can provide isolation for the warhead to better than one part in a thousand. Therefore, the stated safety requirements of a probability of less than one in a million requires two independent strong links in the arming set, and that is the way the ENDS system is designed. Both strong links must be closed electrically—one by specific operator-coded input and one by environmental input corresponding to an appropriate flight trajectory—in order for the weapon to be armed.

ENDS includes a weak link in addition to two independent strong links in order to maintain assured electrical isolation at extreme levels of certain conditions in accident environments, such as very high temperatures and crush. Safety weak links are functional elements (such as capacitors) that are also critical to the normal detonation process. They are designed to fail, or become irreversibly inoperable, in less stressing environments (such as lower temperatures) than those that might by-pass, and cause failures of, the strong links.

The ENDS system provides a technical solution to the problem of preventing premature arming of nuclear weapons subjected to abnormal environments. It is relatively simple and inexpensive, and it lends itself well to probabilistic risk assessment. ENDS was developed at the Sandia National Laboratory in 1972 and introduced into the stockpile starting in 1977.

The weapon without the modern ENDS system that has caused the greatest concern as a result of its means of deployment is the W69 warhead of the SRAM-A missile aboard the strategic-bomber force. (Some of the older models of aircraft-delivered tactical and strategic bombs also raise similar concerns.) Since 1974, concerns have been raised on a number of occasions about the safety of this deployed system. A particular concern is the potential for dispersal of plutonium, or even of the generation of a nuclear detonation, in the event of a fire aboard the aircraft during engine-start readiness drills, or of an impact involving a loaded, ready-alert aircraft (that is, one of the ALFA force), should an accident occur near the landing and take-off runways during routine operations of other aircraft at a SAC base. In spite of these warnings, many remained on alert or in the active stockpile as recently as six months ago. Since then, following public disclosure of the safety concern, the SRAM-A has been taken off the alert SAC bomber force.

Insensitive High Explosives

Nuclear warheads contain radioactive material in combination with high explosives. An accident or incident causing detonation of the high explosive would result in radioactive contamination of the surrounding area.

The consequences of a violent accident, such as an airplane fire or crash, may be very different depending on whether the high explosive is the insensitive (IHE) or conventional (HE) type. In such incidents, the HE would have a high probability of detonating, in contrast to the IHE. The importance of this difference lies in the fact that detonation of the HE will cause dispersal of plutonium from the weapon's pit. In decisions made up to the present, technology and operational requirements were judged to preclude incorporation of IHE in AFAPs and Fleet Ballistic Missiles (FBMs). The small diameters of the cannon barrels (155 millimeters, or 8 inches) pose very tight geometric constraints on the design of AFAPs. As a consequence, there is a severe penalty to nuclear artillery rounds relying on IHE. On the other hand, it was possible to go either with HE or with IHE in choosing the warhead for the Trident II, or D5, missile. Of course, there are also geometric constraints on the Navy's FBMs that are set by the design of the submarine hull. However, the missile dimensions have expanded considerably in the procession from the Poseidon C3 and Trident I (C4), which were developed before IHE technology was available, to the D5 missile, which is approximately 44 feet long and 83 inches in diameter. When the decision was made in 1983 to use conventional HE in the D5 warhead, it was based on operational requirements, together with the technical judgment that the safety advantage of IHE relative to HE was relatively minor, to the point of insignificance, in view of the geographic protection and isolation available to the Navy's FBMs during handling and deployment.

A major requirement, as perceived in 1983, that led to the decision to use HE in the W88 warhead was the strategic military importance attached to maintaining the maximum range for the D5 when it is fully loaded with eight W88 warheads. If the decision had been to deploy a warhead using IHE, the military capability of the D5 would have had to be reduced by one of the following choices:

- Retain the maximum missile range and full complement of eight warheads, but reduce the yields of individual warheads by a modest amount.
- Retain the number and yield of warheads, but reduce the maximum range by perhaps 10 percent; such a range reduction would translate into a correspondingly greater loss of target coverage or a reduction of the submarine operating area.
- Retain the missile range and warhead yield, but reduce the number of warheads by one (from eight to seven).

Missile Propellant

Two classes of propellants are in general use in U.S. long-range ballistic missiles. One is a composite propellant dubbed "1.3 class." The other is a high-energy propellant dubbed "1.1 class." The important safety difference between the two propellant classes is that, although both ignite with comparable ease, it is very much more difficult, if not impossible, to *detonate* the 1.3 class propellant. On the other hand, the 1.1 propellant has the advantage of a 4 percent larger specific impulse, which propels a rocket to greater velocity and therefore to longer range. For example, if the third-stage propellant in the D5 were changed from 1.1 class to 1.3 class with all else remaining unchanged, the decrease in missile range would amount to 100–150 nautical miles, which is less than 4 percent of the maximum range.

The safety issue of concern here is whether an accident during handling of an operational missile—that is, during transporting or loading—might detonate the propellant, which, in turn, could cause the HE in the warhead to detonate, leading to the dispersal of plutonium or even to the initiation of a nuclear yield beyond the 4-pound [of TNT equivalent] criterion.* This issue is of particular concern for the

---

*This particular concern can be avoided if the warheads are removed from the missiles during all

Navy's FBMs. The D5 missile, like its Trident I (C4) predecessor, is designed with through-deck configuration in order to fit within the geometric constraints of the submarine hull and, at the same time, to achieve maximum range with three boost stages. In this configuration, the nuclear warheads are mounted on the postboost vehicle (PBV) in a circular arrangement around, rather than on top of, the third-stage motor. Thus, if the third-stage motor were to detonate in a submarine loading accident, for example, a patch of motor fragments could impact on the side of the re-entry bodies encasing each warhead. The concern is whether some combination of such off-axis multipoint impacts would detonate the HE surrounding the nuclear pit and lead to plutonium dispersal or possibly a nuclear yield. In order to assess this concern, it is necessary to make a reasonable estimate of the probability of accidentally detonating the 1.1 class propellant in the third-stage motor and to calculate or measure the probability of subsequently detonating the HE in the warhead. One would compare the findings of such a study with an analogous study involving a missile with nondetonatable 1.3 class third-stage propellant and/or IHE in the warhead. This comparison would provide the basis to judge analytically the trade-off between enhanced safety and military effectiveness.

Concerning military requirements for the Trident II system, we face the prospect that further reductions in the numbers of warheads will be negotiated in follow-on rounds of the START negotiations. There may then be a need to reduce the number loaded on each missile in order to maintain a large enough submarine force at sea to meet our concerns about its survivability against the threat of antisubmarine warfare. With a reduced loading, a safety-optimized version of the D5, equipped with IHE, nondetonatable 1.3 class propellant, and a fire-resistant pit, could fly to even longer ranges than at present.

Plutonium Dispersal

There are, at present, no quantitative safety standards for plutonium dispersal. The effort now in progress to see if it is feasible to establish such standards is due to be completed in October 1991.* Any proposed standard will necessarily be critically dependent on the type of incident or accident being considered because there is an important difference

---

loading and handling operations.

*This study has since been completed, recommending against establishing such a quantitative standard as impractical.

between the dispersal of plutonium by a fire or deflagration and its dispersal by an explosive detonation. In the latter case, the plutonium is raised to a higher temperature and is aerosolized into smaller, micron-sized particulates, which can be inhaled and present a much greater health hazard because they can become lodged in the lungs. In the former case, fewer of the particulates are small. The larger particulates, although readily ingested, generally pass through the human gastrointestinal system rapidly and cause much less damage. As a result, there is a difference by a factor of a hundred or more in the areas in which plutonium creates a health hazard to humans in the two cases. This means it is necessary to specify both the amount of material and the manner in which it is dispersed in setting safety standards.

Safety Optimized Designs

Important contributions to weapons-systems safety result from equipping the warheads with modern enhanced nuclear detonation safety systems (ENDS) and insensitive high explosives (IHE), together with composite propellants of the 1.3 class in the missile engines. But it remains physically impossible to confirm quantitatively for all contingencies that risks of, say, no more than one in 10^6 or 10^9 have been achieved. What one can do—and this is important to do—is identify the potential sources of the largest safety risks and push ahead with searches for new technologies that do away with them and further enhance weapons safety.

One such technology is a fire-resistant pit (FRP) that would further reduce the likelihood of plutonium dispersal in fire accidents involving warheads equipped with IHE. In particular, current FRPs are designed to provide containment of molten plutonium against the ($\sim 1,000\,°C$) temperatures of an aircraft-fuel fire that lasts for several hours. They may fail to provide containment, however, against the much higher temperatures created by burning missile propellant. They would also fail in the event of detonation of the HE and are therefore

---

*In the event of a detonation of the IHE of a typical warhead or bomb, an area of roughly 100 square kilometers downwind could be contaminated with radioactivity. Published assessments of clean-up costs for such an area vary greatly; they are estimated to be upward of one-half billion dollars. If a chemical detonation were to occur in several warheads, the contaminated areas and clean-up costs would be correspondingly larger. The number of latent cancer fatalities would be sensitive to the wind direction and the population distribution in the vicinity of such an accident. In the event of a deflagration, or fire, the contaminated area would be approximately one square kilometer.

of primary value to safety only if introduced in weapons equipped with IHE. Some of our newest warheads already incorporate FRPs. Beyond that, however, one can envisage advanced weapons-design concepts, familiar in the world of binary chemical weapons, that separate a very hardened plutonium capsule from the high explosive prior to arming the weapon, or that similarly separate the high explosive into two nondetonable components. We do not now know whether such or other advanced design concepts will prove practical when measured against future military requirements, availability of resources, and budget constraints. However, they should be studied aggressively. R&D is not cheap, but the payoff can be very valuable in terms of higher confidence in enhanced weapons safety. The Department of Energy should support such work with the necessary resources.

Panel Findings

The safety criteria that have been specified for modern nuclear weapons are very demanding. The majority of the weapons in the current stockpile will have to be modified to meet them unless they are retired. Moreover, for some weapons, we still lack necessary data to perform credible safety analyses. With a vigorous R&D program at the weapons laboratories in search of new technologies for advanced design concepts, it should be possible to achieve higher confidence in enhanced weapons safety, particularly with respect to plutonium dispersal, for which there currently is no quantitative standard. Although plutonium dispersal is a much less threatening danger than a sizable nuclear yield, it is nevertheless a potentially serious hazard, particularly if the plutonium is aerosolized in a chemical detonation.

Recommendations

1. Adopt and implement as national policy the following priority goals for improving the safety of the nuclear-weapons systems in the stockpile using available technology:

- Equip all weapons in the stockpile with ENDS.
- Build all nuclear bombs loaded onto aircraft—both bombs and cruise missiles—with IHE and fire-resistant pits. These are the two most critical safety features currently available for avoiding plutonium dispersal in the event of aircraft fires or crashes.

There are no technical reasons for the Department of Defense and the Department of Energy to delay accomplishing these safety goals for existing stockpile weapons; they should be given higher priority than they currently receive. For too long in the past, the United States has retained older weapons that fail to meet the safety criteria proclaimed in 1968. The SRAM-A is one such example, but not the only one. It is not sufficient to pull such weapons off the alert ALFA force but to retain them in the war-reserve stockpile, in view of the hazards they will present under conditions of great stress, should we ever need to generate strategic forces in times of heightened crisis.

2. Undertake an immediate national policy review of the acceptability of retaining *missile systems* in the arsenal without IHE or fire-resistant pits in their nuclear warheads and without using the safer nondetonable 1.3 class propellant in rocket stages that are in close proximity with the warheads. Such a review will have to look at each missile system on a case-by-case basis, considering such factors as the way they are handled and loaded and the military requirements, as well as making a technical determination of how important are the choices of IHE versus 1.1 class propellant and the incorporation of fire-resistant pits.

The Trident II (D5) missile system presents a special case to consider in the recommended policy review. It is a new, modern system that is slated to be a major component of the future U.S. strategic deterrent. At the same time, the design choices that were made for the W88 warhead in 1983 raise safety questions: the warheads are not equipped with IHE and are mounted in a through-deck configuration in close proximity to the third-stage rocket motor, which uses a high-energy 1.1 class detonatable propellant. Today in 1990, seven years after these design choices were made, we have a new and better appreciation of uncertainties in assessing, for example, the probability that accidents in handling the D5 missile system might lead to dispersal of harmful radioactivity; the country has different perceptions of its strategic needs in the post–Cold War era; the public has very different perceptions about safety; and the acquisition of W88 warheads for the D5 missile is still in the early stages and has been interrupted for the present and the near-term future by the shut-down of the Rocky Flats plant, where new pits for nuclear primaries are manufactured.

These circumstances present the country with a tough choice: Should we continue with production and deployment plans for the

D5/W88 as presently designed, or should we use the lull in production to redesign the missile with a safety-optimized design incorporating, at a minimum, nondetonable 1.3 class propellant in the third stage and IHE and FRP in the warhead?

This is clearly a critical issue to be resolved by the recommended policy review. It will be necessary to weigh the safety risks of continuing to deploy the present design against the costs and delays of a system redesign in order to allow for making an informed choice. But to allow such a choice to be made, further studies will be needed:

- to provide the data on which to base a more credible analysis of how well, or whether, the D5/W88 meets modern safety standards;
- to estimate the costs and inevitable time delays of implementing any recommended design changes; and
- to evaluate the impact on anticipated national-security requirements if changes to enhance weapons safety result in fewer warheads, lower explosive yields, or reduced maximum ranges of the missiles.

To do this requires a broad and in-depth examination that is beyond our present review.

3. Continue safety studies and, in particular, fault-tree analyses, such as recently initiated and currently in progress for evaluating the safety of the SRAM-A missile and of the current weapon-transportation system. Such fault-tree analyses, which calculate overall risk and safety levels in terms of the individual stops in the operational procedures and the sensitivities of the system components to abnormal environments, provide the necessary analytic tools for evaluating overall systems safety. Very important to such analyses is developing a data base to provide the necessary factual input. The weapons laboratories and military laboratories should give priority to doing the experiments for building such a base. They should also receive the resources necessary to support this effort. We believe that it is no longer acceptable to develop weapons systems without a factual data base with which to support design choices that are critical to the systems safety.

4. Affirm enhanced safety as the top priority goal of the U.S. nuclear-weapons program and direct the Department of Energy and the Department of Defense, in fulfilling their national responsibilities, to develop nuclear weapons for the future that are as safe as practically achievable, consistent with reasonable military requirements. In par-

ticular, the Department of Energy should task and appropriately fund its weapons laboratories to develop truly innovative warhead designs that are as safe as practically achievable. In this connection, the requirement of "inherent" one-point safety should be re-examined. The enhanced safety resulting if the plutonium capsule is physically separated from the IHE prior to arming may well prove to be more important than whatever weight penalty or decrease in reliability—if any—would result from such a design. All advanced design concepts should be studied aggressively. Subsequently, the utility of such designs, together with whatever weight or range penalties they require, would be measured against established military requirements.

Finally, the preceding recommendations are concerned directly with weapons safety, which is the focus of this review. However, it is appropriate to add how very impressed the Panel was by the nuclear weapons security measures that we observed at the Navy Trident II Base at Kings Bay, Georgia, and the Air Force SAC Base at Minot, North Dakota. During the limited period of this study, the Panel had no opportunity to visit field deployments of Army nuclear weapons.

With respect to controlling the use of nuclear weapons, we are satisfied by the technical measures, including permissive action links (PALS), and the serious attention that use controls receive on Air Force missiles and bombs. Great care is also given by the Navy to maintaining a tight system of use controls on its Trident missiles at sea. However, the Navy's fleet ballistic-missile system differs in that, whereas launch authority comes from outside the submarine, there is no requirement for external information to be provided in order physically to enable a launch. It is also important to evaluate the suitability of continuing this procedure into the future.

Index

358